W9-AZA-197

Proposing Men

Proposing Men

Dialectics of Gender and Class
in the Eighteenth-Century
English Periodical

Shawn Lisa Maurer

Stanford University Press
Stanford, California
1998

Stanford University Press

Stanford, California

© 1998 by the Board of Trustees of the

Leland Stanford Junior University

Printed in the United States of America

CIP data appear at the end of the book

FOR BRITTAIN SMITH,

AND IN MEMORY OF

BARRY D. MAURER

Acknowledgments

This book could not have come into being without the considerable efforts of many people. Carol Barash sowed the seeds of my interest in the eighteenth century, while an education in women's studies provided the grounding for historical analysis of gender. By turning me toward the study of men, Julie Ellison pushed my thinking—and thus this book—in a new direction. With her unusual combination of sense and sensibility, Julie has been inspiration, friend, and mentor. James Winn, Adela Pinch, and Michael MacDonald gave incisive direction to the early stages of this work, while the University of Michigan's Women's Studies Program and Institute for the Humanities offered both financial assistance and intellectual incitement during the first years of writing.

Texas A&M University supplied generous research support; the English Department there presented a remarkably congenial and equally stimulating setting for scholarly endeavor. I am particularly grateful to J. Lawrence Mitchell, Department Head, for his timely sensitivity to faculty needs; to Jeffrey Cox and Larry J. Reynolds for their unsparing efforts on behalf of the Interdisciplinary Group for Historical Literary Study; and to Lynne Vallone and James Rosenheim for founding the Eighteenth-Century Discussion Group. Harriette Andreadis opened up her home to me; Howard Marchitello, Pam Matthews, David McWhirter, Mary Ann O'Farrell, and Lynne Vallone all extended, in a variety of ways, intellectual as well as personal sustenance.

Acknowledgments

My work on this book has been tremendously enhanced by a number of eighteenth-century colleagues whose generosity has never failed to invigorate and encourage me. Accompanying their discerning criticism with sympathetic friendship, David Hensley, Wendy Jones, Larry Klein, and, especially, Jill Campbell and George Haggerty have kept me always mindful of the best of academia. Timely support, intellectual and otherwise, has also come from Boston University faculty members George Hoffmann, Jefferson Kline, Alan Smith, Hallie White, and Eve Zimmerman, while Stefanie Hoffmann, Natalie Leiner, Mary Paterno, and Grace Tran provided the practical assistance without which this book could not have been completed. From the start, Stanford University Press has fostered an amiable as well as productive working environment. I am indebted to the expeditious work of Helen Tartar and Jan Spauschus Johnson, as well as to the valuable recommendations of Ann Klefstad and a particularly insightful anonymous manuscript reader. I would also like to thank Joan Sussler, Curator of Prints at the Lewis Walpole Library, for her kind assistance.

Although Barry D. Maurer did not live to see this book attain final form, his presence has continued to infuse its pages. As father and mentor, he possessed the exceptional ability to challenge without judging, to proffer appreciation untainted by expectation. I dedicate this book to him, as well as to my husband, Brittain Smith, whose extraordinary care, attention, and intelligence have made not just this book, but, indeed, every facet of my life, immeasurably richer.

Earlier versions of parts of Chapters 2 and 3 appeared in *Restoration: Studies in English Literary Culture, 1660–1700* 16, no. 1 (Spring 1992), while portions of Chapters 5, 6, and 8 were published in *History, Gender and Eighteenth-Century Literature*, ed. Beth Fowkes Tobin (University of Georgia Press, 1994). I am grateful to the University of Georgia Press for permission to reprint this material.

S. L. M.

Contents

Proposing Men

Introduction

This is not the book I started out to write. In the interstice between that original, uncompleted book and the one you hold, there exists a history that in many ways parallels the story this book wants to tell. It's a tale of learning to look in different places, to see with different eyes, to foreground the background by turning a narrative situation inside out, thereby transforming the seemingly peripheral into the central. The book demonstrates, moreover, its own process of unlearning assumptions: both the conventions of western European thought, which position men as the universal sex, represented as without gender, and the revisionist work of modern feminism, which, in its laudable attempt to liberate women from their attribution as the second or inferior sex, has frequently ignored the constructed nature of masculinity by subsuming it under the monolithic umbrella of an ahistoric patriarchy.[1] All too often, then, gender has come to mean "feminine gender identity," a classification that not only removes masculinity from the critical gaze but also fails to recognize the dialectical nature of gender formation. Indeed, it is this very correspondence—between the work of eighteenth-century ideologies of gender and the ones we retain today—that has made the act of writing this book so difficult and at the same time so satisfying. In particular, this study reveals the pernicious resilience of a modern model of gender that now, as in the eighteenth century, positions women as the natural object of investigation. The process of illumination described by Walter Benjamin in his "Theses on the Philosophy of History," whereby the materialist historian "grasps the constellation which his own era has formed with a definite earlier one,"[2] can only transpire once one has made a decided break with that prior epoch. It can occur only after one has come out from under the enormous shadows cast by the hegemonies of history itself in order then to return to that past, to review its contours with other eyes.

Upon beginning this study, I was party to the very assumptions I aim to challenge throughout this book. In my initial approach to periodical literature, my training as a feminist combined with the emphases of the texts themselves to make a focus on their discourse regarding women seem obvious. Yet the appearance of Kathryn Shevelow's excellent examination of that very topic, *Women and Print Culture: The Construction of Femininity in the Early Periodical*,[3] both forced and enabled me to rethink the beliefs informing my own work. I was able subsequently to trace within these texts, like the pattern in a carpet, the multiple threads of a discourse about men. And I began to find that as I looked more closely at those masculine strands in relation to the previously more dominant feminine ones, the composition itself began to take on altered shapes, changed meanings. Men, I was coming to understand, were not just the carpet weavers: they too, in both subtle and not-so-subtle ways, were part of its design, were stretched and twisted into rigid, although also sometimes pleasing, patterns.

Accordingly, this book argues that men's interest in and concern with women and with the norms of proper femininity served simultaneously to construct a masculine role or identity for the sentimental husband and father of the emerging middle classes. These texts' explicit discourse about women obscured an equally important—and comparably ideological—discussion about men. Yet men's delineation of domestic femininity, based upon an increasing sense of separation between male and female bodies, spirits, and behaviors, functioned also as a key determining factor in the constitution of men's own gender and class identities. In fact, I maintain that the need to reconfigure masculine gender identity along with new forms of patriarchy is what drove much of the discourse about women. Despite its sentimentality, the ideology of masculinity that emerged in this period was no less rigid or destructive than the aristocratic code of honor—exemplified most brutally in the duel—that it supplanted. Indeed, an emphasis upon men's affective and economic familial role did not obviate previous patriarchal attitudes but served to transform them. Precisely because the breadwinner ethos has survived so powerfully into the present day, the value system it espouses has been naturalized, and thus taken out of history. This book aims to return to that moment when the bourgeois family man emerged as the prototype of desirable masculinity. For reasons I will detail more fully in the following chapter, the genre of the social periodical inculcated new and particularly powerful identities for men, as much as it did for women. This book, then, represents an investigation of the intersection of the periodical form with the birth and development of a specific ideology of masculinity in the early part of the eighteenth century.

In our own century, technological advancements have made even the more obscure eighteenth-century periodicals accessible to the scholar. Wanting, on the one hand, to unearth the plethora of fascinating and often overlooked examples of the genre, yet desiring, on the other hand, to reexamine seminal texts, I concentrated on those works that provided a defined authorial persona or personae, having determined that this structure had a notable effect upon the shaping of masculinity. This focus meant, of course, that many important publications were inevitably excluded; it is my hope, however, that the recent surge of interest in the periodical genre will provide such significant works as Edward Cave's *Gentleman's Magazine* (1731–1907) with the attention that they merit. Moreover, the *Tatler* and *Spectator* came to occupy center stage in this study, an appropriation that in many ways matches their influential position both in the eighteenth century and in eighteenth-century studies.

Beginning with an analysis of the factors that contributed to the phenomenal rise of the social periodical, Chapter 1 theorizes the genre's crucial contribution to the construction of a class-specific gender identity that succeeds as ideology not, as is usually assumed, by separating the feminine private sphere from the masculine public one, but by delineating the private as an important locus of masculine control. Marshaling social history, political theory, economics, and sociology in an attempt to account historically for the appearance of the sentimental family, controlled by the man who is at once lover and husband, father and brother, this chapter challenges the doctrine of separate spheres and the ascription of gender roles connected to it. The profound social, economic, and political transformations that so radically threatened existing structures of aristocratic patriarchal authority will be set forth more fully in Chapter 1. Chapters 2 and 3 engage with the response to this threat by examining some of the earliest forms of periodical literature: Peter Anthony Motteux's *Gentleman's Journal* (1692–94) as well as the various enterprises of the bookseller John Dunton, including the *Athenian Mercury* (1691–97), the *Ladies Mercury* (1694), and the *Night-Walker* (1696–97). At the very outset of a mass dissemination of print culture during the beginning of the long eighteenth century, the rise of the social periodical, a protean genre that, in numerous glossy guises, continues today to collude in the foundation of gender and class difference, assisted in supplying new structures for a superannuated form of patriarchal authority. These chapters investigate the ways in which an emphasis upon marital chastity became the focus for a discussion of changing familial relations between husbands and wives, as well as between parents and children. While distinguishing between texts that focus primarily upon the dispersal of information (Chapter 2) and those that emphasize sexual reform (Chapter 3), I nevertheless contend that both information and reformation were crucial aspects of men's fashioning of themselves, as well as of women.

Chapter 4 illustrates a different approach to reconstructing masculinity by tracing the widespread ramifications of the influential representation of the "Merchant-Gentleman." Appropriating enabling ideals from aristocratic codes of honor exhibited in sartorial display, sexual conquest, and the duel, the merchant transforms these mores into the bourgeois virtues of a smartly dressed wife, sexual continence, and honesty in commerce among men. In Chapters 5 through 8 I demonstrate the ways in which the publications of Joseph Addison and Richard Steele in the second decade of the eighteenth century served to solidify the gender and class differences that Motteux's and Dunton's early periodicals anticipate. Whereas Motteux's work in particular as well as Dunton's reflect a crisis in male authority—gender roles are plainly in flux—Addison and Steele supply the resounding resolution of the climacteric. Primarily in the pages of the collaborators' most famous works, the *Tatler* (1709–11), the *Spectator* (1711–12), and the *Guardian* (1713), but also in Steele's plays, pamphlets, and conduct literature, as well as in Addison's explicitly political journalism, masculinity (re)forms itself through the process of reforming women.

Examining male-female relations in the *Tatler*, Chapter 5 argues that the emerging ideology of masculinity, by stressing the worth of women as desirable objects, necessarily delineates men as constantly desiring subjects, a role at odds with the controlling aspect of masculinity embodied in the roles of chaste husband and benevolent father. The possibility of "companionate" or "egalitarian" relations between husbands and wives is thus obviated by the presence of both the stern father and the objectifying rake within the supposedly loving husband. Turning more specifically to the *Spectator* in Chapter 6, I analyze the text's narrative and ideological uses of the rhetoric of "spectatorship" in order to question the liberal fiction of discursive universality by examining its necessary exclusion of women. I claim that by usurping, as part of its ostensibly rational discourse, a discussion of the very private sphere it seeks to define as other, bourgeois identity can retain, on the level of gender, the patriarchal authority it succeeds in opposing on the level of class. Next, I investigate the relationship between what J. H. Plumb has called the "commercialization of leisure" and moral status. Chapter 7 shows that a concurrent need for and anxiety about consumption, in particular the consumption of supposed luxuries, allowed periodical literature to "trade in virtue" by construing itself as an arbiter of manners and morals, thus mediating its own economic interest. The last chapter in this series delineates the effects of changing economic structures on the *Tatler*'s and *Spectator*'s representations of familial virtue and moral value. By representing the trader as a better gentleman than his aristocratic predecessor, these texts were instrumental in developing a discourse of middle-class identity in which masculinity, conceived in familial terms, culminated in the economic and emotional partnership of fathers and sons.

Turning for the first time in Chapter 9 to periodical literature authored primarily by women, I examine the novelist and playwright Eliza Haywood's most successful journal, the *Female Spectator* (1744–46), in order to question the ways in which modern critics have used such texts as evidence for their unproblematic postulation of the emergence, in the early eighteenth century, of a so-called women's magazine. Although Haywood's periodical, allegedly written by a four-member club comprised of an eidolon, a maid, a wife, and a widow, seems to confirm the critical approach of those who read the monthly periodical as a courtesy journal devoted expressly to women's affairs and designed to direct their behavior, I contend that such a view omits half the story. I show that men play an essential part in Haywood's narratives as both women's reformers and targets for reform. By drawing from established archetypes of libertine masculinity as well as from more recent representations of men of the middle ranks, Haywood's tales of seduction, betrayal, misery, and reclamation expose, but simultaneously sanction, the new domestic roles both women and men were being socialized to play.

Banking on the ability to bring learning into living rooms by mingling instruction with amusement, wit with pleasure, the old with the new, periodical literature claimed to create a discursive arena unmarked by differences in class or gender. Yet as we shall see, both formal narrative structures and the subject matter governed by those structures combined to establish and sustain, on the ideological plane, the very distinctions the periodical purports to eschew (and indeed does eschew on the commercial plane). This paradox at the heart of early periodical literature illuminates similar contradictions within representations of early modern masculine identity. Just as the genre's address to a heterogeneous readership consistently belied the purported belief in separate spheres, so too was men's central place within the home artfully obscured by the very discourse of domesticity they were instrumental in enacting.

1 *Periodical Literature and the Construction of Eighteenth-Century Masculinity*

*L*ooking back in 1705 on a checkered career as a bookseller and publisher, John Dunton recalled his initial excitement upon conceiving the idea of a "Question-Project": "Well Sirs," he told his curious companions, "I have a Thought I'll not exchange for Fifty Guineas."[1] Not only was Dunton's brainchild, the popular and, for the time, long-lived *Athenian Gazette* (subsequently titled the *Athenian Mercury*), particularly profitable, but it also established him, in the last decade of the seventeenth century, as the founding father of a new genre: the literary periodical of morals and manners.[2] Interspersed with readers' questions regarding animal husbandry, natural history, mathematics, philosophy, theology, and all branches of science, Dunton's publication printed inquiries of a particularly social nature, concerned with the most intimate details of family and conjugal life. Although the question-and-answer format itself soon ceded to the more elaborate narrative possibilities inherent in the essay periodical, subsequent practitioners of the genre quickly recognized the didactic and remunerative potential in the subject matter temporarily tapped by Dunton's enterprise. By targeting new groups of readers—urban, middle-class, and female—as well as by availing itself of recently established venues for readership such as the coffee-house, the literary periodical rapidly established itself as the most influential genre of the earlier eighteenth century, instrumental in both generating and disseminating a broad nexus of complex values of moral, economic, political, and aesthetic significance.

In particular, the periodical initiated efforts to publicize representations of what I will term "sentimental masculinity," in which the so-called private space of the home supplanted the *polis* as a locus for masculine virtue. Thus in contrast with the work of such earlier critics as Kathryn Shevelow or Terry Eagleton,[3] who have concentrated, respectively, on the role of the periodical in shaping an ideology of domestic femininity and a discursive public arena, this study interrogates the dialectical relationship between private and public, familial and political. I examine the economic relations that underlie and make possible the supposedly affective family, the family that also stands behind the male actor on the political stage or in the marketplace. For the emerging middle classes in England in the late seventeenth and early eighteenth centuries, women's configuration as inherently domestic—their value defined solely by their position as chaste and dependent daughters, wives, and mothers—required, as an ineluctable concomitant, the simultaneous construction of a new form of masculinity in which men's ability to support and monitor a nuclear family determined, in turn, their own worth. This book analyzes the ways in which the periodical genre's instrumental role in promulgating important new representations of exemplary masculinity was intricately bound to its promotion of domestic femininity, made possible through the marriage of men and women.

My argument about gender is therefore inextricably linked to a discussion of class, for the belief system that constructed the ideal woman as sexually chaste, emotionally passive, and economically unproductive depended upon a new form of exemplary masculinity in which a man's worth is tied to his role as exclusive economic provider. Such a configuration applied primarily in the middle ranks, for in aristocratic households neither sex worked for a living, while in the laboring classes both sexes often did. As a genre that materialized in England contemporaneously with this discernible middle class, the social periodical provides evidence for understanding the relationship between gender construction and class values.[4] By focusing on such topics as courtship, marriage, and parent-child relations, periodical literature played a constitutive role in configuring the nuclear family as a place where emotional and sexual gratification supported material gain. In particular, the social periodical offered an ostensibly neutral forum for public debate about private issues where, under the entertaining yet severely moral male gaze of editors and eidolons, men, by reforming women, learned to become the chaste husbands and watchful fathers of the bourgeois home. In addition, while participating in an ongoing critique of licentious aristocratic conduct and attitudes, these periodical texts contributed powerfully to the upward mobility of the middle-class trader. As we shall see, however, men's need to control themselves, both sexually and economically, was inextricably bound up with their role as monitors and reformers of women. Situating discussions of heterosexual and familial relations within a broader economic and political context via readings of the periodicals can demonstrate the ways in which beliefs about social and sexual behavior—for both men and women—provided the basis for a class position. I argue that the periodical's representations of an ideal heterosexuality in the form of conjugal fidelity is simultaneously gendered and class-based.

In the forty years since the publication of Ian Watt's ground-breaking study of the novel genre, scholars have struggled to assess the critical relationship between the rise of the middle classes and the emergence of new forms of print culture.[5] More recently, Anthony Fletcher has shifted the focus of the discussion by situating "a new series of genres," including the novel, the periodical, conduct books for women, and a medical literature centered upon sexual difference, within what he terms "the properly established discourse, from around the 1670s onwards, of modern gender construction."[6] Yet whether they emphasize class, gender, or their ostensible intersection in an ideology of domestic femininity, these approaches have in common the belief that women rather than men provide the site of early modern society's problematics of identity. Even the work of one of our era's most influential critics of sexuality, Michel Foucault, ignores the fact that men's very act of subjecting women to moral scrutiny, here a particularly sexual scrutiny, functions both to shape and to expose, indeed to "subject," men as well as women. Perhaps I can clarify what I have in mind here through an appeal to contemporary feminist film theory, in which the male gaze that cinematically conjures a desired female image for the purposes of male spectatorship becomes, in its own right, the object of scrutiny and thus an important locus for the investigation of male subjectivity.[7]

Foucault's *History of Sexuality*, particularly volumes 2 and 3, usefully analyzes ancient historical representations of male sexual subjectivity as essential to a discourse of masculine virtue. While establishing an important change in the classical view of male sexual behavior, as sexual self-control moves from demonstrating a man's value as a citizen to defining his worth as a husband, Foucault nevertheless shows how the roles of both husband and citizen contributed to the forging of a masculine "ethical subject." Once he goes on to discuss modern European society, however, Foucault's work uncritically assumes a shift in focus from men to women: "in European culture, girls or married women, with their behavior, their beauty, and their feelings . . . become themes of special concern."[8] Foucault takes for granted the supposition that "it is around women that, little by little, the problems come to be centered."[9] While feminists have understandably censured Foucault for focusing exclusively on masculine subjectivity in his two later volumes, ironically his formulation of the shifting locus of sexuality actually fails to acknowledge the relevant problematics of masculinity: "it is women and the relation to women that will be stressed in moral reflection on sexual pleasures, whether in the form of the theme of virginity, of the importance assumed by marital conduct, or of the value attributed to relations of symmetry and reciprocity between husband and wife."[10] *Pace* Foucault, I contend that all of these issues bear distinct and important relevance to the constitution of modern *masculine* sexuality and subjectivity. Moreover, while men's attention to and control over women constitute crucial elements of the emerging companionate masculine role, as well as of the traditional patriarchal one, the identity of the sentimental man depends also upon his careful consideration and regulation of himself.

In the early eighteenth century in England, burgeoning forms of print culture significantly bolstered men's pursuit of self-mastery. With their stylistic accessibility and their modest price, particularly in comparison to books, periodicals, by combining instruction with amusement, afforded readers the irresistible opportunity to improve while enjoying themselves. As legislators of behavior and arbiters of taste, periodical authors inserted themselves into the age's contentious debates about the proper uses of pleasure, employment of leisure, and consumption of the merchandise increasingly available for purchase. Dependent upon the very systems they professed to adjudicate, these authors produced knowledge as a kind of cultural goods. Through the complex mechanisms of taste, which functioned to demonstrate both sensibility and virtue, they regulated social norms along with literary and aesthetic ones.

In this chapter, I examine the implications of this process of regulation on a number of fronts. Beginning with an exploration of the material conditions that contributed to the periodical's success as a moral genre, I then turn to the broader configurations of the debate surrounding virtue by interrogating the emergence, in this period, of supposedly distinct public and private arenas associated, respectively, with men and women. Arguing that the periodical genre both confounds and solidifies the gendering of each sphere, I show how the development of an ideology of sentimental masculinity depends upon the tenacious success of this artificial separation. Finally, I investigate the specific gender arrangements articulated in periodical literature. By advocating increasingly rigid—as well as diametrically opposed—standards for each sex, periodicals played a constitutive role in the development of modern gender identities.

"Instruction Agreeable and Diversion Useful": The Genealogy of the Social Periodical

> Since I have raised to my self so great an Audience, I shall
> spare no Pains to make their Instruction agreeable, and their
> Diversion useful. For which Reasons I shall endeavour to
> enliven Morality with Wit, and to temper Wit with Morality,
> that my Readers may, if possible, both Ways find their
> Account in the Speculation of the Day.
> —*Spectator* No. 10

Like its sister genre, the novel, which recent scholarship has shown to have a complex and wide-ranging prehistory,[11] the social periodical did not spring unmothered from the head of John Dunton. Outside of the teleological account, which views the periodical as little more than a kind of harbinger of the novel itself, critics have paid relatively scant attention to the cultural contexts of the periodical genre. Viewed historically, this concentration on the novel enacts a contemporary prejudice. By galvanizing an important new reading class, the social periodical clearly contributed to the rise of the novel; yet, in its own right, periodical literature exerted a transformative effect on English society by displaying, from its inception, a moral and cultural authority, not to mention a readership, that novels would struggle for decades to achieve. More accessible as well as more influential, periodicals, at least through the first half of the eighteenth century, unquestionably surpassed novels in their ability to legislate cultural norms.

Who were the readers responding with such immediacy to this new form of printed matter? What kinds of circumstances—social and economic, as well as aesthetic and moral—contributed to the genre's meteoric rise? Soon after its appearance, the *Athenian Mercury* reported itself deluged with material and begged readers to hold off sending in new questions;[12] *Spectator* No. 10 famously estimated twenty readers for each published number. Dunton's statement may have been little more than a canny circulation ploy, while historians of literacy have yet to corroborate Addison's liberal figure. Yet the *Tatler* could boast 314 imitations by the end of the eighteenth century, as the genre's immediate success was only surpassed by its lasting influence.[13] What made this literature so popular—and so compelling?

On perhaps the most basic level, these publications provided vital information and advice about everyday life. Powerful kinship structures that had previously legislated sociosexual practices were weakening; they were being transformed into the related, although distinct, institutions of family and state.[14] In the vacuum created by this maelstrom of change, the periodical genre was able to flourish, owing in part to its ability to reconstitute relations that had formerly been delineated in spoken form through kin and community. As J. Paul Hunter writes, "By the late seventeenth century, print had taken on functions formerly left to oral tradition, and the increasing complexity of ordinary life—especially in the city, especially for rising generations—put new demands upon the press. 'Manuals' of all kinds addressed particular problems, and more complex and comprehensive works incorporated various kinds of pragmatic advice."[15] By offering, amid numerous other topics, a wealth of information relating to courtship, love, marriage, and family, periodical literature educated a burgeoning urban population concerning its proper class and gender roles.

While I accept Jeremy Black's general caution in his preface to *The English Press in the Eighteenth Century* against differentiating too rigidly between newspapers and periodicals or magazines, nonetheless the social periodical clearly and self-consciously distinguished itself from the overtly political and partisan newspaper.[16] Thus the *Athenian Mercury*, the most successful of many projects by the innovative Dunton, located itself in the more neutral zone of information dispersal, claiming to "Resolv[e] all the most Nice and Curious Questions proposed by the Ingenious."[17] As the first English periodical to use a question-and-answer format,[18] Dunton's *Athenian Mercury* was also the first of many texts to appeal to new groups of readers seeking information of a particularly social kind. "Seventeenth-century England," according to David Cressy, "appears to have been a partially literate society, in which literacy varied with sexual, social, and economic position, undergoing an irregular transition to widespread literacy."[19] Although social historians vary in their specific assessments of literacy—usually defined as the ability to sign one's name—in particular populations at different periods, they seem to agree that in England in the middle to later part of the seventeenth century, three overlapping groups made significant and steady progress in literacy: those living in or close to London, the middle classes (particularly tradesmen), and women. While Richard Altick describes a significant variation in male literacy in the Tudor and Stuart periods,[20] Cressy writes, "Tradesmen alone made solid gains, reducing their illiteracy to 30 percent by the end of the seventeenth century."[21] Altick emphasizes that the middle classes' steadily growing need for information and guidance in everyday affairs made them the most important new category of readership.[22] Recently, J. Paul Hunter has added several new pieces to the literacy puzzle, arguing that in addition to being urban, the new reader in this period was mobile, ambitious, and young.[23] Isolated from family and community, these young people turned to print, and primarily to the periodical genre, to find both general and specific answers to crucial questions on personal and professional life.

By claiming to distinguish themselves from the dangerously partisan—as well as particularly masculine—politics associated with newspapers, periodicals created a new discursive and ostensibly apolitical space in which to discuss social issues. Earlier scholars of these texts have understandably chosen to associate this realm primarily with women, focusing on the significant emergence of a female readership or on the periodical's influential construction of a particularly bourgeois form of domestic femininity.[24] By contrast, I want to show the inextricable links between the arenas that the works themselves—as well as their subsequent critics—have perceived as separate. As the following section will demonstrate, men's public identity depended upon, and was indeed shaped by, their domestic or familial roles. Correspondingly, the periodical's ploy of trading parliament for petticoats—what Jonathan Swift, in a deprecating reference to the *Spectator*, called "fair-sexing it"[25]—obscured the economic and political underpinnings of their influential representations of men and women.

In addition to promulgating codes of conduct—for both sexes—governing friendship, courtship, marriage, and childrearing, these texts provided rules for dress, speech, leisure, and the consumption of food and drink. The periodical emerged from the interstice between the social norms previously legislated by an oral tradition and the ever-growing body of printed materials, including newspapers, conduct manuals, published sermons, and other forms of religious writing, available to an increasingly literate public. Responding to what Hunter has described as "a voracious public appetite for being told what to do," periodical literature filled an informational and didactic void while at the same time providing the cachet of being "in the know"—being current less with news per se than with the new.[26] Although later authors might have endeavored to mediate the levity associated with novelty by aligning themselves with the more weighty classical tradition, Dunton exploited what he perceived as a societal fascination with innovation: "For Dunton, the word 'Athenian' implied a taste for novelty and restless curiosity, and he used the term in publication after publication over a period of nearly thirty-five years in hopes of capitalizing on the public preoccupation with what was new."[27] The periodical offered its readers an invaluable means of orienting themselves within the dizzying abundance of a rapidly changing world both by making that world familiar to them and by telling them what and how to think about it.

By employing what one critic has aptly termed "speech-based prose"—a kind of conversational middle style whose most influential exemplar was, of course, Joseph Addison[28]—periodical authors not only mirrored the oral conventions of the tea-table or the coffee-house but also made their pronouncements agreeable to readers less versed in the rigors of print. Although historians of literacy understandably emphasize the considerable growth of the reading public, particularly in the seventeenth century, we need also remember that there was still a large portion of the population either unable to read at all or unused to reading. Numerous critics have remarked upon the symbiotic relationship between one segment of that new reading public, the emergent middle classes, and the periodical genre. Indeed, John G. Ames views the "rise and growth of the middle class in general enlightenment, in position and in importance" as possibly the "chief cause of the rapid growth and development of the English periodical both in tone and numbers."[29] By providing opportunities for writers unschooled in the classical tradition, the periodical enabled men from the middle ranks to take an increasingly active role in literary production.[30] Conversely, periodical authors shrewdly targeted this new market of readers. One can extrapolate from this statement by Richard Altick to find a fitting description of the social periodical in general:

> Addison and Steele possessed a combination of qualities which, in retrospect, were exactly calculated to win the middle class to reading: a tolerant humor beneath which rested moral principles as solid as any citizen could wish; a learning that never smelled of the lamp; a relish for life that was never tinged with Restoration profligacy; a prose that was simple yet never condescending. The essays of the *Tatler* and the *Spectator* were made to order both for men to whom the other reading matter of the age seemed either forbiddingly profane or portentously dull and for him who simply had never been accustomed to read.[31]

Narrative structures deployed within the periodical genre provided especial opportunities to teach and delight. Whether in the form of responses to readers' queries or the (often unanswered) pseudonymous letters to an editor, anonymity facilitated readers' entrance into print and allowed periodical texts to fulfill the rapidly expanding need to articulate public norms for what had hitherto been private behavior. As the following chapter will demonstrate, periodical writers often consolidated their authority by incorporating paternal functions into the personae of their editors or eidolons. The use of examples, as Mr. Spectator himself openly acknowledged, was the sugared pill that allowed authors to preach without being preachy:

> It is observed, that a Man improves more by reading the Story of a Person eminent for Prudence and Virtue, than by the

> finest Rules and Precepts of Morality. In the same manner a
> Representation of those Calamities and Misfortunes which a
> weak Man suffers from wrong Measures, and ill-concerted
> Schemes of Life, is apt to make a deeper Impression upon our
> Minds, than the wisest Maxims and Instructions that can be
> given us, for avoiding the like Follies and Indiscretions in our
> own private Conduct. (*Spectator* No. 299)

It is not a large step from example to exemplar: periodical authors also exploited the rhetorical force of their editorial personae as a means of presenting particularly persuasive models for readerly education and emulation. From the editorial board of the *Athenian Mercury* to Addison and Steele's famed eidolons, periodical narrators charmed, cajoled, and coerced their male readers into new ways of fashioning both themselves and those around them. Moreover, periodical authors acted not only to reform their readers' behavior, but also to articulate a supposedly shared as well as ostensibly unified system of values, values embedded most powerfully in norms of gender and class.[32]

Information, however, forms only one aspect of the story. The increase in literacy, fueled by the urban migration related in part to the continued enclosure of common land, intensified the public's voracity for printed knowledge, which in turn made possible significant developments in the printing and bookselling trade.[33] Parliament's refusal to renew the Regulation of Printing Act in 1695 signaled the end of formal licensing,[34] allowing for the growth of a provincial press[35] as well as a tremendous increase in the number of all periodical publications.[36] In sharp contrast to novels, which did not really become accessible to a general reading public until the spread of circulating libraries in the 1740s,[37] periodicals were, from their very inception, especially affordable and thus widely perused, as many readers could supply the penny (or two, after the Stamp Tax in 1712) that would purchase this form of reading matter. Better yet, for the modest price of a beverage, denizens of London could imbibe a variety of such publications—along with the latest gossip—at one of the city's two thousand coffee-houses.[38] Less capital outlay and a shorter interval of return meant that periodicals were cheaper to produce as well as to purchase.[39] Although periodicals had a clear appeal for men like John Dunton, who were already established in the book trade, even writers with no commercial connections or experience could often obtain financial backing from London booksellers, who saw periodicals as a method of advertising their other publications as well as a source of substantial profit in themselves.[40]

As "bureaux of intelligence,"[41] the place where men went "to read the newspaper, hear the day's rumours and argue,"[42] the enormously popular London coffee-houses played a crucial role in the development and growth of periodicals by providing a ready market for reading material: "In the same way as the publisher of a modern novel relies upon the circulating libraries to take a minimum number of copies off his hands, so the publisher of a newspaper in the early years of the eighteenth century counted on the proprietors of the coffee-houses."[43] In recent years, and particularly in relation to the work of Jürgen Habermas, critics have become increasingly interested in coffee-houses and their offshoots, private clubs, as venues for the ostensibly open debate deemed essential to the formation of what Habermas has termed the bourgeois public sphere.[44] Not only was the coffee-house the place where men went to peruse as well as discuss newspapers and periodicals, but its supposed heterogeneity provided both a model and a forum for the kind of diverse readership fostered by periodical literature. By supplying "a mediation between domestic privacy and the grand public institutions of business and state," the coffee-house, like the periodical itself, contributed to the "regulation of body, manners and morals of its clientele in the public sphere."[45]

Coffee-houses played an integral role in the shaping of bourgeois values by providing an ostensibly neutral and open forum for public discussion. Centers for information and intelligence, they also operated within the broader context of a burgeoning entertainment industry catering specifically to a growing and increasingly affluent middle class. Just as the coffee-house offered its patrons an opportunity to profit from their leisure, so too did numerous forms of printed material present the similarly delectable possibility of recreation combined with education. Among the numerous forms of reading matter available for purchase, periodical literature was singularly successful in negotiating the fine line between pleasure and profligacy. As J. H. Plumb writes:

> Addison and Steele discovered the new and growing middle-class audience, an audience which longed to be modish, to be aware of the fashion yet wary of its excess, to participate in the world of the great yet be free from its anxieties, to feel smug and superior to provincial rusticity and old world manners, above all to be deeply respectful of the world of commerce, an audience in which a hunger for culture could easily be induced and one which had both the leisure and the affluence to indulge it.[46]

Adroitly establishing its moral authority through claims to establish as well as to regulate social norms, periodical literature was quick to capitalize on its audience's pressing need to cultivate *"fine Taste,"* a quality Mr. Spectator deems in *Spectator* No. 409 to be "the utmost Perfection of an accomplished Man."[47] Although Addison's treatise on taste, perhaps an attempt to whet his readers' appetites for the extended discussion of the "Pleasures of the Imagination" that was shortly to follow, concerns itself specifically with literary taste, the principles it espouses were to have a more general resonance. Mr. Spectator begins by reminding us of the metaphorical origin of taste in the sense of judgment by drawing the connection between "Mental Taste" and "that Sensitive Taste which gives us a Relish of every different Flavour that affects the Palate." His linking of this "Faculty of the Mind" to a bodily attribute, one of the five senses possessed by all humans, underpins the second, even more important point: that taste is both a natural inheritance and something that must be nurtured and developed: "notwithstanding this Faculty must in some measure be born with us, there are several Methods for Cultivating and Improving it, and without which it will be very uncertain, and of little use to the Person that possesses it." Because all men have it, all men can learn to use it: representing the faculty of taste as simultaneously democratic and in need of tutelage, periodicals like the *Spectator* cleverly carved out an advantageous niche in the eighteenth century's rapidly growing culture industry. As Terry Lovell writes:

> The periodical press which thrived in this commoditized culture set itself the task of taking in hand the new public (and indeed the new cultural producers and presenters) by providing instruction in the niceties of cultural taste and manners through criticism. The *Spectator* adopted a tone not of moral earnestness, but rather of urbane, avuncular good humor, in this its self-appointed task.[48]

In contradistinction to an aristocratic ethos in which birth alone determined one's gentlemanly status, periodicals severed birth and worth by arguing that gentility resides in behavior rather than blood. Thus by purchasing, or even perusing, the right text, eighteenth-century readers could learn to cultivate the taste that might serve as a marker of gentility. Taste, in other words, has become a commodity, something to be bought, owned, and, ultimately, displayed. As Addison's essay reveals, eighteenth-century purveyors of taste did not place the faculty onto some elevated aesthetic plane, detached from the exigencies of everyday life. By contrast, taste—and this is crucial—existed within and served the needs of a world of commerce and commercial relations.[49] Look, for example, at the way Addison describes the exemplary use of imagination in the first of the "Pleasures of the Imagination" series, *Spectator* No. 411:

A Man of a Polite Imagination, is let into a great many Pleasures that the Vulgar are not capable of receiving. He can converse with a Picture, and find an agreeable Companion in a
Statue. He meets with a secret Refreshment in a Description,
and often feels a greater Satisfaction in the Prospect of Fields
and Meadows, than another does in the Possession. *It gives him,
indeed, a kind of Property in every thing he sees,* and makes the
most rude uncultivated Parts of Nature administer to his Pleasures: So that he looks upon the World, as it were, in another
Light, and discovers in it a Multitude of Charms, that conceal
themselves from the generality of Mankind. [my emphasis]

A sociable rather than solitary capacity, imagination makes objects come
alive and turns the things one sees into objects. In Addison's portrayal, sight
becomes a kind of imaginative labor through which the viewer gains ownership of what he beholds, much in the way that John Locke uses the concept
of property in the person to support the contention that what a man takes
from the "State of Nature" to "mix his *Labour* with . . . thereby makes it his
Property": "The *Labour* of his Body, and the *Work* of his Hands, we may say,
are properly his."[50]

As recent work on the subject of taste has demonstrated, concepts of taste
in this period, like those of beauty or pleasure, were situated within and in-
tegrally bound to problems of commerce and consumption.[51] Thus in *The
Romantic Ethic and the Spirit of Modern Consumerism*, Colin Campbell describes taste as "an ethical and aesthetic concept indispensable to consumer
behaviour, both to facilitate choice and to ensure the generation of new
wants."[52] In this persuasive rethinking of the origins of the consumer revolution, Campbell maintains that neither the theory of social emulation nor
the advent of conscious manipulation by advertising and sales techniques
adequately accounts for the new propensity to consume in the eighteenth
century. Instead, he argues that "the consumer revolution was in fact carried
through by means of a specifically bourgeois consumer ethic; a set of values
and beliefs which were distinct to this section of English society, and which
served to justify not only the reading of fiction and romantically motivated
behaviour, but also indulgence in luxury consumption."[53] Campbell's linking of consumption to taste provides an important key for understanding
the periodical's influential role as a legislator of aesthetic, moral, and social
values. For those in the privileged ranks, lavish forms of consumption and
display could manifest superiority by proving that one had enough to expend, but such conduct did not itself determine worth: worth, in the sense
of status, was inherent in birth rather than revealed through behavior. In the

early eighteenth century, however, an important change occurred. A bourgeois critique of aristocratic honor and the concomitant separation of birth from worth meant that consumption took on new meaning. As the concept of class, determined by occupation and earnings, began to supersede inherited status,[54] what one bought with the money one acquired became a means of demonstrating taste and thereby virtue. For those in the middle ranks, proof of the "essential goodness of one's soul" could be found less in the Puritan asceticism of the previous century than in "sensibility, something which required continuing evidence of one's good taste."[55] Campbell depicts the situation as follows: "It was, therefore, precisely because the middle classes had such a strong Puritan inheritance that they were so eager to 'follow fashion' and hence to consume 'luxury' goods with avidity. This they did out of a deep-seated fear that they might be (and be thought to be) lacking in virtue. Their predominant concern was thus to protect their character by manifesting 'taste' rather than improve their status by exhibiting pecuniary strength."[56]

As powerful participants in the creation of bourgeois sensibility, periodical publications served the needs of a burgeoning middle-class readership interested in situating virtue in a particularly commercial context. By their creation of an environment favorable to mercantile relations as well as through specific representations of exemplary tradesmen, periodicals publicized models of masculine excellence dependent upon such bourgeois qualities as honesty, self-control, and the ability to support and educate one's family. By constituting these attitudes toward virtue in terms of gender as well as class, periodical literature played a decisive role in formulating an ideology of separate spheres.

Public Wholes and Private Parts

> What counts here is less the unfolding of a scholarly argument than the political and cultural destinies of societies that have claimed to command universal membership while preserving their partiality. To confound such claims is not necessarily to construct a better universal but to envision a public "whole" that no longer needs shamefacedly to conceal its private "parts."
> —Joan Landes, *Women and the Public Sphere in the Age of the French Revolution*

With its dizzying array of subject matter and its broad appeal to readers of all classes and both sexes, the periodical genre crystallized the sense of possibility inherent in the massive political, economic, and intellectual developments of late seventeenth-century England. Yet rather than breaking down established hierarchies, the genre employed its artful diversity to institutionalize social as well as sexual difference by naturalizing separations between public and private, masculine and feminine. That is, through the use of a wide variety of narrative techniques, including letters, essays, anecdotes, allegories, and examples, periodical literature consistently demarcated two opposing realms of existence and experience, associated, respectively, with men and women. Men, they contended, belonged in the world of action and accomplishment, whether linked to political, civic, or economic affairs; by contrast, they depicted women as "naturally" suited for the domain centered around the household and its activities. The boundary between the two realms was sustained not only by illustrations of men and women who exemplified these gendered ideals but also by portrayals of failure: periodicals censured as "Amazons" those women who transgressed by participating in party politics or taking on too powerful an economic role, while the specter of effeminacy threatened those men who refused to enter the public arena and made pleasure their sole form of business. Paradoxically, and this is where their power lies, these texts presented, as formed, stable, and even immutable, gender arrangements that they were themselves in the very process of constituting—arrangements, moreover, necessarily linked to a concept of separate spheres.

The important studies by Eagleton and Shevelow cited earlier testify to the enduring efficacy of the periodical genre's classifications of masculine and feminine, public and private as both opposed and disjunctive. While these ground-breaking analyses of the periodical genre have attempted to expose its ideological implications, their work falls unwittingly into two different traps. In *The Function of Criticism*, Eagleton, following Habermas, posits the eighteenth-century periodical, in particular Addison and Steele's *Spectator*, as a dominant cultural force in the development of a discursive public sphere in which bourgeois identity consolidated itself in opposition to a repressive aristocratic state. In *Women and Print Culture*, Shevelow, developing the strategy deployed by Nancy Armstrong in relation to domestic fiction,[57] argues that the periodical genre provided a crucial site for the construction of a new ideology of domestic femininity. Her book analyzes the rhetorical strategies through which periodicals inscribed oppositional gender norms, thereby shaping a private sphere for which women were seen as naturally suited. In their treatment of the ideological division between the public and the private, Eagleton concentrates primarily on the former, Shevelow on the latter. Thus, each critic has significantly enhanced our understanding of these texts' biased representation of class and gender relations, respectively.

Yet their failure to theorize the interrelation between public and private causes them to reproduce, and inadvertently to perpetuate, the artificial division between the two spheres.[58] Throughout this book, I shall be pushing against the public/private dichotomy by arguing that masculinity—despite its representation as public, political, and rational—is powerfully and necessarily concerned with the familial, domestic, and emotional. In other words, in the process of becoming "economic man," supposedly distinct from and complemented by "domestic woman," the eighteenth-century bourgeois male did not automatically shed his formerly central place in the household. On the contrary, patriarchal attributes both underlay and were reinstated within a conception of the modern individual who was, necessarily, a family man and not merely—or even primarily—a free agent in a separate public sphere.

As this study will illustrate, periodical literature was instrumental in codifying new and compelling representations of masculinity in which manliness emanated not from glory or savoir-faire but from a man's ability to engage in the labor that could sustain his family while simultaneously enriching his country. By making a man's familial role central to his public identity, this version of exemplary manhood necessarily confounds any comfortable separation between the two supposedly discrete spheres. In a very similar way, the periodical genre was founded upon an ability to establish much-needed criteria for those forms of behavior designated "private" in the sense of personal or intimate; at the same time, the genre derived authority from its ostensibly "public" roles: the immersion of its editors or eidolons in the rapid current of contemporary social, civic, and economic life.[59]

Characteristically, the periodical manages quite effortlessly to span the two worlds while at the same time working to legislate their separation. An examination of *Spectator* No. 10, Addison's famous apologia for the periodical enterprise, reveals the ways in which the genre's articulation of prescriptive social norms depended, paradoxically, upon the imbrication of supposedly discrete public and private spheres. Cognizant that his publication's success depended upon readership, Addison casts his net as wide as possible by breaking down distinctions that had kept erudition in the hands of a privileged, predominantly male elite. Maintaining heterogeneity of topics as well as an open method,[60] Mr. Spectator asserts that he "shall spare no Pains" to make his readers' "Instruction agreeable and their Diversion useful." Sedulously calculating modes of distribution and habits of readership to arrive at an estimated "Threescore thousand Disciples," Mr. Spectator grounds his achievement in the Horatian dictum of *dulce et utile*, pledging "to enliven Morality with Wit, and to temper Wit with Morality." Thus in a gesture of ostensible inclusivity, he will replace traditional learning with more pleasant as well as less restrictive approaches by bringing "Philosophy out of Closets and Libraries, Schools and Colleges, to dwell in Clubs and Assemblies, at Tea-Tables, and in Coffee-Houses."

Mr. Spectator's promotion of new sites for his readers' edification clearly capitalizes on the recent appearance of contemporary venues for reading and discussion—the coffee-house and the club—as well as the existence of places where the sexes might readily mingle. Ability to benefit from the "Speculation of the Day" will be determined, then, by access to these locations rather than by class or gender privilege. Yet it is worth remembering that within this alleged democracy of readership, at least two of the sites mentioned, the club and the coffee-house, were generally restricted to men. Although Mr. Spectator's mention of the tea-table might, at first blush, seem to redress this imbalance by furnishing a site for readership associated almost exclusively with women, the ideology of masculinity I am here elucidating demands that men appropriate even this supposed female stronghold. When Mr. Spectator goes on to recommend that "all well regulated Families . . . order this Paper to be punctually served up, and to be looked upon as a Part of the Tea Equipage," he draws a necessary correlation between the *Spectator*'s instruction of its readers and a man's government of his home. Even if it occurs at the ostensibly female domain of the tea-table, regulation was the province of men. While couching its prescriptions in a rhetoric of love and complementarity, periodical literature, by enforcing regulation as constitutive of masculine identity, demanded that men assert themselves through adroit control of the household as much as through assiduous self-mastery in the realms of business or politics. At least through the first half of the long eighteenth century, the well-regulated family was one directed and controlled by a man. Hearing one of Mr. Spectator's "Morning Lectures" could thus provide a family with a secular counterpart to the religious literature that also functioned to legislate social and sexual behavior.

Mr. Spectator further asserts male primacy in the personal realm, or what Habermas would call the intimate sphere, by arguing that "what passes in *Muscovy* or *Poland*"—the interest in news and politics traditionally associated with the masculine public arena—is both more harmful and less profitable than what his own paper will provide, namely, "the Knowledge of ones-self." Such knowledge transcended the boundaries of public or private, and necessarily included self-control. Men could demonstrate command over party "Hatreds" by espousing instead the ethos of neutrality ostensibly manifested by the periodical genre's explicit differentiation of itself from the partisan newspaper, a process that acted to reinforce the biblical claims of men's superior rationality. By touting its ability to help men dismantle rather than fuel their "Ignorance, Passion, and Prejudice," periodical literature confirmed its own importance while at the same time instilling this ethos in its male readers, who must display such manly control in the home as well as on the streets. As we shall see in Chapter 6, an ideology of political neutrality both revealed and grounded a belief in male superiority founded in incommensurable sexual difference.

Whereas readers of this essay have generally focused upon Mr. Spectator's construction of normative femininity through his delineation of women as the most suitable audience for his publication—"there are none to whom this Paper will be more useful, than to the female World"—we do well to place into that female world those men whom the narrator also designates as particularly in need of his counsel. By aligning women with men who through position or inclination "live in the World without having any thing to do in it" and also with those men who are "altogether unfurnish'd with Ideas, till the Business and Conversation of the Day has supplied them," the periodical fashions a gendered identity for men as powerfully as it does for women. That is, the narrative implies that the ideal man is active as compared to the useless observer, thoughtful as contrasted to the unreflective Blank (as well as to the uneducated woman); most important, the text defines the exemplary man in terms of occupation by an implicit contrast with the excessive leisure granted the female sex: "I hope these my gentle Readers, who have so much time on their Hands, will not grudge throwing away a Quarter of an Hour in a Day on this Paper, since they may do it without any Hindrance to Business." Scholars of literacy and women's labor have shown that the consumer revolution did not eliminate but instead transformed middle-class women's work, as numerous forms of household production were increasingly replaced by no less onerous or time-consuming supervisory duties. Yet the belief in women's leisure, clearly stated by the *Spectator* essay, played a significant role in the ideological construction of both men's and women's gender identities. This ostensible difference between men and women, manifested in particularly economic terms, functioned to support other perceived differences between the sexes, differences that, as supposedly exemplified in physical, moral, and emotional capacities, provided the basis for modern gender.

Unraveling the rope that has kept us bound to this day within these gender configurations necessitates enlarging our understanding of masculinity to include the familial, domestic, and emotional, in addition to the rational attributes that allow men to operate in the political and economic spheres. Thus while periodical literature upholds and indeed enacts new models of domestic femininity, it does so through an ideology of separate spheres that necessarily effaces men's central place in the home while at the same time making that familial role the repressed foundation of citizenship and masculine subjectivity. In a complex and slippery dialectic, the allegedly private sphere of the family appropriates the public qualities of the *polis*, thus transforming the "private vice" of self-interest into the "public benefit" of the national good.[61] Confounding this great divide also means placing the economic function back into the family in order to explicate the ways in which an ideology of male dominance both conflicted with and was reinscribed within images of the sentimental husband. What unites these two seemingly disparate processes is the fact that both arenas—the political and the familial—proffer themselves as universal, yet each depends upon a significant—and, as we shall see, diametrically opposed—exclusion.

In the political realm, the liberal contract theory that had its greatest exponent in John Locke in the late seventeenth century as well as the bourgeois public sphere that emerged, according to Habermas, in the eighteenth century presented themselves as promoting individual rights in opposition to aristocratic authority. Although formulated in different ways—the former posed against an absolute monarch, the latter against an absolutist state—each structure posited itself as universally accessible. Yet both omitted women in ways that were essential to their very constitution.[62] Second, and collaterally in this period, acknowledgment of the family as an economic entity became ever more obscured by the tender discourse of conjugal feeling, as economics shed its origin in the *oikos*, the private domain of the family, and instead became associated with the (masculine) public sphere of the marketplace.[63] Despite important changes in productive relations within the household, the home remained nonetheless an economic unit. Yet the persistent denial of the economic within the familial made possible the ideology of the sentimental family: beneath a rhetoric of love, affect, choice, and emotional interdependence lay the beginnings of a system driven not only by women's economic and psychological dependence upon the labor of their husbands, but also by those husbands' complementary reliance upon their consuming wives as justification for that labor.

Lawrence Stone's influential study *The Family, Sex and Marriage in England, 1500–1800* clearly delineates the patriarchal components within the sixteenth-century nuclear family structure that formed a transition between the kin-oriented family of the Middle Ages and the companionate nuclear family of the eighteenth century.[64] Yet, when he turns to the later manifestation of what he calls the "closed domesticated nuclear family," Stone tends to erase that family's patriarchal component. His assessment of this family type as one in which affective relations became as important as economic concerns and in which the authority of husbands over wives and of parents over children was severely reduced gives too short a shrift to the complex relations between changing economic structures and developing affective ones. Just as Carole Pateman has argued that contract theory reinscribes patriarchal relations in fraternal form,[65] I believe that the sentimental husband of the companionate nuclear family also refigured the patriarch in the form of the husband.

The father and husband of the feudal household ruled by virtue of his ownership over goods, land, and people; he was master to wife, children, apprentices, servants. His economic power, like his political authority, relied upon his position as head of a household. Whereas a variety of changing political, philosophical, religious, and social factors in the seventeenth century might seem to have eroded male domination, I contend, despite Stone's claims to the contrary, that in this period economic changes for the middle classes served to reconstitute the patriarch's economic power—and thus his social, political, and emotional power—in a different form, a form still prevalent today.[66] Despite the eighteenth century's glorification of women's complementary domestic functions, despite the subsequent Victorian idealization of the "angel in the house," and despite contemporary tributes to the power and importance of mothering, earning wages has always earned familial authority; conversely, economic dependence brings with it passivity and emotional compliance. It is therefore as economic man—a position very different from the supposedly disinterested participant in the ancient *polis*, and a role mistakenly perceived as separate from private, domestic functions and relations—that the middle-class husband (and husbander) of the eighteenth century constructed himself as familial patriarch.

What emerges from this dual-faceted distillation of women from the political and men from the familial is nothing less than the modern ideology of separate spheres. In the case of supposed political universality, the extract— that which must necessarily be eliminated—is woman and those attributes marked as feminine, whereas in terms of the family realm, the process operates to fractionate, and thus to exclude, characteristics and functions associated with masculinity. Possessing a formal similarity but a converse content, both political individuality as formulated by Locke and Habermas and the ideal of familial sentiment, as represented by eighteenth-century writers and contemporary historians, contributed to the ideological creation of discrete arenas of human endeavor. These separate realms, by symmetrically excluding in both instances their opposites, came correspondingly to define the proper places for masculinity and femininity.

Despite their vast differences, models of ideal masculinity from earlier

ages—the Christian knight, the Renaissance courtier, the Restoration wit—
shared a belief in the public realm, however broadly construed, as the sphere
of action and thus of virtue. The new model of masculine virtue that
emerged in the eighteenth century, derived from the classical model in
which a man's ownership of property made possible his participation in the
polis, defines the family as a *polis* in its own right. Thus the sentimental man
finds his most satisfying moral opportunities at home. In *The Human Condition*, Hannah Arendt formulates this transition as the movement of private
and public (the former defined as the sphere of necessity, the latter as the
arena of freedom and action)[67] into the single realm of society: "Society is
the form in which the fact of mutual dependence for the sake of life and
nothing else assumes public significance and where the activities connected
with sheer survival are permitted to appear in public."[68]

Arendt's analysis of this new social realm, whose origin "coincided with
the emergence of the modern age and which found its political form in the
nation-state,"[69] inclines toward the possible recovery of a human agency she
perceives as lost in the modern world. Thus while salubriously insisting
upon a melding of the spheres of public and private, Arendt, because she believes that such a process has had negative consequences, fails to draw out
the ramifications of her own argument. Precisely this relationship between
the public and private as manifested in the new category of the social is the
subject of much of this book. The family, conceived as a social rather than a
private phenomenon, became a way for emerging bourgeois man to justify
his involvement in the public sphere, now conceived not as the arena of individuality and action but instead as the place for the accumulation of wealth
and the protection of interests.[70] Despite Arendt's claims to the contrary, this
process transformed rather than effaced the family and, at the same time,
contributed to a metamorphosis of patriarchal structures.

In the discourse of modern masculine individuality that reinscribes patriarchal relations by setting public against private, political against familial, rational against emotional, the costs for women emerge distinctly. We can
clearly observe the relation of women's otherness to men's subjectivity, of
women's economic dependence to men's material ownership, of women's
public silence to men's political voice. What is more difficult to imagine, and
thus to trace, is the concomitant negative effect upon men. While the shift
from economic power as vested in land ownership to the exchange-based relations of mercantile capitalism served to lessen women's productive role and
thus to increase their economic dependence upon men, it also necessitated
men's configuration as the workers whose worth was defined by their ability
to provide for their families. In short, I am claiming that for modern man

the family, as the primary location of the social, replaces the *polis* as the sphere of both virtue and humanness.

Yet I also contend that just as classical man achieved his freedom at the expense of those whose existence was defined by their place within the realm of necessity,[71] so too must modern man construct his own system of difference and inequality. Strange as it may seem, the belief in incommensurability between the sexes reinforces the discourse of equality, precisely because each gender, by fulfilling its supposedly natural and necessary function in its ordained sphere, can lay claim to full participation in the broader realm of human existence. As we shall see, the emergence of the social necessitated a deceptive rhetoric, indeed a duplicitous ideology, of *egalité* not only among all men but also between men and women. In order to construct from the shards of the ancient *polis* a new locus for virtue in the social and thus familial realm, modern man must elevate women, in particular married women, to a level of seeming equality. Such an endeavor was riven, however, by the widening gap between masculinity and femininity as inscribed in literature and as enacted in political, economic, legal, and familial relations.

Historicizing Masculinity

> For every image of the past that is not recognized by the present as one of its own concerns threatens to disappear irretrievably.
> —Walter Benjamin, "Theses on the Philosophy of History"

Studies of the eighteenth century that are informed by an awareness of gender readily acknowledge that emerging notions of masculinity and femininity are constituted in relation to other configurations, in particular to the ideological division into public and private. This topographical mapping of gender formation has spawned a rich and productive critical cartography. Yet, while feminist analyses call attention to the interlocking of each seemingly separate realm—arguing, for example, that the supposedly unproductive family unit is indeed concerned with labor, albeit labor that is unpaid— our critiques, I fear, unwittingly maintain the very dichotomies we attempt to rupture. By neglecting to address the gendering of the divisions themselves, feminist critics, who laudably desire to assert women's cultural and economic productivity within the supposedly unproductive private realm, have tended to accept the notion of gendered spheres without attending to their genealogy. By so doing, we have anachronistically adhered to a nineteenth-century understanding of gender difference—essentializing it, in effect—in order then ourselves to point out its essentialized characteristics.[72]

Instead, the very spaces that, through a hegemonic pursuit of scientific truth, nineteenth-century thought came to codify as rigidly male or female were, in the eighteenth century, just being established.

A dialectical reconceptualization of gender necessitates a thoroughgoing reassessment of the notion of separate spaces in which the public is male and the private is viewed as essentially feminine. Just as Michael Kimmel, one of the founders of men's studies, has argued that the conception of sex roles as mutually exclusive perpetuates ideologically powerful assumptions about masculinity and femininity,[73] the articulation of separate and exclusive spheres of activity and influence serves to reify a distorted view of gender relations. Indeed, postulating a domestic sphere that has been viewed as inherently female becomes a way to obscure the fact that the private, so-called feminine sphere, far from being an autonomous entity distinct from the masculine world of war, politics, and business, is instead a kind of subset, incorporated within the larger domain already classified as male.

Men's crucial place within the sphere supposedly defined by their absence has been artfully obscured by an ideology of gender that unreflectedly positions men as the universal sex, the sex that theoretical discourse has traditionally, but again unconsciously, represented as lacking gender. An understanding of the inevitably relational, even parasitical entwinement of public and private spaces calls attention to the particular nature of men's position with regard to the purportedly feminine, domestic sphere. In keeping with the dialectic of gender formation and critique, however, it does so in order to present more clearly the determining effects of that position upon the strictures women must learn to incorporate in order to be accounted proper, feminine members of a gendered middle class. By the same token, the awareness of women's internalized oppression leads us back, not only to the role men play in contributing to that oppression, but also to men's own inscription within a culture that seems to make oppression inevitable.

Two suppositions ground this analysis. First, I contend that systems of gender established within the eighteenth century constitute masculinity and femininity as incommensurable opposites, which means that men should not possess traits marked feminine, nor should women exemplify attributes denoted masculine. Second, the gendered subject is always and necessarily a subject in process, since for each sex there is no inherent link between anatomy, itself as much a social construction as a biological given,[74] and gender identity. Ann Bermingham succinctly describes the resulting tension: "While a culture's construction of gender difference is always in crisis it is always and everywhere attempting to stabilize itself and to reinstate and reinscribe itself through ideological constructions and social and material practice."[75] As I argue with regard to the periodical genre, such stabilization often took the form of presenting as already created that which was in the process of being fashioned. In other words, periodical texts routinely represent as solidified and accepted gender arrangements that they themselves were instrumental in establishing as cultural standards. In this period, a particular archetype of masculinity succeeded in being seen as normal, natural, and therefore desirable by usurping and incorporating other, comparably powerful representations of masculinity.

Whereas the ideology of sentimental masculinity that this book attempts to explicate configured men and women in ways that were essentially new, eighteenth-century attitudes toward and assumptions about gender also followed fluidly from the biblical and moral traditions of earlier centuries. Thus Anthony Fletcher's impressive work *Gender, Sex and Subordination in England 1500–1800* demonstrates the "continuity in ruling concepts of masculinity from the Elizabethan to the Hanoverian periods," and concludes that "not the programme and content of gender training . . . changed between 1500 and 1800 but merely its mechanism":

> It was not so much that men abandoned the trust that they had long ago put upon God's word in scripture or on the tradition which condoned male power and the use of force but that they sought a framework for gender which rested on something more permanent and more secure than either of those things. The central intention was the proper internalisation of gender values. If they could teach both boys and girls, men thought, to see sexual difference as fundamental and intractable, sustaining their superiority and women's subordination would become easier.[76]

In a similar vein, Michael McKeon titles a recent essay on the emergence of gender difference in early modern England "Historicizing Patriarchy." Asserting that "male domination and the subordination of women are constants" in the long-term process of establishing modern gender ideologies, McKeon contends that "what changes is the form patriarchy takes under different historical circumstances."[77]

✓ These authors strengthen my attempt to demonstrate how a belief in women's inferiority—on physical, emotional, and particularly moral terms— established in an earlier period did not, as many would like us to believe, suddenly dissipate with the emergence of an ideology of the companionate marriage or the egalitarian family. On the contrary, ideas of companionship and complementarity served to reinscribe patriarchal attitudes, albeit in new forms. Men remained the intellectual, moral, and even, surprisingly, the emotional centers of the household, in addition to and as an important foundation of their work in the public realm. Yet it is important to go beyond the psychological limits imposed by such conceptual frameworks as patriarchy (even a well-historicized patriarchy) or the relations of domination and subordination.[78] That is, I wish to show how supposedly companionate relations had as their dark underside a conception of masculinity that, while subordinating women, simultaneously privileged and oppressed men.

Because from the eighteenth century until today, women, and the attendant construction of a feminine gender identity, have borne the primary weight of both popular representations and scholarly analyses of gender, discourses of masculinity have been largely naturalized, all but taken out of history. One means of penetrating the seemingly impenetrable haze of ideologies of masculinity is to look at the contradictions present within the sentimental masculine role I am describing. In the remaining pages of this chapter, I endeavor to explicate the workings of these contradictions in order to set the stage for the textual analyses that follow.

•

For the emerging middle classes of the late seventeenth and early eighteenth centuries, productive work, and with it the notion of occupation, became part of a whole collection of related attributes that served to distinguish the gainfully employed from the landowning aristocracy and gentry.[79] The elevation of middle-class work, particularly in the form of commercial relations, became a crucial component of bourgeois superiority in a number of connected areas. Not only was middle-class occupation figured in particularly moral terms, but commercial man's self-control, understood as frugality, and his access to and application of capital also qualified him to understand and meet the country's needs in the role of citizen. The celebration of occupation came to define a form of masculine identity in gendered terms as well as those of class, as the middle-class man's role as worker distinguished him not only from the aristocrat but also, and with equal significance, from the middle-class woman. As the middle-class workplace became increasing separated from the household, the husband enacted the role of sole or primary breadwinner in the public realm of the market, while his wife remained in the home performing supervisory domestic duties. Studies of this shift in economic relations have stressed its negative, indeed destructive, implications for those predominantly middle-class women who, deprived of their distinct but nonetheless valued role in the family's economic well-being, became increasingly constituted as problematic consumers.[80] By establishing women as the target of men's reforming attention, this "feminization of consumption" both obscured and legitimized men's own essential part in the economic enterprise.

√ Viewing the construction of the masculine provider as a particular historical phenomenon within a specific economic structure enables us to analyze that role both in its traditional aspects, as emerging out of the previous preindustrial and patriarchal household, and in its more modern permutations. For just as the status of breadwinner necessitated newly positive attitudes toward work, it also sanctioned novel ways of configuring the family. Whereas earlier critics concentrate primarily on the shift from the family as a social and economic unit to the family as a private and affective sphere—an emotional haven separate from the harsh or confusing demands of public and economic life[81]—I argue that in this period the middle-class family did not lose its economic function but did modify it, and that it is perhaps more productive to theorize the modern family in terms of this economic transformation, rather than through changes in household size, or the movement from patriarchal to affective paternal roles.[82]

This shift in perspective forces us to confront the fact that men's role as provider was extraordinarily tenuous. In the seventeenth century, such factors as enclosure and the capitalization of labor compelled many men to work ceaselessly for wages that did not fully support their wives and children;[83] in addition, changes in political structure caused men to blame themselves for their failure to realize the possibilities promised by contract theory's valorization of property and labor: "Just when so many Englishmen were losing their economic autonomy, ideological shifts indicated that they had gained increased individual independence."[84] For both working-class and bourgeois men, occupation was fraught with the specters of imminent poverty, debt, or ruin.[85] These economic pressures significantly promoted a process wherein men learned to deny the nurturing aspects of themselves in order to acquire the ruthless determination necessary to the competitive marketplace. Thus while capitalism in many ways taught men to identify their "individual self and achievement with [their] work lives,"[86] such an identification was at best a problematic one.

√ The severe economic and political inequalities that distinguished men from women created a situation in which male-female companionship was really a euphemism for feminine vulnerability, as women learned to please the men they needed to take care of them. As feminist critics have shown with precision and clarity, women suffered in this position of vulnerability. I do not wish to neglect or condone the violence perpetrated, nor do I seek to excuse the perpetrators. Yet for men, such companionship entailed not mutuality but domination and responsibility, as men's labor both caused and mediated anxieties about providing for—and depending upon—their dependents. Economic changes, then, especially in the middle-class household, conspired to create a structure of greater inequality between men and women inconsistent with a companionate relationship between husbands and wives.

The ideological construction of the restricted nuclear family as a realm of personal pleasure, emotional nurturance, and affective individualism distinguished from the demands of the public sphere and the economic market has been variously analyzed by historians, political theorists, and literary critics. What these scholars share, however, is a belief that such changes depended upon a refiguring of the domestic sphere, defined in specific relation to women and the family, with the latter conceived as primarily female-centered. What such analyses leave out, clearly, is attention to men's place within such a shift, and to masculinity and male sexuality as comparably problematic, and equally ideological, structures. I contend that in this period, changing attitudes toward the virtuous deployment of male sexual desire acted to justify male superiority. That is, while female chastity both prior to and within marriage remained an extraordinarily important part of religious, moral, and judicial discourse, men's monitoring of women's sexual behavior was complemented by an appeal to men's own sexual self-control. Attacks upon the sexual double standard served to buttress hierarchical male claims to a superior rationality that had been threatened by the political and philosophical discourses of potential gender equality, in souls if not in bodies.[87] In constructing sexual control as a form of self-control, men could envision themselves as morally superior to the women whom they monitored along with themselves.

But such a position conflicted with the sexual subordination of women that was transferred from patriarchal relations into contractual ones. Although for the middle classes, marriage was posited as a safe and indeed productive repository for male sexuality, the ideal of a tranquil and mutually comforting marital sexuality was riven by the competing pulls of libertine compulsion and moral self-control. The tender and loving husband of the middle-class marriage struggled, therefore, with contradictory constructions of masculine sexuality. Defined by the possession, if no longer the outright ownership, of a woman, male sexual identity was in large part determined by the need for activity and subordination; even the "language of male sexuality that we have inherited is a language of will, performance and conquest."[88] Political identity depended in part upon the conquest and possession of women's bodies; in addition, the economic shift that resulted in men's occupation and women's domesticity also contributed to an ideal of complacent female compliance on both emotional and sexual levels.

Yet conversely, masculinity was also established within a context that defined the regulation of sexual appetites—both outside and within marriage—as proof of self-control and thus masculinity. In a context in which sexuality was increasingly perceived as an unreasonable desire, a threat to the rational sphere of work, conjugal fidelity could function less as a tribute to mutuality and partnership than as a way to constitute masculine identity through domination—of the self, as well as of the other. To be a man, then, meant negotiating between the contradictory poles of erotic conquest and sexual repression, for a man needed a woman in order to be a real man, but real men also needed to control their unruly desires to prove their superior rationality. Chapter 5 argues that periodical literature, by constituting the rake figure as the opposite of the desirable husband for his failure to master and thus channel his sexual appetites, obscures the libertine elements within all men. According to this ideology, every *man* must be at heart, or in mind, something of a rake, if he is to embody the desirable masculine activity that culminates in the conquest and possession of a woman.[89]

Whereas sexual mastery had long been a patriarchal stronghold, in this period active desire for a woman becomes important for another reason: as a way to establish male sexuality as normatively heterosexual. As historians of homosexuality have recently demonstrated, the late seventeenth and early eighteenth centuries witnessed a decisive shift in cultural attitudes toward same-sex attraction between men. From a general type of debauchery akin to adultery and practiced even by men renowned for their exploits with women,[90] sodomy became a behavior associated with a specific kind of individual, who was seen to desire only other men: "What had once been thought of as a potential in all sinful human nature had become the particular vice of a certain kind of people, with their own distinctive way of life."[91] Paradoxically, the presence in London of "molly houses"—clubs where men might meet, have sex with, and even "marry" other men—functioned to make the molly a more visible target of attack and persecution at the same time as it created a homosexual subculture, a refuge from societal opprobrium.[92] The emergence in this period of a specific homosexual identity thereby worked to harden the contours of a masculine sexuality that had earlier admitted more polymorphous possibilities. Just as masculinity and femininity emerged in this period as incommensurable opposites, constituted dialectically and in negation, so too did the concept of heterosexuality emerge in tandem with the category of homosexuality, as a way to define—and thereby to circumscribe—ideal masculinity.[93] In explicit contrast to the homosexual, the newly emergent heterosexual man desires only women—but, importantly, not all women, for that would make him a rake.

Ironically, however, just as men were being taught to direct their sexual desires solely toward women (and one woman in particular), men's life outside the home became more and more determined by relations with other men. In the workplace as well as in such predominantly male establishments as clubs and coffee-houses, men cultivated sensibility and cemented social, economic, and political ties.[94] The visibility and importance of sites for male bonding sparked new skepticism about men who might prefer the company of women. This masculine (anti)type—termed the ladies' man or, more deprecatingly, the fop—focused the period's anxiety about men who did not follow the increasingly rigid cultural rules about male and female difference. That is, before he became exclusively associated with the sodomite or homosexual, the fop represented the man who refused to embrace this new (public) arena for the consolidation of masculine relations and interests. By eschewing male society in favor of the world of gossip and tea-tables, the fops in periodical literature exemplify "effeminacy" in its original sense of men made feminine, softened, by too much contact with women.[95]

The fop served to demarcate class as well as sexual difference by defining the ideal man as economically active in contrast with the leisured ladies' man, whose only business is to be found in his pleasure. However, while men might denigrate the fop, condemning him as a useless member of society, women find him eminently appealing. Women's attraction to the fop reveals the dilemmas within these new gender roles. On a sexual level, the fop threatens the belief in gender incommensurability by raising the possibility that desire might be stimulated by similarity rather than difference. On an economic level, the leisured fop challenges an ideology of separate spheres in which men's active work in the public realm complements and is distinguished from women's existence in the domestic realm. By showing that women's interest in the fop, like their fascination for the dangerous rake, is a false attraction stemming largely from ignorance, however, periodical literature secured its own critical place in educating women into their proper feminine roles. Similarly, periodicals used these masculine antitypes—the rake, the ladies' man, the fop—to fashion an identity for eighteenth-century men built on the foundation of irrevocable difference between the sexes. In the following chapter, I turn to some of the earliest examples of periodical literature to examine the first stirrings of this new masculine ideal.

2 *Chaste Heterosexuality in the Early Periodical*

Society is the main End of *Marriage*, *Love* is the bond of
Society, without which there can neither be found in that
State *Pleasure*, or *Profit*, or *Honour* . . .
—*Athenian Mercury* (Vol. I, No. 13, May 5, 1691)

Man is in some degree termed but half himself, without an
happy conjunction with one of the Fair Sex; he is a kind of
Vagrant and Wanderer; a thing without a Center to fix him;
he is, as it were, a Traveller in the Earth, having no certain
home that can be pleasant to him, his mind is roving, and he
aims at something it covets, but he knows not well what;
innocent Conversation with Male Friends is pleasant to him;
but that does not satisfy, he wants a Cabinet to deposit secrets
in, that he cares not to reveal to Father or Mother, or the
nearest Relation; and surely, let his search be never so curious, he can never find any so trusty as a Virtuous Wife; there
is in such a Marriage so close an Union, that what he intrusts
to her, he intrusts himself with, for she knows his misfortunes
are her own, and she will run any danger and hazard, rather
than betray her trust, no, not by Inadvertancy, her caution
always being great in such affairs; so that without this material part of himself, we conclude that a man is wanting in that
which should make him happy in the world.
—*The Ladies Dictionary* (1694)

This chapter concerns itself with two phenomena that in-
tersected in the last decade of the seventeenth century:
the rise of the social periodical, as a genre designed to be
an arbiter of the morals and manners of the period, and
the emergence of an ideology of what I term "chaste
heterosexuality," in which a monogamous and companionate marital sexuality became the basis for a set of
class values. Although of two seemingly different
worlds, one literary, the other more broadly sociocultural, both developments are products of a single discursive formation: the articulation of a realm in which

pressing personal issues might be discussed and determined. I wish to trace the implications of the relationship between the creation of the periodical genre and the formation of attitudes toward conjugality, with particular attention toward masculinity and male sexuality. As I argued in the previous chapter, the periodical's virtually instantaneous success reflected the need of a burgeoning urban population who, separated from traditional networks of kin and community, came increasingly to turn to print for information as well as counsel. In the process of legislating morals and manners, periodical authors derived their authority both contextually, through a general usurpation of the materials of family life, and structurally, as supposedly neutral editors took on, and in the process reformed, the masculine familial role.[1]

Periodicals' early and consistent devotion to the topics of love, courtship, and conjugal relations patently reinforced the belief that women were to find their *raison d'être* in the bonds of holy matrimony. However, by characterizing romantic love as the highest form of human interaction for both sexes—"*There's no earthly Happiness like mutual Love*, the more intense the one, the greater the other" (*Athenian Mercury*, Vol. 1, No. 4, Apr. 4, 1691)—these texts simultaneously targeted men as a group also in need of guidance in these crucial matters. As represented within marriage, "mutual love" entailed a specific set of experiences, including emotional connection, nurturance, freedom of expression, psychological communion, and complementarity. Viewed as familial and private, these qualities distinguished the marital relationship from men's experiences within the rapidly growing arena of commercial interactions, thus providing what Nancy Armstrong and Leonard Tennenhouse have called "the sanctuary of middle-class love."[2] And yet, the ostensibly egalitarian attitude toward marriage evidenced, for example, in the epigraph above from the *Ladies Dictionary*,[3] also implied a weakening of the traditional foundations of male authority. The social periodical participated discursively in this purported egalitarianism by representing itself as a forum open to all classes and both sexes, thus differentiating itself from its predecessor, the conduct manual.[4] As we shall see, however, both the content and narrative structure of the social periodical simultaneously reinscribed patriarchal authority, albeit in new forms.

In the formal structure of the periodical, editors played a personal part in their correspondence with specific individuals as well as a general role as the text's representatives to a wider audience.[5] Once printed or paraphrased by periodical editors, private narratives became public property. While the editorial position blurred the narrative boundaries between public and private, it nonetheless slotted both male and female readers into increasingly rigid gender relations.[6] The editors of these texts were able to combine authoritarian and affective characteristics in a number of ways—by acting as firm teachers, delineating proper attitudes; benevolent confessors, absolving women from past infelicities; and chivalrous knights, defending women against misogynist attack. Although male editors encouraged and even depended upon women's contributing questions or other forms of writing, women's status as both inferior and subservient to men circumscribed their entrance into print culture in a manner that mirrored their construction as economically dependent and emotionally complaisant.

A curious text composed by Dunton and founded quite explicitly upon men's positioning as women's champions demonstrates how men's textual authority delimits even the most powerful writing women. In October of 1696, the second number of Dunton's publication the *Night-Walker* advertised a forthcoming volume entitled *The Challenge, sent by a young Lady to Sir Thomas—. Or the Female-War*, in which "the Present Dresses and Humours, &c. of the Fair Sex are Vigorously Attack't by Men of Quality, and as Bravely defended by Madam Godfrey, and other Ingenious Ladies, who set their Names to the Points they Defend." Although *The Female-War* was not itself a periodical publication, it continued the debate upon subjects that had long engaged the attention of the *Athenian Mercury*. In the text's Preface, "Philaret" (Dunton's pen name in his 1705 autobiography, *Life and Errors*) explains the publication's history. What had supposedly begun as a personal "Quarrel sometime since between Sir Thomas—&c. and Madam Godfrey—he reflected on the whole Sex, and she as vigorously defended 'em"— escalated into a veritable Battle of the Sexes: "the Gentleman undertook more at large to prove 'em guilty of innumerable Faults and Follyes, (that the whole Sex was made up of Vexation and Vanity, not a Patch or Mask, or Ribbon about 'em; nothing from Top-knot to Shoe-tie, but what needed Reformation) and she to Answer whatever he could urge against 'em." The misogynist tone of the provocation is conventional, even trite; more interesting, however, is the way in which Philaret and the Athenians construct and indeed market this "Litteral War," acting to "succour" Madam Godfrey against the roughness of her "Challenger," even going so far as to answer themselves the "First Paper, that against Love." Refusing, however, to "engage any further in the *Controversy*," the Athenians nevertheless keep the whole project afloat, first by advertising for "*any other Lady to come in and assist their Sex*," then by ostensibly publishing the replies they receive, and finally, by agreeing to serve as a clearinghouse for further challenges, which are to be printed in a forthcoming volume. In this publication, the conditions of production control, and thereby mediate, the representation of women's textual power. While Philaret might write that the "valiant Godfrey . . . wears her pen as others do their Sword," it is clear that these pen-wielding women write only in response to male attack, and only with the gracious support of the male Athenian Society.

Yet such apparently benevolent authority functioned to shape men as well as women. In Dunton's most famous publication, the *Athenian Mercury*, the editorial role served both as a forum through which to disseminate information and as a source of information in itself, in the form of a particular new type of masculinity that combined the role of the husband with that of the father. Not only did Dunton's publication provide "information and instruction presented in an easily digested form,"[7] thus turning the *Athenian Mercury* into "an instrument of popular education and a worthy forerunner of the 'improving' works characteristic of the next century,"[8] but the periodical's editorial structure also reconfigured for an increasingly urban audience the authority that had previously been dispensed through familial networks and relations. In the *Athenian Mercury*, Dunton neither assumes the editorship himself, as in Peter Anthony Motteux's contemporary publication, the *Gentleman's Journal* (1692–94), nor creates a fictional eidolon, such as Richard Steele's Isaac Bickerstaff (*Tatler*, 1709–11). Rather, Dunton invents the "Athenian Society," an anonymous and supposedly august body charged with answering readers' questions. In fact, this illustrious society consisted only of Dunton himself, and—in a literal merger of print and kinship structures—his brothers-in-law Samuel Wesley, who responded to theological and philosophical questions, and Richard Sault, who dealt with questions about mathematics and science. Occasionally, they solicited help from the Oxford Platonist John Norris. Yet the Athenian Society served as a powerful "means of capturing public credence" for Dunton's work.[9] In *John Dunton and the English Book Trade*, Stephen Parks stresses the relation between narrative authority and social class: "Dunton created the Athenian Society for the practical advantage of its prestige; had it generally been known that a bookseller was the chief organizer of the project, the public would have no reason to respect the opinions, or to accept the integrity, of the publication. But the public could be encouraged to trust the pronouncements of an anonymous group of authorities. Dunton understood that the success of his project depended upon his creating the illusion of a body of learned men engaged in replying to questions submitted by readers."[10] By presenting its answers as deriving from a learned Society, the *Athenian Mercury* endowed its pronouncements with the weight of masculine cultural authority, voiced in "the supposedly neutral and impartial language of reason."[11] In the previous chapter, we discerned how a public masculine identity was paradoxically constituted by authority over, and knowledge about, domestic issues. Similarly, at the close of the seventeenth century, one of the key factors underlying the social periodical's enormous cultural influence was the newfound ability to train the light of universal rationality on the particularized domain of the family.

Two exchanges taken from one of the *Athenian Mercury*'s "Ladies Issues"[12] delineate the intersections of editorial, cultural, and masculine authority. The first questioner asks "Whether the *Authors* of this *Athenian Mercury* are not Batchelors, they speak so Obligingly of the fair Sex?" (Vol. 2, No. 3, Jan. 3, 1691). The editors address the question's misogynist implication—that any man who is married to a woman could never speak "obligingly" of women—less in a defense of femininity than in a redefinition of masculinity: "If they are not Batchelors, they are (or wou'd be thought) Gentlemen, and all who pretend to that Name, as well as all civiliz'd Mankind, have ever treated Women with that respect and tenderness which their Beauty or at least their Sex deserve." Not just gentlemen, but indeed all men must participate in this process of respecting women, for it exists in nature and in culture, among men as among beasts: "Nay, we may go yet further, and not only affirm that the fiercest Nations and most barbarous of Cannibals have acknowledg'd and practis'd this piece of *good Breeding*, but even the Beasts themselves teach it us." Here the presence of nature underlines women's supposedly essential function as childbearers, a function that serves to authorize both this benevolent editorial stance and men's ostensible protection of women through the control of their vulnerable bodies. While the following sentence acknowledges the myriad ways in which masculine culture must be indebted to feminine nature, for "Reason as well as Inclination and Custom" demonstrate that "We owe the Happiness of Society, the Defence of Nations, the best Riches of Kingdoms, which consists in the multitude of Inhabitants; nay, even the continuance of the World . . . to that Sex whom we are so willing to oblige," these obligations must take the form of men's guardianship of women.

Such safekeeping necessarily includes redefining men's relationship to the devalued concerns associated with women. When a reader asks "Whether it does not weaken the Credit of the *Athenian Mercury*, that the Authors of it descend to such a pitiful Employment as to take Notice of Feminine Impertinencies?" (Vol. 3, No. 13, Sept. 8, 1691), the editors respond first by pointing out that this "way of Trading is now a little out of Fashion," and therefore the questioner must be "*some sowr, old, surly, or young, disappointed Lover*; or else a grave Philosophical Don, so *perfectly refin'd*, that he's made up of nothing but Spirit and Notion." Implying that such thinking is aberrational rather than customary, this *ad hominem* attack characterizes the reasonable position, by contrast, as the kindness and magnanimity exhibited by the editors themselves. The editors' next step in their answer is to defuse the category of "impertinencies" altogether by claiming that their female readers' questions are both intelligent and important: "Whereas, on the other side, we have Letters upon the File from Ladies, and those without the *boasted Advantages of Learning*, which are of so great Concern, and carry so much weight, that we dare not without considerable *Time* and *Thought* attempt their Answer." Women's concerns, their "Questions of *Courtship, Love, and Marriage*," thus present the editors with an opportunity to amuse and instruct both sexes by mingling, like Horace, "the *Dulce* and the *Utile*, that one might like a gilded Pill or sweeten'd Potion get down the other."

However, lest the questioner remain unsatisfied that attention to women and their questions is indeed an educational task—and one equally important for and to men—the editors continue: "But we scorn to Excuse what needs it not, but rather ought to be glory'd in, since tho' some things of this Nature may be *pure Matters of Gallantry*, yet there are very many Questions which not only have an Influence on the Happiness of particular Men, and the *Peace of Families*, but even the good and welfare of larger Societies, and the whole Commonwealth, which consists of Families and single Persons; the Instances whereof need not be more distinctly remarkt to the Observing Reader." It becomes, therefore, the task of the "Gentleman," particularly in his position as husband and father, to take interest in matters that have been conventionally viewed as trivial: "Questions of *Courtship, Love, and Marriage*" are far more than mere "Gallantry." In a monthly miscellany published concurrently with the *Athenian Mercury*,[13] we find a particularly powerful representation of the ideal gentleman as defined by his sensitive and elaborate defense of women.

These Fatal Virtues of Men: The 'Gentleman's Journal'

Written by the exiled Huguenot Peter Anthony Motteux, the *Gentleman's Journal* (Jan. 1692 to Sept. 1694) has occupied a significant place in literary history as the first monthly English miscellany, consisting of foreign and domestic news, history, philosophy, questions and answers, poetry, music, translations, stories, fables, and book notices.[14] Motteux's biographer, Robert Cunningham, emphasizes the way in which this "unique and amazing miscellany" managed to enlarge and improve upon prior sources, combining, in particular, "the main journalistic trends of the seventeenth century as expressed in the newspaper, the periodical of amusement, and the learned journal."[15] Moreover, the periodical's editorial functions, performed not by a fictional editorial society as in the case of the *Athenian Mercury*, but by "P. Motteux" himself, supplied the model of the civilizing bachelor, a role later energetically assumed by the *Tatler's* eidolon Isaac Bickerstaff. Although Motteux's personal narrative voice is ironically less self-disclosing than Bickerstaff's tattling persona, the impact of the earlier periodical, like that of its successor, depended upon the narrator's relationship to a sphere of cultural authority marked as masculine, yet one that incorporated the concerns, and often the voices, of women.[16] Indeed, like other prototypical examples of English periodical literature, Motteux's journal testifies to a moment of ontological crisis in which gender norms for both sexes were clearly in transition. By examining Motteux's singular form of self-fashioning, a posture that takes as one of its necessary elements a chivalrous as well as sensitive attitude toward women, we can discern the place of these early texts in molding the ideology of intrinsic gender difference that was later to solidify in the pages of the *Tatler* and *Spectator*.

The periodical's French-born editor acknowledges in his publication's first number its reliance upon the format of the *Mercure Galant* (1673–74 and 1678–79), a monthly miscellany written for the Parisian *beau monde*.[17] The French publication couched its varied items in the guise of a letter to a lady who, having left Paris for the provinces, wished to remain informed about all the most recent and fashionable events in the capital.[18] Working within the same model, Motteux chooses a man as his epistolary interlocutor, thereby endowing his publication with its name—*The Gentleman's Journal: or the Monthly Miscellany. By Way of Letter to a Gentleman in the Country*—as well as with a narrative authority derived from the explicit configuration of relations among men. At the same time, however, the editor expresses cautious solicitude for his female readership, claiming that "The fair sex need never fear to be exposed to the Blush, when they honour this with a Reading; 'tis partly writ for them, and I am too much their Votary to be guilty of such a Crime." He concludes that "this is no less the *Ladies Journal* than the *Gentleman's*."[19] Motteux solicits his female readers' participation and also concerns himself with their interests: many of the issues contain essays by the author which address topics of love and marriage, and which support women's claim to knowledge and education. In addition, he explicitly titles the issue for October 1693 the *Lady's Journal* because it consists mainly of pieces written by women. Yet, as I will argue, the deferential, chivalric, even sentimental narrative voice of the *Gentleman's Journal* relies upon the author-narrator's ability to construct himself as a fit representative of a cultural authority firmly delineated as the rightful province of men.

An examination of two sets of prefatory comments enables us to see with particular clarity the explicit as well as covert bases of Motteux's presentation with regard to gender. The first group consists of his dedication to the patron of his inaugural volume and of an address to the unnamed "Gentleman" who is the recipient of his first letter; the second is comprised of Motteux's speech "To the Fair Sex" at the outset of his *Lady's Journal*. Notably, Motteux positions his specific addresses to men within a complex nexus of public and private relationships. Thus he modestly contrasts the lofty social and political status of his periodical's dedicatee, the "Right Honourable William Earl of Devonshire,"[20] with his own more humble aims as his correspondent, claiming that his journals "aspire no higher, than to attend your *Lordship* when you enter into your Closet, to disengage your Thoughts from the daily pressure of Business" or to amuse him when he retires to his "beautiful Seat" in the countryside.[21] Here Motteux's role as purveyor of pleasure to the English nobility depends upon an accepted distinction between the demands of business and the delights of entertainment, a distinction that would be, of course, applicable only to men.

Motteux's awareness of his dedicatee's public roles—he praises the Earl's military success as well as the aesthetic talents that will make his estate "a lasting *Monument* to the Delicacy of your Choice and the Greatness of your Family"[22]—extends as well to the lengthier address to his first male correspondent, where he acknowledges not the correspondent's but his own literary and civic responsibility:

> Sir,
>
>   Indeed you impose too hard a Task on me: Is it not enough that I send you what ever News or new things I meet with to divert you in your solitude, but you must oblige me to print my Letters? ... I know, you tell me, that this may redeem many glorious Actions and ingenious Pieces from obscurity, the first too particular for our *Gazette*, and the latter too short to be printed apart; that a thousand things happen every day which the publick would gladly know: But must I for all that acquaint the World with them, when so many better pens might do it?[23]

Although in his professed reserve Motteux seems to differentiate between private correspondence and public document, the formal structure of the periodical necessarily blurs such distinctions. On the one hand, the journal's letter form, like that of the epistolary novel, provides its anonymous readers with access to the supposedly personal communication between two specific individuals, thereby creating, as Margaret Ezell notes, "an impression of a personal relationship between writer and reader."[24] By endowing the miscellany with a sense of intimacy, the epistolary arrangement serves to disguise its commercial status, as well as to provide a congenial forum for its readers' own amateur literary productions.[25]

And yet, this intimacy reverberates differently for readers of different sexes. On the one hand, male correspondents are treated as equals if not superiors, whose power must be acknowledged as their favor is solicited. Indeed the passage quoted above plays out a mock power dynamic, as Motteux somewhat facetiously begs to be "discharged" from his "rash promise"; later he concedes that since his correspondent has "no mercy," he "must set up for a Journalist." On the other hand, Motteux courts his female audience with an eroticized deference that disguises their construction as cultural others. For Motteux, as later for Steele, the gentleman is constituted less by birth than by behavior, in particular his behavior toward women. The gentleman's need to protect and vindicate women, which in turn demands that women remain fundamentally different from men, functions to limit and even at times to erase women's place in cultural production. Ironically, although Motteux ultimately argues for women's inclusion within the realm of male-defined and male-dominated culture, which would include both literary production and access to education, his own position as gentleman necessarily mitigates such incorporation.

For the month of October, 1693, Motteux renamed his publication the *Lady's Journal* in honor of the women whose contributions comprised the bulk of the issue. In his dedication "To the Fair Sex,"[26] Motteux addresses not any special woman or women, such as a particularly important contributor or a renowned patron of the arts, but instead proffers his declaration to the sex in general. Eliding such contributors as "Mrs. S—" and "A Lady of Quality" and thereby erasing the multiple differences—in experience, education, marital and socioeconomic status—among his correspondents as well as his readers, the editor also unites all women as the grateful recipients of his romantic attention and effusive praise. Motteux sexualizes his relation to his female readers, who, he claims, have responded to his journal as if it were a "*Billet Doux*," writing that "methinks a Dedication to the Fair, has much in it of a Declaration of Love." He asserts that his "two Years Constancy" to the "Fair Sex" has made him, if not their Don Quixote, since "I do not pretend to revive Knight Errantry," at least their "confirm'd Votary," who has "boldly taken the liberty to vindicate you, and proclaim your Perfections."

Indeed, so far from needing to be reformed themselves, women stand as both models of and inspiration for men's cultural production. In addition to contributing examples of their own writing, women have been the Muses who have inspir'd most of the Gentlemen whose Writings have grac'd this Journal: 'Tis you to whom not only they, but all our Sex owe, that Politeness, Easiness, and Delicacy which a converse with you imparts more liberally than the most lavish Nature. She indeed among many Peebles produces some Diamonds, some sprightly valuable Minds among a great number of dull inconsiderable Souls; but still they are rough, till pollish'd by You and Love that set them in their true Light and bid them shine. Thus the greatest Scholars are but Bookish Dunces till their Hearts have taken lessons from your Eyes, and they have commenc'd Batchelors of Love. . . . But when they are read in you as well as in Books, they cast off that awkard Air, and growing polite and complaisant, soon become absolute Masters of those outward endowments that by a happy Metamorphosis, change a rude Mass into a perfect Gentleman.

Less the creators of texts than texts in and of themselves, women become, oxymoronically, a species of cultured nature: not diamonds in the rough but perfectly polished gems whose qualities are more powerful because less studied. Unlike men, whose expressions of wit are "like forc'd Flowers, more due to Art than to Nature" and who are thus doomed endlessly to recycle "antiquated Novelties," Motteux sees women's writing as fresh, original, and of course, natural: "But we may well be jealous of Nature's kindness to you. You owe nothing to the Ancients, and your Wit is all your own." Indeed, like Dryden before him, Motteux uses women's supposedly amateur literary status and lack of classical education to chastise professional male authors: although he claims that women write only for "private diversion," they "can at least equal the best of our profes'd Authors with all their auxiliary Ancients!"[27] Motteux's need to exclude women from the economic sphere, here figured as the profitable aspects of literary production, parallels his need to deny their equally significant participation in the cultural arena. Thus while Motteux argues that gender difference is a social construction rather than a natural reality, and that there are therefore neither physiological nor practical reasons for excluding women from realms designated public, his analysis nevertheless reinscribes gender difference by endorsing a "natural" view of female otherness that describes culture as masculine while positioning women outside its boundaries.

Consequently, Motteux's sense of women's intellectual and artistic abilities as free from the supposed taint of masculine civilization contradicts his insightful grasp of the social bases of women's oppression. A close examination of an essay entitled "The equality of both sexes asserted" elucidates the complex repercussions of Motteux's delineation of virtue as gendered.[28] On a positive note, Motteux's take on male virtue as dependent upon the civilizing influence of women, whose cultural otherness serves as an antidote to male aggression and discontent (thus anticipating the later eighteenth-century designation of women as inherently morally superior), allows him to delineate perceptively the cultural bases for women's exclusion and oppression. Yet, at the same time, this position inscribes women within an ideology that defines them as necessarily apart from, rather than inside of, the institutions of culture and education, of economics and politics.

Beginning with a criticism of "most Men's" approach to the question of women's equality, the tract emphasizes the relationship between men's construction of women and their simultaneous configuring of themselves. Because the issue of women's equality appears to these men as "nothing but an Ingenious Amusement, and a meer piece of Gallantry," they bring to the subject "all the Rhetorical Stores, . . . saying in favor of the Fair, all the refined and flattering things which the mind is able to imagine." Motteux's use of "gallantry," a term commonly employed as a euphemism for adultery, characterizes these men as verbal, if not necessarily sexual, libertines, who defend women by employing the seductiveness that is women's own, and only, asset. Not surprisingly, their vindication emphasizes women's "Charms, which have made even the Gods stoop to their power, and raise them a Throne in every heart."[29] These men then contrast this "glorious" female "Empire" with the dominion of men, "which owes its establishment to nothing but Force, and the authority of Laws made by themselves to their own advantages."

While Motteux denounces the libertine approach as "very glittering and pretty" but lacking in seriousness and "Solidity," he nonetheless assimilates its rhetoric in order to articulate his own analysis of the gendered bases of power. "Force," "Law," and "Language," the last of which will later include "wit" and thus encompass literature and the arts, appear as the three spheres of male control. All three are compared to female "Charms"—women's one avenue to power. And yet, while the flatterers view these charming qualities as inherent in feminine nature, Motteux's next paragraph argues for the social causes of women's inequality: "Should a Woman pretend to preach, or command an Army, it would be a piece of Extravagance with relation to our Manners; yet if we rightly examine the thing, we will find that this only proceeds from Custom, which we persuade our selves to be very well grounded, because it hath always been the same." Men's vested interest in power and control is then internalized by women, who "stick to the Lot which hath been prescribed to them, and confine themselves to their private condition, supposing it their natural state; so that things being settled in that manner by the mutual consent of both Parties, this Order seems to us rather established by Nature, and an Universal Consent, than by the Usurpation of Men." In this passage, women's ambiguous "private condition" denotes both the specific tasks connected with women's biological capacities, in particular childbirth and child rearing, and women's relegation to the private, domestic sphere of home and family as opposed to the public spheres of politics, economics, and (university) education. A later paragraph combines both aspects, as Motteux poignantly asks, "Is it not then an unjust and tyrannical Invasion, to have reduced them [women] to the low and narrow Sphere of domestic management?"

Yet after arguing that women's difference is social rather than biological, and thus making "Nature" a dubious category for distinguishing between men and women, Motteux goes on, paradoxically, to acknowledge decisive biological variations in the sexes. Like those contemporary critics who seek to find in biology an irrefutable ground for the social distinctions manifested in gender, Motteux too elides culture and nature in his attempt to demonstrate women's equality. Thus he asserts that although women are the "weak Sex," Nature has made amends to them "by such advantages as justly compensate their want of strength." One example is the constitution of female "Organs and Fibres," which being more "thin and flexible" than those of men, endow women with "a more lively, delicate, and penetrating Imagination."[30] By positing a biological explanation for women's difference, Motteux can then employ scientific qualities to situate women's cultural abilities outside the realm of culture, as women's finer parts become the cause of "that natural Eloquence which shines in their expressions, and is so uncommon amongst Men, who by the structure of their Organs and Fibres, less fine and flexible, have less delicacy and vivacity."[31]

In the essay's most interesting rhetorical move, the oxymoronic "natural Eloquence" both registers the sign of women's absence from the dual senses of "learned" masculine culture and functions as the civilizing force in the production of culture itself. Motteux writes "that there is something more free, easy and polite, in the conversation of Women; they soften the too great roughness incident to the minds of Men, and the moroseness and pedantry of the Schools. Thus their exclusion from Offices, cannot be grounded on their Incapacity; neither is their Temper inconsistent with all necessary application." Motteux thus predicates his position on women upon a fallacy: the very arena of masculine cultural authority that he argues should be open to women by virtue of their capacity for understanding is necessarily founded upon their exclusion, for as cultural others women serve as the force that defines what Motteux calls the "perfect Gentleman."

In the essay's last paragraph, the idealization of women's innate abilities provides the basis for Motteux's analysis of men's cultural position. His condemnation of men's supposed superiority, strikingly similar to that offered by Virginia Woolf nearly two hundred and fifty years later in her brilliant essay *Three Guineas*, contrasts the "sweets of ease and tranquility" that women "peaceably enjoy" with the "world of toyls" that comprises male existence. In a passage that reads like a less fervent rendering of Bernard Mandeville, Motteux exposes the spheres of male domination as so many destructive delusions:

> [Men] are doomed to Till and Cultivate the Earth, and to the meanest and most laborious Employments. They expose themselves to Fatigues and Dangers in Voyages and Wars; all the labour of the Body, and anxiety of the Mind lies on their side, whilst Women peaceably enjoy the sweets of ease and tranquility. Thus they purchase dear enough their imaginary Empire, and their boasted Superiority costs them a world of toyls, much heavier to be born with, than the Submission of the Female Sex. And, after all, what have those Talents which Men value themselves so much upon, produced? unless it be *Chymera's*, Divisions, Errors and Disputes, the Results of which serve only to darken and confound Truth. They are all the Fruit of their mighty Sciences and Studies. Arts were only invented to provoke Pride and Vanity, and more to spoil the simplicity of Nature, and multiply our Wants and Uneasiness, than for the Ease or Happiness of Mankind. War, which intitles to the highest Merit amongst Men, is an Art which makes them murther one another; and from that barbarous Trade have sprung infinite mischiefs which have over-run the World, swept away whole Nations, and dealt the World into Factions, that make it their whole business to undermine and swallow one another. Savage Beasts are not mortally bent against their different kinds; each Sect, each State, seeks to pull down or sink its Competitor. In this lies their utmost glory and management. The weakness of Women hath not ushered in such a flood of mischief, as these fatal Virtues of Men.

I am hesitant to criticize Motteux's articulation of the violent and competitive nature of male existence, for in his society as well as in ours, the mistreatment of men is held in place by its denial. But I want nevertheless to highlight the ways in which his construction of women as cultural others necessarily distorts the lucidity of his picture. While Motteux's proposed antidote to the social ills created by "these fatal Virtues of Men" is to allow women access to privileged, because hitherto exclusive, masculine spheres, his solution is marred by its infeasibility: it is impossible for women to become part of something whose very existence depends upon their exclusion. Since Motteux's ability to protect the women who can in turn refine men defines his stance as both benevolent editor and virtuous man, women's "natural" status as cultural outsiders necessarily underpins, and thus fundamentally undermines, his otherwise insightful understanding of both men's and women's oppression.

Informing Men: Dunton's 'Athenian Mercury' and 'Ladies Mercury'

Whereas Motteux's author-narrator accentuates the courtly and protective aspect of the desirable man, numerous interactions in the *Athenian Mercury* exemplify the editors' role of paternal advisor. Traditional patriarchal models of parent-child relations, in which children were viewed as part of a father's property instead of desiring subjects in their own right, afforded those children little choice with regard to their future mates. In the late seventeenth century, however, an ideology of sentimental relations between husband and wife necessitated greater participation and choice on the part of potential spouses. Moreover, attitudes that stressed affective over economic marriage bonds meant that men as well as women needed to be educated differently with regard to both spousal choice and conjugal behavior. Even a publication as explicitly directed toward women as the *Ladies Dictionary* contains advice that emphasizes men's responsibility in these areas. The "young Batchellor," it counsels, should "be wary and cautious in his chusing, seeing it is the greatest business of his Life, next to the concernment of his Immortal State." In making his choice, he is instructed to be "well satisfied" of his prospective wife's "Birth, Sober and Religious Education, Frugality and Industry"; once he has managed to select the ideal woman, he is told how to win her hand.[32]

Conversely, these publications also taught women how to find the right men. Thus in response to the marvelous question of "Whether it be lawful for a Young Lady to pray for a Husband, and if lawful, in what Form?," the *Athenian Mercury* offers a half-mocking, half-serious "Prayer for a Husband";[33] I include here the invocation's more sober second section for its astounding catalogue of the characteristics that constitute a desirable husband.

As represented in this petition, not only would the ideal spouse exemplify the bourgeois attributes of self-control, circumspection, and religious virtue, but he would also demonstrate a reciprocal affection for his wife:

> Give me one whose Love has more of Judgment than Passion, who is Master of himself, or at least an indefatigable Scholar in such a Study, who has an equal Flame, a parallel Inclination, a Temper and Soul so like mine, *that as Two Tallies we may appear more perfect by Union.*
>
> Give me one of as genteel an Education as a *little Expense of time will permit*, with an indifferent Fortune, rather independent of the servile Fate of Palaces, and yet one whose *Retirement is not so much from the Publick as into himself*: One (if possible) above Flattery and Affronts, and yet as careful in preventing the Injury as able to repair it: One, *the Beauty of whose Mind exceeds that of his Face*, yet not Deformed so as to be distinguishable from others even unto a ridicule.
>
> Give me one that has learnt to *live much in a little time*, one that is no great Familiar in Converse with the World, nor *no little one with himself*: One (if two such Happinesses may be granted at one time to our Sex) who with these uncommon Endowments of Mind may (naturally) have a *sweet, mild, easie Disposition,* or at least one who by his Practice and frequent *Habit* has made himself so before he is made mine; but as the *Master-perfection and chiefest Draught, Let him be truly Virtuous and Pious; that is to say, Let me be truly Happy in my choice.*

Yet despite the periodical's active role in facilitating the shift from arranged marriages to those of preference, the narrative relations of the periodical do not, in fact, obviate the father's role in the process but merely transform it, as editorial advice acts as both guide and warning. That is to say, periodical literature, while not actually choosing specific mates for its correspondents,[34] nonetheless performs the crucial tasks of legislating to whom, and under what circumstances, its readers might pay addresses, and from whom they might receive them. Moreover, by assertively championing the rights of children, the *Athenian Mercury*, like the periodicals that would succeed it, presents itself as a better kind of father, condemning those mercenary parents or relations who view marriage as an economic institution rather than an emotional one. Indeed, the publication's editors censure not only parents, but any "*He* then or *She* that Marry for so base an End as *profit* without any possibility or prospect of love." Such a person becomes bestial rather than human, "guilty of the highest *Brutality* imaginable . . . united to a *Carkass* without a Soul" (Vol. 1, No. 13, May 5, 1691).

The periodical takes on the role of educating its readers in these new attitudes toward conjugality. As a result, courtship becomes a necessary process of learning to tell the true from the false, of discovering how to distinguish the genuine affection derived from mutual attraction and respect from the feigned attention that results from the desire to exploit and acquire, to obtain temporary sexual satisfaction or permanent material gain. In anticipation of the women's magazines we find today at the grocery check-out, advice about courtship—how to meet, get, and keep your man or woman—occupies a central place in the pages of both the *Athenian Mercury* and the related *Ladies Dictionary*. The thirteenth number of the *Athenian Mercury* is comprised solely of questions regarding the acceptable mores of marriage and courtship, ranging from "Whether it is *lawful* to make *Addresses* to young *Ladies*, without a prior acquainting their *Parents* and *Relatives* therewith?" to "Whether it is lawful to Marry a Person one *cannot Love*, only in compliance to *Relations*, and to get an *Estate?*" The third number of the fourth volume (Oct. 6, 1691) is devoted to a "FORM OF COURTSHIP" for the use of young bachelors; a few weeks later the editors oblige with a similar issue for women, teaching them "how to Behave our selves to the *Men* (Vol. 4, No. 13, Nov. 10, 1691).[35]

Although these texts express a number of different attitudes, obedience to parents often conflicts with a growing emphasis on the marriage partners' choice. While affirming, on the one hand, the importance of parental wishes by stating that "So long as *Parents* are living, they have a greater Propriety over their Children than the Age is generally aware of," the *Athenian Mercury* nevertheless opposes those parental decisions that occur at the expense of children's desires: "We don't say that Parents have that right over their *Children*, as to Marry 'em against their own Consent, the many sad Consequences of such *Marriages* show it impracticable" (Vol. 3, No. 10, Aug. 29, 1691). Indeed, a response from the first "Ladies Number" is even more vehement: "*Parents* are not to *dispose* of their *Children* like *Cattel*, nor to make 'em *miserable* because they *happened* to give 'em *Being*" (Vol. 1, No. 13, May 5, 1691). The shift in emphasis from parents to partners served ostensibly to keep sexual desire within the marital relationship, for, as is made wittily explicit at the end of the diatribe against parents' marrying children against their will, "he who *marries* a Woman he cou'd *never Love*, will, 'tis to be fear'd, soon *Love* a Woman he never *marry'd*" (Vol. 1, No. 13). The same could be, and is, said about a woman: what strikes the modern reader of these texts most forcefully is their sense of parity. The discussion of adultery that occupies many of these pages represents both men and women as victims as well as perpetrators of adulterous liaisons. In response to a question about how a husband ought to behave in relation to an adulterous wife, the editors reply that he should leave punishment for the other world; they end by stating that "Nor, holds this [behavior] only in *Women*, but in *Men* as well as they, since after we have abstracted from Custom and Opinion (both very ill Judges) the crime is much the same in one as the other" (Vol. 2, No. 3, June 3, 1691).

As with queries about courtship, the periodical articulates many of the questions about adultery in terms of both abstract knowledge—for example, "Whether our Laws against Adultery, and the Proof of it, been't too favourable to the Women" (Vol. 3, No. 13, Sept. 8, 1691)—and personal experience: "Whether a Lady having a Man to her Husband that keeps ill Company, and debauches himself with common whores, . . . may not she break the bond of Marriage, by separating herself from him, and marrying again, or by repaying him in his own Coin?" (Vol. 3, No. 21, n.d.). Although the questions themselves are frequently interesting, the replies are fairly standard, carefully toeing the Anglican party line: a separation from bed and board can be obtained, but to marry or have sexual relations while the adulterous spouse is still living is to commit adultery oneself. Thus Gilbert McEwen maintains that in the *Athenian Mercury*, the "rigidity of divorce law is pointed up by the frequency of questions about the circumstances which would permit husband or wife to leave a partner without due legal process."[36] We find the common editorial attitude typified in the response to a woman who asks whether she can leave her marriage to a debauched husband and remarry: "Upon proof of *Adultery*, she may sue out a Divorce from Bed and Board, and an Third of the Estate for maintenance, but the Law allows not a Second *Marriage* whilst he is living" (Vol. 3, No. 21). In spite of his own apparently happy marriage to Elizabeth Annesley, Dunton was clearly fascinated by the topics of adultery and divorce. In *The Athenian Spy*, a miscellany published by Dunton in 1704, "A poor man, unhappily yok'd, petitions ATHENS for some legal way of Unmarrying both himself and others in the same condition." The Athenian Society cheerful accommodates him by printing an extended proposal of "an infallible Method to *Unmarry* those that are *Unhappily Yok'd, by Act of Parliament*, with the *Reasons* that make such a Provision of absolute necessity."

In these publications, editors play a paternal role which serves to educate male readers as well as female readers into positions of domestic responsibility. But although an ideology of chaste heterosexuality posited men's conjugal fidelity as comparable in importance to that of women, sexual threats from within and without had different consequences for each gender. Accordingly, an important aspect of the masculine paternal role involved educating women against the sexual dangers that men posed, a process that served to instruct men about the dangers of other men as well as about the need to control themselves. But educating women posed a difficult, and particularly delicate problem, for while women must know enough to keep out of danger, they must not know too much, since that could become a danger in itself by filling them with "wanton" ideas. Certain avenues to knowledge are represented as extremely dangerous, since young women may identify too closely with what they read and thus be tempted to enact textual scenes, as books become "cunning Lessons, to learn young Maids to sin more wittily."[37]

Yet the editors also hold up knowledge as the surest way to safeguard female virtue. Responding to a man's hesitation about encouraging the studiousness of a young woman "over whom I have some Power," the editors of the twelfth volume of the *Athenian Mercury* reply that "since knowledge depends upon Purity and Simplicity, it seems the safest course Women can take for Security [of] their Purity and Chastity, is, to make Provision of Learning and Knowledge. For 'tis a thing hitherto unheard of, that a Woman was Learn'd, and not Chast and Continent." As evidence for their position, they cite Greek mythology: "the Ancients" represented the chastity of learned women "by *Minerva* the Goddess of Sciences, and the Nine Muses, all Virgins" (Vol. 12, No. 4, Nov. 4, 1693). Although the reply argues that women should be educated on the basis of their similarity to men, it also, and paradoxically, distinguishes women from men by claiming that learning will better equip them to be virtuous wives and mothers. Initially, the editors acknowledge both men's "God-given" power over women by virtue of their superior strength, and men's abuse of that power: "as absolute Power is often accompanied with Tyranny, so he hath not only reserv'd to himself alone the Authority of making Laws (whereunto Women never being called, have always had the worst) but have also appropriated the best things to himself." The editors go on to attack both primogeniture and marital property laws, arguing that in their desire to wield sole economic power, men have "ill provided [for women] . . . in Successions" and have kept women in "Servitude . . . to have themselves Masters of their Estates." Yet women's material deprivation is less detrimental than their intellectual loss, for not only do women possess "Understanding" in common with men, but many of women's distinguishing physical attributes make them not just comparable with, but even superior to men in terms of their ability to learn. Having established intellectual parity between the sexes, the editors argue for women's education in relation to their separate (but hardly equal) realm of authority: "Now if it be true, that Politicks and Oeconomicks are founded upon the same Principles, and there needs as much Knowledge to preserve as to acquire; then since Women are in a Family, what men are in a State, and are destined to keep what men get, why shou'd they not have the Knowledge of the same Maxims, as Men have by Study and Theory; inasmuch as the reservedness and Modesty of their Sex, allows them not to have the experience thereof, by frequenting the World?" As with Motteux, the editors' claim for women's equality comes finally to depend upon a belief in essential difference based upon artificially separated spheres.

Whereas throughout its pages, the *Athenian Mercury* champions women's claim to knowledge as a form of sexual protection, it still regards sexual knowledge as a topic for anxious concern. When an earlier reader, whose sex is undetermined, writes to inquire "Whether it be proper for Women to be *Learned?*" (Vol. 1, No. 18, May 23, 1691), the answer betrays that apprehension by representing women's knowledge solely in sexual terms: "All grant that they may have some Learning, but the Question is of what sort, and to what Degree? Some indeed think they have *Learn'd* enough, if they can distinguish between their *Husbands Breaches* and another *mans.*"[38] Moreover, women must learn not only to defend against the false language of seduction, but they must also discern how to behave in such a manner as not to provoke men, who, "from a double Temptation of Vanity and Desire, are but too apt to turn whatever a Woman Acts to the hopefullest side."[39] Prevention becomes the best "Remedy": "therefore, nothing ought more seriously to be avoided, than such a kind of Civility, as may be mistaken for an Invitation to what is unreasonable."[40]

These texts advise women to be reserved and modest, but, contrary to later ascriptions that we will encounter in the *Tatler* and *Spectator*, the *Athenian Mercury* does not construe these attributes as part of women's nature. Rather, such advice responds to an understanding of male sexuality as an appetite, an urge comparable to those for food and drink, which if not regulated could prove extremely destructive. As the next chapter's reading of Dunton's explicitly sexual periodical the *Night-Walker* will demonstrate, Dunton gives men full responsibility both for their own and for women's deviations from the emerging norms of heterosexual monogamy.[41] When asked "Whether are more inconstant in Love, the Men or the Women?" (Vol. 3, No. 4, Aug. 8, 1691), the editors respond that they see the situation as comparable, "thô Interest makes both the one and the other complain loudest of the contrary Sex." However, they present women's inconstancy as "more *ex-*

cuseable" because men "are generally the *Aggressors*." As evidence, the editors cite the fact that "we have known very few Kings or Princes who have been constant to one Woman: And have instances of some who cou'd not be contented with less than *several hundreds*; whereas we have but comparatively few of the *Female Sex* in that high Station who have been false to their *Lords*, and never heard of any of 'em who kept a *Seraglio of Men*." Biological and cultural differences are here erased; the concept of polygamy represents the inherently aggressive and appetitive quality of male sexuality. In the question that follows, "Whether in a Dishonourable Amour is most to blame, the Man in tempting, or the Woman in yielding?", the answer states it is the man, "because he's the *very Cause of the Evil*" (ibid.). Women are not accused of inherent lasciviousness, as in the earlier misogynist tradition: "The Woman had been *virtuous* had he not tempted her." Because man is positioned as the aggressor, woman must learn to be the defender.

In the majority of interchanges, male and female correspondents ask questions and receive information ranging from the abstract to the deeply personal. As the *Athenian Mercury* progressed, questions developed into narratives, and people began to tell their own stories. In these confessional texts, editors transformed their correspondents' experiences into examples for others. Two interactions demonstrate how a more elaborate narrative structure functioned to delineate specific relations among men. The question from the *Athenian Mercury* (Vol. 5, No. 13, Jan. 12, 1692) reads as follows:

> I Have long liv'd in an unlawful thô successful Amour. I have enjoy'd all the Favours that a lovely young Woman can bestow. I am very sensible of the Sin I commit, as well as the Injury I do the Husband. My Circumstances and Employment are such I cannot quit this Town or Land, nor wou'd willingly expose her Reputation: I therefore give you the trouble of this to beg your Advice what measures I shall take (besides those prescrib'd by Religion) to avoid this *lovely Tempter*, who will not fail to press me to a continuance of my Passion, which I am resolv'd to quit. Your Directions in this Case will very much oblige———*Yours*, &c.

In their reply, the learned editors hold up the letter itself as a moral example, its exemplary nature a sufficient warrant for publication: "This being a thing of more than ordinary moment, as well in its self as from the Influence it may have upon others, we thought fit to print the Letter at large, to let our Gallants see, that there are yet some imitable Examples left, of penitence at least, if not of perfect Virtue." The editors' riposte goes on to acknowledge the man's sexuality, his infringement upon the husband's property rights, the woman's sexuality, and the correspondent's recognition of his "sin." It counsels the correspondent to use his own "conversion" to bring about that of his mistress: the editors tell him to write to her "using the same arguments to convince her, and make her a real *Convert* to *Virtue* and *Honour*, which he found before work'd on his own Mind." Yet such advice, sandwiched between stories of virtuous male behavior (e.g., Joseph and Potiphar's wife) and directions about how the man should respond to his mistress's importunities, seems almost an aside. Rather, the editors emphasize the powerful, almost addictive, nature of the man's sexual desire: "*see her no more*, if possible to be avoided; at least *converse* not with her, nor receive Letters from her, but to the *Fire* with 'em as soon as e'er you perceive they are *hers*, if you are sure of the *Hand* without so much as opening 'em, or else you'l endanger the rekindling a worse Flame in your Breast, than that from which you have sav'd 'em." Indeed his passion metamorphoses for the editors into a form of illness: "As for your self, have a care of *Relapses*, more dangerous than the *Disease*." The primary point I wish to make here is that the specific male-female alliance that initiated the inquiry recedes in favor of the interaction between the editor and correspondent and then, in turn, between the text and other male readers, particularly those "gallants" who exhibit similar behavior. While the correspondent himself does not construe his situation as exemplary, his narrative is shaped by the textual interaction itself into an illustration of virtuous male penitence.

The editors' response to a narrative of female contrition taken from the *Ladies Mercury*, a short-lived periodical enterprise published contemporaneously with the *Athenian Mercury* and usually attributed to Dunton,[42] evinces a set of complex narrative relations that incorporate many of the attitudes we have found throughout these examples of early periodical literature. Just as Dunton capitalized upon a growing middle-class readership with his question-and-answer format in the *Athenian Mercury*, he seemed to recognize a separate and equally lucrative audience in middle- and upper-class women. However, as I argue in Chapter 9, in this period even publications purporting to be aimed specifically at women necessarily included men—whether as editors, examples, or correspondents. As with the "Ladies Issues" of the *Athenian Mercury*, subjects earmarked "feminine" were also of significant concern to men. Although I reserve a full-fledged discussion of the problematic appellation of "Women's Magazine" for the final chapter of this study, I nevertheless want to emphasize that despite the potent success of an ideology of separate spheres, men's place was everywhere. By promising in its inaugural issue not to encroach upon the "learned" territory of the Athenian Society but to deal only with "that little Sub-lunary, Woman,"[43] the *Ladies Mercury* seemed to confirm the belief in a distinct place for each sex. Yet in their claim to leave to the Athenians "that fair and larger field; the Examination of Learning, Nature, Arts, Sciences, and indeed the whole World," the authors simultaneously demonstrate their awareness that men's sphere was "indeed the whole World." (Of course, the fact that the *Athenian Mercury* itself printed questions by women and related to women's concerns reveals even more bluntly the spurious distinction between the two realms.)

The publication's pose of mock-restraint with regard to subject matter is paralleled by its assumed modesty of tone: the dedication "To the Ladies" claims that not only will the periodical answer women's questions, but it "shall likewise make it our study to [omit] the least offensive syllable, that it may give any rude Shock to the Chastest Ear. We declare our selves such Religious Homages of Vertue and Innocence, that We would not force a Blush into a Virgin-cheek, having that true value for Beauty, as to adorn it with no other Vermilion but its own." The simultaneously idealized and condescending position of the introduction manifests itself as well within the specific narrative exchanges. Such protestations of editorial virtue are particularly interesting in light of the questions posed, many of which focus upon decidedly immodest issues—namely, female sexuality both within and outside of marriage.

The initial question in the first number relates a story, told at great length, by "a very young *Woman*, born of Parents of some *little Quality*, but not altogether favour'd with an *extraordinary Fortune*." She is, however, endowed with enough beauty to "balance the slenderness" of her portion; yet she writes that it was her "Calamity, about Two Years Since, [to] be so seduced, as to give up the very *Soul of Beauty*, my *Honour*, to a lewd and infamous Rifler, with whom I secretly continued this vile and unhappy Conversation, for near a Twelve Month together." She then proceeds to tell how a man of "great Honour and Worth" fell "honourably in Love" with her, married her, and how he is the best of husbands to her. The only problem, however, is that her past sits so heavily upon her that although she has attempted in frequent prayers to expiate her sin, nevertheless "a hundred daily and hourly Horrors haunt me, telling my conscious Soul what *Delusion and Pollution I brought to his Bed*, what practised *Cheats* and *Impostures* I have used, all my affected feigned Innocence; Nay, (Heaven forgive me) I practised even the vilest of Arts in his very *Bridal Night Joys*, being in that dearest Scene the highest of Counterfeiters."

Having worn herself away to a "Skeleton" with her worries, she turns to the editors of the *Ladies Mercury* both for advice, since "(from those that know me I must not ask it)," and for confession, "(for since Black and White cannot Blush, I venture under this *Skreen* to make you my *Confessors*.)" Throughout their extensive response, the editors' tone baldly obliterates the sexual nature of the woman's situation. After all, the fact that this "unlawful amour" continued for twelve months seems to imply the woman's acquiescence, at least to some extent: this was more of an affair than a seduction. Treating her as an example for other women, they necessarily erase her sexual past by focusing solely upon her present contrition: "Well, Mournful fair unknown, you have drawn so lovely a Picture of Penitence, that I hope you'l make your whole Sex so in love with the Shadow as to resolve to copy from so excellent an Original." They further deny her agency by construing her as victim rather than participant: "You have exprest your self so much in the Mournful Notes of a Ravish'd *Philomel* or a Bleeding *Lucrece*, that if all the private wounds of Feminine Honour felt Your Remorse and Pain, I am afraid we should have but a sickly Age, and a drooping World."

The editors then respond with advice that is both pragmatic and idealized, as they exculpate her from her supposed crime against her husband by claiming that her "sin when committed was only against Heaven; for Your Honourable Lover was not then so much as thought on, consequently uninterest'd and unconcern'd. When that Honourable Lover afterwards address'd himself, no Obligation even of the most Rigid Laws compel'd you to be your own Accuser." With her initial desire utterly obliterated, they then advise her to turn her newly conceived, penitent sexuality upon her husband, to whom it rightfully belongs: "And as for your part make it your study . . . to exert thy tenderest, kindest, duteous, softest Love in all the opening, blooming, ravishing, melting fragrance, that the whole Paradise of Truth and Faith, with all its endless boundless Joys can give him." The multiple strings of adjectives, worthy of Milton, depict an Edenic chaste heterosexuality powerful enough to erase everything that has preceded it.

Thus women's sexuality is here being re-formed, but at the cost of male ignorance. The editors of the *Ladies Mercury* do not find this problematic: "[Your husband's] confidence of a Virgin-Innocence was an Error of the Favourablest side, and 'twas no part of Yours to unveil the mistake." Rather, they see the husband's innocence as a necessary element in pardoning the woman's action:

> Did you make your self Happy in the honourable Embraces of the best of Husbands by a little Hypocrisie? *Jacob* obtain'd the highest of Blessings, transfer'd even to Posterity, by a false Neck and false Hands, the most notorious of Cheats, and the boldest of Lyes. You brought Guilt to his Bed, 'tis true, but a truly and nobly repented Guilt. Infamy, (the more substantial

and sensible wrong) you brought none, for your sin lyes con-
cealèd from the World. Your Husband, for his part, tasted no
fainter nor weaker Sweets in your Embraces for having a Rose-
bud cropp'd before him: For Ignorance keeps up the Devotion.

It is a fascinating response. By fashioning the woman as both pattern and
victim, and by seeing her repentance as erasing the misdeed, the editors sen-
timentalize and even trivialize her, yet they also endow her with a form of
power in the knowledge of her own experience. But that power is in turn dependent upon the seeming control—both linguistic and moral—of the publication's male editors, under whose alchemical pen even the dross of sexual
license can be converted into the gold of conjugal chastity.

Contrasting the response from the *Ladies Mercury* with the much more
sobering reply to the same question published three weeks later in the
Athenian Mercury (Vol. 9, No. 28, Mar. 18, 1694) exposes the problematic
nature of the former editors' efforts to promulgate an ethos of penitent sexuality.[44] Here the question itself, in the form of the woman's narrative, is
presented much more briefly, and the editors, while first referring to the response from the *Ladies Mercury*, then proceed with their own more conventional answer. They bluntly state that the woman should never have married
her husband in the first place: "You ought to have been the *Wife* of your first
Acquaintance, or else always to have liv'd *unmarry'd*"; furthermore, they
chastise her for being more troubled by the loss of her looks during her marriage than by the loss of her virtue prior to it.

Focusing primarily upon the woman's betrayal of both her husband and
her marriage vows, the *Athenian Mercury* editors criticize the "false Doctrine" evidenced in the *Ladies Mercury* response, which "excuses your *Hypoc-
risie* by the Example of *Jacob*, and might have done as much with your *Whoredom* by that of *Judah* and *Tamar*." They end by pointing to the problems implicit in treating the woman's narrative as exemplary, for she could serve as
an example of whoredom rather than penitence. Ultimately, they attack not
the woman herself, but the judgment and the moral view of the *Ladies Mercury*: "However, from this, and from the whole *stream* of this Gentlemans
Writings, we can't help wishing that his design ben't the *Encouragement* of
some of that Sex in another and a worse Sense than he talks of in his Preface
to it, *viz*. 'That they hope the whole Sex will be so in *Love* with this *Shadow*,
as to resolve to copy from so excellent an original.'"

The exchange between the two publications uses the woman's pained narrative to spark a discussion of men's attitudes and behaviors, in this case
those of the editors themselves. Although one of the publications might have
been titled the *Ladies Mercury*, and although women might have been an im-

portant audience for both periodicals, each text nevertheless offered an important site for discussion among and about men. The publicly private space of the social periodical contributed to the development of a sphere in which men learned implicitly to become proper bourgeois citizens through explicit attention to women as well as to themselves. As informing texts such as the *Athenian Mercury*, the *Ladies Mercury*, and the *Ladies Dictionary* educated women into their proper domestic roles, they also provided a forum for criticizing men by opening for public scrutiny and editorial approbation the societal, and particularly the familial, dangers posed by uncontrolled male behavior. Yet it is not until a later reforming text by Dunton, the *Night-Walker, or, Evening Rambles in Search after Lewd Women, with the Conferences Held with Them, &c.* (1696–97), that this new discourse on masculinity becomes combined with a particularized narrative voice. Although most modern critics classify the publication as pornographic, dismissing it with attitudes ranging from faint distaste to downright opprobrium,[45] the *Night-Walker* serves as a fertile source for exploring the ways in which the form of interaction between narrator and reader inscribes a new model of exemplary masculinity. Unlike the chivalric authorial voice of the *Gentleman's Journal*, Dunton's *Night-Walker*, as we shall see, offers a chastened model for sexual reform within the context of monogamous marriage.

3 *Reforming Men: The 'Night-Walker'*

There is a very large Body of Persons, compos'd of the *Original Society* before-mentioned, with the Additions that have been since made of Persons of Eminency in the *Law*, *Members of Parliament*, *Justices of Peace*, and considerable *Citizens of London* of known Abilities and great Integrity, who frequently meet to consult of the *best Methods* for carrying on the Business of *Reformation*, and to be ready to advise and assist others that are already ingaged, or any that are willing to join in the same Design.
—Josiah Woodward, "An Account of the Societies for Reformation of Manners, in England and Ireland" (1699)

ot yet christened the "Night-Walker," the figure of the man walking the streets in search of wanton women first appeared in an uncharacteristically lengthy narrative published in the third volume of the *Athenian Mercury* (No. 3, Aug. 4, 1691). Touted earlier in the same volume (No. 1, July 28, 1691) as a forthcoming "Gentleman's *. . . Account of his late Six Nights Rambles*, with the Confessions he has got from those Creatures about their first Engagements, their Struggles *with Conscience*, and about the Methods of their stiffling [sic] it by their *Habits in Lewdness*," the chronicle subsequently assumed the form of a response to the question of "Whether the present offers at a Reformation are like to prove effectual? and what are the best methods to detect the vile haunts and practices of those Lewd Women called *Night-Walkers*?"[1] Dunton was here, as in many other matters, perspicaciously topical, for 1691 was the year in which was founded the first London association to obliterate vice.[2] Emerging five years later as a periodical in its own right, the *Night-Walker* ran for eight numbers of approximately twenty-eight quarto pages apiece and sold for

sixpence.[3] Each issue details the various nocturnal adventures of the narrator, who, although concerned initially with reforming "Lewd Women," soon comes to turn his attention upon men. In fact, what emerges from the narrative grid comprised of the narrator's descriptions in conjunction with the stories of the men and women he encounters is a pattern of *male* corruption and deceit. We find countless stories of servant maids and young gentlewomen debauched by masters or master's sons and left, often pregnant and always without resources, to fend for themselves; of women who, upon being forced by avaricious parents into marriages with wealthy older men, turn to adultery to satisfy the desires their husbands cannot; and of wives of publicans or tradesmen who must use their own charms to sell their husbands' wares.

By ignoring the context from which this periodical emerged, most critics have failed to take seriously the significance of Dunton's text for interpreting late seventeenth-century intersections of gender, sexuality, textuality, and class.[4] The assessment of Walter Graham, one of the earliest twentieth-century critics of the periodical genre, exemplifies both the norm and the exception; he notes, on the one hand, Dunton's "effort to exploit the reforming trend of his time," and on the other hand he dismisses the publication as "worthless . . . save as it illustrates the very general interest in the correction of morals which preceded the *Tatler*."[5] Graham concludes that "Dunton's declaration of war on 'the chief prostitutes in England, from the pensionary miss down to the common strumpet,' . . . whether dictated by religious or mercenary motives, added another impulse to the wave of reform."[6] Graham's equivocation—"religious *or* mercenary motives"—typifies the attitude of most critics who have, if only in passing, passed judgment on the *Night-Walker*: like Graham, they treat the two positions as mutually exclusive, whereas I will demonstrate that Dunton's genius lay precisely in his ability to combine the moral with the mercenary, to profit from reform.

A Grub Street "modern" whose tremendous output and notorious eccentricity made him an easy target for such "ancients" as Swift and Pope,[7] Dunton has traditionally been relegated to the musty halls of obscurity or to the critical cat-calls of scurrility.[8] Of all his abundant literary endeavors, only the *Athenian Mercury* has received serious critical attention. However, if we extend what Graham calls religious motives to include a general didactic or reforming aim, such a collection of attributes—didactic and remunerative—characterizes not just Dunton's idiosyncratic publications but the majority of eighteenth-century periodical literature.[9] As I will argue, the *Night-Walker*'s fervent engagement with the period's concern for sexual reform both paralleled and exploited the strategies of Dunton's contemporaries, in particular those members of the various societies for the reformation of manners. At the same time, the periodical's stance on a number of issues diverged significantly from that of the reforming societies. The *Night-Walker's* treatment of prostitution as an economic phenomenon as well as a moral one, its explicit attention to men rather than women as the perpetrators of sexual misconduct, and its focus on the behavior of men of the highest social status as well as those from the lower and middle ranks, all served, ironically, to align the periodical with such subsequent reformers as Daniel Defoe and Bernard Mandeville, whose own works exposed the hypocrisy of the societies' methods and criticized their ineffectiveness. In his long-lived periodical, the *Review* (1704–11), Defoe attacked the societies' double standard of class, maintaining that "it is Unreasonable and Unjust, an Injury to the common people, and a Dishonour to the Gentry and Nobility to make Laws . . . against Vice and Immorality, while you execute those Laws upon the Poor, Mean and Common People only, and your selves go Unpunished in the open Commission of the Same."[10] Mandeville, by contrast, censured not the societies' duplicity but their inefficiency when confronted with the "Torrent of Lewdness" that is male sexual desire. In *A Modest Defense of the Public Stews* (1724), in which he proposes a plan for licensed and regulated houses of prostitution, Mandeville aims not to extirpate male lust but to channel it more judiciously: "The *Public Stews* will not encourage Men to be lewd, but they will encourage them to exercise their Lewdness in a proper Place, without disturbing the Peace of the *Society*, and with as little Detriment to themselves as possible."[11]

Whatever their shortcomings, the several societies for the reformation of manners that emerged in the last decade of the seventeenth century testified to a strongly perceived need on the part of certain sober citizens in and around London to address an increasing secularization of moral authority in the years after the Restoration. In *Sin and Society in the Seventeenth Century*, John Addy employs the surviving consistory court records of Chester diocese from the years 1600 to 1730 (some 10,500 files) to trace the "standards of morality and social relationships" that existed during this period.[12] Addy's case studies reveal the ways in which both church and community were intimately involved in legislating sexual behavior: "Authority demanded that Englishmen and women must be compelled by law to live what seventeenth-century society considered to be a Christian life. The vast bulk of office causes that came before the consistory court were concerned with licentious living, fornication, adultery, premarital pregnancy, failure to marry after a betrothal, or refusal to cohabit after marriage, together with some scolding, back-biting, and brawling between neighbours. These composed a goodly proportion of court business."[13] Addy observes that the courts' concern with scandalous living rather than heresy might have had much to do with the fact that although the putative father was by law responsible for the maintenance of a child born out of wedlock, such fathers were often difficult to identify, thus thrusting the burden of care onto the parish whose "respectable parishioners disliked paying rates to maintain children illegally begotten."[14]

Yet the courts' ability to prosecute their business was seriously hampered in the years after the Restoration. Although the Church itself was restored to its pre-Civil War organization and the church courts reinstated, "the prerogative courts of High Commission and Star Chamber were not. This meant that the coercive power which had upheld and enforced the sentences imposed by the church courts was missing." Offenses previously punished by steep fines or humiliating sentences could now be penalized only through penance and excommunication. Moreover, Parliament weakened even this latter remaining prerogative by enacting frequent general pardons.[15] The inability of the church courts to enforce moral norms created a gap that was quickly filled by citizens who began to form their own religious societies in order to impose the moral laws that the church courts could not. Richmond Bond describes the resultant London Society as "a prominent body with royal sponsorship and noble support which strove to enforce neglected statutes and identify offenders, to regulate conduct and to direct righteous zeal against common evils."[16] Drawing on the punitive techniques of the church courts, the Society's methods combined actual prosecution before magistrates "shamed into enforcing laws regarded by some as obsolete"[17] with public humiliation in the form of an annual broadside "Black List" publishing the names of those malefactors caught and punished by members of the Society. Furthermore, the reformers appealed to the zeal and curiosity of both their own members and interested outsiders by printing thousands of tracts, including the Society's yearly sermon.[18]

In his largely overlooked reforming text, Dunton too capitalizes upon the relationship between discourse and reform, between the need for self-regulation and the management of others. Before moving to a specific examination of the *Night-Walker*, however, I wish to turn for a moment to Dunton's own history, which, like the history of his time, provides an important context for rethinking Dunton's periodical. Born in 1659 and raised in Aston Clinton, thirty miles from London, John Dunton inherited the name and was slated to inherit the profession of his father, grandfather, and great-grandfather—minister in the Church of England. Yet his "unsettled and mercurial humour"[19] distracted him from the scholarship requisite to the clergy and prevented his following the path of "lineal descent."[20] His father apprenticed him at the age of fifteen to a bookseller, Thomas Parkhurst, so that he might be "at least a friend to Learning and the Muses, if I would not join myself to them by some nearer affinity."[21] Dunton's break from the patrilineal pattern was furthered by the fact that Parkhurst was both a Londoner and a prominent Presbyterian. Dunton subsequently solidified his connection to the Dissenting community through his marriage in 1682 to Elizabeth Annesley, daughter of the Reverend Samuel Annesley, whose religious writings Dunton was later to publish along with the works of many of the minister's nonconformist congregants.[22] The first four books Dunton released under his own imprint in 1682 had religious themes;[23] moreover, an advertisement from that year describing books sold by Dunton "list[ed] twenty-three titles, for the most part sermons and devotional works, which were to form the basis of Dunton's trade for several years."[24]

Thus while Dunton's move to London and away from the clerical profession may have "disrupted the family pattern,"[25] his thwarted religious orientation surfaced in alternative ways. Like those reforming societies that claimed to have transcended sectarian difference "in the common cause of Christianity,"[26] Dunton, in his career as author, publisher, and distributor, managed to incorporate a wide range of beliefs and affiliations under the united rubrics of morality and profitability. One item in particular, an anonymous pamphlet issued in 1694, two years prior to the first installment of the *Night-Walker*, demonstrates Dunton's involvement—as well as investment—in the reforming cause. Published by the Society for Reformation and entitled "Proposals for a National Reformation of Manners," the pamphlet may even have been authored by Dunton himself, but in any case he certainly incorporated many of its attitudes and techniques into his subsequent periodical. The work displays such typical reforming strategies as "The *Instrument* for Reformation," a blueprint for organizing new societies and encouraging fresh membership,[27] and the publication of a "Black List" of those prosecuted, comparable to one the Society itself published annually.[28]

In the Preface to the *Night-Walker*'s inaugural issue, the narrator lends himself credibility by citing his "very good Correspondence" with numerous representatives of moral authority, including "*Justices Clerks, Constables,* [and] *Watchmen,*" as well as "*with some of the Society for Reformation,* many of which have sent us in *Considerable Lists* of such persons of *both Sexes* as have come within their Cognizance, with an *Account of their particular Crimes.*"[29] Encouraging readers' participation in his design by asking them to send "such *Instances* as occurr to them" to his printer, James Orme, the narrator solicits readers' stories in the same way that the reforming societies encouraged the efforts of their own members. Yet he also distinguishes himself from their methods by claiming that his "Design is to Reform, and not to Expose, and shall therefore refrain from making use of *Names*, tho' now and then we may make use of *Initial Letters*, to let the more *Notorious Criminals* know, that we could name them if we please" (ibid.). While the Night-Walker clearly relies upon the reforming power inherent in the public nature of print, his aim, as I will discuss more fully below, is primarily to instill in his readers, particularly his male readers, the discipline of self-regulation.

Moreover, his explicit dedication of the fourth number of the first volume "To the GENTLEMEN of the Society for Reformation" betrays his ambiguous relationship to that august group by, on the one hand, cheering their efforts—"Gentlemen, take heart and redouble your Courage"—while, on the other hand, hinting at their failures when he remarks on the enormity of their task, since "the Corrupt nature of men is such, that it is much easier to debauch a whole Nation than to reform a few Parishes" (Dec. 1696, A₂v). The narrator concludes by cleverly insinuating himself into the ranks of the Reforming Society as a (more efficacious) mouthpiece for their endeavors: "And as there are no persons so capable of discovering *Lewd Houses and Persons as your selves*, it would be a peice of good Service to the publick, if you would communicate from time to time, your discoveries of that nature to the *Undertaker of this Work*; There's reason to think that the exposing of those Persons, and their practises in this manner once a *Month*, together with some Arguments against those Courses, would be more effectual to restrain or at least to expose those Enormities than the printing of your *Black Lists once a year*" (A₃).

In the publications of these societies, public discourse, couched in the approbative language of legal, religious, and royal authority, becomes a way of inviting individuals to participate in their actions. In Josiah Woodward's "Account of the Societies for Reformation of Manners," which first appeared in 1699, three years after Dunton's *Night-Walker*, information functions as a means of inciting readers' involvement: "I ask leave to present the World with a *short Scheme* of the *Design*, and some *Account* of the *Managers* of it, that the well-disposed part of the Nation, that have hitherto been Strangers to it, may, by the Knowledge thereof, be induced to join in so good a Work."[30] The exposition that follows, in which Woodward describes societies comprised respectively of legal authorities, tradesmen, constables, informants, housekeepers and officers, religious enthusiasts, and ministers,[31] encourages the reader to find his proper niche within social, professional, and religious hierarchies. By contrast, Dunton's periodical uses private behavior—that of the Night-Walker himself—as a means to public reform. The Night-Walker functions as his own organization, a society of one, yet he enlarges his scope both by incorporating into his periodical the narratives of the lewd women and men he attempts to reform and by encouraging the private participation of readers who must learn to survey not the streets of London, but the nooks and crannies of their own homes and their own psyches.

Unlike the reforming societies, which routinely attacked prostitutes while turning a blind eye to the mistresses of upper-class men, the *Night-Walker* claims in its very title to continue publishing "'till a Discovery be made of all the chief *Prostitutes* in *England*, from the *Pensionary Miss*, down to the *Common Strumpet*." Paradoxically, however, Dunton's periodical both criticizes and upholds the sexual class system. By showing the link between feminine sexual degradation and economic necessity, the *Night-Walker* exposes destructive male appetites for sex and money while at the same time institutionalizing monogamous marriage as the only acceptable place for both male and female sexuality.[32] Depicting the exemplary marriage as one between equals in age and socioeconomic status, the text attacks those middle-class fathers who use their daughters to bolster their own economic standing. The companionate ideal also functions to denounce the libertine behavior of aristocrats, male or female, who separate sexual pleasure from its proper place within the family unit. Using seduction as a means to gain or display power, aristocratic sexuality stands in contrast to the prototype of middle-class love, in which sexual attraction between spouses cements the domestic relationship both emotionally and economically.

The very title of the periodical embodies tensions inherent in its narrative structure. "The Night-Walker" refers on one level to the narrator, the man who supposedly walks the streets of London and its surroundings at night, and who interrogates women and men, usually in one-on-one situations, in order to show them the error of their ways. "The Night-Walker" is also the title of the periodical, which itself attempts to do publicly, with the readers of the text, what the narrator does privately with its characters. Accordingly, whether one reads to find one's own situation represented in the pages of the periodical or simply to gain from someone else's story the warning that prevents entry into such disastrous circumstances in the first place, the actual process of reading the work serves a moral function. Whereas male and female readers alike can align themselves with those needing to be reformed, it is important to note that, whether incidents related by the Night-Walker or independent stories submitted for publication, the periodical's narratives place only men in the position of moral reformer.[33]

The text's configuration of moral authority as masculine is complicated, however, by a third meaning of the publication's title: a night-walker was of course a prostitute. This ambiguity exposes a fundamental ambivalence about men in their role as reformers, as well as about the structure of the periodical itself: Dunton's narrator is, in fact, himself a kind of prostitute as he solicits women in order to preach to them. In addition, the periodical propositions its readers through an appeal to their more prurient interests, as it prints its stories of debauchery.[34] The Night-Walker places himself initially in the role of client in order to catch a woman in the act of solicitation, for he "cannot any other way prove the Crime upon such Persons with whom he confers but to *sound their Inclinations* and no man of Common Sense will suppose that any modest Woman will go in to a Tavern or publick House with a Stranger upon an Invitation in the Streets" ("Conclusion to the Criticks," Vol. 1, No. 4, 26). Once that interaction has been completed, however, he moves from the role of immoral customer to that of moral solicitor, since the woman's acquiescence gives him "reason to conclude that they who accept of such proffers are subjects fit enough for his Reproof, without offering any further Tentation" (ibid.).[35] And yet, whose "Tentation" is, or is not, being addressed here? While ostensibly talking about the inducement he offers to "lewd women," the narrative conveniently erases any possible temptation to the Night-Walker himself, namely, the provoking of his own sexual desire, as well as the likely arousal on the part of the reader who imagines the consummation that the Night-Walker coyly denies. The Night-Walker's behavior thus becomes a model for that of his male readers, who are encouraged to emulate his denial. Furthermore, the erotic situations portrayed in the text function as a paradigm for the appropriate reader response: male readers, stimulated by the narratives, then learn to control that arousal. Through the reading process, voyeurism metamorphoses into a method of self-control.[36]

A second "Conclusion to the Criticks" (Vol. 2, No. 2, Feb. 1697) addresses once more the potential of readerly arousal. As an answer to the supposed accusation that "by representing the Practices of Unclean Persons, those who are ignorant of them are taught the way of being Lewd," the Night-Walker cites numerous Old Testament stories whose manner of telling offsets their dangerous matter: when the Bible relays these events, "at the same time it tells us how odious they were in the Eyes of God." The Night-Walker claims the same moral stance, asserting, moreover, that his publication has effected actual transformations: "there are Persons really Guilty who have found themselves toucht with the matters of fact related in the *Night-Walker*." By contrast, he cites literary forms such as "the Common Plays, profane Songs, and such Wicked Books, as the *English Rogue*, the *London Jilt*, and others of the Sort, which are spread throughout the Nation like so much Poyson, and have not contributed a little to promote that raging sin of Uncleanness, because those vicious Practices are therein Represented without any reproof." But the distinction between moral and licentious is not quite so hard and fast, for Dunton then acknowledges the way in which, in his own texts, he exploits the reformative potential of lascivious narrative:

> Therefore it was thought that a Design of this Nature re-
> counting the same Intrigues in a more modest manner, and ex-
> posing the Inconsistency of 'em with Religion or Good Morals
> might be very subservient to the design of a Reformation, as
> being so adapted as to entice the persons who have read those
> sorts of Books abovementioned with but too much intention,
> to read these also with the reproofs annexed, for who knows
> but that according to *Herbert*
>
> > *A Verse may catch him who a Sermon flies,*
> > *And turn Delight into a Sacrifice.* (18–19)

The text construes the act of reading, when properly circumscribed, as having the potential to create change. The reforming process becomes evident in the first number, dedicated "To the *Whore-Masters* of *London* and *Westminster.*" The medium of print, as an institution for moral control, works in conjunction with other such institutions as law and religion: "By the *Laws of God* you are excluded from Heaven, and by the *Laws of the Land* you are entitled to Punishment and Disgrace" (A₂). Bolstered by civil and religious authority, the Night-Walker attempts to reform these men by appealing to their gender and class identities. Acknowledging both the injustice and the harm of the sexual double standard, he tells them that they would not want their wives, sisters, or mothers doing what they do, "a plain Demonstration that you hate that Vice in others, which you indulge in your selves" (A₂v); and argues, more importantly, that the repercussions of infidelity are different for women than for men. To encourage adultery by example is to risk the loss of personal as well as class integrity and privilege, since

> you give your Ladies occasion to repay you in your own Coin;
> and as you make bold with their *Waiting-women, Chamber-*
> *maids, and your Pensionary-mistresses,* they to quit you as good a
> Common, will make bold with your *Gentlemen, Valet de Cham-*
> *bres, or some Sparkish Gallants*; and by this means your Estates
> and Honours shall be Inherited by a spurious Brood, and the
> Ancient Honour and Gallantry of the *English Nobility* and *Gen-*
> *try* miserably tarnisht. (ibid.)[37]

Sexual misconduct works here by contagion, spreading first across gender lines, as "Wives and Daughters" are "infected with [men's] bad Examples," and then across class boundaries, for "seeing it is also plain from Experience, that the Practice of the Great ones have always an Influence upon those of the Commons, if these Enormities be not Reformed the whole Nation, in time, will become Vile and Despicable in the Eyes of God and Man" (A_3). After citing biblical as well as historical precedent for this process of infection, the narrator retreats from these "publick Instances," which "may have but small Weight," and encourages his readers "to retire a little into your *own Bosoms*, and consider what are the Fruits you reap by your Debauches" (A_4). The narrative blurs distinctions between public and private, individual and social, moral and economic, as it links the destruction of individual happiness—"the *ruine of your Health, Estates and Reputations*"—to "the Peace of your Families" through an appeal to men's supposed beliefs in "impartial Justice" as well as to "*Liberty* and *Property*": "how will you reconcile those Principles with defiling your Neighbour's Bed, *debauching of poor Maids*, and exposing of 'em, and your spurious Issue by them, to Poverty, Reproach and Punishment?" (ibid.). An important part of the effect of this personal appeal depends upon asking the reader to respond as an owner of property—not only of an estate that needed to be passed down to the rightful inheritor, but also of women, who were themselves a form of property in need of protection because in constant danger of being defiled.

If the dedication "To the Whore-Masters" functions like a sermon by appealing to its readers' inner conscience, the Preface that follows sets up the periodical itself as a kind of external conscience, the type of public monitor of private action that will reach full bloom in the *Tatler*'s Isaac Bickerstaff's devising of himself as "Censor of Great-Britain."[38] Declaring that his aim is "not to minister Fuel to *Wanton Thoughts*, or to please the *prophane Pallats* of the *Beaus* and *Sparks* of the Town, but to display *Monthly* their Abominable Practices in lively Colours, together with their dismal Consequences, in order to frighten or shame them out of them if possible" (B_1), the narrator highlights the power of representation in the process of reform. The individualized quality of the interactions is crucial to the endeavor as a whole. Not only does it enliven the narrative, but, even more significantly, it locates the process of reform itself in a personal sphere, albeit one circumscribed by institutions of authority, not least of which is the emerging genre of the periodical. The reformation process, as an individual act, then becomes linked to another individual act, that of reading. Reading, in addition to teaching men by example, can become itself an act of self-regulation. Within the terms established by these narrative structures, the periodical challenges such behaviors as are allowed by the sexual double standard, while simultaneously circumscribing women's sexuality within the boundaries created by economic necessity and class privilege. By linking moral and economic issues, the periodical establishes a particular kind of reformatory tone, for it was only men whose "property" was at stake. Men's economic and social interest in women's chastity necessitates men's responsibility for the sexual control of women, as well as the need to regulate their own desires. Yet both forms of control depend upon the *Night-Walker*'s acknowledgment of women's sexual needs and desires.

Bernard Mandeville's treatise, *A Modest Defense of the Public Stews*, provides a means of analyzing the implications of this acceptance of female sexuality. Mandeville argues that because women, like men, have been physiologically endowed with the capacity for sexual pleasure,[39] their continence is always tenuous since, he punningly remarks, "Female Chastity is, in its own Nature, built upon a very *ticklish* Foundation." Such a foundation, he contends, ultimately overrides the constraints of modesty, honor, or reputation, since "there is in the Passion of Love a certain fatal *Crisis*, to which all Womenkind are capable of being wrought up." Thus, whether a woman is "Virtuous or not Virtuous, when this Passion is once rais'd to the *critical* Height, it is absolutely irresistible." Mandeville's assertion that "Female Virtue cannot effectually be secured" supports his earlier syllogistic assertion that "The only way to preserve Female Chastity, is to prevent the Men from laying Siege to it, But this Project of the *Public Stews* is the only Way to prevent Mens laying Siege to it: Therefore this Project is the only Way to preserve Female Chastity."[40] Mandeville's argument, therefore, depends upon a frank and open acceptance of female sexuality, yet that acceptance, in welcome contrast to much twentieth-century practice with regard to such issues as rape, pins responsibility for sexual transgression firmly upon men. Similarly, the *Night-Walker* directs its reforming gaze upon men both by situating women as men's property and by calling attention to the pernicious effects of men's reprehensible behavior. Like Mandeville then, the periodical censures not the women who have been forced into prostitution, but the mercenary fathers and brothers or the lascivious masters who have reduced them to that state.

Moreover, Dunton's text employs women's sexuality as a way to talk about class relations. Throughout the *Night-Walker*, female unchastity functions both as indication and consequence of the overstepping of class boundaries. Despite his vehement assertions of novelty, Dunton did not originate the idea of using women's sexual (mis)behavior as a metonym for the breakdown of class hierarchies. Dunton might have known one of the most influential antecedents, Juvenal's sixth satire, in its original Latin or in its translation by Dryden in 1692. Yet, whereas Juvenal's diatribe primarily attacks the decadent upper classes of Roman society, Dunton concerns himself with those from the middle ranks who misguidedly emulate their betters.[41] Moreover, women's ability to tell their own stories uncovers the various ways in which prostitution and adultery are often the products of economic misfortune, usually caused by the unrestrained appetites of men. In "Prostitution and Reform in Eighteenth-Century England," Vern Bullough opposes the attitude of the religiously oriented writers of the sixteenth and seventeenth centuries, who viewed the prostitute as a sinner, to the more progressive view of those eighteenth-century reformers who perceived her as "a victim of her economic situation," recognizing, like Dunton's Night-Walker, "that prostitution for many was an economic necessity."[42] In a similar vein, Roy Porter and Lesley Hall assert that "Enlightened culture tended to exonerate sexual misdeeds. Analysing crime, Henry Fielding exempted girl prostitutes from blame for their offences: they were 'whores through necessity.'"[43]

The indigence underpinning adulterous sexuality becomes most apparent in the narratives of working-class women. One such woman, who accosts the Night-Walker and is subsequently shown the error of her ways, is in turn propositioned by him for her story, "for sincere Repentance was always accompanied by a penitent confession both to God, and those whom we have offended." She tells him

> That she was Chamber-Maid to a Knight's Lady; and her Master being a dissolute Man, had after much Importunity, debaucht her; that her Lady assoon as she understood it, turned her off; that her Master had for some time after allowed her a Pension to maintain her, but his Estate being but low, and his Family numerous, she had had nothing from him for some time; and that what she had formerly done upon the account of a dishonourable Love, she did now practise to procure Bread, but through God's Assistance would rather starve than do so any more. (No. 1, 17)

Although the Night-Walker counsels this woman, like many others who are financially destitute, to "go and sin no more, lest a worse Evil should befal her" (18), he does not describe the kinds of things honest women might do to keep from starvation.[44] The problems of the options he does present, to another young woman in the second number—to "submit either to work at her Needle for a livelihood, or to go a Servant into an Honest Family" (24)—go surprisingly unexamined in light of the previous story. Anthony Fletcher trenchantly describes the precarious situation of the female domestic servant, whose "sexual exploitation . . . was an accepted social phenomenon":

> Its occurrence was inherent in the double exercise of power, as master and man, that characterized master-servant relationships in the patriarchal system. . . . A servant who had yielded to her master's advances was always in an extremely vulnerable position. If she told what happened there was the disgrace of the loss of her honour. By doing so, she risked her master's punishment or ill usage, even the loss of her job. Here was the crux of household patriarchy so far as young women were concerned: the system made rejection of a determined master difficult yet the consequences, if they found themselves to be with child, were dire.[45]

Economic distress was also an issue for women in the middle ranks who, deficient in practical skills, could be precluded from channeling their sexual and domestic energies into the "proper" path of marriage when lacking a suitable portion. One woman confesses to the Night-Walker that "she had an easie tender Education, but her Brother grew extravagant, and instead of paying hers and her Sisters Portions, he spent all; and she having no way left to get her Bread, and *not being able* to work, took up *this Course*," to which she has become gradually hardened (No. 1, 3). Combining women's marital unmarketability with their acknowledged sexual desire leads to a further problem, as in the case of the woman who, when asked why she does not choose to marry, replies that "Nature has fitted me for a Mans Bed; but no Man would make me his Wife without Money, and therefore you cannot blame me for satisfying the Appetite of Nature, and purchasing Money thereby too" (No. 4, 21).[46]

The text attacks not just rapacious brothers and mercenary suitors, but also those fathers who use marriage solely as a form of economic gain. One woman practices adultery not to earn her bread, but to satisfy her sexual desires. She tells the Night-Walker that her husband was "an Elderly Man, to whom she never had that Affection which a Wife ought to have to an Husband"; she was, however, "forc'd by her Covetous Father to marry him because of his Riches." After her marriage, she had been "betray'd by her Love" to a "young Man of a lower Fortune, whom her Friends would not suffer her to marry." Having been "overcome by his Temptations; and he being now married, and removed to another Corner of the Kingdom, she had so habituated herself to that wicked Course, that she became an easy Conquest to other Assailants," but resolves upon the Night-Walker's "Reproof . . . to become a Reformed Woman" (No. 1, 16). Because women's sexual desire is culturally acknowledged, the periodical assumes that "Temptations" will become irresistible if sexual needs are not being met within marriage.[47]

In light of the previous chapter's reading of the *Athenian Mercury*, it comes as no great surprise to find that the Night-Walker professes a keen sense of the destructive effects of bad matches made by avaricious parents. Thus the narrator writes that magistrates should act to remedy the "Covetous Temper of some Parents, who force their Children many times to Marry against their Wills, meerly for the Sake of Riches, without any regard to suitableness of Temper, Age, Constitution, or Religion." This behavior, the narrator contends, leads "twice as many persons" to be "guilty of Unclean Practices, and ruined this way as are brought to Poverty by Marrying without the Consent of Parents" (Vol. 2, No. 2, B_1–B_1v). Ironically, however, he appears oblivious to the ways in which alternatives to marriage, especially domestic service, could function as another form of prostitution.

In the *Night-Walker*, however, even the lusty enactment of servant women's desires, as in the story of one unrepentant woman who, seduced by her master, "lickt the Butter off my old Mistress's Bread with a very good Appetite" (No. 4, 15), can still be less of a threat to society at large than the contagion of men's desire. The introduction to the second number likens male lust to the evils of "*Pride, Gluttony, Covetousness, Sabbath-breaking, and Libertinism in General,*" condemning these related vices as "sometimes the Occasion; and sometimes the Consequences of Whoredom and Uncleanness" (1). Monogamous marriage, however, can serve as a structure in which to refocus rather than deny such appetites and inclinations, as the sexual drive serves the legitimate purposes of procreation and the desire for money and power benefits not just one's immediate self but also one's heirs. Thus affluence becomes linked with sexual regulation on the part of men as well as women.

The *Night-Walker* makes this important point explicit in two different places: a letter published in the second number, describing "a Certain Citizen who became Pimp to his own Wife," and the "Epistle Dedicatory" to Vol. 2, No. 2, directed to "The *Magistrates* of *London* and *Westminster*." In both passages (and the language and tone are so similar it seems reasonable to assume that Dunton authored both), what is being attacked is the overstepping of class boundaries in the form of tradesmen's wives who emulate persons of quality, particularly in their dress. Yet the sexual consequences of such promiscuity, from cuckoldry to economic ruin, provide a subtext that serves to attack aristocratic female sexuality as inherently destructive as well as to promulgate a proper form of middle-class behavior that, as we shall see, connects economic prosperity with women's absence from the public realm.

In the epistolary narrative, the wife's presentation in public, "according to the present mode [of] exposing her self in her Shop deckt and dressed more like a Lady or Person of Quality than a good Housewife, who minds the affairs of her household," serves to attract the attention of "a certain *Lascivious Gentleman*" who "fixt his eye on her as passing by" (10). This man then devises a plan to lend her husband money in return for the company of his wife; the liaison accomplished, the "Gentleman" demands back his 400 pounds, ruining the tradesman in the process. The narrator describes these "Citizens Wives, who sit Trickt and Trim'd, and Rigg'd in their Shops as if they had more mind to expose themselves to Sale, than their Goods" as participating in a dangerous form of economic exchange, as their behavior acts as a temptation to those "*Lascivious Sparks*" who then come to "*treat with them*" not for the "Goods in their Shops" but rather for the women themselves (12). Eliminating this display, the narrator claims, would also eliminate the problem, and thus he proposes as a solution that women be relegated to the domestic sphere:

> If our Citizens Wives were reduced to their plain Head-
> dresses and Green Aprons as it used to be formerly, and busied
> themselves with the Education of their Children, and Govern-
> ment of their Maids, leaving the Shops to their Husbands, ex-
> cept where it cannot be otherwise, the Court end of the Town
> would not have such just occasion as they now have to excuse
> their own Wantonness from the example of the City, nor
> would there be that Emulation betwixt the Gentry and the
> Citizens. (12–13)

In a similar passage in the dedication to city magistrates, which stresses the relationship between sexual misconduct and other forms of criminal behavior, the narrator reiterates his earlier theme, that men's attention to "Lewd Women" destroys familial prosperity as "the lewd Husband or Father spends upon them Sluts what should maintain his Wife and Children" (A$_4$). But the middle-class woman's desire to emulate "persons of Quality" also comes in for attack, for "it many times comes to pass that most of her Portion, which ought to be imployed in her Husbands Trade is spent in furnishing her House, and maintaining her in answerable Apparel, which attracts the Eyes of loose Sparks towards her" (A$_4$v-B$_1$). Such dress then "exposes her to those Tentations, that should never perhaps have otherwise come in her way." Rather, women should absent themselves from the commercial sphere, "imploying themselves like *Solomon*'s good Housewife" in supervisory domestic roles (B$_1$).

These passages position women's capacity to regulate the household as necessary to the success of the family unit as well as a significant method of limiting sexual temptation on the part of the women themselves and the men whose gaze is irresistibly drawn to them. Although this attitude might seem to emphasize desirable domestic femininity, it is important to note that Dunton articulates his beliefs within a particularly masculine context. Both the letter and the dedication to city magistrates, all of whom are men who represent legal authority, do not appeal to women but are instead "a warning to our Citizens, to take heed how they expose their *fine Wives in their Shops*" (No. 2, 11). Ironically, the success of Dunton's own periodical endeavors— both the *Night-Walker* and the earlier *Athenian Mercury*—depended upon his ability to turn exposure, in the form of the titillating details of people's lives, into moral instruction. Casting new light upon Horace's dictum of *prodesse et delectare*, Dunton's publications, with their blunt style and forthright explanations of their own workings, reveal some of the tensions inherent in the genre as a whole. By combining the seductive appeal of narrative with the righteous authority of conduct literature, Dunton's periodicals licensed the dissemination of pleasure as they bolstered their own circulation. In the decades that followed, Joseph Addison and Richard Steele produced more artful, as well as aesthetically more complex, configurations of the teach-and-delight precept. Yet, as the following chapters will demonstrate, their influential works refined the process that Dunton had already begun, as they transformed readers' fascination with intimate matters into an occasion for public moral edification and private economic gain.

4 *Reconstructing Honor*

> The Excellency of this Principle [of Honour] is, that the Vulgar are destitute of it, and it is only to be met with in People of the better sort, as some Oranges have Kernels, and others not, tho' the out-side be the same. In great Families it is like the Gout, generally counted Hereditary, and all Lords Children are born with it. In some that never felt any thing of it, it is acquired by Conversation and Reading, (especially of Romances) in others by Preferment; but there is nothing that encourages the Growth of it more than a Sword, and upon the first wearing of one, some People have felt considerable Shoots of it in four and twenty Hours.
> —Bernard Mandeville, *The Fable of the Bees*

*I*n the previous two chapters, readings of some of the earliest social periodicals suggested that definitions of masculinity were in flux in the late seventeenth century. Such texts as the *Athenian Mercury* and the *Night-Walker* portrayed the chaste and loving husband as a powerful new type of desirable masculinity. Often contrasted to images of the spendthrift libertine, this ideal figure consistently opts for marriage as a means to channel potentially dangerous sexual and economic appetites, thus benefiting both his own family and society at large. Within these publications, as well as those that were to follow, the sentimental nuclear family increasingly becomes a site for the integration of men's personal and sexual needs—the passions—with the economic interests necessary to the formation of a bourgeois ruling class. Bold refiguring of the concept of honor was an essential element in periodical authors' transformation of men's familial role. The notion of honor, customarily a genteel stronghold, was rewritten in ways that appealed to both Christian virtue and burgeoning commercial values. Attacking notions of honor derived from a feudal ethos, which endorsed bragging, aggression, and competition and expressed itself most powerfully in the code of honor that condoned or even demanded the practice of dueling, were such writers as Daniel Defoe, Richard Steele, and Joseph Addison. They proffered, in the early decades of the eighteenth century, an alternative form of heroism, one manifested in humility, charity, and benevolence as well as in the particularly commercial values of honesty and credibility. By challenging the belief that aristocratic birth entails noble behavior as well as the view that the well-born are the only people capable of virtuous thought and action, their works redefined masculine excellence, and thus contributed significantly to the codification of a new form of masculinity.

These authors' revision of male virtue promulgated a pattern of ideal—and active—masculinity in the figure of commercial man. By explicitly contrasting this new type to the landowner who, under a system of primogeniture, can only obtain his property—and thus achieve his prosperity—at the expense of siblings as well as children, these writers came to depict the man who possessed a mercantile fortune as occupying a unique place within a family system extrapolated into a national one. Indeed, one of the most striking aspects of the rhetoric of mercantile exemplarity is its expression in familial terms. In his explicitly political journal, the *Englishman* (1713), Richard Steele depicts the merchant as the model son who then grows up to become the ideal father: "The Course of Wealth within ourselves makes a Distinction between Brethren, but the Merchant is the Child of *Britain* who enriches his whole Family."[1] Not only does the merchant secure honors and privileges formerly accorded only to the man of landed property, but he also enlarges his moral territory by expropriating the sphere of domestic relations. The family provides the most crucial element of differentiation between aristocratic and commercial man, as it serves both to demand and to justify men's participation in the economic sphere.

Exponents of the capitalist model of virtue succeeded in part by claiming for the realm of the social—that is, the spheres of public and private as previously conceived—some of the moral value and the activity hitherto ascribed solely to the public realm. This new model locates courageous individuality not on the battlefield or in the *polis* proper—arenas from which the possessor of wealth without landed property had been officially excluded—but on the high seas and in the alleys of the Royal Exchange, in coffeehouses and around tea-tables. Perhaps most important for my purposes, this new form of active masculinity operates not by distinguishing itself from the private realm, as in the classical model, but, alternatively, by integrating the public and the private. Thus the heroic mercantile man broadens his sphere of ethical subjectivity by extending it into the home, where he can monitor and reform his own behavior and also that of others—particularly his wife and children. By replacing the leisured gentleman with the breadwinner who is at the same time a faithful husband and protective father, this emerging ideology of masculinity functions, in turn, to mediate between attitudes necessary to a flourishing mercantile system and those affective values appropriate to the sentimental family. Indeed, numerous literary representations define merchants and traders by their exemplary ability to meet private needs while simultaneously enhancing the public good. Richard Steele's discussion of the mercantile Cornelii family in *Spectator* No. 192 (1711) questions traditional forms of honor as embodied in wealth or title while expressly proposing new characteristics of exemplary masculinity: "It is not in the Power of all Men to leave illustrious Names or great Fortunes to their Posterity, but they can very much conduce to their having Industry, Probity, Valour, and Justice. It is in every Man's Power to leave his Son the Honour of descending from a virtuous Man, and add the Blessings of Heaven to whatever he leaves him."

The ostensible moral superiority of mercantile men was significantly bolstered by discussions of honor. As a *sine qua non* of aristocratic prerogative, traditionally associated only with those of genteel birth, honor when redefined could provide powerful ammunition for the middle ranks' incursion into the realm of cultural power. By attacking this privileged stronghold, and by positing in its stead a code of honor based on notions of benevolence, cooperation, and, as I shall show, increasingly rigid gender difference, writers from the emerging middle classes postulated a new vision of ideal manhood, one constructed at the crossroads of difference as delimited by both class and gender. The historian Donna Andrew asserts that the discursive middle-class attack on the aristocratic code of honor became successful only at the end of the eighteenth century, as a greater acceptance of commercial values sanctioned the construction of a moral system that was an alternative to, rather than simply a critique of, the aristocratic model of honor.[2] Yet I contend that the earlier part of the century witnessed a similar process. By positing the merchant as a kind of national hero, whose individual economic transactions provide untold national benefit, periodical writers could extract for themselves the status attached to the elite while at the same time censuring their habits. Thus attributes formerly deemed essential to national welfare—class loyalty, courage in battle, lavish display—are instead represented as inimical to such prosperity. Whereas the attempt to codify a new masculine ideal finds particularly powerful representation in periodical literature, other kinds of writing also contributed to the formation of this prototype. I end this chapter with a reading of Richard Steele's final play, *The Conscious Lovers*:

although published and performed in 1722, a decade after Steele's journalistic apotheosis, the comedy, like the periodicals that preceded it, breaks new ground in its articulation of a sentimental ideal.[3] Concerned with the themes and problems I will be tracing throughout this chapter, *The Conscious Lovers*, in the character of its protagonist, Bevil junior, provides an extended example of the new man who, by resisting aristocratic imperatives with regard to sexual conquest and the duel, manages instead to unite affective and paternal characteristics in the name of "conscious love."

•

In the late seventeenth and early-to-mid eighteenth centuries, changes in both material practice and psychological attitudes contributed to a situation in which agriculture and commerce could be viewed as complementary rather than conflicting economic interests. While the "landed" and the "moneyed" interests were often posed as mutually exclusive by their respective proponents, historians have increasingly demonstrated the ways in which "commercial enterprise was changing the face of the old agrarian society."[4] Although few wealthy merchants may have actually bought their way into the elite through the purchase of a large country home and estate,[5] they nevertheless began to exert a powerful influence upon the make-up of English society, as well as upon the country's economic and social policy. The genteel aspirations of those in the middle ranks often provided an easy target for vicious satire;[6] other representations, by contrast, depicted a more fluid assimilation of aristocratic habits and values on the part of the middle classes.[7] The very *idea* that successful merchants might ascend into the elite ranks supplied an important sense of possibility: whether myth or demographic fact, the potential for upward mobility allowed for a drive, and a concomitant sense of self-esteem, not available to someone whose life and occupation were fixed at birth. While the story of the merchant-gentleman, like that of Horatio Alger in nineteenth-century America, may have been largely a fiction, particularly in its implication that such movement was universally available if only one worked hard enough, the narrative could nevertheless function as an ideological wedge, forcing open what may, in earlier times, have looked like locked doors. In other words, it was necessary that the merchant penetrate, if only theoretically, the ranks of the elite in order to be able to claim some of its status for the worker who can also function as a gentleman.

It is critical to realize, then, that the story of the merchant-turned-gentleman possesses an ideological power disproportionate to its material realization. A related process, one I term appropriation, overtly asserts mercantile difference while at the same time claiming for merchants characteristics traditionally associated with the leisured classes. Mr. Sealand, the exemplary merchant in Steele's *The Conscious Lovers*, typifies this process when in a conversation with an older landed gentleman, Sir John Bevil, he states that "we Merchants are a Species of Gentry, that have grown into the World this last Century, and are as honourable, and almost as useful, as you landed Folks, that have always thought your selves so much above us."[8] Here Mr. Sealand dignifies the merchant in a particularly radical way: the merchant is not just "as good as" his purported superior; rather, he is of the same rank, a "Species of Gentry." Separate but equal, the merchant has it both ways: he retains his difference, yet obtains a status hitherto unrealizable, for he is part of a group that has only recently come to prominence, "grown into the World this last Century." While the merchant has achieved his new position through both cultural and personal assimilation, the latter often through marriage,[9] he also stands apart by virtue of his economic position. This new mercantile elite, while not a significant force in terms of status and traditional political power structures, possessed a potent cultural importance in its role as exemplar of a new form of desirable masculinity, a masculinity made possible by precisely those characteristics—work for profit and accumulation—that differentiated them from the traditional landowning elite, whose income derived mainly from rents.

Interestingly, a description of Mr. Sealand from Steele's periodical publication *The Theatre* (1720),[10] which utilized most of the dramatis personae from the unfinished *Conscious Lovers*, represents the merchant as the literal merger of land and sea implied by his surname: "This Gentleman was formerly what is call'd a Man of Pleasure about the Town; and having, when young, lavish'd a small Estate, retir'd to *India*, where by Marriage, and falling into the Knowledge of Trade, he laid the foundation of the great Fortune, of which he is now Master." In this version, Mr. Sealand's claim to gentility resides primarily in his ability to outshine the traditional elite on their own terms: "He is a true Pattern of that kind of third Gentry, which has arose in the World this last Century: I mean the great, and rich Families of Merchants, and eminent Traders, who in their Furniture, their Equipage, their Manner of Living, and especially their Oeconomy, are so far from being below the Gentry, that many of them are now the best Representatives of the ancient ones, and deserve the Imitation of the modern Nobility."[11] This account of Mr. Sealand, like that of the exemplary Paolo of *Tatler* No. 25,[12] effortlessly combines the manners of a gentleman with the honesty of a trader: "He is a Man that does Business with the Candour of a Gentleman, and performs his Engagements with the Exactness of a Citizen."

By omitting Mr. Sealand's prior possession of an estate, Steele would significantly alter his portrayal of the exemplary merchant by the time of the play. In *The Conscious Lovers*, the protagonist Bevil junior describes Mr. Sealand as "a Younger Brother of an Ancient Family, and originally an Eminent Merchant of *Bristol*; who, upon repeated Misfortunes, was reduced to go privately to the *Indies*. In this Retreat Providence again grew favourable to his Industry, and, in six Years time, restored him to his former Fortunes."[13] This Mr. Sealand seems to have inherited no estate; as in the numerous examples depicted by Defoe or the *Spectator*, he has made good solely through mercantile enterprise. Moreover, while the *Theatre*'s narrative represents Mr. Sealand's commercial expertise as deriving in part from connections made through marriage, in the play's rendition he labours alone: his wife and child travel to the Indies only after he has rebuilt his wealth by his own efforts.

Yet it is nevertheless important to note that while the dramatic Mr. Sealand avers a parity of honor—long a genteel stronghold—between merchant and gentry, he still acknowledges an inferiority of service: "we Merchants . . . are as honourable, and almost as useful, as you landed Folks . . . " A third process, what I call the paradigm of the "merchant as hero," poses merchants as more useful, and thus implies that they are more honorable, than men of the landed classes. It is precisely the merchant's economic position—the characteristic that distinguishes him most notably from the traditional elite classes—that allows his proponents to present him as the better man, able to contribute to the nation's defense and prosperity while simultaneously improving himself and his immediate family.[14] In a strategy that we will also see employed with respect to the duel, authors represent traditional means of power as outmoded, even destructive: Mr. Spectator's friend, the merchant Sir Andrew Freeport, "will tell you that it is a stupid and barbarous Way to extend Dominion by Arms; for true Power is to be got by Arts and Industry."[15] Defoe's conduct manual, the *Complete English Tradesman* (1726), argues that "war and encroachment" have added nothing to England's realm since Queen Elizabeth's time, that civil wars and rebellions have rather "torn [England] in pieces." Thus "the rising greatness of the British nation is not owing to war and conquests, to enlarging its dominion by the sword, or subjecting the people of other countries to our power; but it is all owing to trade, to the increase of our commerce at home, and the extending it abroad."[16]

In one of the most famous articulations of this viewpoint, *Spectator* No. 69, Addison uses a visit to the bustling Royal Exchange to illustrate Mr. Spectator's belief that "there are not more useful Members in a Commonwealth than Merchants." The merchants in this essay judiciously combine personal prosperity with public—which is to say British—benefit: "I am wonderfully delighted," Mr. Spectator tells us with tears in his eyes, "to see such a Body of Men thriving in their own private Fortunes, and at the same time promoting the Publick Stock; or in other Words, raising Estates for their own Families, by bringing into their Country whatever is wanting, and carrying out of it whatever is superfluous." Just as an ideology of sentimental patriarchy couches the benefit of one man in the name of the welfare of the family as a whole,[17] so too does a rhetoric of mercantile benevolence cover up the exploitative nature of the transactions through which the "*English* Merchant converts the Tin of his own Country into Gold, and exchanges his Wooll for Rubies" as the "*Mahometans* are clothed in our *British* Manufacture, and the Inhabitants of the Frozen Zone warmed with the Fleeces of our Sheep." In this discourse, supposedly natural processes justify British commercial practice. Thus Mr. Spectator claims that "Nature seems to have taken a particular Care to disseminate her Blessings among the different Regions of the World, with an Eye to this mutual Intercourse and Traffick among Mankind, that the Natives of the several Parts of the Globe might have a kind of Dependance upon one another, and be united together by their common Interest." While the statement that "Almost every *Degree* produces something peculiar to it" might seem to imply a symmetry of trade among nations, the appropriative nature of England's own benevolence soon emerges quite nakedly from Mr. Spectator's assertion that his "Friend Sir Andrew calls the Vineyards of *France* our Gardens; the Spice-Islands our Hot-Beds; the *Persians* our Silk-Weavers, and the *Chinese* our Potters." Mr. Spectator represents all nations as "naturally" profiting from those British merchants who, like beneficent fathers, "knit Mankind together in a mutual Intercourse of good Offices, distribute the Gifts of Nature, find Work for the Poor, add Wealth to the Rich, and Magnificence to the Great."

Effecting a democracy of expenditure in which all men are created equal through their ability to purchase and consume,[18] the merchant-as-hero epitomizes the benevolent and seemingly egalitarian family relations made possible by commerce. Numerous essays contrast a situation of cooperation, indeed often of partnership between father and son or among brothers, to the rivalry inherent in primogeniture, the system of inheritance increasingly practiced by the landed elite in this period. Other ostensibly injurious habits associated with the elite, in particular dueling and adultery, could be censured under the same rubric of the destruction of moral values, and posed as necessarily intrinsic to the elite system. However, while the status of the "New Man" was increasingly defined by his ability to provide for his family in material, social, and spiritual terms, his identity was also threatened by the specter of ruin that massed in dark clouds above the head of every man engaged in commercial practices. For unlike an economic system based upon rents, commercial relations were "inherently unstable" since there was no real guarantee, or formal process, to regulate the mechanisms of credit.[19] Although on the one hand, the mercantilist view that societal well-being depended upon economic well-being served to elevate the trader by exposing the fiction of gentlemanly disinterest,[20] on the other hand the trader could be viewed as a dangerous figure precisely because he pursued his own interests within an economic system now defined by mobility of property, rather than stability of the same.[21] J. G. A. Pocock argues that through the development of government stock and public credit, the property that had previously provided the political individual with a "material anchor" by seemingly guaranteeing him "leisure, rationality and virtue" became instead "not merely mobile but imaginary." According to this view, "specialised, acquisitive and post-civic man," far from being concerned with public welfare, "does not even live in the present, except as constituted by his fantasies concerning a future."[22]

Such fantasies functioned to feminize the trader by associating him with "such archetypally female goddesses of disorder as Fortune, Luxury, and most recently Credit herself."[23] The potential effeminacy of commercial relations, and the connection, as we shall see, between a merchant's credit and a woman's virtue, signal an apprehension that is in part assuaged by twin class and gender assertions: that the merchant is a kind of national hero, and that there is a natural opposition between men and women. Although John Barrell might claim that in a credit economy all men were necessarily vulnerable, it seems nevertheless true that some men were more vulnerable than others. In *Spectator* No. 218, written by Steele, Mr. Spectator reflects upon the nature of "Fame" in relation to "the different Orders of Mankind who have any thing to do with it": "Glory, which respects the Hero; Reputation, which is preserved by every Gentleman; and Credit, which must be supported by every Tradesman." Because credit, like a woman's reputation, is constituted less by actions in and of themselves than through their perception by others, the trader, alone among the three types of men discussed, must rely almost entirely upon other people. Most vulnerable because most dependent, the trader is the "most unhappy of all Men, and the most exposed to the Malignity or Wantonness of the common Voice."[24]

Whereas any comparison between tradesmen's defenselessness in the face of aspersions about their credit-worthiness and women's susceptibility to rumor and gossip impugning their chastity remains implicit in Steele's essay, Daniel Defoe makes the connection in no uncertain terms: the *Complete English Tradesman* discusses "the peculiar value of credit and a good name among tradesmen" in language and terms conventionally associated with female virtue. "Credit," he writes in a tone redolent of the conduct manual, "is so much a tradesman's blessing that it is the choicest ware he deals in, and he cannot be too chary of it when he has it, or buy it too dear when he wants it."[25] Just as chastity defines feminine virtue, and by extension, female existence, so too does credit provide the "life and soul" of the trader's business, requiring "his utmost vigilance to preserve it."[26] To men in other positions slander may be "injurious," but a tradesman "is immediately and unavoidably blasted and undone."[27] Defoe makes explicit Steele's tacit comparison: "A tradesman's credit and a virgin's virtue ought to be equally sacred from the tongues of men; and it is a very unhappy truth, that as times now go, they are neither of them regarded among us as they ought to be."[28] Moreover, his elaboration of this image clearly evokes accustomed representations of the fragility of virginity: "A tradesman's reputation is of the nicest nature imaginable; like a blight upon a fine flower, if it is but touched, the beauty of it, or the flavour of it, or the seed of it, is lost, though the noxious breath which touched it might not reach to blast the leaf, or hurt the root."[29]

For both Steele and Defoe, control can function as a powerful means of alleviating the trader's precarious psychological state. By mastering his private self, as well as by regulating the women—wives and daughters—connected to that self, the trader can mitigate the powerlessness experienced in the public realm. Although his prosperity depends upon action, his behavior at home or in the streets must be as carefully weighed, measured, and accounted for as any business transaction. Such conduct provides an unmistakable contrast to the aristocratic code of masculinity, in which deliberation is synonymous with cowardice. Exemplified most brutally in the duel, this ethos stipulates that honor must be earned, and maintained, through the willingness to sacrifice one's life. In a kind of ironic counterpoint to the self-negation implied in Woody Allen's statement that he wouldn't want to belong to any club that would have him for a member, this club consists of men who must seem to devalue their own lives in order to merit inclusion in the elite. For aristocratic men, the duel serves as the primary means through which they might prove their courage and vindicate the potential disgrace incurred by their own behavior or that of their womenfolk. Men of the middle ranks, by contrast, are counseled to protect themselves and their families by other means altogether—means that would enrich, rather than deplete, the nation's resources. And like England herself, the man of true honor must rely not upon "Arms" but upon "Arts and Industry"—and the art of self-control most of all. In their attempt to abolish what they believed to be the barbarous practice of dueling, eighteenth-century periodical essayists redefined gentlemanliness itself.

In his *Review of the Affairs of France*, Daniel Defoe devoted significant attention to the custom he described as a "Genteel Way of Murther,"[30] while Joseph Addison and Richard Steele addressed the "Chimerical Monster" in a number of impassioned essays in their *Tatler*, *Spectator*, and *Guardian* papers, thereby continuing the trend begun by Steele in his early conduct treatise *The Christian Hero* (1701).[31] This solicitude reached its apex in Steele's *The Conscious Lovers*, a play the author made no "Difficulty to acknowledge, . . . was writ for the sake of the Scene of the Fourth Act," an anti-dueling episode "wherein Mr. *Bevil* evades the Quarrel with his Friend."[32] In their work, Defoe, Addison, and Steele challenged not only the custom itself but also what they perceived to be the numerous mistaken attitudes that allowed it to flourish. We find those attitudes elucidated in *Guardian* No. 161, in which Addison uses the character of "Timogenes" to illustrate the practitioner of "mistaken Honour":

> *Timogenes* wou'd smile at a Man's Jest who ridiculed his Maker, and, at the same Time, run a Man through the Body that spoke ill of his Friend. *Timogenes* wou'd have scorned to have betray'd a Secret, that was entrusted with him, tho' the Fate of his Country depended on the Discovery of it. *Timogenes* took away the Life of a young Fellow, in a Duel, for having spoken ill of *Belinda*, a Lady whom he himself had seduced in her Youth, and betrayed into Want and Ignominy. To close his Character, *Timogenes*, after having ruined several poor Tradesmen's Families, who had trusted him, sold his Estate to satisfie his Creditors; but, like a Man of Honour, disposed of all the Mony, he could make of it, in the paying off his Play Debts, or to speak in his own Language, his Debts of Honour.

The four areas addressed by the essay describe, in microcosmic form, the central issues at stake in the debate over honor, for Timogenes exemplifies the antithesis of the gentleman as (re)defined by Addison and Steele. To begin with, Timogenes elevates friendship above the dictates of religion and the laws of the state, both of which condemned the duel as murder. In blatant opposition to Steele's "Christian Hero," the man of (false) honor cannot turn the other cheek; forgiveness is not in his repertoire. Next, and relatedly, Timogenes will put the secret of a friend above the welfare of his country, again placing private interests above social and civic ones. Accordingly, honoring a friend's secret amounts to dishonoring the claims of society at large. Third, by actually killing someone in a duel, Timogenes reveals the contradictions inherent in the code of honor as it applies to sexual behavior.

That is, Timogenes assassinates a young man who had spoken ill of a woman Timogenes had himself debauched and then betrayed. We witness how one element of honor, the need to protect the reputation of one's women, conflicts with the need to seduce (and then of course abandon) as many women as possible. Since the code of honor and the code of the rake are one and the same, honor among men necessarily entails the dishonoring of women, a point conveniently ignored by the code's practitioners. Finally, Timogenes abuses the trust—here meaning both "to put confidence in" and "to lend without security"—of traders, thereby impoverishing them, along with their families. When it comes time to make reparation, he repays "Debts of Honor"—that is, gaming debts—to men of his own class while continuing to abuse those in the trading classes. The ability to take advantage of the debtor-creditor relationship was a favorite theme of Addison and Steele;[33] here false honor means scrupulous attention to one kind of claim, and licensed denial of another.

As Addison sums up these characteristics, the men of mistaken honor "establish any thing to themselves for a Point of Honour, which is contrary either to the Laws of God, or of their Country; who think it more honourable to Revenge, than to forgive an Injury; who make no Scruple of telling a Lie, but would put any Man to Death that accuses them of it; who are more careful to guard their Reputation by their Courage, than by their Virtue." Addison's juxtaposition of courage and virtue reveals an integral element of the debate. While he had earlier claimed that "The great Point of Honour in Men is Courage, and in Women Chastity," he nevertheless goes on, in the course of that discussion, to argue that those qualities are not inherent but socially constructed: they represent the traits that make men and women most desirable to each other (*Spectator* No. 99).[34] Moreover, he points out that the code of honor often demands an exercising of "a false kind of Courage," as men are forced to defend the mere reputation of virtue rather than its actuality.[35] Thus Addison argues that virtuous honor rather than courage should function as the proper criterion for worth.[36] In the earlier *Tatler* No. 25, Steele had also questioned conventional notions of the relationship of honor to courage by claiming that if honor were really about courage, then the man who refused to duel would actually be more courageous—and thus more honorable—than the duelist, because he would be going against the dictates of convention. Claiming to know that "all Men fight *against their Will*," Steele's eidolon Isaac Bickerstaff alleges the superior bravery of his own daring to "talk very freely on a Custom which all Men wish exploded, tho' no Man has Courage enough to resist it."[37]

Reconstructing honor, on the part of those male writers who saw themselves as simultaneous reformers of the elite and champions of the trading and professional classes, meant severing the link between status and behavior. Steele writes, "It is to me a very great Meanness, and something much below a Philosopher, which is what I mean by a Gentleman, to rank a Man among the Vulgar for the Condition of Life he is in, and not according to his Behaviour, his Thoughts and Sentiments, in that Condition" (*Tatler* No. 69). *Tatler* No. 202 goes on to advocate the proposition that "Heroick Virtue," formerly the sole province of those "whom Fortune has elevated to the most conspicuous Stations," should be available to all men: "I would have every Thing to be esteemed as Heroick which is great and uncommon in the Circumstances in the Man who performs it."[38] By arguing, then, that the "Appellation of Gentleman is never to be affixed to a Man's Circumstances, but to his Behaviour in them" (No. 207), the *Tatler* set the stage for the possible portrayal of the trader as gentleman, as the widening gap between gentle birth and genteel behavior allowed for the displacement of aristocratic notions of honor and their replacement with a new notion of what—or who— might constitute the ideal man. The *Spectator*'s numerous portrayals define traders by their ability to meet private needs while simultaneously enhancing the public good, which in turn allows them to embody most fully the gentlemanly attribute of being "useful to others" (*Tatler* No. 207). The aristocratic duelist, by contrast, places individual or status concerns above those of the nation at large, as desires for personal reputation or class consolidation become the justification for breaking the laws of civil society.

Sexual desire—control over it and access to it—played an important part in the debate over honor. In eighteenth-century society, chastity functioned as women's version of honor.[39] Yet while the *Tatler* and the *Spectator* continue to emphasize the absolute necessity of female chastity, they add another piece to the picture. Proposing in *Guardian* No. 45 to "recommend Chastity as the noblest Male Qualification," Steele, in the persona of Nestor Ironside, creates another important distinction between the nobility and the middle ranks. In contrast with the emotional and physical abuse and neglect associated with aristocratic libertinism, commercial man's ostensible ability to regulate any untoward sexual desires as an integral part of his dedication to his family's welfare contributed toward making him both a concerned father and a caring husband. In addition, I would maintain that the fear of feminization associated with the trader and exacerbated in large part by his dependence upon others is here displaced onto the aristocrat who is feminized by his inability to control the sexual passion that might either lead to a challenge or prevent him from negotiating his way out of one.[40] One need only think of Steele's character Bevil junior, to whom we will return below, or of Richardson's hero Sir Charles Grandison, to note the ways in which the exemplary man is he who refuses to womanize or duel, thus challenging the code of honor by calling attention to the mistaken notions upon which it is based.

The discourse I am describing also feminized the duelist by presenting him as one entirely dependent upon the opinion of others. Numerous periodical essays depict the man who subscribes to the code of honor as a vain and shallow fop, in marked contrast to the true "Man of Honour, [who] wants no Man's Opinion to make him such."[41] The earlier *Tatler* had explicitly differentiated desirable male and female behavior by construing the former as based upon wise and virtuous action, the latter upon pleasing others. Whereas a woman needs to be seen in order to become real, the man of "clear and worthy Spirit" should "be able to disengage himself from the Opinions of others, so far as not to let the Deference due to the Sense of Mankind ensnare him to act against the Dictates of his own Reason" (*Tatler* No. 138). The essay from Steele's *Theatre* No. 16, cited above, revolves around this all-important distinction between internal value and external aspect.[42] Since "the Vulgar, both great and small, are charm'd with the Appearance instead of the Thing itself," the periodical's eidolon, Sir John Edgar, must "make this Matter rightly understood" by delving beneath the seemingly smooth surface of culturally sanctioned behavior. He writes that while "the Person ordinarily so called [Honorable], is he who is esteem'd to be such by other Men," the term must be redefined to put private conviction above outward appearance: "Him therefore we will call truly honourable who knows himself to be a Man of Honour; no Distinctions, Titles or Apellations can give this illustrious Character, which can flow only from a Man's own Life and Actions. There is as much difference between Title and Honour, as between Heraldry and Morality, as between a Man's Person and his Cloaths."

In direct contradiction to the aristocratic code that defined honor solely in terms of a man's behavior toward others and their approbation of him, Steele delineates his revised form of honor as that sense of integrity that can easily distinguish rational decision, here constituted as explicitly private, from conventional belief. The self-made man, who must carve space and meaning from the granite of a value system usually portrayed as impenetrable, is thus distinguished from, and portrayed as superior to, the man whose value is ascribed at birth. The new man of honor stands resolutely upon his own merits, "without Regard to the Favours or Injuries of Fortune" (ibid.). Yet while fashioning himself as an autonomous being, independent of others, the exemplary man must act with scrupulous attention to those who depend on him for material and psychological sustenance. In an important facet of the bourgeois redefinition of honor, a man's value is to be determined by private action, in particular with regard to those below him. In contrast to the classical model of virtue, which deemed that men were to be judged by their conduct in the public arena, Steele writes that "Mens Actions are only indisputably sincere, as they concern their Inferiors; and Husbands, Fathers, and Masters, are the Characters by which we most certainly know the real Men" (ibid.). Steele's passage thus reconceives *noblesse oblige* in an explicitly familial manner, as he domesticates masculinity without erasing its origins in patriarchal authority.

Although Steele devotes two issues of the *Theatre* and sections of seven numbers of the *Tatler* to the topic of dueling,[43] one essay in particular epitomizes the relationship of gender and class to the reconstruction of honor. In *Tatler* No. 29, Bickerstaff's correspondent "Tim Switch" castigates women for encouraging the "Tyranny in Love" which, derived from chivalric gallantry, manifests itself in the form of dueling. Although Switch facetiously compares feudal times, in which "your Heroick Person, or Man of Gallantry, was indispensibly oblig'd to starve in Armour a certain Number of Years in the Chase of Monsters, encounter them at the Peril of his Life, and suffer great Hardships, in order to gain the Affection of the Fair Lady," to the modern methods in which men must employ "single Combat, as the only Proofs they are able to give their own Sex, and the Ladies, that they are in all Points Men of nice Honour," Bickerstaff nonetheless takes his correspondent's remarks seriously, commenting that the "Evil" of dueling "proceeds only from the Force of Custom." He further agrees with his contributor when he notes that this female despotism "is a little too severe, that we must demonstrate our Affection for 'em by no certain Proof but Hatred to one another, or come at them (only as one does to an Estate) by Survivorship." Steele's metaphor here typifies the opposition between aristocratic customs, as manifested in primogeniture and the duel, and those commercial forms of inheritance and behavior in which wealth was disposed equally among all offspring and men often went into business with their sisters' husbands or the brothers of wives.

In the domestic ideology that holds a prominent place in these texts, good women act to bring men together both economically and emotionally; the ideal woman is one who soothes rather than foments competition among men. In the same number, Bickerstaff unmasks the particularly destructive nature of the female-mandated rivalry on the part of unmarried women by taking literally the expressions in a "Billet-Doux." Humorously claiming that "Were such a Lover once to write the Truth of his Heart, and let her know his whole Thoughts, he would appear indeed to have a Passion for her;

but it would hardly be call'd Love," Bickerstaff, in best Orwellian style, puts meaning back into a conventional discourse long emptied of content:

> *Madam,*
>
> I have so tender a Regard for you and your Interests, that I'll knock any Man in the Head whom I observe to be of my mind, and like you. Mr. *Truman* the other Day look'd at you in so languishing a Manner, that I am resolv'd to run him through to morrow Morning: This, I think, he deserves for his Guilt in admiring you; than which I cannot have a greater Reason for murdering him, except it be that you also approve him. *Whoever says he dies for you, I will make his Words good, for I will kill him* [my emphasis]. I am,
>
> > *Madam,*
> >
> > > *Your most Obedient,*
> > >
> > > > *Most Humble Servant.*

Making good on one's word was, of course, one of the standards of the code of honor; according to Addison's critique in *Spectator* No. 99, the "great Violation of the Point of Honour from Man to Man is giving the Lie. One may tell another he Whores, Drinks, Blasphemes, and it may pass unresented, but to say he Lies, tho' but in Jest, is an Affront that nothing but Blood can expiate."[44] By demonstrating that to take literally the word of a man of honor means to murder another man, Steele illustrates the tenuous as well as destructive nature of this form of masculinity.

In his *Review*, Defoe offers a comparable criticism of the effect of female sexual behavior upon men when he tells the story of "two Gentlemen of *Bretaign*, who had liv'd in continual Quarrels about a Mistress, which it seems both of them enjoy'd."[45] Because the woman, whom Defoe terms "Madam *La Coquette*," failed to distinguish between the men, but instead "dispens'd her Favours with such Circumspection, that each thought, as is usual in such Cases, himself entire Master of her, and the other only his Rival," the men live in a state of continual discord, until one verbally and physically abuses the other. Taken before the Court of Magistrates established by Louis XIV to adjudicate matters of honor, the offender is ordered "to have the like Number of blows given him, with a Cane, in the Middle of the Town, by a Woman of the Meanest and most infamous Character that could be found," while "the Mistress they Quarrel'd for" is "Banish'd the Province." By deporting the offending woman, the magistrates manage to achieve harmony between the two men, for Defoe concludes that "Tho' the Justice of this Sentence is very Particular, yet that which is more Remarkable in it is, that this Gentleman not only submitted to the Sentence for that perhaps he could not help, but liv'd afterwards in very good Correspondence with his Antagonist, and they were never known to differ afterward." Defoe's anecdote implies that without the irritating presence of women—particularly those women whose sexuality is not controlled by one particular man—men can bond rather than battle.

And yet, while the story of the two gentlemen suggests that men's sexual rivalry clearly underlies the combat of the duel, another narrative—one that Defoe likes so much he tells it twice—displays how the superior claims of rationality can triumph even over the passion aroused by jealousy. In the first version of the tale,[46] Defoe describes a man who, suspecting that his wife "was no Honester than she should be," surprises her in bed with another man. When the man responds that he is "obliged to give Satisfaction" if the husband wishes it, the latter replies, *"Let me lie with your Wife first, and then I'll fight you withal my Heart; 'tis my Wife has affronted me, says he, and not you; and I know how to deal with her*: and so turn'd her out of Doors." Claiming that he "can pass [his] Word that this Gentleman was no Coward," Defoe goes on to expose the senseless nature of the conventional response: "it can never be Rational, That because my Wife will let another Man lie with her, therefore I should take my Life at an even Rate, and lay an equal Wager, who shall be kill'd for it." Earlier in the essay, he had compared dueling to gambling, stating that "Fighting a Duel is just throwing the Dice for a Man's Life," yet goes on to note that it is a game in which the cards are clearly stacked against one, for "'tis not a great deal of odds, that both shall not fall." He emphasizes the utter illogicality of the custom: "Now to me there seems no manner of Correspondence between the thing and the Cause of it; if both had forfeited their Lives to the Law, and one might have been spar'd, there had been some Reason to try who should be the Man, but in this Case I give a Man two opportunities to Mischief me against my one; the Affront is the first, and an even Chance for my Life is the second."

Steele, too, stresses reason as the basis for moral action. In his final play, *The Conscious Lovers*, which he adapted from Terence's comedy *The Andrian Woman*, Steele creates a hero who exemplifies the belief that "there is nothing manly, but what is conducted by Reason, and agreeable to the Practice of Virtue and Justice."[47] Steele espoused a categorical condemnation of the heroes of satirical Restoration comedy, whose attractive wit, he believed, condoned such vices as adultery, irreverence, and profanity. Yet unlike Jeremy Collier, the notorious author of *A Short View of the Immorality and Profanity of the English Stage* (1698), Steele did not advocate a wholesale abolishing of the theater. In keeping with his zeal as a reformer, Steele recognized early on the powerful ethical potential of "Theatrical Representations": "I am convinced," he writes in the persona of Isaac Bickerstaff, "that the impulses I have received from Theatrical Representations, have had a greater Effect, than otherwise would have been wrought in me by the little Occurrences of my private Life. . . . It is not the Business of a good Play to make every Man an Hero; but it certainly gives him a livelier Sense of Virtue and Merit than he had when he entered the Theatre" (*Tatler* No. 99).

Specifically, Steele saw drama as a powerful tool for social change through virtuous imitation: "By emphasizing a character's magnanimous response to his own adversity or generous response to the adversity of someone else, a playwright could show him to be a fit subject for spectators' emulation."[48] A potent believer in the force of sympathy, Steele attempted to elicit from his audience an emotional response that could translate into moral action.[49] Like the ostensibly unified narrative voice of periodical literature, such response presents itself as universal, classless, and available to all, when in reality what it promulgates are such middle-class values as "chastity, marital fidelity, financial economy, charity, civic responsibility, benevolence, . . . and mercantile expansionism."[50] By functioning as a model of self-control in express combination with compassionate reform, Steele's hero, Bevil junior, exemplifies such mores, in spite of his nominal position as a member of the gentry.

Like Richardson's comparable paradigm, Sir Charles Grandison, who, despite his own status as baronet, also epitomizes bourgeois values, Bevil junior falls chastely in love with the woman he rescues from the clutches of a debauched man. Indiana Danvers, the daughter of a Bristol merchant who had succeeded in recouping severe economic losses in the East Indies, had, while an infant, traveled with her mother and aunt to join the merchant there. When their ship is boarded by privateers, Indiana's distressed mother sickens and dies. Initially cared for by her aunt, the young girl is subsequently adopted by the ship's captain. When he dies intestate, having made no provision for Indiana, his fortune reverts to his brother, who is in love with Indiana, now a beautiful young woman. The brother attempts to use Indiana's dependent economic situation to coerce her into sexual compliance. However, Bevil junior rescues her in the nick of time through an exploit he expressly describes as an act of God: "Providence at the Instant interpos'd, and sent me, by Miracle, to relieve her" (I.ii.201–2). By paying off the captain's brother, he obtains Indiana's liberty and establishes her, along with her aunt, Isabella, in a comfortable London residence. Isabella is highly suspicious of Bevil junior's motives: "Still he is a Man, and therefore a Hypocrite" (II.ii.53–54).[51] Indiana, on the other hand, trusts entirely in her rescuer's good intentions, despite the fact that he has made no overt profession of love to her. The reader knows that she is correct in so doing, for Bevil junior keeps silent strictly out of obedience to his father, who wants him to marry the great fortune Lucinda Sealand, thereby "doubling our Estate" (IV.ii.120). In contrast to a work like Jane Austen's *Pride and Prejudice*, where the moral center revolves around the female character's developing recognition of her own vanity, blindness, and partiality, in this play the didactic point rests upon the intellectual and emotional processes through which Bevil junior struggles to reconcile love and duty.

In the end, he succeeds in getting the girl while still managing to please his father. When Indiana is discovered to be Mr. Sealand's long-lost daughter (he had changed his name from Danvers after the loss of his first fortune), he promises her half of the generous portion previously attached to Lucinda, his daughter from a second marriage. Yet the happy ending requisite to comedy tells a larger tale. Bevil junior earns his marital bliss through exemplary self-control, having twice restrained passionate sexual desire, first out of respect for Indiana's chastity and innocence, next out of "tender Obligations" (I.iii.233) to his father. Bevil junior's chastity marks his character as distinct from that of Pamphilus, the protagonist of the Roman comedy on which Steele's play was modeled. In Terence's *The Andrian Woman*, Glycerium, the character Steele will transform into Indiana, never appears on stage; more important, she is pregnant by the time the play begins. In addition, whereas Pamphilus's economic welfare depends solely upon his father's approbation of his marriage, Bevil junior already possesses an estate inherited from his mother. By removing any possible mercenary motive, Steele augments the force of Bevil junior's exemplary sexual restraint.[52]

While the silence imposed by Bevil junior's compliance with his father's desire for a rich match functions, ironically, to expose Bevil junior to the opprobrious title of "keeper," Bevil junior's response to Indiana's question—whether a man can do "any extraordinary Kindness or Service for a Woman, but for his own sake" (II.iii.105–6)—elucidates the important contrast between the rake's desire for immediate gratification and the exemplary man's ability to receive vicarious pleasure through benevolence to others. Bevil junior's "Delight" is "incapable of Satiety, Disgust or Penitence" (II.iii.149–50); indeed, the money he spends upon sustaining Indiana and her aunt is no more, he claims, than what other men might "lay out upon an unnecessary Stable of Horses" (II.iii.133–34). Bevil junior's expenditure "exalts and raises" (II.iii.148) rather than demeans him; moreover, he claims that such behavior is available to all men: "your Hero, Madam, is no more, than what every Gentleman ought to be, and I believe very many are—He is only one, who takes more Delight in Reflections, than in Sensations: He is more pleased with Thinking, than Eating; that's the Utmost you can say of Him" (II.iii.128–32).

However, both the sexual implications of Bevil junior's equine example and the clearly unintentional double entendre "exalts and raises" belie his dispassionate pose, revealing the unconscious at work within the conscious lover. Bevil junior's profession of disinterestedness is of course disingenuous, for he is indeed in love with Indiana; moreover, his economic support serves to keep her innocent by preventing her from possible dependence on other, less "rational" men. Indiana closes the second act with a couplet that summarizes not only the import of the play, but also the ideologies of male-female relations that underlie its exemplary masculinity:

> As Conscious Honour all his Actions steers;
> So Conscious Innocence dispels my Fears.
>
> (II.iii.204–5)

While at first blush Indiana's trust in the goodness of her protector may seem to run counter to the sexual awareness preached relentlessly in the conduct and periodical literature of the period, her modesty, which serves as her protection, functions also as a prescription for dependence: women must rely on men to rescue them from other, less controlled men, or to revenge the wrongs done to them by those other men (often in the form of the duel). Thus women's emotional, physical, indeed psychological dependence—a necessary aspect of the gendered construction of feminine modesty and virtue—demands men's constant action. While Bevil junior might declare that pleasure is to be found in benevolent action, and that such pleasure rivals, if not surpasses, the satisfaction derived from gratifying the senses, I maintain that the exemplary man gets to have it both ways. At the play's end, Sealand rewards Bevil junior with his new-found daughter, glorying in the young man's ability to be simultaneously "A Lover to her Beauty, and a Parent to her Virtue" (V.iii.241–42).

In the relationship with his hot-headed friend, Charles Myrtle, Bevil junior exemplifies the trials as well as the rewards of conscious control. In the fourth act, Myrtle misinterprets a note that Lucinda Sealand, with whom he is desperately in love, has sent to Bevil junior, and so challenges his friend to a duel. In the play's Preface, Steele makes no "Difficulty to acknowledge, that the whole was writ for the sake of the Scene of the Fourth Act, wherein Mr. *Bevil* evades the Quarrel with his Friend, and hope[s] it may have some Effect upon the *Goths* and *Vandals* that frequent the Theatres, or a more polite Audience may supply their Absence." Yet while Bevil junior does indeed sidestep the duel, prompting his repentant and chastened friend to acknowledge that "there is nothing Manly, but what is conducted by Reason, and agreeable to the Practice of Virtue and Justice" (IV.i), the scene is a closer call than Steele's didactic comment would seem to acknowledge.

We know that Bevil junior, like Steele's eidolon, Isaac Bickerstaff, has no qualms in expressing his opinion of the evils of dueling: "I have often dared to disapprove of the Decisions a Tyrant Custom has introduc'd to the breach of all Laws, both Human and Divine" (IV.i.113–15). However, in contrast to Sir Charles Grandison, who makes good on his vow never to raise his sword but in his own defense (although he manages to wreak mighty havoc with just a sword handle), Bevil junior, provoked by Myrtle's insinuations about Indiana's chastity, initially—and surprisingly—accepts the challenge, as the passionate man overtakes the rational one: "You have touch'd me beyond the Patience of a Man" he cries, and agrees to fight (IV.i.152). In an earlier scene, when asked by Bevil junior whether Crispo or Griselda were the "more agreeable Entertainment," Indiana, in keeping with her circumstances and her gender, chooses the patient Griselda (II.iii.152). Although the exemplary man must assume the womanly virtue of patience—just as he must challenge the sexual double standard and practice chastity—such patience directly contradicts the particularly masculine imperative to protect, indeed to champion, women's innocence. This part of the aristocratic code, what C. L. Barber has termed "reflected reputation,"[53] remains unchallenged by the middle-class critique of the duel. If anything, this form of benevolent patriarchy is in fact solidified by an ideological discourse that promotes women's utter economic, and thus psychological, dependence upon men.

No superior rational process serves to rouse Bevil junior from his chivalrous stupor, for, as I am arguing, the stance is itself inherent in the masculinity he embodies. He regains his "sense" only through the accidental interruption of Tom, his servant, and recalls his "Obligation to the best of Fathers, to an unhappy Virgin too, whose Life depends on mine" (IV.i.165–66). Bevil junior's remembrance seems purely pragmatic: he recognizes that he can protect Indiana better alive than dead. He then gives Myrtle Lucinda's letter, the token of their mutual innocence, and transforms his own humiliation into the desire to humble his friend: "When he [Myrtle] is thoroughly mortify'd, and Shame has gotten the better of Jealousie, when he has seen himself th[o]roughly, he will deserve to be assisted towards obtaining *Lucinda*" (IV.i.181–84). At the play's end, Bevil junior does indeed reward his now-chastened friend by asking Sealand to bestow Lucinda upon Myrtle as a way to "overpay" his own earlier protection of Indiana (V.iii.244). "Competition ceases," Myrtle declares (V.iii.282); Bevil junior pronounces them "no longer Rivals now, but Brothers" (V.iii.280).

The bonds of marriage link the two men not only to each other, but also to a common father—Mr. Sealand. By the final scene, Mr. Sealand, who has acquired two new sons along with his lost daughter, displaces Sir John Bevil as the play's pivotal father figure. Reconfirming as well as reconfiguring the patriarchal order, the merchant embodies the kind of fraternal alliance in which fathers, sons, and brothers support rather than compete with each other. Thus while Indiana Danvers, as the play's incognita figure, might well serve, as James Thompson has argued, to rank "individual worth above class status" by manifesting a beauty and virtue unconnected, at least initially, to societal position,[54] she also functions as the means by which the men around her can prove their own worth. Indeed, her given name clearly retains the signs of her father's exploits in the Indies, despite the fact that her family name, her patronymic, has been "Toss'd on the Seas" (V.iii.136), set adrift along with the family to whom she belonged. Bevil junior's ability to decode that name and thus to facilitate the discovery of her true parentage allows him to assume the role of tender husband while still retaining the place of obedient son. It is his own father, Sir John Bevil, who, at the play's end, says to his newly endowed future daughter-in-law: "I congratulate my self, as well as you, that I had a Son, who could, under such Disadvantages, discover your great Merit" (V.iii.226–28). Bevil junior's actions thereby manage to unite sexual desire with filial obedience, just as his marriage to Indiana represents the melding of land and (overseas) trade signified by Sealand's assumed name. I have argued earlier that in and of himself, this merchant epitomizes a crucial component of commercial man's ability to appropriate those honorable characteristics previously associated solely with the well-born. It is precisely the relationship between Sealand and Bevil junior, however, between the merchant and the gentleman, that best manifests an ethos in which the family serves to unite passions and interests.

5 *Father, Husband, Rake: Contradictions of Masculinity in the 'Tatler'*

I shall take it for a Maxim, That a Woman, who resigns the Purpose of being pleasing, and the Man, who gives up the Thoughts of being Wise, do equally quit their Claim to the true Causes of living.
—*Tatler* No. 175

As we have seen, the late seventeenth and early eighteenth centuries witnessed the dramatic unfolding of a domestic ideology that conceived the two sexes as complementary in their distinct spheres and functions and thus equal in their ability to fulfill a necessary role in the natural as well as the cultural order. Yet in spite of—or perhaps in response to—the developing belief in parity, men's ability to dominate and govern the female sex remained a central element in masculine gender identity. "The real man," writes Anthony Fletcher, "was able to possess his wife's body through regular sex and her mind through authoritative control of her behaviour and of how she spent her time."[1] Although men's efforts to teach women to internalize, rather than simply to capitulate to, patriarchal dictates meant a softening of previously harsh attitudes and an accompanying attention to women's need for improvement through education, such changes transformed without eliminating a misogynistic tradition in which women's supposedly uncontrolled sexual desires posed a severe threat to the order of male dominance. At the same time, a continued emphasis upon sexual prowess as a measure of masculinity conflicted with the emerging ideology of chaste heterosexuality, described in earlier chapters, in which men solidified their class and gender interests by demonstrating exemplary self-control.

As one of the eighteenth century's most influential texts in terms of "in-still[ing] a sentimental domestic ideal that redefined the qualities desired by one sex in the other,"[2] the *Tatler* (1709–11), written primarily by Richard Steele, reveals the pointed sword within the velvet scabbard of sentimental masculinity. For the developing middle classes in England in the early eighteenth century, women's fabrication as inherently domestic was linked to the simultaneous construction of a new form of masculinity that combined aspects of the patriarchal father with the more tender attributes of the bourgeois husband. By emphasizing women's importance as desirable objects, this view of masculinity unavoidably represents men as continually desiring subjects, a position that conflicts with the authoritative aspect of masculinity pioneered in Dunton's idea of self-regulation and embodied more generally in the role of the father/patriarch. In the ensuing chapter, I explore the ways in which the reforming narrative voices of the *Tatler*, construed as explicitly male, become both expressions of and influences upon the construction of ideal masculinity.

Grasping masculinity and femininity as dialectical rather than dualistic constructs allows us to examine the problems present within both conventions, as each incorporates attributes of old paradigms while at the same time creating new ones.[3] "In the beginning of the [eighteenth] century," writes Nancy Cott, "when spokesmen for the new professional and commercial middle class began explicitly to oppose aristocratic pretension, vanity, and libertinism, reforming writers such as Daniel Defoe, Jeremy Collier, Richard Steele, and Samuel Richardson portrayed sexual promiscuity as one of those aristocratic excesses that threatened middle-class virtue and domestic security."[4] The *Tatler* clearly distinguishes characteristics of middle-class domestic masculinity from the behavior of "your Men of Wit and Pleasure," who look upon a "kind Husband" as a "Clown, and a good Wife as a Domestick Animal, unfit for the Company or Conversation of the *Beau Monde*" (No. 159). Ironically, however, an understanding of sentimental masculinity that configures women as pleasing objects, thereby forcing men into the role of constantly desirous sexual subjects, actually perpetuates the libertine behavior that it purportedly rejects. At the same time, within the familial sphere the relationship between fathers and daughters necessitates the repression of male desire, as exemplified in the dual nature of the male gaze, which, when turned upon women, is at once judgmental and erotic—both the stern glance of the patriarchal father and the titillated look of the aroused boy or man. In addition, the pressing need to secure for his daughter an advantageous marriage (often to an older man not unlike himself) exacerbates the opposition in the father between the moral "no"—to his own desires, as well as to those of his daughter—and his libidinous, aesthetic "yes." In other words, the father's stance of denial must simultaneously include approval, for to be marriageable, his daughter must be chaste; but to be desirable, she must also be alluring.

The *Tatler* and the later *Spectator* (1711–12) both described and enacted numerous representations of archetypal familial relationships.[5] Reading the family plots of these texts from the perspective of the father's relationship to his daughter and the husband's to his wife exposes the contradictions both within prescribed male functions themselves and within our historical understanding of them. For not only have we masked the processes by which men become conditioned into their social and familial roles, but the very ways in which we understand gender construction also serve to reify the already existing separations between male and female. Thus Michael Kimmel argues that the sex-role socialization model of gender relations, by minimizing the extent to which gender relations are based on power, reproduces "the very problems it seeks to understand" by positing "two fixed, static, and mutually exclusive role containers with no interpenetration."[6] In this context, it is important to recognize the sentimental family as an ideological structure that acted to perpetuate the gender differences that, as I argue in Chapter 1, were only beginning to emerge in their particular forms at the beginning of the eighteenth century. By concentrating, then, on this new type of family man, I hope to make manifest the discursive means through which men, framed within an ideology of masculinity, were limited to their prescribed roles as women's guardians, protectors, reformers, and providers.

The notion of a companionate marriage in which women's domestic functions inside the household serve to complement those of men in the public sphere conceals the fact that men's supposedly new role only modifies the patriarchal functions of the father and husband and does not eliminate them. In the sentimental nuclear family of the late seventeenth and early eighteenth centuries, the father retained his position as head of the family by virtue of his inclusion within a sphere that incorporated the domestic world of women and children, home and family. In this situation, the seemingly egalitarian relationship between husbands and wives proves to be instead more of an extension of the highly asymmetric relationship between fathers and daughters. In other words, the separate but equal status accorded to domestic femininity is nothing more than an ideological myth.[7] As eroticized objects, dependent upon male attention, education, and approval to realize their limited role as wives and mothers, women lack the requisite components of humanness: rational capacity and active participation in the civic and political realms.

In addition, expressions of desirable male sexuality are formulated in dual relation to prescriptions for female sexual behavior. In order to insure a daughter's marketability and an heir's legitimacy, a man's duties must include monitoring the sexual behavior of his women and protecting them from the dangers of other men. Indeed, the exemplary man must learn to repress his own sexual longing, whether it be incestuous desire for the daughter or lust for other men's property.[8] It follows from a concept of intrinsic gender opposition, which postulates that it is women's nature to be pleasing, that all women—whether daughters, wives, or mothers—depend upon the approving male gaze to confer upon them "the true Causes of living" (*Tatler* No. 175). Yet if women can never escape their designated role as desired objects, men too are trapped within their configuration as desiring subjects, whose sexualized response to women becomes an integral part of their own sense of themselves as men.[9]

In keeping with the theory that women must be what men are not and vice versa, a decent woman must take a passive position vis-à-vis relationships—so much so, in fact, that the *Tatler* would have us believe, paradoxically, that modesty with regard to sexual desire is both natural and culturally dictated: "Nature has formed us with a strong Reluctance against owning such a Passion," writes "Diana Doubtful" in a letter to the *Tatler* (No. 98), "and Custom has made it criminal in us to make Advances." As Patricia Meyer Spacks frames the situation, "Men were the wooers, women the wooed; a woman who allowed her interest in a man to become apparent before he declared his in her risked disgrace."[10] Women's enforced passivity thus leaves the active role exclusively to men. If women must repress their desire in order to be accounted proper, and therefore marriageable, then by the same token men in romantic relationships are forced into a position of constantly expressing their desire, a circumstance that aligns them with the libertine whose existence is defined by sexual conquest. These contradictions within the ideological construction of masculinity, as a set of beliefs about proper male attitudes and behavior inscribed within a changing set of familial structures, find discursive representation within the pages of the *Tatler*.

The periodical genre promoted a particular kind of vision, a reforming gaze, delineated in manifestly gendered terms. The acts of evaluation necessary to reformation depended upon teaching people how to think and understand by seeing—so the theory goes—what is really there. Yet, according to convention, these capacities depended upon a rational faculty designated as exclusively masculine. One influential expression of this belief, with its concomitant declaration of reciprocity between the sexes, occurs in the Marquis of Halifax's "Advice to a Daughter" (1688). Again, note the way in which inequality becomes equality via complementarity:

> You must first lay it down for a foundation in generall, that there is inequality in the Sexes, and that for the better oeconomy of the World, the men, who were to bee the Law-givers, had the larger share of reason bestowed upon them; by which means your Sex is the better prepared for the complyance that is necessary for the better performance of those duties which seem to bee most properly assigned to it. . . . Wee are made of differing tempers, that our defects may the better bee mutually supplyed: your sex wanteth our reason for your conduct, and our strength for your protection: Ours wanteth your gentleness to soften, and entertain us.[11]

In defining the piercing glance of the social censor as explicitly masculine, the *Tatler* implicitly defines the feminine as that which is to be looked at, as well as that which becomes real only within the reflection of the male gaze. Therefore, although the *Tatler* carefully scrutinizes both men and women in its pages, each sex's relationship to the "mirror of truth"—an image I shall explore shortly—differs.[12] Moreover, by valorizing the male perspective, the periodical sets itself up as a model of correct vision. Let us examine the foundations of this site upon which is built an omniscient narrative voice that is then explicitly gendered as male, thereby aligning truth with the male point of view.

Steele chose as the supposed author of his first periodical the character of Isaac Bickerstaff, invented by Jonathan Swift to satirize the quack astrologer John Partridge.[13] Steele endowed his persona with a history, a large and various family, and a wealth of social experience. Bickerstaff, the character, mingles freely with the polite world of London, enjoying a correspondence that includes many women. Yet his advanced age—sixty-four—allows him a seemingly detached stance with regard to sexual desire. Discussing the delicate subject of women's "transgressions," Bickerstaff writes that "He that is past the Power of Beauty, may talk of this Matter with the same Unconcern as of any other Subject" (No. 201). Bickerstaff's narrative authority as "an old Man," I would thus argue, underlies and enhances his other roles as "a Philosopher, an Humorist, an Astrologer, and a Censor" (No. 271).

The "lucubrations" of Isaac Bickerstaff both embody and depend upon the idiosyncrasies of his character. As a visionary, both in the sense of his ability to foretell the future (part of the legacy inherited from his Swiftian incarnation) and as a man with a vision, a clear-cut sense of how society should be, Steele's eidolon demonstrates numerous forms of insight. Some of these manifestations are part of his character roles. In addition to his astrological abilities, Bickerstaff is a physician, "Having taken upon me to cure all the Distempers which proceed from Affections of the Mind" (No. 34). Modeling himself after the Roman censors, Bickerstaff has also assumed the title of "*Censor* of *Great Britain*," which entails categorizing and distinguishing people by type, from "Rakes" to "Pedants"; looking "into the Manners of the People . . . to check any growing Luxury, whether in Diet, Dress, or Building"; and finally, "punishing Offences according to the Quality of the Offender" (No. 162). Moreover, he plays the role of father to his half-sister Jenny Distaff.

Steele also employs manifold devices that allow Bickerstaff access to a literal vision not possessed by mere mortals. Pacolet, who first appears to Bickerstaff in the thirteenth number as his guardian angel, performs in person, albeit invisibly, the work of moral reformation that Bickerstaff attempts to do through writing. As Bickerstaff's familiar, Pacolet allows him—and us—to see the inner workings of a variety of people. Bickerstaff employs Pacolet as a messenger, a teacher, and a species of strong-arm to carry out his dictates as censor.[14] Although Pacolet receives no mention after No. 167, his function is in part filled by Bickerstaff's own ability to render himself invisible through his use of the "Ring of *Gyges*," which was mentioned first in Plato's *Republic* and later by Cicero. Bickerstaff's possession of this wondrous talisman enables him to enter the chamber of the "beauteous Flavia" in order to witness her coquettish response to a love letter (No. 139). In No. 243 Bickerstaff uses the ring for moral rather than mercenary purposes: he turns himself invisible not, as Gyges did, to become king but instead to "get a thorough Insight into the Ways of Men, and to make such Observations upon the Errors of others as may be useful to the Publick, whatever Effect they may have upon my self." In these narratives, Bickerstaff's ability to make himself disappear works to literalize the periodical's *modus operandi*, baring its devices. As the erasure of Bickerstaff's corporeal body acts to diffuse and naturalize his ethical sensibility, so too does the periodical's promotion of an ethos of universal morality function to subsume its distinct ideological agenda.

In No. 237, Bickerstaff unmasks deception in a slightly different way. Falling asleep after having read *Paradise Lost*, he dreams he has been granted Ithuriel's spear, which shows the things it touches as they really are. Although Bickerstaff remarks that the spear would be a tremendous advantage to "a Minister of State," he chooses to employ it at "a Place of publick Resort," a setting, in other words, that permits him to comment upon social as well as political mores. When touched by the spear, a demure woman becomes lascivious; a woman boasting of her virginity immediately goes into labor; a loving husband and wife to whom he gives a "gentle Tap" reveal their true colors, as "the next Instant saw the Woman in Breeches, and the Man with a Fan in his Hand"; a touch reveals "Whigs disguised in Tories and Tories in Whigs"; a Bible-toter commences, when touched, to pick Bickerstaff's pocket. In this sequence only Bickerstaff himself remains immune to the spear's corrective tap, since, in matters of truth, we are given to understand that his vision is already twenty-twenty. In addition, the *Tatler* uses exemplary types, both negative and positive, to educate its female readers into becoming not just objects, but objects of the right kind. The periodical deems a woman whose only pleasing characteristic is physical beauty less desirable than one who combines beautiful or even plain features with modest good nature.[15] For men, however, to be an object is itself wrong. Thus a male type such as the "Ladies' Man," who takes pleasure in being looked at, becomes a target of scorn and even distaste.

As with the earlier *Night-Walker*, it is not just the ability to see but also the possession of a forum in which to tell that underlies the *Tatler*'s ability to reform manners and morals. By expanding the circle of the neighborhood or village into the whole of London's literate classes, the *Tatler* can increase the audience for information that had previously been transmitted by word of mouth. In the third *Tatler*, while criticizing the Society for the Reformation of Manners for its severity regarding plays, Bickerstaff (here closely allied with Steele) nonetheless names himself a member. While Bickerstaff distinguishes himself from both the society and his reforming predecessor, John Dunton's Night-Walker, by claiming that rather than "punishing Great Crimes, and exposing the Abandon'd," he will genteelly note "Indecorums, Improprieties, and Negligences," he, even so, employs a comparable strategy in his claim to expose inappropriate behavior publicly: "After this Declaration, if a fine Lady thinks fit to Giggle at Church, or a Great Beau come in Drunk to a Play, either shall be sure to hear of it in my ensuing Paper: For merely as a well-bred Man, I cannot bear these Enormities." While "Enormities" may be satirical, "well-bred" is not. In his role as arbiter of taste and behavior for the rising middle classes, exemplified in his title of "Censor of Great Britain," Bickerstaff cleverly includes the ability to institutionalize scandal: not only can he see, he will also tell.[16]

But what is it that Bickerstaff sees? How does he translate his vision to his readers, and in the process instill in them the proper kinds of insight and, by extension, the correct forms of behavior? It is by learning to look at women,

as well as to become simultaneously the mirror in which women are represented, that men can learn to constitute themselves as ethical subjects. As I
have argued, this male speculative position is at least two-sided. Incorporated within the stern gaze of the father as social censor is the eroticized
glance of the man as desiring subject. But this visual position itself depends
upon and forms part of the configuration of women as inherently different
from men, designed with opposite attributes and designated for separate
responsibilities.

A closer look at the visions comprising the whole of *Tatlers* 100 and 102
(written by Joseph Addison) demonstrates more clearly the ways in which
the marking of the reforming gaze as male depends upon this rigid ascription of gender roles. Bickerstaff experiences his first dream-vision after he
has spent the evening in the garden of Lincoln's Inn, philosophizing upon
"the unequal Distribution of Wealth, Honour, and all other Blessings of
Life." His access to this domain of masculine legal authority inspires his
dream of a rightful distribution of life's good fortune. Within the mirror
held by a goddess who combines Justice and Truth, men's positions as property owners, fathers, and leaders are re-viewed. In order "to restore and appropriate to every one living what was his Due," the goddess pronounces the
first edict, "*That all Titles and Claims to Riches and Estates, or to any Part of 'em,
should be immediately vested in the rightful Owner.*" As men hold up the "Instruments of their Tenure," the rays of the goddess's mirror set fire "to all
Forgery and Falshood." This process, which serves also to bring to light
"Writings and Records which had been hidden or buried by Time, Chance
or Design," occasions "a wonderful Revolution among the People," as does
the second command, "for the whole Body of Mankind to separate themselves into their proper Families." The results of the second edict allow Addison to satirize the sexual mores of his contemporaries as well as their material propensities: "You might see a Presumptive Heir of a great Estate ask
Blessing of his Coachman, and a celebrated Toast paying her Duty to a *Valet
de Chambre.*"

But the final edict is the most important one: "*That all the Posts of Dignity
and Honour in the Universe should be conferred on Persons of the greatest Merit,
Abilities and Perfection.*" These attributes consist, we learn, not in looks,
strength, or wealth, for their claimants, unable "to bear the Splendour of the
Mirror which played upon their Faces," fall back into the crowd. Rather, it is
the men of "Virtue, Knowledge or Capacity in Business, either Military or
Civil," who form the ranks of leadership, with the highest posts granted to
those "who were Masters of all Three Qualifications in some Degree." As
John Berger reminds us, men are important both to each other and to

women for "the promise of power" they embody: "A man's presence suggests what he is capable of doing for you."[17]

Whereas this text values men for their ability to act, and to act upon each other, women must be judged by different criteria altogether. Bickerstaff's sexually evaluative gaze informs the vision's continuation in No. 102. Even before the goddess proclaims the standards by which women are to be measured, Bickerstaff himself has already marked the fair sex as pleasing objects: "So charming a Multitude filled my Heart with unspeakable Pleasure; and as the Celestial Light of the Mirror shone upon their Faces, several of them seemed rather Persons that descended in the Train of the Goddess, than such who were brought before her to their Tryal." Yet tried they must be. The very qualities upon which these women base their claims are worth noting, for all demonstrate some aspect of women's relations to men: "Some boasted of the Merit of their Husbands; others of their own Power in governing them. Some pleaded their unspotted Virginity; others their numerous Issue. Some valued themselves as they were the Mothers, and others as they were the Daughters, of considerable Persons." When the goddess declares that beauty will be the ultimate arbiter, the women continue to present themselves as objects to be surveyed. Initially, however, it is neither Bickerstaff nor the goddess who is to determine the outcome: "The Ladies were yet better pleas'd, when they heard, that in the Decision of this great Controversy, each of them should be her own Judge, and take her Place according to her own Opinion of her self, when she consulted her Looking-glass."

Yet not only do women fail to see what they really look like, for better or for worse, but the confrontation with reality infuriates them: "It is impossible to describe the Rage, the Pleasure, or Astonishment, that appeared in each Face upon its Representation in the Mirror: Multitudes stared at their own Form, and would have broke the Glass if they could have reached it." By showing the disparity between women's image of themselves and the "true" picture as presented in the mirror, the narrative constitutes women's vision as unreliable. Women as unreliable viewers of themselves then become elided with women as unreliable viewers of truth or reality, and thus women in need of the corrective male gaze. Of course, women's position is untenable. There is no objective standard for pleasing; one is successful only as one positively affects an other or others. Thus the only woman who could possibly possess a clear picture of herself would be one whose sense of self-worth did not consist in being pleasing or beautiful, but this is a Catch-22; since pleasing others is what defines female worth, such a creature would no longer be a woman.

Once women are shown what they really look like—for example, the

"Lady who was thought so agreeable in her Anger, and was so often cele-brated for a Woman of Fire and Spirit . . . fancied she saw a Fury in the Glass"—the women who are satisfied with their images are asked "to sepa-rate, and place themselves at the Head of their Sex." Whereas the men were earlier divided as to virtue, knowledge, and business, the women are distin-guished as "Maids, Wives, and Widows" in order to be tested more fully. Two edicts serve further to diminish their ranks, as a way "to make an Ex-ample of two Extremes in the Female World; of those who are very severe on the Conduct of others, and of those who are very regardless of their own." Thus "all Females addicted to Censoriousness and Detraction, should lose the Use of Speech," and in terms of "the loose Part of the Sex, That all should immediately be pregnant, who in any Part of their Lives had ran the Hazard of it."

In the vision of men, the reassessment of family is important with regard to the rightful attribution of their property; for women, who are themselves property, loose behavior threatens the men who possess them. Loose speech poses a different danger for reasons that are by now familiar: *Tatler* No. 102 condemns women's censoriousness because it encroaches upon a territory marked as male. By contrast, men might trespass with impunity upon female ground: the periodical's title enacts precisely that male confiscation of the fe-male domain. After stating in the *Tatler's* first number that he is going to tell men of "strong Zeal and weak Intellects . . . what to think," Bickerstaff turns his attention to women: "I have also resolved to have something which may be of Entertainment to the Fair Sex, in Honour of whom, I have invented the Title of this Paper." The *Tatler's* narrative authority is thus founded upon a mode of discourse, as well as a form of interaction, designated originally as both female and undesirable.[18] Although the edict pairs the term "Censori-ousness" with "Detraction," seemingly in order to specify women who make negative judgments about others, the term itself, like its root, "censor," im-plies any kind of critical judgment. To judge is to view others. This is, how-ever, an unseemly position for women, whose construction as pleasing ob-jects allows them only to be viewed. Granted, women must indeed view themselves to some extent for the purposes of reforming their behavior, but when they do, they must inevitably assume the gaze of their male censor.

Men, on the other hand, should not be self-conscious. Whereas a woman needs to be seen to become real, the man of "clear and worthy Spirit" should "be able to disengage himself from the Opinions of others, so far as not to let the Deference due to the Sense of Mankind ensnare him to act against the Dictates of his own Reason" (No. 138). The negative example given in the number is that of "Will Glare," who is "so passionately intent upon being admired, that when you see him in publick Places, every Muscle of his Face discovers his Thoughts are fixed upon the Consideration of what Figure he makes." Yet the position of the exemplary man, who is the same in his house as he is on the public streets, is onerous to achieve: "It is therefore extremely difficult for a Man to judge even of his own Actions, without forming to himself an Idea of what he should act, were it in his Power to execute all his Desires without the Observation of the Rest of the World" (ibid.). Because a man must himself "execute all his Desires" while a woman is dependent upon a man for both the expression and fulfillment of her own, the self-consciousness necessary to women becomes a liability to men.

This different stance concerning the *regard d'autre* relies upon a clearly delineated view of gender opposition. One of the *Tatler's* most famous statements regarding gender difference occurs in the context of a discussion about the danger of men's unrestrained passions within marriage. Steele, in his persona as Bickerstaff, writes that in marriage

> a Man should, if possible, soften his Passions, if not for his own Ease, in Compliance to a Creature formed with a Mind of quite a different Make from his own. I am sure, I do not mean it as an Injury to Women, when I say there is a Sort of Sex in Souls. I am tender of offending them, and know it is hard not to do it on this Subject; but I must go on to say, That the Soul of a Man and that of a Woman are made very unlike, according to the Employments for which they are designed. The Ladies will be pleased to observe, I say, our Minds have different, not superior Qualities to theirs. (No. 172)

In this example, the rhetoric of complementarity transforms blatant inequality into a supposed equality through recourse to function as well as to nature. By making "Souls" depend upon "Employments," Steele's argument constructs those employments as natural, God-given, and inherent rather than as socially constructed and male-defined. Moreover, if women's souls are qualitatively different from those of men, it follows that the attributes assigned to them be defined in gendered terms: "The Virtues have respectively a Masculine and a Feminine Cast. What we call in men Wisdom, is in Women Prudence. It is a Partiality to call one greater than the other. A prudent Woman is in the same Class of Honour as a wise Man, and the Scandals in the way of both are equally dangerous" (ibid.).

In addition, inherent gender difference supplies the reason for men's and women's contrasting willingness to be reformed. In No. 139 Bickerstaff ruminates upon "the many Nights I have sat up for some Months last past in the greatest Anxiety for the Good of my Neighbours and Contemporaries," noting that "it is no small Discouragement to me, to see how slow a Progress I make in the Reformation of the World." Although his tone is satirical by virtue of its melodrama, the analysis that follows is wholly serious. To give women credit, he notes that they have indeed been better subjects than men, for "their tender Hearts are much more susceptible of good Impressions, than the Minds of the other Sex." Women respond emotionally, men intellectually: although this is hardly a new perspective, the sentimentalized configuration of that difference is worth noting, as is its explanation with reference to separate spheres: "Business and Ambition take up Men's Thoughts too much to leave Room for Philosophy: But if you speak to Women in a Style and Manner proper to approach them, they never fail to improve by your Counsel." Of course the "you" refers here exclusively to men: although men may be too busy to pay much attention to their own reformation, an integral part of their "Business" must be their attention to women. In deference, therefore, to this greater receptivity in women, Bickerstaff writes that "I shall therefore for the future turn my Thoughts more particularly to their Service, and study the best Methods to adorn their Persons, and inform their Minds in the justest Methods to make them what Nature designed them, the most beauteous Objects of our Eyes, and the most agreeable Companions of our Lives" (ibid.).

Although the *Tatler* grants women minds to inform as well as bodies to adorn, it nevertheless encompasses both minds and bodies within the larger process of teaching women to become pleasing objects. Yet the woman who takes too much pleasure in her own beauty becomes something less than ideal. Termed a coquette and discussed often within the pages of the *Tatler*, this female type is "one who lives in continual Misapplication of her Beauty," just as her male counterpart, the rake, is "the Man who lives in the constant Abuse of his Reason" (No. 27).[19] The coquette transgresses gender boundaries by presuming to judge herself instead of leaving that office exclusively to men. In No. 126, Bickerstaff juxtaposes Lydia, who "has all the Charms that can adorn a Woman" and whose "Attractions would indeed be irresistible, but that she thinks them so, and is always employing them in Stratagems and Conquests," with Belvidera, who exerts "an invincible Prejudice in Favour of all she says, from her being a beautiful Woman, because she does not consider her self as such when she talks to you." Although Belvidera is exemplary because she does not abuse the power of her beauty by using it for her own self-aggrandizement,[20] Bickerstaff does nonetheless counsel women to exert the force of their charms when it is for the purposes of gaining or retaining men's desire for them. Just as the "Mirror of Truth" posits the male gaze as the only real confirmation of women's attractiveness and thus their worth, so too does the expression of male desire provide the only legitimate arena in which women can experience their own sexual passion.

No. 147, in which Addison retells a passage from the *Iliad*, provides an example of the acceptable use of female sexuality within marriage. The allegory, Bickerstaff writes, is designed "for the use of several of my Fair Correspondents, who in their Letters have complained to me, that they have lost the Affections of their Husbands, and desire my Advice how to recover them." He then recounts, following closely upon his source, the steps Juno takes to rekindle Jupiter's love for her. She bathes and perfumes herself in ambrosial liquids, combs her hair, dresses herself to greatest advantage, and finally goes to Venus to ask for the loan of "those Charms with which she subdued the Hearts both of Gods and Men,"[21] claiming that she will use them to reconcile the estranged deities who cared for her in infancy. Juno is of course successful in her attempt to excite Jupiter with her beauty; in fact, he becomes so enamored that he cannot wait even to get to Juno's chamber, but instead creates a golden bower for them atop Mt. Ida. Although Addison is less detailed than Homer in rendering Jupiter's previous sexual infidelities, all of which have paled before his present desire for Juno, his modesty does not minimize the triumph of heterosexual monogamy, in all its Edenic undertones, that is here enacted.[22]

And yet the fable's larger context mitigates the allegory's representation of behaviors that are "so indispensably necessary in every Female who desires to please, that they need no further Explanation." In the *Tatler*'s version, Juno, "seeing her *Jupiter* seated on the Top of Mount *Ida*, and knowing that he had conceived an Aversion to her, began to study how she should regain his Affections, and make her self amiable to him." In the *Iliad*, however, it is Hera who conceives the dislike: "Then she saw Zeus, sitting along the loftiest summit / on Ida of the springs, and in her eyes he was hateful" (14, 157–58). Zeus defends the Trojans while Hera supports the Greeks; her desire is to "beguile," rather than be reconciled with, her husband:

> And now the lady ox-eyed Hera was divided in purpose
> as to how she could beguile the brain in Zeus of the aegis.
> And to her mind this thing appeared to be the best counsel,
> to array herself in loveliness, and go down to Ida,
> and perhaps he might be taken with desire to lie in love
>   with her
> next her skin, and she might be able to drift an innocent
> warm sleep across his eyelids, and seal his crafty perceptions.
>
> (161–65)

Thus all of Hera's actions occur within the context of deception: she seduces to achieve her own will, rather than to fulfill that of her husband. It is therefore highly ironic that Addison uses the story both to exemplify feminine "Discretion" and to upbraid those married women who do not devote enough attention to retaining the desire of their husbands.[23] In the same number, Addison calumniates those "Housewives who are never well dressed but when they are Abroad, and think it necessary to appear more agreeable to all Men living than their Husbands." In addition, he criticizes "those prudent Ladies, who, to avoid the Appearance of being over-fond, entertain their Husbands with Indifference, Aversion, sullen Silence, or exasperating Language." Following Homer's Hera rather than Addison's Juno, these women maintain a public appearance that conflicts with their private domestic behavior.

Bickerstaff's claim, noted earlier, of being able to take an impartial and thus necessarily sharply critical view of women because as an old man he is "past the Power of Beauty" (No. 201), is double-edged, for it demonstrates men's extreme vulnerability to women's attractions. The traditional belief in women's power to arouse, confuse, and distract men makes imperative men's ability to control women's use of their sexual desirability.[24] Yet men are dependent upon women's construction as pleasing objects in order to make themselves feel and act like men. It thus becomes necessary to build into the notions of both femininity and masculinity some safeguards against the abuse of that situation. Women must therefore direct their desire exclusively toward the pleasing of men, only pleasing themselves as they succeed in fulfilling their respective roles as "Mothers, Sisters, Daughters, and Wives" (No. 42). Men, for their part, must guarantee the constant availability of such women by making it their job to teach their daughters, as well as often their wives, to become exemplary, that is, both pleasing and chaste, women.

As with Dunton's *Night-Walker*, the act of reading turns into a process of regulation. For a woman, reading the *Tatler* meant becoming a desirable object and thus a desirable woman to the extent to which she internalized the periodical's pronouncements and narrative examples. Yet, as I am arguing, the social periodical ideologically constructed the male reader as well. For him, reading the *Tatler* meant identifying with Isaac Bickerstaff, as a character older, of the world, opinionated, and benevolently paternalistic in his dictates. Kathryn Shevelow notes that through Bickerstaff's "interconnected functions as a correspondent, a persona, and a figure of wise male behavior," Steele asserted his eidolon's "authority to articulate the periodical's moral standards and reformist sentiments."[25] The familial model for this interaction, best reflected in the papers detailing the relationship between Bickerstaff and his young half-sister Jenny Distaff, is that of a father to a daughter. Shevelow has argued persuasively that this relationship takes its model and moral authority from the genre of father-daughter conduct literature, which in the seventeenth century and well into the eighteenth provided norms for female behavior and feminine gender identity.[26] Jenny Distaff's education, from a flighty, feisty, pleasure-loving young woman into the dedicated, loving, and obedient wife of Tranquillus—a trader whom Bickerstaff has chosen for her—serves as a model for the *Tatler*'s female readers, just as Bickerstaff's patriarchal attitudes and actions provide a paradigm for correct male behavior.

The two Staffs are related through a common father: Isaac is a product of his first marriage, Jenny of his third. The forty-year age difference and the implied death of their father create a situation in which, as Bickerstaff acknowledges, Jenny relates to him "rather like a Daughter than a Sister" (No. 75). With Jenny, Bickerstaff can play father without having also to play husband, a circumstance that underlines the paternal element in the male-female relationship. As a bachelor, Bickerstaff, like the eidolons of the *Spectator*, *Guardian*, and *Lover*, rests outside of the ultimate jurisdiction of the domestic realm, while still retaining privileged access to it.[27] As a dutiful daughter, however, Jenny is highly problematic. In her first essay, she sets out to expose the double standards and "unreasonable Expectations" placed on female behavior by criticizing some papers she finds in her brother's closet (No. 10). She begins her second essay by professing to agree with Bickerstaff's assertion that men's vices are to be blamed upon "Women's secret Approbation of Libertine Characters in them," stating with regard to herself that "no Vow shall deceive me but that of Marriage" (No. 33). And yet, by spending the remainder of the essay recounting the story of her own near-seduction at the hands of both a male and a female libertine, she exposes the threat to female chastity that results from her own unwillingness to abide by the rules of proper feminine behavior. Jenny vehemently condemns that behavior, as she had earlier denounced the "Batchelor's Scheme for Governing his Wife" presented in No. 10: "The First Thing he makes this Gentleman propose is, That she shall be no Woman; for she is to have an Aversion to Balls, to Opera's, to Visits: She is to think his Company sufficient to fill up all the Hours of Life with great Satisfaction: She is never to believe any other Man Wise, Learned, or Valiant; or at least but in a Second Degree."[28]

In No. 75, Bickerstaff further describes Jenny's unfeminine nature when he puts aside "public Dissertations" to discuss "a Domestick Affair of great Importance, which is no less than the Disposal of my Sister *Jenny* for Life." In Bickerstaff's portrait, Jenny prides herself upon intellectual rather than domestic abilities: "Her Wit she thinks her Distinction." She "therefore knows nothing of the Skill of Dress, or making her Person agreeable. It would make you laugh to see me often with my Spectacles on lacing her Stays; for she is so very a Wit, that she understands no ordinary Thing in the World." Taking snuff, reading plays and romances, ignoring her looks, and having opinions: these attributes mark Jenny as unwomanly, and therefore in need of reform. Although he himself has been unsuccessful in changing Jenny's ostensibly masculine behaviors, Bickerstaff intends to cause the desired change through his choice of her marriage partner: "I have dispos'd of her to a Man of Business, who will soon let her see, that to be well dress'd, in good Humour, and cheerful in the Command of her Family, are the Arts and Sciences of Female Life" (ibid.).

Bickerstaff's "disposal" of Jenny is to my mind the most revealing aspect of this remarkable passage. As a wit, a reader of literature, and a young woman out and about in the world (witness her adventure in No. 33), Jenny seems more likely to make her own choice of a marriage partner than to have one chosen for her. Yet early in the number, Bickerstaff writes that "I have indeed told her, That if she kept her Honour, and behav'd herself in such Manner as became the *Bickerstaffs*, I would get her an agreeable Man for her Husband." His having complete choice enables him to correct the imbalance in Jenny's nature and behavior much in the way that one of his aristocratic ancestors cured the "Spindle-Shanks" incurred by too much inbreeding by marrying "*Maud* the Milk-Maid." A kind of master eugenicist, Bickerstaff explains why he "found it absolutely necessary to cross the Strain," for "a Fine Gentleman, who extremely admir'd her Wit, and would have given her a Coach and Six" would have been an unsuitable match for Jenny: "had they met, they had eternally been Rivals in Discourse, and in continual Contention for the Superiority of Understanding, and brought forth Criticks, Pedants, or pretty good Poets." Rather than encouraging Jenny's unfeminine lack of care for herself or a household, Jenny's ideal suitor, the "Man of Business" whom Steele names "Tranquillus" (No. 79), will allow Jenny to flourish as a properly domesticated woman, one versed in the arts of household management rather than those of literary criticism.

Bickerstaff's control over Jenny's conjugal arrangements also manifests itself in narrative terms, as all of the discussions of Jenny's marriage and marital situation—Nos. 75, 79, 85, 104, and 143—are recounted by Bickerstaff. (When Jenny once again takes over, in No. 247, it is to answer a woman's letter, not to comment upon her own situation.) Bickerstaff's supervision of Jenny allows him both to retain his primary claim over her and to use Tranquillus as a kind of extension of himself. Thus while Jenny might demonstrate her reformation by emulating Tranquillus, Bickerstaff can nevertheless claim full credit for her transformation because it was he who chose Tranquillus for her (No. 104). In "The Father's House and the Daughter in It," Lynda Boose takes issue with Levi-Strauss's now-classic explication of daughters as objects of exchange, gifts given in return for social benefit, by arguing that instead of being the cause for exchange, such gift-giving might function as a psychic defense against its necessity: "For losing one's daughter through a transaction that the father controls circumvents her ability ever to choose another man over him, thus allowing him to retain vestiges of his primary claim. . . . The bestowal design places the daughter's departure from the father's house and her sexual union with another male into a text defined by her obedience to her father—not preference for an outside male."[29] Thus, while Jenny's love for Tranquillus depends upon the kind of sexual bond prohibited between her and her half-brother, the potency of the connection can, however, be mediated by the fact that she directs that sexual love toward a man whom her brother has selected.

In earlier numbers, Bickerstaff prepares Jenny for her forthcoming marriage by telling her, in good conduct-book style, that "there is no Mean in the State you are entring into, but you are to be exquisitely happy or miserable, and your Fortune in this Way of Life will be wholly of your own Making" (No. 79). Then, after their marriage has taken place, he takes her to task for an argument with her husband in which she has taken pleasure in her "Power to give Pain" (No. 85). Bickerstaff here sees Jenny as still in need of reform, an object yet to be molded, in this case by himself. But in No. 104, when Jenny comes to dine with her brother when Tranquillus has gone out of town, Bickerstaff notices a significant alteration in her manner. The change first evinces itself, appropriately enough, in her name, which serves to mark both ownership and loyalty: "I perceived she expected to be treated hereafter not as *Jenny Distaff*, but Mrs. *Tranquillus*." Jenny, however, has taken on more than just her husband's name; she has also incorporated his thoughts and mannerisms: "upon talking with her on several Subjects, I could not but fancy, that I saw a great deal of her Husband's Way and Manner in her Remarks, her Phrases, the Tone of her Voice, and the very Air of her Countenance."

In this passage, Bickerstaff's "fancy" manifests his own wish to see in Jenny the signs of her reform. While *she* might attribute her supposed change to her husband, Bickerstaff nonetheless assumes credit for the transformation he perceives: "This gave me an unspeakable Satisfaction, not only because I had found her an Husband, from whom she could learn many Things that were laudable, but also because I looked upon her Imitation of him as an infallible Sign that she intirely loved him." Indeed this point is made again in *Spectator* No. 605: "It is a nice Reflection, which I have heard a Friend of mine make, that you may be sure a Woman loves a Man, when she uses his Expressions, tells his Stories, or imitates his Manner."[30] It is interesting to observe the mimetic chain operating here: readers imitate characters who in turn are imitating each other. What seems particularly noteworthy, however, is the way in which a woman's imitation of her husband is represented as a sure sign of love, and thus a positive thing, whereas in many other cases women's imitation of male behavior becomes an occasion for stringent criticism. When women are kept safely in the domestic realm, however, conjugal mimesis can be seen as an advantage rather than a threat, as it reinscribes masculine superiority, and thus patriarchal authority.

When Jenny does finally speak to Bickerstaff of her marriage, "the natural Shieness of her Sex" prevents her from talking of "the greatness of her own Passion." Yet, Bickerstaff has "easily collected it" from the representation she gives of her husband's feelings. Once again Jenny is subsumed within her husband. She tells Bickerstaff that "I have every Thing . . . in *Tranquillus* that I can wish for; and enjoy in him (what indeed you have told me were to be met with in a good Husband) the Fondness of a Lover, the Tenderness of a Parent, and the Intimacy of a Friend." Jenny's emotional response to her situation "transports" Bickerstaff, who goes on to demand of her the confirmation of his own attitudes: "And is there not, Dear Sister, said I, more Pleasure in the Possession of such a Man, than in all the little Impertinencies of Balls, Assemblies, and Equipage, which it cost me so much Pains to make you contemn? She answered, smiling, *Tranquillus* has made me a sincere Convert in a few Weeks, tho' I am afraid you could not have done it in your whole Life."

Yet Jenny's wholesale embracing of Bickerstaff's attitudes, as channeled through Tranquillus, also constitutes a source of friction, since the apparent transforming agent is the sexual relationship with her husband—the one thing she gets from him that is prohibited between her and her half-brother. The conflict is resolved, however, when that sexual attraction proves problematic by preventing the uxorious trader from performing his proper—which is to say admonitory—masculine role. Tranquillus is too infatuated with Jenny to be effectively firm in his financial dictates: in No. 143 Jenny visits her brother in the carriage he knows to be beyond their means (and comparable, ironically, to the "Coach and Six" that the "Fine Gentleman" would have given her). Himself presumably unhampered by such partiality, Bickerstaff can contentedly resume his reformation of Jenny, as he proceeds to intercede both in conversation with Jenny herself and in a letter to her husband, whom he lectures on the subject of "Modesty in the Enjoyment of moderate Wealth." Bickerstaff even extends his advice to the broader audience: in the next issue (No. 144), he employs his position as "Censor of Great Britain" to discuss the proper employment of carriages, thereby providing an especially clear example of the way in which the monitoring of the supposedly limited domestic sphere can expand to include the whole of the country.

The paternal relation of Isaac Bickerstaff to his sister/daughter and to his brother/son-in-law serves to educate both Jenny and Tranquillus into their proper domestic roles. The husband-wife relationship, modeled after the bond between the father and his daughter, is marked by a desire for inclusion: the husband's incorporates his wife's "interests" as she internalizes her husband's beliefs. Here control of others—men's control over women—functions as an effective form of self-control. We find this need for mastery manifested as well in three other examples from the *Tatler* of men's learning to reform women. In following these narratives, male readers are compelled to emulate not specific instances, for the examples given are extreme rather than mundane, but the views of masculinity they embody. While the narrative virtuosity of the stories acts as a smokescreen for the hidden ideology, what the male reader is left with is a sense of the pressing need for control—over his own behavior, but especially over that of women.[31]

For whether by direct example, as with Jenny Distaff, or through stories, often presented as responses to readers' queries, men are being taught to control women. In the periodical's second number, a man mends the marriage of his beautiful but shrewish niece by prescribing a cordial that she must hold in her mouth while in the company of her husband. Told in full in the form of a poem titled "The MEDECIN: A Tale—for the Ladies" (written by William Harrison), the story functions also as a tale for the men. Here it is significant that not the husband but an older avuncular figure (comparable to Isaac in his relation to Jenny) finds a solution that serves in turn to rekindle the husband's absent sexual desire, when he arrives home to find his shrill wife, for once, silent:

> Thus the Fond Pair to Bed enamour'd went,
> The lady pleas'd, and the good Knight content.

The double meaning of the phrase "The lady pleas'd" manifests precisely the melding of desires advocated by the text: by pleasing her husband, the lady can herself be pleased. Unfortunately, once the bottle is emptied, the fights recommence. When the wife flies "poste-haste" to her uncle for replenishment, he gives the moral:

Why Neece, says he,—I prithee apprehend,
The Water's Water,—Be thy self thy Friend;
Such Beauty would the coldest Husband warm,
But your provoking Tongue undoes the Charm:
Be silent, and complying,—You'l soon find,
Sir *John*, without a Med'cin, will be kind.

Just as women are to take their hint from the silent wife, men, by emulating her uncle, learn witty solutions to women's transgressions.

In No. 23, the contrast between an ineffectual husband and a wise uncle becomes that between a first and second husband. The exemplary man turns his wife dutiful by seeing through her "little Arts"—the counterfeit "Convulsions" she had used to manipulate her first spouse. When she falls into a fit over some china he has refused to buy,[32] he privately whispers into her ear, *"My Dear, This will never do: What is within my Power and Fortune, you may always command, but none of your Artifices: You are quite in other Hands than those you pass'd these pretty Passions upon."* She then collapses for real, at which point he tells her he will leave until she is more sincere. She gets up, pulls him into a closet and "thank'd him for her Cure; which was so absolute," Bickerstaff writes, "that she gave me this Relation her self, to be communicated for the Benefit of all the voluntary Invalids of her Sex." While this sentence might demonstrate how completely this woman has taken her own medicine, it is nevertheless important to remember that she is reformed by the intervention of a man, and an experienced, fatherly one at that. Like "The Medecin," this exemplary narrative reads more as a tale for men than for women—alerting them to feminine artifice and teaching them how to counteract it so that they may become, like the man in the story, "absolute Master."

A third example from a late *Tatler* (No. 231), while presented as Bickerstaff's personal experience, simply retells the story of Katherine and Petruchio from *The Taming of the Shrew*. Here another man cures his wife's bad temper by simulating one of his own, thus turning his wife into "the most meek and humble Woman breathing." Although in this periodical, women's dissembling is a subject for alarm (and it is implied that a good husband has a moral responsibility to cure his wife of such behavior),[33] men are allowed—even encouraged—to trick women in the name of reforming them. The active part that husbands are exhorted to play with regard to refractory wives is, I would argue, a direct extension of the paternal responsibility that keeps daughters chaste, silent, and obedient and thus marriageable. Jenny Distaff, the difficult daughter who becomes an exemplary wife, and the women "tamed" in the narratives discussed above are initially outspoken, even dominant: their desires rule their household situations. As such, they provide powerful threats to domestic stability. I find it hard to believe that, as Richmond Bond writes of Bickerstaff, "the wise old man's lectures, suavely administered, were no doubt warmly and gratefully accepted by the *Tatler*'s female readers."[34] Rather, it would seem that the gratitude was on the part of the men, whose reading of the *Tatler* (and later, the *Spectator*) taught them both what they were expected to do with their daughters and wives and, even more important, how to do it.[35]

The *Tatler* also disseminates notions of ideal masculinity *a contrario* through numerous representations of bad fathering. The most blatant example of paternal misbehavior comes in the story of the "unhappy *Teraminta*," who has been abducted and sequestered away by the libertine Decius (No. 45). Although Teraminta is the daughter of a friend of his, Bickerstaff can hardly recognize her: her formerly "decent and modest" dress has been replaced by "the most sumptuous Habit, as if she were going to a Ball"; her "serene and beautiful" expression has changed to one that is "abject and disconsolate." She proceeds to tell him her story, both as an emotional unburdening and as a possible means of escape. On first glance, Teraminta's story appears to be a cautionary tale for those women who, through their love of flattery, "expose" themselves to the "solicitations" of such dangerous men as "the abandon'd *Decius* . . . wickedest of all men living." Yet it was the death of her father, rather than any vices of her own, that precipitated all of her problems: "When your Friend my Father died, he left me to a wide World, with no Defence against the Insults of Fortune, but rather a Thousand Snares to intrap me in the Dangers to which Youth and Innocence are exposed." In a corrupt society, in which, as Teraminta describes it, "Honour and Virtue are become mere Words, and us'd only as they serve to betray those who understand them in their native Sense," a young woman is especially in need of a father's wisdom and guidance. Like Jenny Distaff, who in No. 33 recounted her own near-fatal adventure at the hands of libertines, Teraminta has no visible mother; there is, moreover, not the least expectation that a mother might fulfill any of the functions she describes herself as needing, including education, protection, and moral stability. As a "ruined" woman, Teraminta stands testament to her father's failure to fulfill his paternal responsibilities, for he has neglected to assign the appropriate guardian to replace himself.

Teraminta has lost her father and, as a telling consequence, her virginity, not to mention the possibility of acquiring a husband. The transmission of the daughter from father to husband depends upon the father's ability to vouch for her intact status: Bickerstaff says he will provide a husband for Jenny "if she has kept her Honour." If, as I am arguing, the bond between husband and wife is in large part an extension of that between father and daughter, marital happiness—for both men and women—depends upon the father's ability to fulfill his proper duty toward his daughter.[36] And not only is the ideal husband an extension of the ideal father, but the woman's proper role as wife also depends upon her successful fulfillment of her daughterly duties: to love and obey her father, to be his "Friend and Companion" as well as an object of pleasure. The father's position as his daughter's protector, "both as to Fortune and Innocence,"[37] allows him to displace any potentially dangerous sexual feelings by assuming the presence of those feelings on the part of (all) other men. The positions of rake and father are thus contradictory and complementary, as each calls up, and feeds upon, its opposite.

A final example, taken from the related *Spectator*, depicts a dutiful daughter whose filial affection appears dangerous. No. 520 prints a letter from a bereaved widower, describing his passionate "Affliction." While in the throes of bittersweet reminiscence about his beloved wife, the writer is "broken in upon by a charming young Woman, my Daughter, who is the Picture of what her Mother was on her Wedding-Day." The order of his description, in which she is first a woman, and a charming one at that, and only afterwards his daughter, exemplifies the ambivalence of the father's position: "The good Girl strives to comfort me; but how shall I let you know that all the Comfort she gives me is to make my Tears flow more easily? The Child knows she quickens my Sorrow, and rejoices my Heart at the same Time." The father's semantic regression—from "charming young Woman" to "good Girl" to "Child"—testifies to an attempted denial that is, finally, impossible: "When she kneels and bids me be comforted, she is my Child; when I take her in my Arms, and bid her say no more, she is my very Wife, and is the very Comforter I lament the loss of." In contrast to the lover-like reunion of Indiana and her father Mr. Sealand in Steele's play *The Conscious Lovers* (1722), or the de-eroticized but permanent "Affection" of Fidelia and her father in *Spectator* No. 449, this father-daughter embrace ends in dismissal, and a refusal to conflate overtly what coexist covertly: the roles of wife and daughter. "I banish her the Room," the widower concludes, "and weep aloud, that I have lost her Mother, and that I have her." It is only in the more gratifying role of husband that the man can incorporate elements of both father and rake. Within marriage, patriarchal power relations stay intact, and sexual desire can be both acknowledged and acted upon, as the object of pleasure becomes, "silent and complying," the devoted wife.

6 *Their Proper Spheres: Engendering Difference in the 'Spectator'*

When the Wife of *Hector*, in *Homer's Iliads*, discourses with her Husband about the Battel in which he was going to engage, the Hero, desiring her to leave that Matter to his Care, bids her go to her Maids and mind her Spinning: By which the Poet intimates, that Men and Women ought to busie themselves in their proper Spheres, and on such Matters only as are suitable to their respective Sex.
—*Spectator* No. 57

With its notable ability to admonish as it entertained, the *Tatler*, particularly in the character of its redoubtable narrator, Isaac Bickerstaff, exerted a significant influence upon a discourse that constituted male exemplarity in explicit relation to wives and daughters. By contrast, the *Tatler*'s equally renowned successor, the *Spectator* (1711–12), figures desirable masculinity most powerfully in representations of benevolent relations among men—on political, economic, and familial levels. From the celebrated Spectator Club, in which such traditional adversaries as a rural squire and a city merchant exist in relative harmony, to the exemplary Cornelii family, where father and sons live and work together like brothers (No. 192), we see men from different generations, diverse worlds—as well as from opposing worldviews—lay aside their distinctions in order to assemble contentedly beneath the gleaming dome of a munificent rationality. Even the journal's production history reveals a form of cooperation between men. Despite the fact that Addison and Steele, like countless other distinguished pairs, have become as fused in the mind as they are on the tongue, we should recall that "Addison and Steele's

Tatler" was in fact primarily the production of Richard Steele. By contrast, Joseph Addison shared equal responsibility for the *Spectator*'s original 555 numbers.[1]

While both publications promoted an ideology of separate spheres that construed the military, political, and economic realms as exclusively masculine, in the *Spectator*, a greater emphasis on male relations demanded an even more powerful demarcation between the sexes. By building upon the doctrine of gender difference publicized by the *Tatler*, which promulgated an incommensurability of bodies, spirits, functions, even virtues, the *Spectator* worked to consolidate men's interests by creating and then effacing an artfully conceived female Other. Whether occupying their "proper sphere" by living as creatures "designed wholly domestick" (*Spectator* No. 449) or transgressing gender boundaries through such "Amazonian" behavior as participation in party politics, women allowed for particularly powerful forms of male bonding—in the coffee-house, the marketplace, even the household. The supposedly nonpartisan, apolitical stance of both the Spectator Club and the periodical itself depended upon women's exclusion both from the club and from the realm of politics, thus configuring women as the common enemy against whom and in the name of whom men of conflicting interests could unite.[2]

Eighteenth-century writers described men acting in both public and familial spheres. By pretending that these overlapping parts of each man's life were separate, politicians consolidated their class interests. In their claims of neutrality and rationality, the authors of the *Spectator* did something quite similar, defining the interests of their own class as universal. They implied that rational men might put aside their class differences, engage in a free exchange of ideas, and thus arrive at a truth that would magically counterbalance aristocratic corruption. From our perspective today, their claims about the universal capacity for social criticism available to all men reveal an assumption that "all men" are well-educated, progressive, affluent Whigs. Of course, Addison and Steele's implied definition of "all men" excluded many men on the basis of class, education, or political ideology; yet this relegation pales in comparison with their even more sweeping banishment of women. As Terry Eagleton unwittingly puts it, what "makes criticism's tacit assumption of superiority tolerable, as what makes the accumulation of power and property tolerable, is the fact that all men possess the capacity for it."[3] "All men" indeed, for eighteenth-century women scarcely had rights to material property,[4] and few men were willing to grant that they had the capacity to think.

While claiming, then, to offer all of its readers an opportunity to learn the moral and critical capacities associated with spectatorship, the periodical nevertheless espouses a universal voice, in the form of a spectatorial "we," that incorporates women while simultaneously objectifying them. Or to put it differently: in the gendered world of spectatorship, men possess the critical gaze while women remain the passive article to be scrutinized. As one might expect given the title of the later periodical, the spectatorial relationship between men and women, which we observed also in the *Tatler*, becomes even more pronounced in the *Spectator*. Although in No. 34 Mr. Spectator claims that "My Readers too have the Satisfaction to find, that there is no Rank or Degree among them who have not their Representative in this Club, and that there is always some Body present who will take Care of their respective Interests," it is notable that the interests of women are supposedly taken up by Will Honeycomb, an over-the-hill Ladies' Man who represented a stereotypical masculine figure already thoroughly satirized in the *Tatler* and soon to come in for its share of attack in the *Spectator*. In the Spectator Club, then, women's interests turn out to be little other than men's sexual interest in women.

As homosocial roles exacerbate heterosexual difference, individuals who fail to conform to an ideology of separate spheres become targets of virulent attack. Accordingly, the pages of the *Spectator* represent two things as especially odious: the crossing of gender boundaries, in the form of women who dress as men or men who act like women, and women's involvement in party politics. Sempronia, who mingles her toilet with political talk (No. 45), is an example of the dangerous "Fopperies" that will be a consequence of the peace with France;[5] in a slightly later issue, Mr. Spectator's attack on women's use of patches to signify party affiliation unites the two elements when he writes that women should "distinguish themselves as tender Mothers and faithful Wives rather than as furious Partizans," for "Female Virtues are of a Domestick turn. The Family is the proper Province for Private Women to Shine in" (No. 81). Making both narrative and ideological use of the rhetoric of spectatorship, the *Spectator* endeavors to return both men and women to their proper places in a gendered order.

•

In the *Tatler*, Bickerstaff's mastery results from his specific roles as astrologer, physician, moral censor, and, especially, brother-father; as a man who goes everywhere and speaks to everyone, he both delights in and is empowered by his publicly loquacious character. In the periodical's last number, however, Steele claims that this authority has been lost or certainly compromised by his eidolon's loss of anonymity: "I shall not carry my Humility so far as to call my self a vicious Man," Steele writes under his own name, "but at the same Time must confess, my Life is at best but pardonable. And with no greater Character than this, a Man would make but an indifferent Progress in attacking prevailing and fashionable Vices, which Mr. *Bickerstaff* has done with a Freedom of Spirit that would have lost both its Beauty and Efficacy, had it been pretended to by Mr. *Steele*."[6] It seems hardly coincidental, then, that the next periodical persona is narratively distinguished by his public silence, as well as by his position as an observer rather than as a worldly participant. The reforming vision necessary to both texts' construction of exemplary masculinity is achieved in the *Tatler* on an individual level. In the *Spectator*, however, the process of correct sight becomes assimilated into the text in general, and in specifically gendered ways. In the *Spectator*, both the exemplary characteristics of the narrator and the benevolent relations of the Spectator Club inscribe moral authority as masculine.[7] The periodical's eidolon is an unnamed, anonymous "Spectator" who limits his speech to the confines of his all-male club. Moreover, while serving as the periodical's principal narrator, Mr. Spectator also represents himself as the spokesman for his "Society" of spectators, who ostensibly share in the periodical's production (Nos. 1 and 2).

In *The Narrative Act*, Susan Lanser distinguishes between a "public narrator" who shapes our perception of the fictional world and addresses a reader-figure or audience "outside" the text and a "private narrator, . . . usually a character in the text, bound to the fictional world, . . . [whose] speech activity is directed to a more limited audience—a fictional character or group—rather than to the textual equivalent of the reading public."[8] She acknowledges, however, that her terms are "somewhat metaphoric . . . because obviously all fictional narration is 'public' in the sense that it was written to be published and read by an audience." What she claims to be differentiating between, then, are "fictional narrative acts designed for an apparently public readership and those narratives designed for reception only by other characters or textual figures."[9] The narrative situation of the *Spectator*, however, is one in which it is impossible to make such distinctions. In the overlap between "public" and "private" exists the "reader-construct" who is simultaneously a figure within the text—a spectator of Mr. Spectator and an implicit member of the Spectator Club—and a figure outside of it—a spectator of the *Spectator*, as well as of the world. The discursive relations made possible by this narrative ambiguity are crucial to the attitudes toward masculinity embodied in spectatorship. Just as Bickerstaff reconstitutes gossip and tattle into materials for the reformation of manners and morals, so too does Mr. Spectator exploit the possibilities inherent within spectatorship as a theme, a process, and a rhetorical position.

Mr. Spectator's description of his own neutrality encompasses both a personal and a party political level. His spectatorial position enables him to know far more than he could ever experience practically: as he tells us in the periodical's inaugural issue, he has been "a Speculative Statesman, Soldier, Merchant and Artizan," and is "well versed in the Theory of an Husband, or a Father." His role of spectator also imparts to him the moral detachment to "discern the Errors in the Oeconomy, Business, and Diversion of others, better than those who are engaged in them; as Standers-by discover Blots, which are apt to escape those who are in the Game." In addition, his feigned political disinterest becomes a model for civic interaction in general: "I never espoused any Party with Violence," he tells us in the same number, "and am resolved to observe an exact Neutrality between the Whigs and Tories." As one might suspect, the Spectator Club enacts this allegedly neutral position as well, particularly in the characters of Sir Roger de Coverly, the Tory squire, and Sir Andrew Freeport, the Whig merchant. While acknowledging that his friends are "of different principles," one "inclined to the *landed* and the other to the *moneyed* Interest," Mr. Spectator nevertheless claims that in both Sir Roger and Sir Andrew, political "Humour" is "so moderate . . . that it proceeds no farther than to an agreeable Raillery, which very often diverts the rest of the Club" (No. 126). In the case of both the Spectator Club and its eponymous spokesman, an explicit denial of economic and political interests mediates the divisive potential of individual desires. The ostensibly unified "we" of moral spectatorship thus transforms a multiplicity of voices into "the capacious, bland, homogenizing language [that] is able to encompass art, ethics, religion, philosophy and everyday life."[10]

Mr. Spectator's representation as a man removed from economic exigency and personal ambition situates spectatorship as an exemplary moral position. When Mr. Spectator writes, "In short, I have acted in all the parts of my Life as a Looker-on, which is the Character I intend to preserve in this Paper" (No. 1), he is inviting his readers to emulate the moral stance made possible by his status as a leisured gentleman, one who can play all roles while being financially dependent upon none. Mr. Spectator's own lack of occupation reveals his otherwise effaced status as a member of the gentry, living on income derived from the "small Hereditary Estate" that "has been delivered down from Father to Son whole and entire, without the Loss or Acquisition of a single Field or Meadow, during the Space of six hundred Years." In other words, Addison and Steele must stringently deny economic interests, in this case those of the educated, property-owning gentry, in order to uphold the notion of a detached, and therefore moral, spectatorial position. This disavowal of individual interests and of particular points of view with regard to spectatorship highlights the difference between men's and women's relation to the Spectator Club: women are supposedly included but are absent; men are supposedly neutral but are partisan.

Particularly interesting here is the way in which the journal elevates rarified aspects of the terms "speculation" and "speculative" to a position of authority comparable with, if not superior to, the sway of experience. Consequently, Mr. Spectator's being "well versed in the *Theory* of an Husband, or a Father" as well as a *"Speculative* Statesman, Soldier, Merchant and Artizan"* magically metamorphoses into a substantial form of experience, despite—or because of—the fact that he has acted "without ever medling with any Practical Part in Life" (No. 1; my italics). The voyeurism implicit in the act of reading mirrors the eidolon's own neutral spectatorship, thereby masking, once again, the periodical's own existence as an economic enterprise, just as Mr. Spectator erases his own class and party concerns. Whatever their reasons for reading the text, the *Spectator's* "Threescore thousand Disciples" (No. 10) must either buy the paper or buy admission to a place, for example a coffee-house, that was itself a subscriber. Just as Mr. Spectator's professions of political and economic detachment veil the particular interests of his own class position, so too does the periodical's claim to "enliven Morality with Wit, and to temper Wit with Morality" (ibid.) obscure its existence as a commercial enterprise, one dependent upon the approbation of those it is intended to instruct. Charles Knight calls our attention to the way in which newly emerging systems of production and distribution allowed the *Spectator's* eidolon to create the illusion of an intimate community: "[Mr. Spectator] can maintain an independent role appropriate to his function as the analytic observer of society at the same time as the specialized process of distribution—through the business arrangements of printer and bookseller, through subscription and delivery, through the hawking of numbers, through a postal service that radiated from London, and through coffeehouses—brings him more immediately than ever before to a wide and responsive audience."[11] While the *Spectator's* profession of moral authority necessarily relies upon its disavowal of economic interest, the periodical nevertheless remains a kind of trader, circulating not goods but the good.

Like Mr. Spectator and the periodical itself, the Spectator Club, with its disparate membership, becomes the model for a new form of male interaction, one ostensibly removed from both economic and political considerations. John Brewer notes that although today the word "club" may conjure up "the impression of a venerable, neoclassical edifice filled with leather armchairs, musty volumes, and antediluvian males," in the eighteenth century "the term 'club' was understood as a verb, rather than as a noun, '*to club together*' meant to pool one's financial resources for almost any collective activity."[12] What united the members of most clubs was the possibility of mutual gain: "Joining a club enabled the tradesman to extend the ambit of his acquaintance to meet potential customers, creditors and partners in a highly convivial, amicable atmosphere."[13] While the spectatorial position claims to acknowledge and appreciate the multiple voices, opinions, and experiences represented by the members of the Spectator Club, however, the text's actual discursive practice subsumes diversity under the monolithic "we" of the detached critical perspective. Mr. Spectator's apolitical posture masks a position that becomes normative by virtue of being moral. Moreover, by eliding the differences between national opinion and the attitudes of the individuals who comprise that nation, Addison and Steele, through their eidolon, construct a perspective that claims to benefit England as a whole while simultaneously meeting the needs of her individual citizens. By contrast, Mr. Spectator finds men "sowered with Party-Principles" (and thus tastelessly brandishing their personal interests) incapable of such a viewpoint, for they are "alienated from one another in such a manner, as seems to me altogether inconsistent with the Dictates either of Reason or Religion" (No. 125).

Accordingly, while in *Tatler* No. 100 self-interest warps men's image of themselves in the "Mirror of Truth," here party zeal prevents men from "discerning either real Blemishes or Beauties." Mr. Spectator's employment of a visual, and aesthetic, metaphor should come as no surprise, for it is only from a position of supposed disinterest that the spectator can truly see: "A Man of Merit in a different Principle, is like an Object seen in two different Mediums, that appears crooked or broken, however streight and entire it may be in it self." What should unite men, he implies, is precisely their capacity to see things as they really are. The ability to see and thus to ascribe value, an ability made possible only by the suspension of interest, is what Mr. Spectator proposes in the form of an "Association" in which virtue would be the criterion for inclusion within a national whole: "we should not any longer regard our Fellow-Subjects as Whigs or Tories, but should make the Man of Merit our Friend, and the Villain our Enemy." Here politics recedes completely behind a veil of universal moral judgment, the natural ability to distinguish excellence from corruption.

Two issues later (No. 127), the interactions of the Spectator Club itself exemplify their spokesman's virtuous association. Richard Sennett has argued for a distinction between the discourse of the public coffee-house, in which a man entered, paid his penny, was told the rules of the house, and sat down to enjoy himself—talking—to anyone and everyone,[14] and that of the private club, as an institution "based on the idea that speech gave most pleasure when one had selected the audience, excluding those whose personal lives were distasteful or alien."[15] According to Sennett, the private speech of the men's club, a privacy that meant speech was agreeable "only when one controlled whom one was speaking to," threatened the suspension of social rank so necessary to the free speech of the public sphere.[16] The fictional representation of the Spectator Club, however, collapses the distinction between public and private speech. First, and most obviously, the periodical's narrative structure necessarily exposes private discourse, even the intimate and exclusive conversations of the Spectator Club, to the public scrutiny of anyone who could pay his penny.[17] Next, the composition of the club itself, in which two of its members—the Tory squire and the Whig merchant—hold severely conflicting economic and political views, directly subverts the supposed intimacy and safety of the club structure. And yet, by taking a structure ostensibly built upon a sociable similarity—as exemplified in Addison's discussion in *Spectator* No. 9 of assemblies united by a common theme, such as the "Club of Fat-Men" or those comprised of men with the surname "King" or the Christian name "George"—and peopling it instead with disparate types, Addison turns the squire and the merchant into collaborators rather than competitors.[18] Furthermore, this brotherhood extends to the interests they represent. Just as land and trade interests are deemed necessary to, rather than in conflict with, each other's success, as "the Trader is fed by the Product of the Land, and the landed Man cannot be cloathed but by the Skill of the Trader" (No. 174), so too are the opinions and attitudes of their representatives portrayed as mutually compatible (No. 126). Thus the Spectator Club transforms dissent into diversion; in its setting, enemies become friends.

Yet the supposedly nonpartisan, apolitical stance of both the Spectator Club and the periodical itself represents a definite political position, a position that depends upon women's exclusion both from the club and from the realm of politics. As I have argued in Chapter 1, a conception of gender defined by difference demands that qualities attributed to one sex be eradicated in the other. Men's imperative participation in the political and economic workings of society parallels, but cannot overlap with, women's work in the home. Consequently, while masculine consolidation necessitates a view of women as inherently different from men, it depends as well upon including women's interests within those ascribed to men, so that women's natural place in the domestic sphere can vindicate men's efforts in the public realm.

Under an ideology of conjugality, then, women are figured as both self and other, men's soul-mates and their objects of desire. To be alluring, women must be different from men: in *Spectator* No. 435, Addison writes that "I would fain have [women] consider with themselves whether we are not more likely to be struck by a Figure entirely Female, than with such an one as we may see every Day in our Glasses." Yet women's difference also threatens male power. In his *Second Treatise*, Locke writes of husbands and wives who may share common interests, but who hold diverse opinions; he solves the problem, however, by stating that "the last Determination . . . naturally falls to the Man's share, as the abler and the stronger."[19] While the *Spectator*'s rationale for male dominance may be somewhat more subtle, the periodical's depiction of powerful women as Amazons serves the similar purpose of bolstering claims of male superiority. In the *Spectator*, both the pleasure and the danger of gender difference are beautifully embodied in the liminal figure of the Amazon, who demonstrates the masculine qualities of physical strength, military prowess, and economic independence, but who is at the same time sexually desirable to men. Characters who scorn the emotional and dependent relations of conjugality, Amazons represent all women who stray from feminine complaisance.

By taming the Amazon, the *Spectator*'s narratives restore women to their proper place in the domestic household. First, however, the periodical must establish that place in explicit distinction from the political realm. No. 57 reveals how this institution of gender difference affects both sexes, for masculinity as well as femininity are threatened when women stray from "their proper Sphere." The previous chapter analyzed the basis of this inherent gender opposition as exemplified within the male-female relations of the *Tatler*, but in the *Spectator* an emphasis upon collaborative male relations necessitates an even more powerful delineation of gender difference. Such cultural cross-dressers as political women and domestic men menace particularly, for the "Faults and Imperfections of one Sex [when] transplanted into another" can appear not just "ridiculous" but "black and monstrous."[20] Because the *Spectator* defines "Party Rage" as a "Male Vice," women's partisan behavior appears doubly odious, dangerous both in itself and to women's supposed nature: "Party Rage" is "made up of many angry and cruel Passions that are altogether repugnant to the Softness, the Modesty, and those other endearing Qualities which are natural to the Fair Sex . . . there is nothing so bad for the Face as Party Zeal."

In addition to destroying women's beauty, one of the attributes deemed essential to their function as pleasing objects, political ardor also impedes women's ability to gratify through conciliation: the female sex, Mr. Spectator contends, was formed to "temper" and "sooth" men, not to inflame in them "those Passions which are too apt to rise of their own Accord." By remaining, like Hector's wife, safely tucked away with their maids and their spinning, women also provide men with a haven from the vicissitudes of public life. Accordingly, women's first loyalty should be to men. Just as most women have no property or legal person apart from first father and then husband, so too should women's political convictions bolster, rather than contradict, the beliefs of the men upon whom they depend. In his satire on women's use of patches to demonstrate political affiliation (No. 81), Addison writes with obvious scorn that some women "adhere so stedfastly to their Party, and are so far from Sacrificing their Zeal for the Publick to their Passion for any particular Person, that in a late Draught of Marriage Articles a Lady has stipulated with her Husband, That, whatever his Opinions are, she shall be at Liberty to Patch on which side she pleases." But women's job is not to hold and express opinions; rather, women ought to function as the pleasant resting spot for the male spectatorial gaze: "the most amiable Object that the Eye of Man can possibly behold" (No. 435).

In *Spectator* No. 41, Steele distinguishes between *Picts*—women who paint—and *British*—women who don't—in order to prescribe the ways in which women's bodies should signify the direct expression of their thoughts and feelings. By humorously appropriating the term *"Pict,"* Steele imparts a decidedly blue undertone to the artful tints of white and red, implying, moreover, that such makeup can make monstrosities out of otherwise attractive women. Thus whereas the "*British* have a lively, animated Aspect, . . . *Picts*, tho' never so Beautiful, have dead, uninformed Countenances." In contrast to those prettily blushing women whose faces "are flushed with agreeable Confusions, according as the Objects before them, or the Ideas presented to them, affect their Imagination," the Picts "behold all things with the same Air, whether they are Joyful or Sad; The same fix'd Insensibility appears on all Occasions."

Although Steele values the exposure of feminine feeling and perception for its natural quality, he also counsels women to "study the agreeable *Statira*" as a "Pattern for improving their Charms." Statira's own allure stems most evidently from her ingenuousness: "She is Graceful without Affecting an Air, and Unconcerned without appearing Careless. Her having no manner of Art in her Mind, makes her want none in her Person." Statira's lack of mental art—one is tempted to say thoughts or opinions—enables her body to serve as the unmediated expression of her mind, a process exemplified in the slightly misquoted lines from Donne's poem, "Of the Progress of the Soul (the Second Anniversary)," with which Steele ends the paper:

> How like is this Lady, and how unlike is a *Pict*, to that Description Dr. *Donne* gives of his Mistress?
>
> . . . *Her Pure and Eloquent Blood*
> *Spoke in her Cheeks, and so distinctly Wrought,*
> *That one would almost say her Body Thought.*

The delicate nerves and fibers that supposedly equip women for the emotional proficiency requisite to sensibility function here to circumscribe and limit them.[21] The conceit that women think with their bodies rather than their minds naturalizes women's expressive capacities while simultaneously erasing their rational faculties.

In addition, male control over the deployment of the female body—legally, sexually, aesthetically—and women's internalization of men's standards effectively mitigates the threat of women's sexuality. In No. 45, the sight of a woman in her bed when such morning visits were the fashion affects even the staid Mr. Spectator, who, he claims, has "no Expectations from Women" (No. 41). In order to efface his own desire, he displaces his reaction onto the woman herself, attributing *his* confusion to shock at *her* lack of modesty: "The Lady, tho' willing to appear undrest, had put on her best Looks, and painted her self for our Reception. Her Hair appeared in a very nice Disorder, as the Night-Gown which was thrown upon her Shoulders was ruffled with great Care. For my part, I am so shocked with every thing which looks immodest in the Fair Sex, that I could not forbear taking off my Eye from her when she moved in her Bed, and was in the greatest Confusion imaginable every time she stirred a Leg or an Arm." Constructing femininity through the use of disciplinary practices related specifically to the body,[22] the *Spectator* attempts to turn women's sexual power into a force that unifies, rather than disorders and divides, men.

In a number of different *Spectator* essays, Addison employs the term "Amazon" to delineate pejoratively those independent women who use their bodies to wrong ends, women who eschew the sexual and social control fundamental to a patriarchal order by claiming their bodies as their own. No. 57 describes an encounter between "the fierce and beautiful *Penthesilea*" and Camilla, "one of the greatest Beauties in the *British* Nation," who, despite her attractiveness to the male sex, distressingly "values her self more upon being the *Virago* of one Party, than upon being the Toast of both."[23] Yet Camilla, the virago or female warrior, and Penthesilea, the woman named for the Amazon queen who fought with Achilles, meet not, as might be expected, upon a battlefield but rather "across a Tea-Table," where a mishap fortuitously prevents the impending contest: "in the height of her [Camilla's] Anger, as her Hand chanced to shake with the Earnestness of the Dispute, she scalded her Fingers, and spilt a dish of Tea upon her Petticoat. Had not this Accident broke off the Debate, no Body knows where it would have ended." In Addison's narrative, the discrepancy between the Amazonian signified—literary examples of fighting women—and its signifiers—these two women whose battle is aborted by a spilled cup of tea—renders each part ridiculous. Moreover, the fact that these unquestionably beautiful women have chosen opinions over the male admiration they are certain to receive designates them as unwomanly without even the epithet of Amazon or virago. Paradoxically, this ascription serves to align them with those older women to whom Mr. Spectator grants unfettered political rein precisely because their opinions do not impede their proper role with regard to men: "I would give free Liberty to all superannuated motherly Partizans to be as violent as they please, since there will be no danger either of their spoiling their Faces, or of their gaining Converts" (No. 57). Implicit in this statement is the view that women lack the requisite intellectual skills to convince through any means other than beauty: as Addison will write a few years later in his openly partisan journal *The Freeholder*, "Arguments out of a pretty Mouth are unanswerable."[24] Thus we find that the modern sense of virago—"a bold, impudent (or wicked) woman; a termagant; a scold" (*OED*)—a meaning also in use during Addison's time, suggests that the aggressive attitudes of a beautiful woman who engages in party politics can make her bold and wicked as well, as, once again, morality upholds normality.

A second "Body of *Amazons*" are the women who patch for political purposes (No. 81). By staging their performance in the theater audience in terms notable for their bellicosity, Addison wittily diminishes, through a strategy of mock-heroic exaggeration, the import of such behavior. Having "placed themselves in the opposite Side-Boxes" in imitation of warring camps, these women "seemed drawn up in a kind of Battel Array one against another"; using their patches "as Party Signals to distinguish Friends from Foes," they manifest their antagonism by "cast[ing] Hostile Glances upon one another." By contrast, exemplary women prevent war among men rather than engaging in it themselves: "Party Rage in Women . . . only serves to aggravate the Hatreds and Animosities that reign among Men, and in a great measure deprive the Fair Sex of those peculiar Charms with which Nature has endowed them." Removing the difference between men and women upsets the so-called natural order; women can retain their beauty, and men their rational capacity, only when a benevolent neutrality keeps such attributes on opposites sides of the gender divide. Consequently, while Addison's philosophy continuously positions men and women into discrete rather than overlapping roles, we sense the fragility of both the roles themselves and of their spheres of enactment; they are in constant danger every time a woman picks up a patch.[25]

Continuing in the same paper, Mr. Spectator describes the way in which women's allegiance to men once acted to reconcile two warring peoples: "When the *Romans* and *Sabines* were at War, and just upon the point of giving Battel, the Women, who were allied to both of them, interposed with so many Tears and Intreaties that they prevented the mutual Slaughter which threatned both Parties, and united them together in a firm and lasting Peace." Yet it is interesting to note what gets left out of this account of ostensible feminine compassion: namely, the Roman men's violence and the Sabine women's acceptance of it. The Sabine women had been raped and abducted by the Romans; the Sabines attacked them to get their women back. The battle was effectively prevented because the Sabine women were unwilling to support their male kinsmen's claim, preferring instead to remain with their captors. By emphasizing domestic magnanimity rather than military strife, the *Spectator*'s story of the Sabine women authorizes all women to show political interest only when such "Zeal for the Publick" has been reconstituted as part of their private work as "tender Mothers and faithful Wives."

Women's bodies are not meant to be the site of political display that might instigate or enhance contention among men. In Chapter 4 I argued that these periodical texts criticize dueling in part because it pits men's love for women against men's relationships to other men. Women are "created as it were for Ornament" (No. 104); accordingly, they must decorate and display their bodies in such a way as to make them desirable to the male sex. Yet ironically, women's proper use of ornament, while naturalized into an inherent capacity, must at the same time be properly learned, for as Mr. Spectator notes, "Women, tho' themselves created as it were for Ornament, are often very much mistaken in this ornamental Part of Life." In a three-part series written by Addison, Mr. Spectator uses "a little Manuscript which is lately fallen into [his] Hands" as a basis for speculations about natural and learned gender characteristics. This "summary Account of two different States which bordered upon one another"—"a Commonwealth of *Amazons*, or Women without Men" and "a Republick of Males that had not a Woman in their whole Community" (No. 433)—allows him to discourse upon the natural traits of men and women as well as upon the effect of each sex on the other.

Initially, he claims that without the presence of the opposite sex, both men and women would appear very different from the way we find them now. "Man would not only be an unhappy, but a rude unfinished Creature, were he conversant with none but those of his own Make"; and women would be "Sower and Unamiable, Sluttish and Censorious," for "it is the Male that gives Charms to Womankind, that produces an Air in their Faces, a Grace in their Motions, a Softness in their Voices, and a Delicacy in their Complextions." If the earlier battle between the virago and the Amazon queen (No. 57) made both of the women, and thus their political pretensions, appear ridiculous, this more elaborate version of the Amazon myth renders such independent women impotent. That is, whereas the story clearly grants women a duly valued "civilizing influence" upon men, at the same time it revokes women's autonomy by curtailing their opportunities to wage war, govern, or support themselves. Thus in spite of eighteenth-century women's unacknowledged contributions to the economy or their clandestine participation in the military,[26] women's presence in both arenas, like their involvement in party politics, impinges upon men's designated role as protectors and providers. Moreover, the Amazons' manifest bodily strength blatantly challenges a gender order in which men's physical superiority had long justified their cultural dominance.[27]

Simultaneously fierce and alluring, the Amazons depicted in these essays symbolize the untamed desire within all women. Mr. Spectator declares in No. 433 that women "talk, and move, and smile, with a design upon us; every Feature of their Faces, every part of their Dress is filled with Snares and Allurements." Yet Addison mitigates the predatory threat of women's bodies by telling a story in which the presence of men acts insensibly to form women into beautiful objects. By transforming this "Commonwealth of *Amazons*" from a nation of women warriors into a group of dutifully ornamental wives, the fable nullifies women's power while simultaneously naturalizing their domestic behavior.

In the "Female Republick" detailed in No. 434, girls go to school to learn boxing and cudgeling; no woman is allowed to marry until she has killed her man;[28] the women play with lions instead of lap-dogs; and an afternoon's entertainment consists in wrestling rather than tea drinking. Most particularly, women dress not to please, "but to look terrible, to which end they would sometimes after a Battel paint their Cheeks with the Blood of their Enemies." These women's ability to look "terrible," and thus to excite both "fear or terror" and "some feeling akin to dread or awe" (*OED*) is manifested in their complete lack of any sense of themselves as pleasing objects: "If they found Lace, Jewels, Ribbons, or any Ornaments in Silver or Gold, among the Booty which they had taken, they used to dress their Horses with it, but never entertained a Thought of wearing it themselves." It is not until a joint attack against a difficult foe has united the male and female republics for longer than their customary mating period that men and women begin to live together, instead of in separate camps. Men's desire to appeal to women becomes the basis for the development of "Architecture, Painting and Poetry among this Savage People":

> From this time the Armies being Chequered with both Sexes, they polished apace. The Men used to invite their Fellow-Soldiers into their Quarters, and would dress their Tents with

Flowers and Boughs, for their Reception. If they chanced to like one more than another, they would be for cutting her Name in the Table, or Chalking out her Figure upon a Wall, or talking of her in a kind of rapturous Language, which by degrees improved into Verse and Sonnet.

But if delighting women results in men's learning to create *objets d'art*, women's desire to please men culminates in their learning to turn themselves into elegant commodities. In a particularly telling turn, the following passage represents the love of finery and adornment most often ascribed as natural to women as a product of men's own interest in such female display:

When they had taken any Spoils from the Enemy, the Men would make a Present of every thing that was Rich and Showy to the Women whom they most admired, and would frequently dress the Necks, or Heads, or Arms of their Mistresses, with any thing which they thought appeared Gay or Pretty. The Women observing that the Men took delight in looking upon 'em, when they were adorned with such Trappings and Gewgaws, set their Heads at Work to find out new Inventions, and to out-shine one another in all Councils of War or the like solemn Meetings.

Addison's story of the Amazons offers a fascinating insight into the male understanding of separate spheres. A society in which "the Women had learnt to Smile, and the Men to Ogle" reveals that men's reforming of women applies also to themselves. Women's institution as pleasing objects and men's as desiring subjects actually defines a state of difference, one that contains, moreover, "the most Flourishing and Polite Government in the Part of the World which they Inhabited." Men, therefore, must invest in women's difference to the extent to which they fear what would happen if women refused to fashion themselves in accordance with men's desire.

The *Spectator* establishes women's desirability to men as the most important part of their existence, as well as the characteristic that most distinguishes them from men. Just as "Party Zeal" makes women unattractive by damaging their complexions (No. 57), the "*Amazonian* Hunting-Habit" sported by "a certain Equestrian Order of Ladies" (No. 104) erases sexual difference and is thus particularly threatening to male viewers of women. Rather than attempting to look like men, women should be "what Nature design'd them; and to see their Mistake when they depart from this, let them look upon a Man who affects the Softness and Effeminacy of a Woman, to learn how their Sex must appear to us when approaching to the Resemblance of a Man."

Women's literal cross-dressing also forms the subject of No. 435, the third in Addison's series on gender construction. Although Mr. Spectator claims to have talked in the previous number about "the Mixture of two Sexes in one Commonwealth," in reality there should be no mixture whatsoever. The "Amphibious Dress" of those women who combine "two Sexes in one Person" challenges the rigid demarcation of gender difference: "I think it however absolutely necessary to keep up the Partition between the two Sexes, and to take Notice of the smallest Encroachments which the one makes upon the other." Addison carries this martial language into a later paragraph, when Mr. Spectator explains his theory that women's sartorial singularity always has "some Evil Intention; and therefore [I] question not but the Design of this strange Fashion is to smite more effectually their Male Beholders." Although on the one hand the essay criticizes women for their desire to attract men (recall the "Snares and Allurements" of No. 433), on the other hand Mr. Spectator attempts to "set them right" with regard to proper dress by saying that women who look like men are less appealing and even monstrous—amphibious creatures, neither male nor female.[29]

What seems particularly interesting about this passage is its assumption that sexual attraction is entirely heterogeneous: why should difference rather than similarity be the main criterion even of heterosexual desire? In her reading of William Wycherley's Restoration drama *The Country Wife* (1675), Eve Kosofsky Sedgwick argues that heterosexual relations in the play "have as their *raison d'être* an ultimate bonding between men; and that this bonding, if successfully achieved, is not detrimental to 'masculinity' but definitive of it."[30] These passages from the *Spectator*, which characterize male heterosexual desire in relation to an explicitly differentiated femininity, moreover one defined in terms of "Dress, Words, and Actions" (No. 104), raise, I think, similar questions about the "ultimate bonding" that is supposed to be taking place within heterosexual relations. As I will argue in Chapter 8, the flourishing of a class-based theory of gender incommensurability, so successfully promulgated in this period by the *Tatler* and *Spectator* themselves, will mean, ironically, that the highest form of human relations exists not between men and women but rather among men, in particular the blood-linked liaison of fathers and sons.

This ideology of gender stipulates that if women remain in "their proper Sphere," acting only in the "Characters" of a "Sister, Daughter, or Wife" (No. 104), their behavior will enhance rather than inhibit the free range of male enterprise. And yet, precisely because Addison and Steele recognize, on some level, the permeability of those boundaries they are so intent upon solidifying—between masculinity and femininity, between the political and the domestic—even women's willing removal to the so-called domestic sphere presents cause for anxious concern. Since the "Dress, Words, and Actions" that define femininity are themselves fraught with multiple meanings on political as well as socioeconomic levels, it becomes incumbent upon men—as well as upon the male eidolons of Addison and Steele's periodicals—to "keep a watchful Eye over every Part of the Female Sex, and to regulate them from Head to Foot" (*Guardian* No. 109). By examining the processes of such regulation, particularly with regard to women's bodies, the next chapter analyzes the ensuing relations among economic debates about the importation and use of so-called luxury items, the gendering of consumption and leisure as particularly feminine, and the periodicals' development of a moral authority construed as both male and middle-class.

*Trading in Virtue:
Attacks on Luxury, Leisure,
and Fashion in the 'Tatler,'
'Spectator,' and 'Guardian'*

The evident fact of women's appetite for consumer pleasures
had always gone hand in hand with attempts to control it.
—G. J. Barker-Benfield, *The Culture of Sensibility*

*I*n the early part of the eighteenth century, a marked increase in the availability of a wide range of consumer
goods, in particular items perceived as "luxuries,"[1] produced a powerful sense of anxiety in a number of different groups. Consumption's potential for blurring distinctions between classes clearly troubled members of
the elite, who justified their superior place in the social
hierarchy through what Georges Bataille has termed
"unproductive expenditure."[2] Yet those in the middle
ranks, who even in the seventeenth century had provided the largest market for new and imported goods,[3]
were increasingly caught between the economic need to
consume as a way to display social status as well as
credit-worthiness, and the moral need to resist lavish expenditure, as such resistance was what distinguished
them from a supposedly profligate aristocracy and gentry.[4] Both groups made numerous attempts to alleviate
this anxiety, two of which I explore here. First, conspicuous consumption manifested in dress became discursively marked as a particularly feminine phenomenon
and occupation. Thus "eighteenth-century moralists
singled out girls and women in their attacks on luxury
expenditure, complaining of girls buying silk ribbons,
hats, jewellery and dresses to suit every change in fash-

ion," despite the fact that "men equally participated in the luxury consumption of dress."[5] By displacing the need for public display onto (increasingly passive and economically unproductive) wives and daughters, men of the middle ranks could meet social requirements while still retaining the moral high ground. Men of both socioeconomic groups attempted to allay the apprehensions of a disorder stemming from consumption's possible elision of class distinction by establishing even more firmly the differences between the sexes. As Kaja Silverman writes, "sexual difference has become the primary marker of power, privilege and authority, closing the specular gap between men of different classes, and placing men and women on opposite sides of the great visual divide."[6] A belief system that defined femininity as all that masculinity was not (and vice versa), and subordinated women's supposedly inherent capacities to those of men, helped to reestablish the hierarchical distinctions threatened by economic developments.

Periodical literature, as I have demonstrated, played a constitutive role in the process of engendering gender difference. Moreover, since periodicals were themselves commodities—items to be purchased and consumed—authors' strategies for masking their texts' participation in, and dependence upon, the consumer revolution provide us with important insights into the connections between economic interests and gender roles. In this chapter, I argue that Addison and Steele mediated their own commercial stake in the periodical enterprise, a stake that included both the solvency of specific publications and the broader Whig mercantile interests supported by both men, by construing their journals as arbiters of universally acceptable morals and manners. Proffering entertainment as instruction, they transformed luxury into necessity.[7] While employing diverse narrative strategies, the *Tatler*, *Spectator*, and *Guardian* share a claim to moral and literary authority determined in large part by the self-defined admonitory roles of their pointedly male eidolons. Whether performed in Isaac Bickerstaff's Court of Justice, inside Mr. Spectator's private and all-male club, or around Lady Lizard's tea-table, these roles continue to enact gender difference by establishing women as the proper objects of visual as well as ethical scrutiny and men as their obligatory scrutinizers. Men who confound this standard by presenting *themselves* as objects to be observed and admired are unequivocally censured. Women's role as the visible target of surveillance did not, however, in any way obviate the need to survey men. By advancing the ancient belief, here adumbrated by Bernard Mandeville, that luxury "effeminates and enervates the People, by which the Nations become an easy Prey to the first Invaders,"[8] Addison and Steele's writings continually position consumption and display as practices inimical to the strength—psychological as well as physical—requisite to masculinity.[9]

Thus at the same time as satirical essays, prose treatises, mock-heroic poems, and fictions debated the various merits and pitfalls of female luxury
consumption, periodical literature conducted a similarly light discussion,
with serious undertones, of *men's* attire, attitudes, and actions. For every dissection of a "Coquet's Heart" we find a parallel perusal of a "Beau's Head";[10]
"Fops," "Dappers," "Coxcombs," "Pretty Fellows," "very Pretty Fellows,"
and "Ladies' Men" litter the periodicals' pages in numbers equal to their female counterparts. Heated essays couple detailed discussions of women's
hoop petticoats, headdresses, tuckers, card-playing, and fondling of lap-dogs
with comparably particularized deliberations about men's red-heeled shoes
and amber-tipped canes, their snuff-taking and drinking, their uselessness or
value to society at large. After discussing the ways in which attitudes toward
luxury and leisure become, in this period, imbricated with gender norms, I
will turn to Addison and Steele's three most important periodicals to analyze
how each traded in virtue through a complicated and ambivalent discussion
of luxury apparel and leisure activities—for both women and men.

•

As I have shown in the previous chapter, clothing serves both to establish
and to subvert gender identity. In her analysis of the oxymoronic "Female
Warrior" of popular ballads, Diane Dugaw aptly notes that such a figure is
able to cross over gender boundaries in part because those boundaries are
produced precisely through such categories as dress: "The Female Warrior
heroine shows that the early modern era explored to a somewhat startling
degree the extent to which being a woman (or a man) is conventionally determined from the outside. For the ballad heroine reefing and steering are
not a matter of ability—any girl can learn to sail—but of costume: provided
she dress like a sailor, she will be taken for one." Thus the ballads "highlight
the extent to which gender markers are actually customary and primarily external—a social construction."[11] Such social constructions also existed
within specific economic contexts. As Louis Landa and Laura Brown have
argued, the woman's body, "deckt with all that Land and Sea afford," provided late seventeenth- and early eighteenth-century writers with a convenient torso on which to drape both the celebratory and the alarming aspects
of overseas trade.[12] While duly noting the dour complaints of those "balance
of trade" mercantilists who viewed all consumption of imported goods as
detrimental to the nation's welfare, Landa clearly sides with those writers
who extol the benefits of what he salubriously describes as "economic expansion" as well as those women whose adornment provides its *raison d'être*.
Brown, on the other hand, is unambivalent in her desire to uncover the ideological underside of those economic relations she defines as "imperialist";

her study attempts to demonstrate the ways in which, as "women become the proxies for men, object and agent of accumulation are reversed, and thus the female figure is made to bear responsibility for empire."[13]

Yet despite their radically different economic and political agendas, Landa and Brown share an explicit focus upon femininity and the female body as the locus of literary debate and the repository of cultural meaning. While attempting to bring to light what has been obscured both by mercantilist doctrine itself and by such celebrants as Landa, Brown's important contribution unwittingly instates a different omission. Although I agree that men's concerns about the brutal nature of commercial expansion found a convenient scapegoat in the body of the woman who, in the eighteenth century, came increasingly to display its spoils, I believe that Brown's pioneering argument does not go far enough. While the significant tension between commerce and morality was indeed resolved—at least in part—by displacing the immorality associated with the consumption of luxury goods onto women, such a displacement was also a necessary part of the process of masculinization that is the focus of this book. In other words, throughout literary and economic discourses about luxury, leisure, and expenditure, men also functioned as direct objects of scrutiny; they had, moreover, a ubiquitous role as the overseers of the women whose own duty was increasingly identified with consumption. Men, therefore, learned to maintain a position of moral authority both by monitoring women's purchases and by attending to their own.

Thus the "Man of Fashion," like the figure of the Rake, provided Addison and Steele with a powerful antitype of desirable masculinity. Identified with the attention to appearance essential to the ideal woman, who must be pleasing in order to be female, the fashionable man is feminized through his similarity to women, a characteristic embedded in the very denomination of "Ladies' Men": "these pretty Gentlemen [who] are not made for any Manly Imployments, and for want of Business are often as much in the Vapours as the Ladies" (*Spectator* No. 536). By naming as effeminate those men of leisure whose main "Business in this World is to be well dressed" (*Tatler* No. 166), periodical literature ascribes a class basis to masculinity: the "real" man is the active, economically productive man of the middle ranks. Effecting a clear (though spurious) distinction between the man of business and his leisured wife, and thus between his production and her consumption, periodical literature neutralizes men's participation in the enterprise of expenditure, thereby allowing them to retain the detached perspective fundamental to both their gender and their class position. By setting out the sartorially resplendent man of leisure as a spectacle to be ridiculed rather than admired,[14] periodical literature played a significant part in fashioning men as well as women for the roles that would best benefit developing consumer capitalism.

With the separation of the home from the workplace, women of the middle ranks came increasingly to embody attributes of gentility no longer appropriate for their male counterparts. When the fashionable pastimes previously accessible only to the elite became available to those of the prospering middle ranks, bourgeois women began to employ their expanded leisure time in many ways new to them. They drank tea, coffee, and chocolate; they acquired chinaware and looking-glasses; they bought luxury fabrics for dresses and draperies. Thus the lavish expenditure and sartorial display associated with both men and women of the elite classes became encoded as particularly feminine occupations, even characteristics;[15] and the pursuit of fashion, clearly a luxury endeavor, came to define not only the aristocratic "Lady of Fashion" but all women. The English word "mode," whose meaning in the sense of "fashion, prevailing fashion or custom" was adopted from the French in the seventeenth century, is etymologically connected through a Latin root (*modus*) to the adjective "modest," one of whose definitions refers explicitly to the "attributes and behaviour" of women: "Governed by the proprieties of the sex; decorous in manner and conduct; not forward, imprudent, or lewd, 'shamefast'" (*OED*). While this signification stresses the sexual aspects of women's "modest" behavior, I submit that the word's semantic field reveals another element in the construction of female gendered identity (and thus of male identity). Although women's desire to follow the mode might cause such outrages against modesty as the enormous hoop petticoat that cannot fit through Bickerstaff's doorway (*Tatler* No. 116), in this period women's attention to fashion rapidly becomes an issue as paradoxically vexed as that of their chastity: simultaneously natural to them, inherent in their very femininity, it is also something that must be zealously monitored by men.

As the expanded purchasing power of the middle ranks combined with a greater availability of goods and activities, leisure and its associated diversions functioned less as a way of distinguishing the elite from the middle and lower classes than of differentiating women of the middle ranks from their male counterparts. In this context, the goods these women bought and the entertainments in which they participated came to bear the weight of a massive accumulation of economic, political, and moral considerations dealing with the importation, manufacture, and consumption of luxury items, in particular those that comprised the intricate "machinery" of women's dress.[16] Louis Landa's essay "Pope's Belinda, the General Emporie of the World, and the Wondrous Worm" usefully describes the contemporary economic milieu surrounding both the dress and dressing table of Pope's heroine. On the one hand, such objects as Belinda's silk petticoat or her tortoiseshell combs would "testify to the vast expansion of England's trade in the seventeenth century . . . Belinda and her kind were the wealthy consumers whose demands gave an impetus to the merchants trading in all parts of the world."[17] Yet on the other hand, for those economic theorists who believed that the country's welfare depended upon maintaining parity between imports and exports, "the lady of fashion was frequently the object of criticism, a danger to the national economy":

> In the mercantilist philosophy perhaps the most cogent doctrine was that a nation should have a favorable balance of trade. As a corollary, national frugality was deemed a virtue. Any action that caused bullion to flow out of the country was held to be harmful, particularly the importation of luxuries. Though there were arguments to the contrary from the apologists of the great trading companies, many of the more stringent economic writers complained often of the fashionable lady who insisted on dressing herself in calicoes, linens, velvets, laces, damasks, brocades, and satins imported from around the world, all at the expense of England's great staple, wool.[18]

For economists and moralists alike, the notion of national growth and prosperity through increased spending by those of all economic ranks "threatened to undermine a class discipline and a system of social control previously bolstered up by the patriotic and ascetic elements in orthodox mercantilist theory."[19] Such dangers were in part assuaged by the ideological alignment of the nation's welfare with that of the (middle-class) nuclear family. And yet, as the outraged contemporary response to the publication of Bernard Mandeville's *The Fable of the Bees* demonstrated,[20] accepting the public benefits of private vices was no easy task for either late seventeenth-century economic writers or early eighteenth-century periodical essayists. Despite the fact that Landa's essay cites Addison's *Spectator* No. 69 as the apogee of "sheer pleasure in the spectacle of the lady of fashion,"[21] Addison shared with his collaborator Steele an awareness of the problems inherent in the consumption of luxuries, whether imported or domestic.

While recognizing the importance as well as the dangers of the burgeoning consumer revolution in which their works were implicated, Addison and Steele sought at the same time to mitigate their apprehensions by scrupulously classifying, then carefully monitoring, the appearance and behavior of readers from all classes and of both sexes. Women's expanded role as consumers marked them as a particularly urgent target for such concern, for women had to buy, but what they purchased was not always what men desired. Thus women, who are both valued as necessary members of the British commonwealth and trivialized as volatile consumers of its products, occupy a liminal and contradictory position with regard to the economic and political realms. How to regulate women's purchases, and by extension women themselves, was a key issue for the men who wrote these texts and those who read them.

An examination of two lesser-known and explicitly political periodical publications, by Steele and Addison respectively, reveals each author's ambivalent treatment of women's economic role. In Steele's *The Spinster: In Defence of the Woollen Manufactures*, published in December 1719 at the height of contention among the domestic wool, silk, and cotton industries,[22] Steele expressly contrasts the periodical's eidolon, "*Rachel Woolpack*, Spinster," with the "modern *English* Lady" whose dress she inspects. While the latter is categorized by her leisurely schedule—"eleven a-clock in the Forenoon . . . is her break of Day"—the spinster is defined by the labor that supplies her title.[23] Rachel Woolpack notes, moreover, that the word's expansion to describe legally all maiden or single women in Britain "intimates that a Woman's chief Praise consists in Domestic Industry, and in Simplicity, rather than Variety of Dress."[24] Here "Domestic Industry" nicely amalgamates the more literal meaning of women whose livelihood was derived from manufacturing performed in the home with the broader sense of domesticity implied, for example, in Addison's *Spectator* No. 81 when he writes that "Female Virtues are of a Domestick turn. The Family is the proper Province for Private Women to Shine in." Numerous scholars have noted the correlation between women's loss of a productive economic role and the negative connotations attached to the term "spinster" in the early eighteenth century.[25] By ambiguously conflating the increasingly marginalized female spinner with the domestic woman who purchases rather than produces woolen goods, Steele establishes such domesticity as women's ultimate profession.

Moreover, the spinster's "simplicity . . . of Dress," contrasts forcefully with the elaborate costume of the "fine Lady," whose "several Dresses, with several suitable Undresses" Steele, in the increasingly transparent guise of Rachel Woolpack, goes on to examine. He moves from head—"A black *French* Silk Alamode Hood"—to foot—"Shoes, *English*"—in order to tabulate the nineteen articles that comprise only one of her five "necessary" outfits, calculating that "Foreigners sell this Lady to the Value of a thousand

Pounds, where the English sell her to the Value of five." He adds that "any Company, or Person, Trade, or Trader, on the *British* side of the Channel, will find it hard to ballance this Loss to our Country by what they sell of *English* Cloathing to Foreigners."[26] He is careful to note that he criticizes not trade in general but merely the imbalance between import and export, and cites "that excellent Eulogium" of the overseas trader in *Spectator* No. 69 as evidence of his pro-mercantile stance.[27]

Yet wedged between the anatomized articles of fashionable dress and the celebration of the merchant we find an appeal to women who, while not themselves spinsters, are also differentiated, at least potentially, from the fine lady whose sartorial splendor is ruining her nation's economy. Steele recommends to these women "the Imitation of the *Spartan Dame*, now represented on the Stage, where they will find the Duty of a Lady not restrain'd to domestick Life, but enlarging the Concern for her Family into that of her Country." This address, like that in Addison's earlier *Freeholder* (1716), clearly acknowledges women's powerful role within the domestic economy: "When a Woman of Honour and Understanding takes this Matter seriously into her Thoughts, she will consider how far her Fortune and Person may influence or support a Fashion, destructive to the Society of which she is a Member."[28] We find such a woman epitomized in Lucinda Sealand, a character best known for her role as the heiress in Steele's play *The Conscious Lovers* (1722), but who appeared two years earlier in Steele's periodical *The Theatre*.[29] In the name of stage reform, the periodical's narrator, Sir John Edgar, proposes in the third number an assembly of "Auditors of the Drama," comprised of people from different sectors of society, "to approve, condemn, or rectify whatever shall be exhibited on the *English* theatre."[30] Lucinda, who hopes to be chosen as representative of the "Front-Boxes," exemplifies an ideal domestic woman: at ease among "great Families" yet "no Stranger to Houshold Affairs." Most important, she is a "great Favourer of the Woollen Manufactures; and she intends on the Election-Day to appear in a White Stuff Suit, lin'd with Cherry-colour'd Silk." Like the model reader of *The Spinster*, Lucinda can combine an attractive appearance with public spirit: "For, besides the Consideration of her Country's Good, she has skill enough to know that no Woman is the better dress'd for being in rich Clothes, and that 'tis the Fancy and Elegance of an Habit, and not the Cost, that makes it always becoming to the Wearer." In addition to providing in herself an example of the fashionable yet patriotic female theatergoer, Lucinda will even refurbish the actors themselves by introducing "Dresses of our own Growth and Labour" on stage.

Like Steele, Addison acknowledged women's political and economic clout. His *Freeholder*, the Whig party organ in the early years of George I,[31] also addresses women as potentially useful and usefully attractive citizens, capable of benefiting the nation while pleasing its men. Yet while Addison expressly devotes nine of the periodical's fifty-five numbers to the topic of women's significant place as "Members of the Body Politick" (No. 32), women's own bodies consistently subvert that role. Women prove useful not for their rational capacity but for their sexual potential, for since "Arguments out of a pretty Mouth are unanswerable," he contends that "Ladies are always of great use to the Party they espouse, and never fail to win over Numbers to it" (No. 4). In the same number, Addison observes that in those countries where "Arbitrary Government and Popery" reign, women's bodies are uniformly victimized: tortured by foot binding, burned in suttee, or considered chattel. In Persia, for example, "it is a usual Thing when a Man sells a Bale of Silk, or a Drove of Camels, to toss half a dozen Women into the Bargain." It is noteworthy that all of the countries mentioned in this number—China, the East Indies, Persia, Turkey, Spain, Italy, and France—were involved in trade with Britain during this period, and provided the items, in particular silks and cottons, that were the targets of heated debate. Addison seems almost to conflate these countries' mistreatment of their women with the destructive potential of their goods—bought and worn, of course, by those ostensibly free English women whose bodies are supposedly their own. Addison soon attempts to circumscribe that liberty by encouraging his female readers to use their bodies solely in promoting the Whig cause: "It is therefore to be hoped that every fine Woman will make this laudable Use of her Charms; and that she may not want to be frequently reminded of this great Duty, I will only desire her to think of her Country every Time she looks in her Glass" (No. 8). Proper participation in party politics thus transforms the denigrated mirror into a serviceable tool; and the narcissism for which women are commonly calumniated becomes a "laudable Use of . . . Charms."

In the periodical's early issues Addison seems to revel in the sheer possibility of such a process. No. 8 repeatedly employs the zeugma to describe a draft for a "*Female Association*" formed for the "Good and Safety of our Constitution":

> And we do hereby engage ourselves to raise and arm our Vassals for the Service of His Majesty King *George*, and Him to Defend with our Tongues and Hearts, our Eyes, Eye-Lashes, Favourites, Lips, Dimples, and every other Feature, whether natural or acquired. We promise publickly and openly to avow the Loyalty of our Principles in every Word we shall utter, and

every Patch we shall stick on. We further promise, to annoy
the Enemy with all the Flames, Darts, and Arrows with which
Nature has armed us. . . . We are determined in so good a
Cause to endure the greatest Hardships and Severities, if there
shou'd be Occasion; and even to wear the Manufacture of our
Country, rather than appear the Friends of a foreign Interest
in the richest *French* Brocade.

And yet, while Addison here politicizes women's every physical feature, gesture, and item of clothing by enlisting them in the Whig struggle, women themselves remain trivial objects, targets of satire rather than compatriots. Through a strategy of mock-heroic diminishment, the *Freeholder* papers devoted to women minimize their power by exaggerating it. For example, No. 15 enumerates the ways in which women have employed fans in the service of their country; Addison notes that "Fans are much more innocent Engines for propagating the Protestant Religion, than Racks, Wheels, Gibbets, and the like Machines, which are made use of for the Advancement of the Roman-Catholick."[32] The comparison effectively erases women's historical participation in religious wars; moreover, the shocking disparity—in spite of the attempted humor—between instruments of torture and those of seduction belies Addison's comfort with the "Female-Patriots" he had lauded earlier in the same number: "It is with great Pleasure that I see a Race of Female-Patriots springing up in this Island. The fairest among the Daughters of *Great Britain* no longer confine their Cares to a Domestick Life, but are grown anxious for the Welfare of their Country, and show themselves good Stateswomen as well as good Housewives."

Like their enterprising efforts in the area of consumption, women's active involvement in the political realm presupposes a sense of self-assurance that clearly threatens male control. By No. 38, the Freeholder's farewell to his female readers, his initial delight in women's ability to combine patriotism with domesticity has turned to repugnance at the loss of femininity caused by political association: "there is nothing which makes the Sex more Unamiable than Party-Rage." The very women who had earlier succeeded in numerous forms of political seduction are in danger of forfeiting their looks altogether and thus becoming a liability to their party as well as to their country: "The finest Woman, in a Transport of Fury, loses the Use of her Face. Instead of charming her Beholders, she frights both Friend and Foe." Women's ability to be "good Stateswomen as well as good Housewives" has clearly proved illusory, for Addison disparages even the term itself: "A States-woman is as ridiculous a Creature as a Cott-Quean."[33] To restore order, he returns to the doctrine of separate spheres promulgated throughout the *Spectator*: "Each of the sexes should keep within its particular Bounds, and content themselves to excel within their respective Districts."

In these texts, the consistent undermining of women's role as "Members of the Body Politick" betrays a persistent anxiety about the effects of that role on their bodies. The attempt to trivialize women's use of attractions can serve to mask the significance of their consuming role in a developing capitalist economy: "the vagaries of fashion disturbed the ultra-sensitive moralists of the day; but they also disturbed the politician, for every change of style in dress had economic consequences, and these could be damaging to native industries."[34] Moreover, belittling of women camouflaged the fact that for women, seemingly frivolous attention to looks could in fact become a matter of survival, dependent as they were on the approbation and concomitant economic support of fathers, lovers, or husbands. Representations of the adornment process as natural to women obscure that process's cultural and economic components, as the activity of women's embellishment establishes gender difference at the same time as it supports economic enterprise. If an interest in dress and appearance is culturally coded as part of women's nature, then fashion can be severed from any particular economic class and attributed to femininity itself (and any woman who deviates from such behavior is viewed as somehow less than woman). Women's supposed intrinsic desire to please not only constitutes a feminine gender identity but defines a masculine one as well. By distinguishing female passivity from the gainful employment of middle-class men, periodicals attribute a homologous femininity to those men with both the leisure and the economic means to attend to their own dress and to ladies' tea-tables. Masculinity, then, describes an active process that includes both economic production and control over women. Reading the *Tatler*, *Spectator*, and *Guardian* exposes the ways in which each text, by aligning itself with this supervisory role fundamental to domestic masculinity, obscures its significant part in the creation of both gender and class values.

Dead Men and Petticoats

> In a Nation of Liberty, there is hardly a Person in the whole
> Mass of the People more absolutely necessary than a Censor.
> —*Tatler* No. 144

To read the *Tatler* is to be plunged into a teeming pool of eighteenth-century urban life, where proper names and place names, types of people, forms and venues of entertainment, items of foreign news, articles of dress and aspects of behavior swim ceaselessly through the 271 issues. While Steele, with occasional help from Addison, presents this discursive world as one of disorder and confusion, it is less a world turned upside down than one that has outgrown its borders or spilled over its edges. Yet the *Tatler*'s universe of constant movement, boundless novelty, and continual "Exorbitances" (No. 113) boasts a lone figure—its narrator, Isaac Bickerstaff—who has assumed the role of ordering chaos and applying method to madness. Bickerstaff's technique is majestically simple: he goes everywhere, sees everything (or has it reported to him), and then informs his readers of what he has seen. The tumultuous world he inhabits and depicts thereby inflects, necessarily, both the form and the content of his lucubrations. In the publication's first number Bickerstaff describes the procedure through which particular themes will be affiliated with specific sites: "All Accounts of *Gallantry*, *Pleasure*, and *Entertainment*, shall be under the Article of *White's Chocolate-house*; *Poetry*, under that of *Will's Coffee-house*; *Learning*, under the Title of *Graecian*; *Foreign* and *Domestick News*, you will have from St. *James's Coffee-house*; and what else I have to offer on any other Subject, shall be dated from my own *Apartment*." Such a format preempted, at least initially, the kind of unified essay later perfected by Addison, and facilitated instead a peripatetic conglomeration of frequently diverse topics. In a different sense, the conceit of the *Tatler*'s physical allocation of subject matter to various coffee-houses emphasized the gendered nature of Bickerstaff's reforming roles, for these so-called public spaces were, of course, restricted to the male sex.[35]

In Chapter 5 I argued that Bickerstaff's reforming vision functioned to accentuate both the gendering of physical spaces and the promotion of unequivocal and discrete roles and characteristics for each sex. In this section, I wish to pay particular attention to one of Bickerstaff's many corrective characters, one that I have mentioned often in passing—his role as censor. His account of the genealogy of this position (No. 162) paradoxically confounds the very public/private distinction he is so intent upon establishing. Bickerstaff, he informs us for the first time, is a failed public servant; continuously unsuccessful in his "many Endeavours to get a Place at Court," he resolved, late in life, "to erect a new Office, and for my Encouragement, to place my self in it. For this Reason, I took upon me the Title and Dignity of *Censor* of *Great Britain*, reserving to my self all such Perquisites, Profits, and Emoluments, as should arise out of the Discharge of the said Office." He thus appropriates the language and authority of the state (as well as the financial benefits attached to state office)[36] in the service of a private goal and personal advantage.

The position itself blends a government-sanctioned need for surveillance with objects of scrutiny residing mostly within the private realm. The first part of Bickerstaff's "Duty," as modeled upon that of the Roman censors, was to review and classify "the People"; he numbers among his own aggregation "the *Dappers* and the *Smarts*, the *Natural* and *Affected Rakes*, the *Pretty Fellows* and the *very Pretty Fellows*." As we shall soon see, these types of men are distinguished by their lack of "that publick Spirit, which ought to be the first and principal Motive of all their Actions" (No. 183). He goes on to note that in the ancient Greek and Roman empires, all "Gallantry" had its source in attention to the country's welfare, for it was "impossible to be in the Fashion without being a Patriot." In eighteenth-century Britain, by contrast, Bickerstaff consistently positions attention to attire and the rationality associated with public (or even private) service as mutually exclusive—as, for example, when he decrees that "*Harry Lacker* is so very exact in his Dress, that I shall give his Estate to his younger Brother, and make him a Dancing-Master" (No. 66).

The second part of the censor's office, "to look into the Manners of the People, and to check any growing Luxury, whether in Diet, Dress, or Building" (No. 162),[37] establishes even more forcefully the interpenetration of spheres. By placing such resolutely personal conduct under the official eye of the law, for the censor was also empowered to punish "Offences according to the Quality of the Offender," the occupation of the Roman censors and Bickerstaff, their eighteenth-century disciple, sanctions the slackening of one kind of difference, that between public and private, in order to arrange other distinctions even more securely. Bickerstaff's judgments and dicta on the apparel of both sexes serve as a way to establish not only proper dress codes but also codes of behavior in keeping with the supposed natural differences between the sexes. Yet to do justice to Bickerstaff's engagement with these issues would require not merely part of a chapter but a volume in itself, since one might argue that the function of censor determines the character of both Bickerstaff and the *Tatler* as effectively as those of "spectator" or "guardian" establish the dispositions of their respective eponymous narrators and texts. My reader, then, must bear in mind that the scope of this discussion permits me to select only a few examples out of a multitude of possibilities, for my perusal of the *Tatler* found at least 100 numbers that dealt in some way with topics related to dress, leisure, and luxury.

"Tom Modely," the subject of *Tatler* No. 166, "is one of those Fools who look upon Knowledge of the Fashion to be the only Liberal Science"; he belongs, Bickerstaff claims, at the "Head" of the type he designates as "*Insipids*":

> By being habitually in the best Company, he knows perfectly
> well when a Coat is well cut, or a Periwig well mounted. As
> soon as you enter the Place where he is, he tells the next Man
> to him who is your Taylor, and judges of you more from the
> Choice of your Periwig-maker than of your Friend. His Busi-

> ness in this World is to be well dressed; and the greatest Cir-
> cumstance that is to be recorded in his Annals is, That he
> wears Twenty Shirts a Week. Thus, without ever speaking
> Reason among the Men, or Passion among the Women, he is
> every where well received; and without any one Man's Esteem,
> he has every Man's Indulgence.

By declaring Tom Modely's unseemly attention to appearances to be part
and parcel of the fruitless, even ruinous quality of his life, Bickerstaff characterizes him, along with those other men he reviles as "Expletives in Human Society," by his thorough lack of the rational capacity that would enable
him to benefit, rather than deplete, the British commonwealth. Yet the consuming interest in "News and Scandal" that renders Modely and his insipid
cohorts a "constant Plague" to men of business makes them at the same time
"the Heroes of Visiting Days." These men are valued by *women* for their
ability to participate in activities gendered female: "they help the Design of
the Meeting, which is to pass away that odious Thing called Time, in Discourses too trivial to raise any Reflections which may put well bred Persons
to the Trouble of Thinking."

In this period, both bodily adornment and social uselessness have increasingly become characteristics associated with women. In No. 109, for example, Bickerstaff's condemnation of the empty and even destructive existence of a "Visiting Lady" becomes a reproach to the entire female sex: "As
for my Part, I think most of the Misfortunes in Families arise from the tri-
fling Way the Women have in spending their Time, and gratifying only their
Eyes and Ears, instead of their Reason and Understanding." Since femininity takes meaning in opposition to those traits marked as masculine, modish
men are governed by a paradox: they can no longer be men. Bickerstaff
solves this ontological dilemma with a stroke of his censor's stylus: he pronounces them dead.[38] By taking literally the tenet "That *every Worthless Man
is a Dead Man*" (No. 96), a notion that he claims to be "as old as *Pythagoras*,"
Bickerstaff corrects social ills and, in the process, solidifies gender norms.
While Bickerstaff's criteria for distinguishing between the living and the
dead seem at first to apply to individuals of both sexes, the characteristics
that he ascribes to the deceased are, ironically, those that describe behaviors
firmly identified with aristocratic and bourgeois femininity: "In the Number
of the Dead, I comprehend all Persons of what Title or Dignity soever, who
bestow most of their Time in Eating and Drinking, to support that imaginary Existence of theirs, which they call Life; or in dressing and adorning
those Shadows and Apparitions, which are looked upon by the Vulgar as real
Men and Women." The next sentence augments this point, for not only does

it exclude from the ranks of the living most middle- and upper-class women, but its declaration also extinguishes a portion of the male population: "In short, whoever resides in the World *without having any Business in it*, and passes away an Age, without ever thinking on the Errand for which he was sent hither, is to me a Dead Man to all Intents and Purposes; and I desire that he may be so reputed" (my italics).

Bickerstaff's dictum, then, humorously promulgates a serious set of values. He seems to revel in his new-made power: the following issue (No. 97) opens with his proud claim of "Having swept away prodigious Multitudes in my last Paper, and brought a great Destruction upon my own Species." We as readers are encouraged, of course, to share Bickerstaff's celebratory, and censorial, point of view, and thus to laugh at (and out of existence) those men, who, like the character of "*Quid nunc,*" exist "without entring into the Business of Life" (No. 10). Yet it is important to note the violence of Bickerstaff's attack, a violence, moreover, that applies also to those men who are alive. While Bickerstaff's narrative implies by contrast that relations of public utility and personal benevolence characterize the spheres of action occupied by living men, both commercial and political activity are of course governed by such unbenign issues as power, profit, and dominance. The satirical tone of Bickerstaff's declaration that "every Worthless Man is a Dead Man," not to mention its subsequent execution in the "Court of Justice," should not blind us to the cruel, inexorable choice men are socialized to accept: be productive or die. Furthermore, such death applies only to males. Women, we shall shortly see, can be judged, but they may not be judged lifeless for behaviors construed as intrinsic to their very nature.

Shortly after he has made his life-and-death pronouncement, Bickerstaff reports upon the "Pleasure" he has taken in "dispatch[ing] a great deal of Business," especially because it was business turned "to the Publick Emolument" (No. 103). His satisfaction, we find, results from his having presided at a "Court of Justice" in which he adjudicated men's "Pretensions" to such foppish luxury items as "Canes, Perspective-Glasses, Snuff-Boxes, Orange-Flower-Waters, and the like Ornaments of Life." In keeping with the conviction that such adornments are the proper province of women, Bickerstaff carefully monitors men's possession and usage of the above goods. While the entire number manifests the wit that attests, at least in part, to the periodical's immense popularity, Bickerstaff's penultimate suppliant, who requests the continued use of his perspective glass, is the most interesting for our purposes. The interaction begins with physical comedy, as Bickerstaff states that "there came in a well-dressed Man, with a Glass-Tube in one hand, and his Petition in the other. Upon his entring the Room, he threw back the

Right Side of his Wig, put forward his Right Leg, and advancing the Glass to his Right Eye, aimed it directly at me. In the mean while, to make my Observations also, I put on my Spectacles; in which Posture we surveyed each other for some Time." And yet the man's ability to read, without the glass, the petition he has brought soon belies his avowal of near blindness. Thus while he argues for the retention of his glass by claiming that "it is the Joy, the Pleasure, the Employment of my Life, to frequent publick Assemblies, and gaze upon the Fair," Bickerstaff apprehends that "his Use of a Glass was occasioned by no other Infirmity but his Vanity, and was not so much designed to make him see, as to make him be seen and distinguished by others." The censor thereby "refused him a License for a Perspective, but allowed him a Pair of Spectacles, with full Permission to use them in any publick Assembly as he should think fit."

The case of the perspective glass focuses a number of related concerns. To begin with, it establishes the professedly useless man, whose "Employment" is pleasure, not as a spectator of women, but as himself a spectacle.[39] This latter position Bickerstaff deems an unseemly one for men, whose sexuality, and thus masculinity, must be determined in large part through the libidinous gaze of the rake. Consequently, Bickerstaff's proffered spectacles correct not the man's poor eyesight but his failure properly to discern an important component of the masculine gender role. Moreover, the text utilizes such recently obtainable commodities as perspective glasses to distinguish desirable from fruitless masculinity—no small feat, for it simultaneously marks the living and the dead. These glasses, whose use, like that of canes, snuff-boxes, and perfumed handkerchiefs, must be licensed by a censor, denote the leisured lifestyle inimical to active masculinity.[40] In the moralizing mode, the number concludes with Bickerstaff's reflection upon the importance of being vigilant: "however slightly Men may regard these Particularities and little Follies in Dress and Behaviour, they lead to greater Evils." Today the snuff-box, tomorrow the world.

In No. 116, however, Bickerstaff holds court for the ladies, having earlier bemoaned the fact "that while I am busie in correcting the Folly and Vice of one Sex, several Exorbitances break out in the other" (No. 113). Although Bickerstaff names as the "Criminal" in the case a young lady "who was taken up as she went out of the Puppet-Show about Three Nights ago," the defendant is less a particular woman than her hoop petticoat, which assumes superhuman, even architectural, proportions.[41] Not only is the petticoat too wide to fit through Bickerstaff's door, but, once it has been separated from its wearer and mounted on an "Engine of several Legs, that could contract or open it self like the Top of an Umbrello," it is also too colossal to be fully extended in Bickerstaff's "great Hall"; after the petticoat has been "drawn up by a Pully" to the hall's ceiling and spread out upon the "Engine," Bickerstaff comments that "it formed a very splendid and ample Canopy over our Heads, and covered the whole Court of Judicature with a kind of Silken Rotunda, in its form not unlike the Cupolo of St. *Paul's*." Bickerstaff's farcical manipulations of the unwieldy article provide a further entrenchment of gender difference: "By framing the hoop petticoat as a structural or mechanical device, its critics indirectly characterized women as incompetent 'architects' and 'mechanics.' Women rejected their 'natural' shape—and, by extension, their natural function, procreation—and failed in inappropriate, masculine roles, offending both the sense and sensibility of the age."[42] In addition, while Bickerstaff might attempt to elevate the skirt metaphorically as well as literally by comparing it to the dome atop St. Paul's cathedral, we should also recognize that the petticoat's placement puts both Bickerstaff and his court in the titillating position of being able to look up a woman's skirt, a situation that reveals, once again, the rake within the censor.

Bickerstaff's interaction with the young woman, who turns out to be a sensible as well as "very beautiful young Damsel," is relatively brief. While his discovery that she sports the petticoat only "to look as big and burly as other Persons of her Quality," for she had begun "to appear little in the Eyes of all her Acquaintance," might contain interesting moral implications, he does not dilate upon his findings, but simply dismisses his "pretty Criminal" by acknowledging that he always "give[s] great Allowances to the Fair Sex upon Account of the Fashion." As I have noted earlier in this chapter, fashion was of course entangled with economics; Addison, the author of this well-known essay, makes the association explicit when he has Bickerstaff call in a "Council for the Petticoat" who defend the object against its detractors by expounding upon its material benefit to Great Britain. The council argues first that this outsized garment, because six times larger in area than its predecessor, the "common Petticoat," would occasion a "prodigious Improvement of the Woollen Trade! and what could not fail to sink the Power of *France* in a few Years." In addition, the council maintains that both the "Rope-Makers," who provide material for the "Stiffening of the Drapery," and the "*Greenland* Trade[rs]," who supply its whalebone ribbing, would benefit tremendously from the increased demand for their goods necessitated by the swollen petticoat.

Bickerstaff, however, dismisses their appeal, arguing that while the "monstrous Invention" might bolster the mercantile interest, it simultaneously exhausts the family budget: "These Arguments would have wrought very much upon me, . . . had I not considered the great and additional Expence which such Fashions would bring upon Fathers and Husbands; and therefore by no Means to be thought of till some Years after a Peace." While the judicious expenditures sanctioned by men serve, ostensibly, to unite personal interest with the national good, the expense of the hoop petticoat, as an article of dress sported by women largely in the teeth of male opposition,[43] appears irrational as well as exorbitant. Bickerstaff is quick to note, however, that his casting off the hoop petticoat does not make him "an Enemy to the proper Ornaments of the Fair-Sex." He asserts that "On the contrary, as the Hand of Nature has poured on them such a Profusion of Charms and Graces, and sent them into the World more amiable and finished than the rest of her Works; so I would have them bestow upon themselves all the additional Beauties that Art can supply them with, providing it does not interfere with, disguise, or pervert, those of Nature."

Bickerstaff's attempt to regulate women's adornment reveals the contradictory elements within women's positioning vis-à-vis nature and the natural. To begin with, the "Hand of Nature"—itself an interesting locution in its bodily personification of a supposedly abstract force, its elision of biology and culture—has poured "Charms and Graces" upon women in such profusion as to send them into the world "more amiable and finished than the rest of [nature's] Works." While Bickerstaff, in a show of great generosity, subsequently grants that women might "bestow upon themselves all the additional Beauties that Art can supply them with," his appended stipulation, "providing it does not interfere with, disguise, or pervert, those of Nature," instantly obviates any simple use of such "additional Beauties" on the part of women, for if "finished," they need no ornament; consequently, any ornament, no matter how tastefully displayed, will by necessity "interfere with, disguise, or pervert" those natural ornaments with which women are born. Moreover, even the adornment that is presumably natural to the female sex is culturally dictated, for Nature is of course a manmade institution. Thus women, trapped within these various contradictions, inhabit a no-woman's land between, on the one hand, a shifting yet ineluctable nature, and, on the other, a morally suspect artifice. These permutations of femininity present a perplexing challenge to the women who must embody them, for while any use of adornment might be too much, none at all is certainly too little. In the absence of any rational middle ground, women must depend on men to arbitrate their choices.

The final paragraph of the essay performs such a mediation:

> I consider Woman as a beautiful Romantick Animal, that
> may be adorned with Furs and Feathers, Pearls and Diamonds,
> Ores and Silks. The Lynx shall cast its Skin at her Feet to
> make her a Tippet; the Peacock, Parrot, and Swan, shall pay

> Contributions to her Muff; the Sea shall be searched for
> Shells, and the Rocks for Gems; and every Part of Nature fur-
> nish out its Share towards the Embellishment of a Creature
> that is the most consummate Work of it. All this I shall in-
> dulge them in; but as for the Petticoat I have been speaking of,
> I neither can, nor will allow it.

Here Bickerstaff delineates, in sumptuous diction, the various "Part[s] of Nature" that should, in his schema, contribute toward women's proper "Embellishment." The passage contains elements already familiar to us from the
prior paragraph: incongruity—why should a "Creature that is the most consummate Work" of nature need further elaboration from the nature it supposedly transcends?—and, in its opening phrase, a confluence of culture and
nature, as "Romantick," with its connotations of literature and the human
imagination, is aligned to the "Animal." In addition, the abstract "Hand of
Nature" has metamorphosed into the specific creatures whose skins and
feathers comprise articles for women to wear; nature's other opulent goods—
pearls, diamonds, ores, silks—also actively contribute their "Share" to
women's adornment. Laura Brown's reading of this final paragraph as a "ra-
tionalized version of imperial expansionism" registers the way in which "Addison's female figure disappears behind or within or beneath the numerous
treasures and rarities with which she is adorned." Brown argues that the passage, wherein "all of nature seems to cooperate in this process of adornment
and erasure," exemplifies the "most common trope" of eighteenth-century
mercantile capitalism, in which "the agency of the acquisitive subject and the
urgency of accumulation are concealed and deflected through the fantasy of
a universal collaboration in the dressing of the female body."[44] This trope of
collaboration, she then maintains, permits men to make women accountable
for the entire mercantile enterprise: "Women wear the products of accumulation, and thus by metonymy they are made to bear responsibility for the
system by which they are adorned."[45] Like Bickerstaff, Brown is interested in
looking beneath the "monstrous" petticoat. While he finds a desirable young
woman, she discovers the ways in which women's fetishized adornment acts
to conceal "the activities and motives of male mercantilists and the system-
atic, bureaucratic, piratical, or mercenary dimensions of imperialist expansion."[46] But because she is content simply to reinstate men's culpability,
Brown neglects the very masculine structures she has so cogently elucidated.

These structures are present by virtue of their absence. What Landa has
termed Bickerstaff's "apostrophe to women" addresses itself primarily to
men.[47] Concealed within the passage's figurative language, which attributes
agency to the animals themselves, and its passive grammatical structure,

which eliminates agency altogether, we find men: the men who must kill the lynx, pluck the peacock, probe the sea for shells, and excavate the rocks for gems. Such actions depleted the men who performed them as much as the women who supposedly benefited from them. While Brown excoriates imperialism for its disguised exploitation of human beings, in particular women and slaves, and thus for its cavalier exhaustion of both human and natural resources, I allege that men, constrained by the breadwinner role that was forcing them into the life-threatening pursuits associated with imperialist accumulation, were also being stripped of aspects of their own humanness, in particular the emotive capacity increasingly displaced onto women. In the process of censuring women's manifestation of the very attributes they have ascribed as intrinsic to them, men condemn themselves to the debilitating practices that make possible such display.

Cultivating Nature: Mr. Spectator as Gardener

The Mind that lies fallow but a single Day, sprouts up in Follies that are only to be killed by a constant and assiduous Culture.
—*Spectator* No. 10

Early in the *Spectator* series, Mr. Spectator responds to several readers who have solicited his censure of some recent affectations of dress. By carefully tilling his rich periodical soil, he establishes, through an implied contrast to his illustrious predecessor Bickerstaff, his own moral position not as the censor of Great Britain but rather as its husbandman:

> To be brief, there is scarce an Ornament of either Sex which one or other of my Correspondents has not inveighed against with some Bitterness, and recommended to my Observation. I must therefore, once for all inform my Readers, that it is not my Intention to sink the Dignity of this my Paper with Reflections upon Red-heels or Top-knots, but rather to enter into the Passions of Mankind, and to correct those depraved Sentiments that give Birth to all those little Extravagancies which appear in their outward Dress and Behaviour. Foppish and fantastick Ornaments are only Indications of Vice, not criminal in themselves. Extinguish Vanity in the Mind, and you naturally retrench the little Superfluities of Garniture and Equipage. *The Blossoms will fall of themselves, when the Root that nourishes them is destroyed.* (No. 16; my italics)

While Bickerstaff was content, indeed delighted, to pick the gaudy blooms, examine their color and scent, then press them in his censor's book, Mr. Spectator's detached, even magisterial disposition situates him, paradoxically, in a more active relation to the tender shoots that grow in the human psyche. If Bickerstaff's role of cultural overseer was predicated upon the belief that luxury, because inherent in the human condition, could never be eradicated, yet might be suppressed through vigilant classification,[48] Mr. Spectator's concern for the "Passions of Mankind" demands his application of "Remedies to the first Seeds and Principles of an affected Dress, without descending to the Dress it self." Mr. Spectator conducts no court; his own speculations, as well as those of his abundant correspondents, warn more than they judge. *Spectator* No. 478, in which a male contributor offers his "amusing Thoughts" upon visiting the London shops, typifies the periodical's penchant for moral meditation as well as its characteristic urbanity. In the letter, a detailed plan for the fanciful construction of a "Repository builded for Fashions, as there are Chambers for Medals and other Rarities," is preceded by a discourse upon luxury worthy of Bernard Mandeville, as the correspondent considers that

> it must be very surprizing to any one who enters into a Detail of Fashions, to consider how far the Vanity of Mankind has laid it self out in Dress, what a prodigious Number of People it maintains, and what a Circulation of Money it occasions. Providence in this Case makes Use of the Folly which we will not give up, and it becomes instrumental to the Support of those who are willing to labour. Hence it is, that Fringe-Makers, Lace-Men, Tire-Women, and a Number of other Trades, which would be useless in a simple State of Nature, draw their Subsistence; tho' it is seldom seen that such as these are extremely rich, because their original Fault of being founded upon Vanity, keeps them poor by the light Inconstancy of its Nature. The Variableness of Fashion turns the Stream of Business, which flows from it now into one Channel, and anon into another; so that different Sets of People sink or flourish in their Turns by it.

Mr. Spectator's dispassionate stance and affable manner soften, yet cannot conceal, the authority behind his reformist agenda. In eighteenth-century parlance, the meaning of culture in the sense of "cultivation of intellectual or aesthetic faculties" unquestionably possessed an overt moral component, as Terry Lovell reminds us.[49] Another reader (No. 127), while acknowledging Mr. Spectator's earlier "Resolution . . . to avoid descending to Particularities of Dress," asks him to make an exception of one of the fair sex's "great Extravagancies": the petticoats which, having begun "to heave and swell" before the Spectator's departure from London (he has gone to visit Sir Roger de Coverly on his country estate), "are now blown up into a most enormous Concave, and rise every Day more and more." The writer attributes to Mr. Spectator an authority worthy of any censor when he writes that "In short, Sir, since our Women know themselves to be out of the Eye of the SPECTATOR, they will be kept within no Compass." The correspondent's choice of imagery reveals, ironically, the corrective for women's bodies. Whereas women, "kept within no Compass," might thereby transgress the prescribed boundaries of their proper sphere or orbit, the compass as drawing instrument provides the needed antidote by putting control back in the hands of men; women become, then, not just charted but encompassed, literally circumscribed, by men's directives. As the letter goes on to establish, it is not Mr. Spectator's eye but his pen that wields such power: "I am apt to think the Petticoat will shrink of its own Accord at your first coming to Town, at least a Touch of your Pen will make it contract it self, like the Sensitive Plant, and by that means oblige several who are either terrified or astonished at this portentous Novelty." As in its earlier trial by Bickerstaff (*Tatler* No. 116), the petticoat achieves a life of its own; here, however, it functions as a biological rather than an architectural or even economic phenomenon. The plant that will, supposedly, shrink at the Spectator's touch will also, it is implied, grow until checked; women's natural luxuriance, then, demands the constant attention of the men—including the Spectator himself—who must work to monitor, and thus to modify, the "great Extravagancies" that female flesh is heir to.[50]

Mr. Spectator's fertile use of horticultural imagery both fosters and conceals a deep-rooted dependence on the cultural categories of nature and the natural, for the biology that supposedly underlies problematic (and thereby unnatural) human behavior is itself a social construct. A passage later in No. 16 displays this conflation of nature and culture when Mr. Spectator comments, "To speak truly, the young People of both Sexes are so wonderfully apt to shoot out into long Swords or sweeping Trains, bushy Head-dresses or full-bottom'd Perriwigs, with several other Incumbrances of Dress, that they stand in Need of being pruned very frequently, lest they should be oppressed with Ornaments, and over-run with the Luxuriency of their Habits." Addison's marvelous conceit delights by virtue of its visual aptness: such sumptuary extrusions seem indeed to resemble the "shoot[ing] out" of plants, and to need the gardener's pruning for optimum development. Yet this yoking together of diverse elements does more than showcase Addison's wit. By likening "the Young People of both Sexes" to exuberant plants, the metaphor represents a human, culturally inflected interest in display as a biological phenomenon; moreover, it transforms people into aesthetic objects to be arranged by the gardener's hand.[51]

An examination of the tilling, seeding, and pruning of Mr. Spectator's garden reveals a set of complex processes through which social norms are planted and nurtured. The process of cultivating nature—correcting its extravagances and deviations—implies, of course, the acceptance of a set of inherent, and thereby proper, characteristics for all living creatures. For humans in particular, these qualities are marked by gender: what is good for the goose cannot, then, be good for the gander. *Spectator* No. 128 elucidates, perhaps more completely than any other number, the text's justification of gender difference by recourse to biology: "Women in their Nature are much more gay and joyous than Men; whether it be that their Blood is more refined, their Fibres more delicate, and their animal Spirits more light and volatile; or whether, as some have imagined, there may not be a kind of Sex in the very Soul, I shall not pretend to determine." Such physiological traits define masculinity as well as femininity, for "As Vivacity is the Gift of Women, Gravity is that of Men." This corporeal distinction, itself culturally loaded, meshes seamlessly with a behavioral imperative that vindicates men's public, productive role and demands women's private, nurturing one: "By what I have said we may conclude, Men and Women were made as Counterparts to one another, that the Pains and Anxieties of the Husband might be relieved by the Sprightliness and good Humour of the Wife. When these are rightly tempered, Care and Chearfulness go Hand in Hand; and the Family, like a Ship that is duly trimmed, wants neither Sail nor Ballast."

At the time of writing No. 128, Mr. Spectator is in the country visiting Sir Roger; he looks once again to nature for his example of domestic interdependence: the male bird alone sings, and his song "amuses and diverts" his mate while she sits upon her nest. For humans, according to Mr. Spectator, these roles are reversed, due, in large part, to the nature of what he terms their "Contract": "in the feather'd Kind, the Cares and Fatigues *of the married State, if I may so call it*, lie principally upon the Female. On the contrary, as in our Species the Man and Woman are joined together for Life, and the main Burden rests upon the former, Nature has given all the little Arts of soothing and Blandishment to the Female, that she may chear and animate her Companion in a constant and assiduous Application to the making a Provision for his Family, and the educating of their common Children" (my italics). This turn to nature establishes both men's and women's economic and psychological roles as biological imperatives. And yet, Addison's self-conscious use of the very human institution of marriage to describe the conduct of birds exposes the permeable membrane between the supposedly bounded areas of nature and culture. While the argument from nature can provide a grounding for such seemingly fundamental attributes as gender, the periodical's need constantly to authorize gendered comportment belies such behavior's indigenous quality.

By expatiating upon the traditional view of women as lacking the rational ability to control their seemingly voracious appetites—for clothing as well as for sex[52]—the *Spectator* furthers the belief in men's need assiduously to regulate the female sex. No. 265 ingeniously elaborates the conceit of women's presumably natural empty-headedness by observing that "when in ordinary Discourse we say a Man has a fine Head, a long Head, or a good Head, we express our selves metaphorically, and speak in relation to his Understanding; whereas when we say of a Woman, she has a fine, a long, or a good Head, we speak only in relation to her Commode." If the essay suggests that the term describing men's intelligence derives from an associative process whereby the physical head comes to represent the mental activity going on within it, the essay simultaneously establishes women's cerebral vacuity through the operation of synecdoche, as the whole head is subsumed by its millinery part.

Because the "light minds" of women are, by nature, "taken with little things,"[53] women stand in serious and constant danger of being attracted not only to inappropriate attire but also, and even more dangerously, to the wrong men. "I have often reflected with my self," writes Mr. Spectator, "on this unaccountable Humour in Woman-kind, of being smitten with every thing that is showy and superficial; and on the numberless Evils that befall the Sex, from this light, fantastical Disposition" (No. 15). Thus in No. 311 Mr. Spectator receives a letter from the aptly named "Tim Watchwell," who has taken every precaution to protect his nubile daughter from the snares of those men he terms "Fortune-Stealers." Mr. Spectator's response confirms his correspondent's need for vigilance in the face of female vulnerability: "The young innocent Creatures who have no Knowledge and Experience of the World, are those whose Safety I would principally consult in this Speculation. The Stealing of such an one should, in my Opinion, be as punishable as a Rape. Where there is no Judgment there is no Choice." As other essays clearly demonstrate, even adult women lack the judgment that will enable them to make proper choices when it comes to men:

> In short, they consider only the Drapery of the Species, and
> never cast away a Thought on those Ornaments of the Mind,
> that make Persons Illustrous in themselves, and Useful to

> others. . . . A Girl, who has been trained up in this kind of
> Conversation, is in danger of every Embroidered Coat that
> comes in her Way. A Pair of fringed Gloves may be her Ruin.
> In a word, Lace and Ribbons, Silver and Gold Galloons, with
> the like glittering Gew-Gaws, are so many Lures to Women of
> weak Minds or low Educations. (No. 15)

Here Addison's ingenious personification of articles of male dress itself in-
carnates women's attention to male "Drapery"; these preternaturally active
coats, gloves, and lace, like the objects in Pope's "moving Toyshop of [the]
Heart,"[54] both embody and satirize women's predilection for turning objects
into people.[55] Moreover, since most women possess "weak Minds" by nature,
and many suffer "low Educations" through parental neglect,[56] the majority
of the female population stands in dire need of corrective guidance.

Men's supposedly natural possession of such attributes as weight, gravity,
and reason ideally suits them for such a role. However, despite our contemporary awareness that such positioning is culturally constructed, as much a
product of nurture as nature, critics have largely ignored the problematics of
men's placement within this arrangement. Men's disciplinary role demands
that they be everything that women are not, and that they employ that difference in an attempt to balance women's propensity for those activities associated with leisure, pleasure, and imagination. Thus while women, as I
have argued throughout, necessarily depend upon men to confer upon them
that badge of femininity earned by their ability to please, men cannot be so
easily delighted, for delight implies approval, and men must improve in order to approve.

In addition, not only must men perform the incessant and often arduous
tasks associated with cultivating the female species, but women's preference
for those men who repudiate the part of reformer rather than enacting it also
presents a constant challenge to masculine authority. In No. 128, Mr. Spectator remarks that "if we observe the Conduct of the fair Sex, we find that
they choose rather to associate themselves with a Person who resembles
them in that light and volatile Humour which is natural to them, than to
such as are qualified to moderate and counter-ballance it." The most popular men, therefore, are those who reflect in themselves the supposedly intrinsic attributes of women: "It has been an old Complaint, That the Coxcomb carries it with them before the Man of Sense. When we see a Fellow
loud and talkative, full of insipid Life and Laughter, we may venture to pro-
nounce him a female Favourite: Noise and Flutter are such Accomplishments as they cannot withstand."[57] Whereas men of sense might demonstrate their worth through such achievements as great learning or noble

heroism, economic success or political renown, the coxcomb manifests only "Accomplishments," a term generally reserved for the genteel endeavors of women. "A Woman's Man," Mr. Spectator informs us, "is very knowing in all that passes from one Family to another, has little pretty Officiousnesses, is not at a Loss what is good for a Cold, and it is not amiss if he has a Bottle of Spirits in his Pocket in case of any sudden Indisposition" (No. 156). He is exemplified, moreover, in the Spectator Club's Will Honeycomb, who "is very ready at that Sort of Discourse with which Men usually entertain Women. He has all his Life dressed very well, and remembers Habits as others do Men. He can smile when one speaks to him, and laughs easily. He knows the History of every Mode, . . . In a Word, all his Conversation and Knowledge has been in the female World" (No. 2).

The belief that women delight in men who mirror them finds an objective correlative in No. 392, a contribution describing "The Transformation of *Fidelio* into a Looking-Glass." Fidelio's reflective qualities render him "'the Confident and Darling of all the Fair'"; he informs us that "'No Ball, no Assembly was attended till I had been consulted.'" Yet while the malleable Ladies' Man succeeds insofar as he continues to feed women's inherent egotism, such achievement is indeed fragile. Fidelio meets an untimely death at the hand of his paramour, the appropriately named Narcissa, who stabs him with a bodkin when, true to his name, he reflects a visage severely altered by smallpox. Fidelio's Ovidian metamorphosis results from the ministrations of the god of love: "'*Cupid*, who always attends the Fair, and pity'd the Fate of so useful a Servant as I was, obtained of the *Destinies*, that my Body should remain Incorruptible, and retain the Qualities my Mind had possess'd. I immediately lost the Figure of Man, and became smooth, polish'd, and bright, and to this Day am the first Favourite of the Ladies.'" Thus while in this essay female desire remains essentially heterosexual, women are seduced by similarity rather than difference, a desire that contrasts, however, with that of those men for whom difference becomes erotically charged. The tale of Fidelio confirms Mr. Spectator's earlier aggrieved statement that "the Passion of an ordinary Woman for a Man, is nothing else but Self-love diverted upon another Object: She would have the Lover a Woman in every thing but the Sex" (No. 128).[58]

And yet, whereas women find attractive those men who mimic rather than modify their "light, fantastical Disposition," an ideology of intrinsic gender difference necessarily characterizes men who emulate women as antithetical to most other men: "The Woman's Man is a Person in his Air and Behaviour quite different from the rest of our Species: His Garb is more loose and negligent, his Manner more soft and indolent; that is to say, in both these Cases there is an apparent Endeavour to appear unconcerned and careless" (No. 156). Such indifference serves to distinguish the Woman's Man from the family man—the man who must take upon his shoulders the "main Burden . . . [of] a constant and assiduous Application to the making a Provision for his Family" (No. 128). Not only does the Ladies' Man share rather than improve women's "empty" hours of leisure,[59] but his unregulated sexual appetites make him constitutionally unsuited for controlling the passionate excesses of women. In "A Few Kind Words for the Fop," Susan Staves reminds us that "Despite common twentieth-century directorial practice, it is important to recognize that there is no necessary connection between foppery and male homosexuality." While Staves's discussion, taken primarily from dramatic literature, remarks the fop figures' "lack of strong sexual appetite," describing them as "asexuals who like to spend their time with the ladies,"[60] periodical literature, by contrast, portrays fops as a significant sexual threat to "Men of Sense." As Mr. Spectator says in his initial description of Will Honeycomb, "where Women are not concerned, he is an honest worthy Man" (No. 2).

Numerous papers present the fundamental incompatibility of these disparate orders of men. No. 151 describes men of fashion as the "most infamous Rogues in Nature, with Relation to Friendship, Love, or Conversation"; the essay dourly maintains that "where-ever this is the chief Character, the Person who wears it is a negligent Friend, Father, and Husband, and intails Poverty on his unhappy Descendants. Mortgages, Diseases, and Settlements are the Legacies a Man of Wit and Pleasure leaves to his Family." No. 479, a disquisition on husbands, observes that "He that sincerely loves his Wife and Family, and studies to improve that Affection in himself, conceives Pleasure from the most indifferent things; while the married Man who has not bid adieu to the Fashions and false Gallantries of the Town, is perplexed with every thing around him." We find the most extended example in a number late in the first *Spectator* series, detailing Will Honeycomb's unexpected marriage to "a plain Country Girl" (No. 530). Here "the gay, the loud, the vain *Will Honeycomb*, who had made Love to every great Fortune that has appeared in Town for above thirty Years together," exchanges the qualities that had made him a consummate Ladies' Man for "the sober Character of the Husband." Will's description, in a letter he sends to the Spectator Club, of the humble woman with whom he has fallen in love—she has no portion, but a great deal of virtue—both relies upon and furthers the conventional opposition between country and town, in which the former is associated with goodness, innocence, and bodily health and the latter with affectation, false privilege, and mercenariness:

> The natural Sweetness and Innocence of her Behaviour, the
> Freshness of her Complection, the unaffected Turn of her
> Shape and Person, shot me through and through every time I
> saw her, and did more Execution on me in Grogram, than the
> greatest Beauty in Town or Court had ever done in Brocade.
> In short, she is such an one as promises me a good Heir to my
> Estate, and if by her means I cannot leave to my Children what
> are falsely called the Gifts of Birth; high Titles and Alliances: I
> hope to convey to them the more real and valuable Gifts of
> Birth; strong Bodies and healthy Constitutions.

Will's reformation consists, in effect, of a multileveled (re)turn to nature.
His bride seduces through her lack of seduction: her flourishing body, like
that of a robust cow or mare, effectively sells itself. The profligate Will
Honeycomb has found his proper niche; and the man who has made love to
all women has finally mated for life. Moreover, marriage transforms his
usual pleasurable business, which had constituted him women's counterpart
and thus a devalued man, into the more profitable enterprise of superiority
in the domestic realm: he resolves that "It shall be my Business hereafter . . .
to act as becomes the Master of a Family." The adjectives with which he describes his new role underline his conversion into an exemplary family man:
"I shall endeavour to live hereafter suitable to a Man in my Station, as a Prudent Head of a Family, a good Husband, a careful Father (when it shall so
happen)."

However, while Will Honeycomb has at last discovered his beneficial
place in the natural order, the coxcomb as a type errs precisely through his
deviation from this norm: "Nature in her whole Drama never drew such a
Part; she has sometimes made a Fool, but a Coxcomb is always of a Man's
own making, by applying his Talents otherwise than Nature designed, who
ever bears an high Resentment for being put out of her Course, and never
fails of taking her Revenge on those that do so" (No. 404). Once again we
see the ways in which nature is ever at the service of culture: here we have
Nature as revenge tragedian. Endowing nature with a vindictive bent confirms, of course, the belief in a rightful employment of nature's gifts. As we
have seen, the attribute of gender functions most frequently and forcefully
to determine proper behavior in all spheres.

On an economic level, the notion of a gendered division of labor depends
first upon separating the home from the workplace and then upon designat-
ing that home as a site of consumption rather than production. The distraught letter that comprises the whole of *Spectator* No. 328 illustrates how
men's exclusive productive role relies momentously upon women's proper

implementation of their domestic duties.[61] The writer, whose possession of a "healthy vigorous Constitution, a plentiful Estate, no inordinate Desires, . . . a very virtuous lovely Woman, who neither wants Wit nor good Nature, and . . . numerous Offspring" should render him "a happy Man," confides to the *Spectator* that he is instead "the most anxious miserable Man on Earth," on the verge of "being ruin'd and undone, by a Sort of Extravagance which of late Years is in a less Degree crept into every fashionable Family." This domestic improvidence, we soon discover, results from the correspondent's wife's misguided application of the "Accomplishments we generally understand by good Breeding and a polite Education." The problem is not that she takes pleasure in singing and dancing, painting or embroidering, among numerous other talents, but that "what is only design'd for the innocent Amusement and Recreation of Life, is become the whole Business and Study of hers." Business and study, the writer implies, belong to the world of men; women, on the other hand, should have accomplishments rather than achievements.

Whereas during this woman's six months in town she spends large amounts of her husband's money in taking lessons with the best masters and having her pictures mounted by the most renowned framers, these expenditures pale in contrast to the damage she does to the family budget during her half year in the country. Her residence there functions as a kind of factory, in which she manufactures items for home use: in addition to being skilled at pickling and preserving, concocting medicinal preparations, and brewing fruit wines, she is, her husband tells us,

> a great Artist at her Needle, [and] 'tis incredible what Sums she expends in Embroidery: For besides what is appropriated to her personal Use, as Mantuas, Petticoats, Stomachers, Handkerchiefs, Purses, Pin-cushions, and Working-Aprons, she keeps four *French* Protestants continually employ'd in making divers Pieces of superfluous Furniture, as Quilts, Toilets, Hangings for Closets, Beds, Window-Curtains, easy Chairs, and Tabourets: *Nor have I any Hopes of ever reclaiming her from this Extravagance, while she obstinately persists in thinking it a notable Piece of good Housewifry, because they are made at Home, and she has had some Share in the Performance.* (my italics)

While this woman's textile output is admittedly excessive, I would nevertheless maintain that the problem lies in the mode rather than the quantity of her production. That is, the husband's plaint highlights the shift from an earlier manifestation of "good Housewifry," in which women did indeed participate in the manufacture of goods for home use, to a system in which such labor becomes inappropriate, even ruinous. In exposing, albeit in exaggerated terms, the dangers incurred when women fail to make the transition from producers to consumers, this letter concurs in constructing a division of labor that burdens men as it constrains women.

Although devastatingly clear about women's rightful duties, Mr. Spectator is equally firm in his supposition that "Every Man has one or more Qualities which may make him useful both to himself and others: Nature never fails of pointing them out" (No. 404). And yet, while the attempt to force character seemingly results in men who are deserving targets of ridicule, as "tasteless and insipid" as "an unwilling Plant, or an untimely Sallad,"[62] I contend that in the garden of masculinity, even those men who conscientiously fulfill their roles as active producers languish under a dual anxiety: they themselves have become conflated with the goods they work so assiduously to provide and, moreover, those possessions are more important to women than are the men themselves. As my earlier discussion of the *Tatler*'s "monstrous" petticoat indicated, men's responsibility for the pruning of women's dress meshed with their own emerging role as primary producers in a capitalist economy. While this role depended, in part, upon men's construction of women as the *raison d'être* for the imperialist enterprise, thus obscuring men's own role in relations of production and consumption, I argued that this process had a powerful and often detrimental effect upon men. Under capitalism, not only do relations of exchange transform the *products of human labor* into commodities, goods detached from the actual processes of production and given an existence independent of their producers, but these relations, I contend, ironically render *men themselves* commodities by ignoring or erasing men's own laborious role in the production process. Fetishized in their role as producers, men become less than human, conflated with—and often judged as lesser than—the goods their money buys.

Two numbers from the *Spectator* disclose men's unmistakable distress about the psychological repercussions of their financial role. No. 252, a letter from a troubled husband, reveals the methods whereby women exploit the masculine vulnerability that derives from men's dependence on women's role as consumers. The intimate nature of the epistolary presentation and the man's distraught state render even more palpable his loss of humanness. Responding to a previous essay (No. 247) satirizing women's rhetorical skills, this correspondent laments the way his own wife has used emotional wiles to manipulate him. While the earlier paper turned to biological causes, speculating that women's "Talent of a ready Utterance" might possibly derive from the "Juices," "Fibres," or "Muscles" of their agile tongues, this letter attributes women's considerable eloquence to "the silent Flattery of their pretty Faces, and the Perswasion which even an insipid Discourse carries with it when flowing from beautiful Lips, to which it would be cruel to deny any thing." This tenderhearted husband goes on to enumerate the uses to which his wife applies these "Springs of Rhetorick," which include tears and fainting fits:

> You must know I am a plain Man and love my Money; yet I have a Spouse who is so great an Orator in this Way, that she draws from me what Sums she pleases. Every Room in my House is furnished with Trophies of her Eloquence, rich Cabinets, Piles of China, Japan Screens, and costly Jarrs; and if you were to come into my great Parlour you would fancy your self in an *India* Warehouse: Besides this, she keeps a Squirrel, and I am doubly taxed to pay for the China he breaks. She is seized with periodical Fitts about the Time of the Subscriptions to a new Opera, and is drowned in Tears after having seen any Woman there in finer Cloaths than her self: These are Arts of Perswasion purely Feminine, and which a Tender Heart cannot resist.

The importuned goods, the pet squirrel, the opera subscription, and the rivalry over dress categorize this woman as a complete "Lady of Fashion." In contrast with the exemplary wife, who describes her husband as "the End of every Care I have; if I dress 'tis for him, if I read a Poem or Play 'tis to qualify my self for a Conversation agreeable to his Taste" (No. 254), the acquisitive spouse portrayed employs her husband as a means alone. Forced continuously to expend rather than husband his resources in the name of domestic peace, this man laments not so much fiscal ruin as emotional abuse.

No. 499, a letter written for the periodical by Will Honeycomb (back in his infamous days), presents such mistreatment in satirical rather than sentimental terms. Will's dream version of the Siege of Hensberg transforms a narrative displaying women's conjugal fidelity into a story revealing such devotion's mercenary underside. In the original tale, the general whose army has surrounded the German city allows its married women to depart taking with them only what they can carry on their backs. These virtuous women convey, of course, their own husbands. Yet in Will's rendition, what women value most is not their spouses but the material goods or leisured pleasures those men have provided: "The first of them had an huge Sack upon her Shoulders, which she set down with great Care: Upon the opening of it, when I expected to have seen her Husband shot out of it, I found it was filled with China Ware." Additional sacks contain a "Gallant," a "Favourite Monkey," a "huge Bale of Cards," a "*Bolonia* Lapdog," and a "Bag of Gold." While other pleasures are indeed present, material goods clearly predominate: Will notes that "All the Place about me was covered with Packs of Ribbands, Brocades, Embroidery, and Ten thousand other Materials, sufficient to have furnish'd a whole street of Toy-shops." One wife, when forced to choose between a "great Bundle of *Flanders-Lace*" and her husband, unfalteringly selects the lace: "finding herself so overloaden that she could not save both of them, she dropp'd the good Man, and brought away the Bundle."[63]

Will's version of the story makes manifest the anxiety both implicit in and assuaged by the original anecdote. While in the initial tale the women's exemplary behavior saved their husbands from certain death, Will's version, in which the men are left behind (and therefore killed) once they have provided the goods, transforms the metaphorical destruction of men's humanness into the literal annihilation of men's lives. Revealingly, the only husband Will espies "among this great Mountain of Baggage" is a "lively Cobler" who had earlier beaten his wife into submission: he "kicked and spurr'd all the while his Wife was carrying him on, and, as it was said, had scarce passed a Day in his Life without giving her the Discipline of the Strap." We should not overlook the serious anxiety that evinces itself in what Will presents allegedly as men's humorous dilemma: either beat your wife into submission or risk being replaced in her affection by material goods.[64] Moreover, taken in conjunction with its analogue, namely, the narratives from the *Tatler* describing the "death" of unproductive men, this tale reveals that men are indeed trapped between Scylla and Charybdis: damned if they don't produce, but equally damned if they do.

In his closing comments upon Will's contribution, Mr. Spectator endeavors to temper its overtly misogynistic tone by informing his readers that Will, like other "Men of Wit and Pleasure of the Town, . . . shews his Parts by Raillery on Marriage." Yet Mr. Spectator's other feeble attempt at mitigation, the statement that in order to abuse women, "the Writer is obliged to have recourse to Dream and Fiction," falls distressingly flat when one recalls the plethora of essays, some the most renowned in the *Tatler*, *Spectator*, and *Guardian* series, that rely on just such dreams and visions. Mr. Spectator's inability to counter the sentiments Will expresses reveals, then, men's fears about the true answer to the question "What does Woman want?" A second letter by Will Honeycomb dealing with the same theme, "those dear confounded Creatures *Women*" (No. 511), effectively restores domestic order by producing the kind of women clearly desired by men. In this subsequent letter, Will relates and elaborates upon two narratives, the first taken from Herodotus's description of the Persians' method of selling all their young unmarried women and the second a story from Le Comte in which a Tartar general "set to Sale" all the women in a conquered Chinese town by placing them in a sack to be purchased "*unsight unseen*" by merchants. In both accounts, women rather than men reassuringly serve as the sex to be assessed and acquired. This time Mr. Spectator has no need to apologize, for Will's claim of having learned "to talk in thy [i.e., the Spectator's] own way" means that he, like his moralizing friend, can educate all men in the process that will render women docile objects to be purchased rather than the unruly subjects who purchase in their own right. By concentrating upon on the admittedly egregious treatment of women entailed by this dynamic, critics have overlooked its potential damage to men.

Designing Women: The Guardian

If my Readers make as good a Use of this Work as I design they should, I hope it will never be imputed to me as a Work that is vain and unprofitable.
—*Guardian* No. 158

Last in Addison and Steele's periodical triumvirate, their *Guardian* (1713) presents, in its narrator Nestor Ironside, a figure who upholds the moral and ancestral lineage of his illustrious forebears. In No. 98, Ironside comments upon his attempt to "fill the Place" of his "two renowned Kinsmen and Predecessors": "*Isaac Bickerstaff* of famous Memory" and "a Gentleman of the same Family, very memorable for the Shortness of his Face and of his Speeches," that is, the Spectator. He notes, moreover, with "some secret Pride," that "this way of Writing diurnal Papers has not succeeded for any space of Time in the Hands of any Persons who are not of our Line."[65] Ironside's concern in demonstrating relationship should not surprise us, for he founds his personal claim to moral authority, and thus the periodical's general conceit, upon the expertise garnered from many years as faithful guardian to multiple generations and both sexes of the Lizard family. With the exception of his years at Oxford, where he met the family patriarch, Sir Ambrose, who began the lengthy alliance by appointing him guardian to his young son, Ironside's experience has transpired almost exclusively within the environment of the Lizard family and their Northamptonshire estate. Moreover, Ironside's account of their history soon discloses that they have functioned for the last sixteen years as a kind of matriarchy, run not by Sir Marmaduke, Ironside's original ward, but by his widow the Lady Aspasia, whose nine children form Ironside's current charge at the time he writes the *Guardian* papers (No. 2).

The *Guardian*'s discourses take place, then, at quite a reach from Bicker-staff's London lucubrations; in addition to the contrast between country and city, we find in each periodical a very different arrangement of public and private. Whereas the *Tatler*'s numerous departments, as I described earlier, were organized around the London coffee-houses that were designated as public spaces but were available only to men, Ironside announces in the *Guardian*'s second number that "I am to let the Reader know, that his chief Entertainment will arise from what passes at the Tea Table of my Lady *Lizard*." Although in this period both the drinking of tea and the gossip and scandal often assumed to accompany it were activities customarily associated with women,[66] Ironside manages to temper any possible allegations of effeminacy by constituting himself a connoisseur of, rather than a participant in, women's pleasures.[67] While Ironside's comfortable presence within a predominantly female and thus traditionally devalued milieu might at first glance seem to distinguish him from Addison and Steele's more male-centered eidolons, their common blood reveals itself in his ability to transform a limited, personal position into one that will seemingly benefit the nation at large. Not only does he inform us that a "Series of History of Common Life" culled from his experiences with the generations of Lizards will be "as useful as the Relations of the more pompous Passages in the Lives of Princes and Statesmen," but he also claims that the situation surrounding Lady Aspasia herself warrants the attention of a broad range of readers: "As there is no Circumstance in Human Life, which may not directly or indirectly concern a Woman thus related, there will be abundant Matter offer it self from Passages in this Family, to supply my Readers with diverting, and perhaps useful Notices for their Conduct in all the Incidents of Human Life" (No. 2).

At first glance, the *Guardian*'s forthright acknowledgment of the domestic sphere's centrality to "Human Life" appears a welcome change from the patriarchal sentiments espoused, albeit with seeming deference, in the *Tatler* and *Spectator*. And yet, a closer look reveals unmistakable traces of masculine dominance. Women's household existence is indeed central to the *Guardian*'s rubric, yet becomes so only when narrated by a man. As "a Woman thus related," Lady Aspasia relies upon her association to husband and children, but she is also "related," placed into discourse, by the man who chronicles her history. Ironside's curatorial role operates equally powerfully in relation to her daughters, who form the more "delicate part of [his] Guardianship" (No. 5): "the Female Part of a Family is the more constant and immediate Object of Care and Protection, and the more liable to Misfortune or Dishonour, as being in themselves more sensible of the former, and from Custom and Opinion for less Offences more exposed to the latter." Accordingly, the periodical's narrative situation manifests, perhaps more distinctly than in any other publication by Addison and Steele, an underlying ideology in which women's inherent vulnerability demands the assiduous patronage of men. Both Nestor Ironside's private role as steward to the Lizard family and his civic persona as custodian of the British nation act in tandem to publicize men's need to guide and govern their wives and children. Moreover, the coupling of men's management of their families with men's regulation of society at large constitutes guardianship as a specifically masculine role, for women's domestic supervision, no matter how competently performed, can never translate into action within the public sphere.

If guardianship is a gendered phenomenon, in the case of Ironside it also becomes a remunerative source of material for publication. The "Cares, Passions, Interests and Diversions" of the Lizard family described in No. 2 provide ample grist for the Guardian's mill; virtue itself becomes a commodity when Ironside trades on the unsullied excellence of the "intelligent and discreet Lady *Lizard*" as a means of selling his papers to the public. Not only does he bank upon the moral wares furnished by the worthy example of the Lizard family, but he also accumulates the interest accrued through his connection to them. As we shall see, the Guardian trades on his own virtue when dealing with the thorny issue of male and female sexuality. Like his predecessors, Ironside finds in women's dress an abundant source of critique. Although the "monstrous Petticoat" still manages to project itself into the *Guardian's* pages,[68] the periodical's numerous dissertations upon that important garment known as the "tucker" concern themselves more urgently with the implications of women's abridging, rather than augmenting, articles of clothing.

While Ironside's discussion of fashionable excesses reiterates many of the *Tatler's* and *Spectator's* most prevalent themes, including women's inborn love of trifles and men's vulnerability to women's material desires, the tone in which he voices these reproaches differs, falling somewhere between the shrill Bickerstaffian plaint and the Spectator's more modulated utterance. Since he purports to use his close involvement with the Lizard family as the basis for his general commentary, Ironside's pronouncements conjoin the personal experience professed by Isaac Bickerstaff with the detached rationality attributed to spectatorship. In his early discussion of the Lizard women, he acknowledges his ability to have it both ways when he states that "if it were possible for a Man, who has never entered into the State of Marriage, to know the Instincts of a kind Father to an Honourable and Numerous House, I may say I have done it. I do not know but my Regards, in some Considerations, have been more useful than those of a Father; and as I wanted all that Tenderness, which is the Byass of Inclination in Men towards their own Offspring, I have had a greater Command of Reason when I was to judge of what concerned my Wards" (No. 5). Ironside thus surpasses Mr. Spectator's claim to being "very well versed in the *Theory* of an Husband, or a Father" (No. 1, my emphasis) by espousing an emotional affinity that is at the same time impartial.

His study of women's dress similarly combines personal and abstract considerations. While taking a fervent interest in the minute particulars of his female wards' dress—"I make it my Business," he tells us, "when my Lady *Lizard*'s youngest Daughter, Miss *Molly*, is making Cloaths, to consider her from Head to Foot"—he founds his concern upon general beliefs in the virtue or vice of specific modes, for he continues: "[I] cannot be easie when there is any doubt lies upon me concerning the Colour of a Knot, or any other part of her Head-dress, which by its Darkness or Liveliness might too much allay or brighten her Complexion. There is something loose in looking as well as you possibly can; but it is also a Vice not to take Care how you look" (No. 10). Later in the same number, his position as supervisor of Miss Molly translates into the more general role of guardian to all women when he proposes that he shall give "the Female World" his "Opinion at large by way of Comment upon a new Suit of the *Sparkler*'s [his nickname for Miss Molly], which is to come home next Week. I design it as a Model for the Ladies; she and I have had three private Meetings about it."

Ironside's "design" emerges in the movement from "private Meetings" with his young ward into a prevailing and universal "Model for the Ladies." His less than modest proposal relies upon and thus develops his unquestioned right to translate private into public, and thereby to legislate the appearance of all women. Moreover, he provides a pattern for those men whose position as husbands and fathers demands such an arrangement of both women and themselves. In a later number, Ironside informs his readers once again that it is his "Design to keep a watchful Eye over every Part of the Female Sex, and to regulate them from Head to Foot" (No. 109). While the Guardian and his correspondents scrutinize a number of female zones, one area in particular seems to receive the most direct and extensive notice in the periodical's pages. *Guardian* No. 100 inaugurates Addison's series of writings about the tucker,[69] a discussion that reveals, of course, what lies beneath it, namely, women's breasts:

> There is a certain Female Ornament by some called a Tucker,
> and by others the Neck-piece, being a slip of fine Linnen or
> Muslin that used to run in a small kind of ruffle round the up-
> permost Verge of the Womens Stays, and by that means cov-

ered a great part of the Shoulders and Bosom. Having thus given a Definition, or rather Description of the Tucker, I must take Notice, that our Ladies have of late thrown aside this Fig-Leaf, and exposed in its Primitive Nakedness that gentle Swelling of the Breast which it was used to conceal. What their Design by it is they themselves best know.

Ironside quickly responds to his own disingenuous question by professing an immunity to the proffered temptations. Reversing the Pygmalion myth, he asserts that "For my own Part, their Necks, as they call them, are no more than *Busts* of Alabaster in my Eye." His statement places women's breasts at a twofold remove, first semantically, through use of the euphemistic "Neck," and then aesthetically, by recourse to the even greater displacement made possible by both sculpture—the *"Busts* of Alabaster"—and poetry: "I can look upon *'The yielding Marble of a snowy Breast,'*" he continues, "with as much Coldness as this Line of Mr. *Waller* represents in the Object it self."

Proceeding in the same number, Ironside informs his audience that this insensibility to female charms distinguishes him in important ways from the rest of the male species: "But my fair Readers ought to consider, that all their Beholders are not *Nestors*. Every Man is not sufficiently qualified with Age and Philosophy to be an indifferent Spectator of such Allurements." Thus the very characteristics that equip him for guardianship exempt him from the lustful behavior he attributes to normative masculinity: "The Eyes of young Men are curious and penetrating, their Imaginations of a roving Nature, and their Passions under no Discipline or Restraint." One might assume that it is not only men's eyes that are wont to penetrate. Since penetration in the form of acumen is a quality deemed necessary to ideal masculinity, however, Ironside must negotiate the fine line between the roving eye of the rake and the discerning eye of the connoisseur.

Ironside's seemingly candid disapproval of women's "throwing off" their tuckers necessarily faces the same dilemma as any censure of so-called vice: how does one denounce something without simultaneously bringing into sharper view that which one condemns? By setting up "Every Man" as "not Nestor," and thus at the mercy of importunate desires, Ironside fixes his own virtuous self-control as the characteristic that can allow for readerly titillation. In other words, the Guardian's seemingly disinterested gaze serves as the polarized lens through which other, more passionate men might look into the sun without sustaining ocular damage. Not only does Ironside trade on his virtue to sell his male readers the delights of women's breasts in the plain brown wrapper of his own chaste example, but his continence also enables him to peddle a particular ideology of masculinity whereby men's possession of women mediates men's problematic sexual desire.[70] Thus the Guardian's professed concern about tuckerless *women's* inability to defend themselves against the "sawcy familiar Glances" of "every impudent staring Fellow" betrays an even greater anxiety about *men's* behavior in relation to such women. His response to the "trouble[d]" observation "that the Leaders in this Fashion were most of them married Women" baldly, and to our eyes disturbingly, reveals his sense of married women's proper deportment: "What their Design can be in making themselves bare I cannot possibly imagine. No Body exposes Wares that are appropriated."

Accordingly, those female "charms" covered by the tucker should be exposed only insofar as they allow women to sell themselves in the marriage market. Also in No. 100, Ironside gives an example of one man's fitting utilization of female "Allurements" in the story of the Spartan legislator Lycurgus. The passage itself, like the costume it describes, combines a tempting visual image with the more restrained view of women as sexual property:

> As that great Law-giver knew that the Wealth and Strength of a Republick consisted in the Multitude of Citizens, he did all he could to encourage Marriage: In order to it he prescribed a certain loose Dress for the *Spartan* Maids, in which there were several Artificial Rents and Openings, that upon their putting themselves in Motion discovered several Limbs of the Body to the Beholders. Such were the Baits and Temptations made use of, by that wise Law-giver, to incline the young Men of his Age to Marriage. But when the Maid was once sped she was not suffered to tantalise the Male Part of the Commonwealth. Her Garments were closed up, and stitched together with the greatest Care imaginable. The Shape of her Limbs and Complexion of her Body had gained their Ends, and were ever after to be concealed from the Notice of the Publick.

Here the carefully crafted "Rents and Openings" in the Spartan virgins' garments function as a metaphor for those openings that no man but a husband should have access to. The stitching together of those same garments upon marriage (in a process I find troublingly reminiscent of the sewing up of women's labia that accompanies genital mutilation) symbolizes both the closing up of those bodies to all men but the husband and the closing off of women's access to the public realm. "Public" women were of course prostitutes; a woman's ownership by one man should preclude her availability to all others. As the final number in the tucker series, to which I will turn shortly, demonstrates, the private property that is a married woman ought to be available only to the penetrating gaze of her husband, just as he must retain sole access to the more literal form of penetration considered his conjugal right.

An analysis of Ironside's description of the Tucker as "the *Decus et Tutamen*, the Ornament and Defence of the Female Neck" (No. 109) starkly divulges women's position as commodity, for "Decus et Tutamen" was the motto "milled on the edges of five-guinea pieces, crowns, and halfcrowns from the Restoration till the nineteenth century, signifying an 'ornament and a safeguard' against clipping."[71] The somewhat contradictory meanings implied by the two nouns, one indicating display and the other protection, manifest the problematic duality of men's sexuality in relation both to women themselves and to the lustful appetites of other men. That is, the woman whose attributes must at first be visible enough to attract the gaze and incite the desire of a prospective husband must not be permitted to exercise those charms upon other men. By associating women with coins, Ironside's "decus et tutamen" metaphor seems to mitigate the implied contradiction by constituting women's bodies as currency to be possessed, and thus controlled, by men. Married women's status as men's property remains problematic, however, for in Britain as opposed to ancient Sparta, men seem less able to control their women's self-display. A disconsolate letter from an aggrieved husband who writes that "Instead of being acquainted with her [his Wife's] Person more than other Men, I have now the least share of it" (No. 134), reveals the consequences of women's taking their position as alluring objects a little too seriously once they have become wives and therefore private property.

As a "*Turkey* Merchant," the author of this letter is familiar with the process of buying and selling; indeed he recognizes that women possess a market value comparable to that of the goods in which he trades. Thus he criticizes the *Guardian*'s method of reform, which relies on an appeal to its readers' morality, and proposes instead a more pragmatic way of handling the problem: "Now, Sir, if I may presume to say so, you have been in the wrong to think of reforming this Fashion, by showing the Immodesty of it. If you expect to make Female Proselytes, you must convince 'em, that, if they wou'd get Husbands, they must not show All before Marriage. I am sure, had my Wife been dressed before I married her as she is at present, she would have satisfied a good half of my Curiosity." The theatrical metaphor he subsequently employs reveals his awareness of the importance of visual display in inciting male desire: "Many a Man has been hindered from laying out his Mony on a Show, by seeing the principal Figures of it hung out before the Door."

The merchant's prior sojourn in the Middle East allows him to compare Turkish habits, in which "the Women show nothing but their Eyes," to his own country's practice: "Upon my return to *England* I was almost out of Countenance to see my pretty Countrywomen laying open their Charms with so much Liberality, tho' at that time many of them were concealed under the modest Shade of the Tucker." Moreover, his contact with the ostensibly exotic women and customs of the east creates the frame within which he can discuss English women's "foreign" habits. In spite of their visible differences—Turkish women are muffled, while English women go bare—the merchant's narrative ironically aligns his European wife, "a very fine Woman, who always goes in the Extremity of the Fashion," with the "otherness" associated with the Orient. This woman, then, refuses to acquiesce to what the merchant believes should be British conjugal norms. He tells Ironside that while he was at first "pleased to think, as every married Man must be, that I should make daily Discoveries in the dear Creature, which were unknown to the rest of the World," the latest fashion, which calls for the abbreviation if not downright removal of the chastening tucker, has made her charms available to the observation of all men: "But since this new airy Fashion is come up, every one's Eye is as familiar with her as mine; for I can positively affirm, that her Neck is grown eight Inches within these three Years."

His attempt to view the situation with humor cannot, however, entirely allay his anxiety, for since he is no longer the sole spectator of his wife's body, he fears what will happen when other men respond as he did when first exposed to her numerous beauties. According to the most recent mode, not only have corsets come down but skirts have also gone up, creating another source of alarm: "And what makes me tremble when I think of it, that pretty Foot and Ankle are now exposed to the sight of the whole World, which made my very Heart dance within me when I first found myself their Proprietor." His apprehensions are given concrete form by the "parcel of Rascally young Fellows in the Neighbourhood" who, since "in all appearance the Curtain is still Rising, . . . are in hopes to be presented with some new Scene every Day." In this representation, the merchant's wife becomes a kind of striptease artist whose performance functions as a carnivalesque spectacle, perversely reversing what its author perceives to be the proper order of domestic sexual relations: "When she is at home she is continually muffled up, and concealed in Mobbs, Morning-Gowns, and Handkerchers; but strips every Afternoon to appear in Publick."[72]

Yet precisely because women fail to monitor themselves, it becomes men's sacred duty to regulate them. Thus the Turkey merchant's irritated plaint, while seeming to be the narrative of a man who has lost control, operates rather as an example *a contrario*, reconfirming the strict code of conjugal chastity broken by the merchant's wife. His letter, then, acts as the symptom of a larger problem that runs through each of the three publications we have been examining. In its acknowledged inadequacy, the missive avows all too clearly the necessity for masculine supervision, a process that in this particular text lies veiled beneath the supposedly more gentle rubric of guardianship. The letter's opening paragraph exposes, however, the ways in which Ironside's Guardian is merely a later incarnation of Bickerstaff's Censor. The merchant tells "Good Mr. *Ironside*" that the Lion, the overtly masculine symbol of his periodical,[73] has "grown a kind of Bull-beggar among the Women where I live. When my Wife comes home late from Cards, or commits any other Enormity, I whisper in her Ear, partly betwixt Jest and Earnest, that *I will tell the Lion of her*." As a "Bull-beggar," "something to frighten people, especially children,"[74] the beast seems to serve as a means of parental admonition, but the merchant's epistolary appeal reveals an additional function for the lion's roar. Ironside, like the Night-Walker before him, reforms through public exposure; to be told of, placed into narrative, can amount to a powerful form of chastisement. Here the Turkey merchant, himself a careful consumer, trades upon the discursive virtues of guardianship as a way to restore his defunct power and, in the process, to espouse the benefits of such control for all men.

8 *Multiplying Affinities: Economic Interests and Familial Passions*

Next to that natural *self-love*, or care of his own preservation, which every one necessarily has in the first place for himself; there is in all men a certain natural affection for their children and posterity, who have a dependence upon them; and for their near relations and friends, who have an intimacy with them. And because the nature of man is such, that they cannot live comfortably in independent families, without still further society and commerce with each other; therefore they naturally desire to increase their dependencies, by multiplying affinities, and to enlarge their friendships, by mutual good offices, and to establish societies, by a communication of arts and labour: till by degrees the affection of single persons, becomes a friendship of families; and this enlarges itself to society of towns and cities and nations; and terminates in the agreeing community of all mankind.
—Samuel Clarke, "A Discourse on Natural Religion" (1706)

From Rae Blanchard in 1929 to Kathryn Shevelow in 1989,[1] critics have examined the ways in which Addison and Steele's periodical publications, in particular the *Tatler* and *Spectator*, acted to define and influence their female audience in the process of constructing a new ideology of domestic femininity: "Through the work of their authoritative yet benign male personae, these early essay periodicals established a definition of feminine nature, rewarded the behavior that adhered to this definition and punished the behavior that did not." In particular, these texts "created a situation in which women readers were cast into these roles of daughters and wives in the act of reading the periodicals 'properly.'"[2] What, however, was the comparable effect on male readership? In Chapter 5 I argued that women's new domestic position necessitated the development of particular attitudes and forms of behavior on the part of men, who were responsible for keeping their wives and daughters chaste and obedient. By learning to emulate the position of patriarchal authority enacted through the *Tatler*'s exemplary narratives, men trained themselves to be virtuous husbands and fathers. In Chapter 6 I analyzed the ways in which an ideology of gender difference supported the *Spectator*'s representations of neutral relations among all men, as women's exclusion from the public realm helped to shape men's social roles as well as their family life. In this chapter I contend that for the developing middle classes of the early eighteenth century, economic man is necessarily domestic man, as the family serves to demand as well as to justify men's participation in the economic sphere.

The idea of commerce presents a way to explore the intersections of economic and social, public and private. In use only since the sixteenth century (the earlier term was "merchandise"), "commerce" can mean the exchange of goods or products, the act of buying and selling—in short, trading. But commerce also denotes the exchange of letters and ideas, or even more broadly, communication in general, exemplified in the expression "to be of good commerce"—to be agreeable in intercourse, pleasant to meet (*OED*). The very breadth of the term reminds us that the economic exchange of both goods and services is necessarily a social transaction, such that commerce becomes a way to define, or redefine, what it is to be a man. The *Tatler*'s representations of commercial man (and, more explicitly, those of the *Spectator*) can thus become a way to rethink the separation of gender and class. I agree with the historians Leonore Davidoff and Catherine Hall when they argue that "gender and class operate together, that consciousness of class always takes a gendered form." By dismantling traditional separations of public and private, their study demonstrates how "middle-class men who sought to be 'someone,' to count as individuals because of their wealth, their power to command or their capacity to influence people, were, in fact, embedded in networks of familial and female support which underpinned their rise to public prominence."[3] Beginning in the late seventeenth century, England's mercantile expansion, the development of London as a center of international commerce, and the concomitant "birth of a consumer society"[4] contributed toward constituting trade, traders, and trading as essential components of contemporary discourse as well as debate. While the development of a coherent and solidified middle-class identity may have been a later phenomenon, writers of the late seventeenth and early eighteenth centuries were certainly concerned with describing, and often promoting, behaviors and values for both men and women that would later be termed "middle class."

The process of tracing these shifts in notions of value and virtue is extremely problematic, for these changes were simultaneous rather than sequential, the categories themselves not unified and discrete but contradictory and fluid. In this period, merchants and professional men were often recruited from the ranks of the gentry; successful younger sons could often do better financially than elder brothers.[5] What needs to be emphasized are the tensions among two different embodiments of exemplary masculinity: the gentleman of landed property, who could "claim the public virtue of disinterestedness"[6] and the "gentleman trader," who reconfigures aristocratic benevolence and generosity in new form. As texts written by men who span both worlds, the *Tatler* and particularly the *Spectator* can be read as barometers of the dialectical process of class consolidation. In the *Spectator*, the denial of Whig economic and political interests makes possible the triumph of those interests. The *Spectator* responded to the period's all-important question of how to make commercial man virtuous man by developing a new ideology of commercial relations articulated in family terms, and, correspondingly, a new ideology of familial relations couched in economic language. The process of "multiplying affinities" described by Samuel Clarke in the epigraph extends a private form of "natural affection" for self and family into a public network of collectively advantageous economic relationships: "the agreeing community of all mankind."

Whereas the *Tatler*'s guiding familial dynamic manifests itself in the relationship between fathers and daughters, developing into that between husbands and wives, I contend that in the *Spectator* another relationship dominates—the one between fathers and sons. This homosocial bond parallels, even epitomizes, the masculine consolidation, toleration, and nonpartisan spirit exemplified by the Spectator Club. The essentiality of gender difference disseminated by the *Tatler* and maintained throughout the *Spectator* constitutes the father-daughter, husband-wife relationship as one of permanent inequality, because it is based upon the fixed characteristic of sex. In the relationship between father and son, however, the imbalance is only temporary, structured by disparities in age and experience. In *The Sexual Contract*, Carole Pateman argues that both Locke and Rousseau "agreed that the natural duty of parents to care for their children gave them rightful authority, but, they argued against Filmer, paternal power was temporary." As Pateman notes, however, for Locke "children" become "sons": "Once out of their nonage, at the age of maturity, sons become as free as their fathers and, like them, must agree to be governed."[7] She cites Locke's *Second Treatise* for emphasis: "We are *born Free*, as we are born Rational; . . . Age that brings one, brings with it the other too. And thus we see how *natural Freedom and Subjection to Parents* may consist together, and are both founded on the same Principle. A *Child* is *Free* by his Father's Title, by his Father's Understanding, which is to govern him, till he hath it of his own."[8]

The ability to regard the father-son relationship as only temporarily unequal gains increasing importance in the early eighteenth century, as England's shift from a rural, landed economy toward a commercial, trade-based system allowed for representations of new, noncompetitive relations between fathers and sons, as well as often between the oldest son and his male siblings. While Mr. Spectator's "Ambition to make the Word *Wife* the most agreeable and delightful Name in Nature" (No. 490) seems to typify the periodical's approbation of the marital relationship, the text's narratives, as I will demonstrate, consistently delineate the ideal form of human relationship not by husbands and wives but by fathers and sons. Trade transforms the original but temporary inequality of the father and son into a "partnership" between brothers, thereby illustrating the move, described by Pateman, from paternal or traditional patriarchy to fraternal patriarchy. To recast Freud's famous anthropological narrative, the brothers no longer need to kill the father, they just go into business with him.[9]

The *Spectator* provides a plethora of examples of such male bonding. We witness relationships of collaboration rather than competition on both structural and narrative levels. Structural examples range from the factual collaboration of Addison and Steele to the fictional joint authorship of the Spectator Club; textual examples include numerous stories of cooperation among friends and family members. Although social historians and literary critics usually focus on bonds between husbands and wives or on the general relations of parents to children, I believe that a consideration of male relations is equally important to an understanding of the ideology of the family. Building upon the general discussion of the merchant found in Chapter 4, the first section of this chapter investigates the contrasts within the *Tatler*'s and the *Spectator*'s numerous representations of commercial relations. Next I explore the connections between early eighteenth-century economic beliefs and conceptions of family relations, in order to explicate the contradictory ways in which the family serves to integrate passions and interests. The chapter culminates in an analysis of the masculinity best reflected in the partnership between fathers and sons. This discourse, begun in the *Tatler* and realized more fully in the *Spectator*, educated its male readers into their familial roles, which became simultaneously the expression of a class position.

The Trader as Gentleman

> Trade is so far here from being inconsistent with a gentle-
> man, that, in short, trade in England makes gentlemen, and
> has peopled this nation with gentlemen.
> —Daniel Defoe, *The Complete English Tradesman* (1726)

The *Tatler* confounded the assumption that only a man of high birth could be a gentleman by severing the link between status and behavior, thus setting the stage for the portrayal of the trader as gentleman. In the later *Spectator*, however, we find a more complex depiction of the manipulations involved in this representation. As we observed in Chapter 6, the *Spectator* serves as the *locus classicus* for the traditional gentlemanly virtues espoused by and in spectatorship, in particular the economic disinterest and political neutrality epitomized by its eidolon, Mr. Spectator. On the other hand, through its numerous portrayals of tradesmen who are defined precisely by their ability to meet private needs while enhancing the public good, the periodical simultaneously undermines the position that only disinterested men can be virtuous, once again confounding the very ideology of separate spheres it seeks to establish. Moreover, the careful and industrious methods demanded by commercial activity developed precisely the capacities for thrift, self-control, and discipline that also enabled a man to prosper in the domestic sphere by allowing him to channel his desires properly. Within the context of the family, judicious expenditure of labor provided the material basis for a useful and moral life, culminating in both tangible and spiritual goods, while the monogamous expenditure of sperm resulted in the legitimate offspring to inherit such goods and thus continue the family enterprise.

Whereas the *Tatler* discusses the question of whether a trader may also be a gentleman, the *Spectator* enacts the debate by personifying the tradesman in the form of club member Sir Andrew Freeport, for whom, incidentally, Freeport, Maine, home of the trading firm of L. L. Bean, is named. Although the club's inclusion of other, more traditional types of male virtue, as embodied in the country squire, the ladies' man, or the soldier, might seem to accentuate our sense of the merchant's difference, the *Spectator* creates a new ideology of male desirability both by distinguishing the trader from his predecessors and by incorporating into his representation some of the characteristics of these earlier, and often more aristocratic, models of manliness. The *Spectator*'s reconfiguration of the trader as gentleman thus meant successfully appropriating qualities previously assigned solely to the owner of property.[10] The diversity of roles presented within the Spectator Club supplies—paradoxically, it might seem—a forum in which one specific position, that of the benevolent and successful trader, emerges as preeminent. The trader's prominence is made possible in part by the characteristic neutrality of the narrative presence: through the supposedly transparent spectacles proffered by Mr. Spectator, we are meant to see an image of Sir Andrew that may have some "Blots," but is nonetheless superior. Less concerned with the issue of neutrality and the problem of representing diversity, the *Tatler*'s narrator, by contrast, is proud of his worldly status and the partiality it provides him. Although the *Tatler* presents trade as one of many professions that benefit society as a whole, its merits are not emphasized in and of themselves.

The two periodicals exhibit three increments in the gradual elevation of the trader. The first stage, represented by the *Tatler*'s story of a trader by the name of "*Tom Trueman*" (No. 213), describes a "Hero of Domestick Life" whose standing as an example of "Heroick Love in the City" derives, surprisingly, from his ability to transcend his mercantile position. Trueman wins his woman, and his role as gentleman, by denying characteristics associated with commerce. His story begins conventionally: while a young apprentice, Trueman falls in love with his master's daughter. The family business, however, is failing, due, the young man suspects, "to the ill Management of a Factor, in whom his Master had an entire Confidence." To remedy the situation, our hero leaves his beloved to go on a quest, and spends the remaining years of his tenure with a "Foreign Correspondent" in order to become "acquainted with all that concerned his Master." He learns his lessons so well that he is able to save his master the terrific sum of "Ten Thousand Pounds." Soon afterward, Trueman inherits "a considerable Estate" from an uncle; he then returns to England and requests his sweetheart of her father. Along with his daughter, the grateful merchant offers Trueman the money he had saved him, "with the further Proposal of resigning to him all his Business." Trueman refuses both, however, and retires "into the Country with his Bride, contented with his own Fortune, though perfectly skill'd in all the Methods of improving it." In this tale, Trueman must eschew the practice of trade in order to claim the position of gentleman.[11]

Rather than advocating complete renunciation of commerce in favor of an assumed gentility, Bickerstaff's account of the renowned tradesmen Paolo and Avaro (*Tatler* No. 25) presents a transitional case. This narrative portrays both men as actively employed in business, yet the exemplary man demonstrates characteristics associated with the country squire or aristocratic lord in addition to those qualities necessary to the successful merchant. In order to help a friend determine with whom to apprentice his son, Bickerstaff visits these "two eminent Men in the City," noting that "not only the Fortune of the Youth, but his Virtue also, depended upon this Choice." While Paolo and Avaro are "equally wealthy," they deviate in the "Use and Application of their Riches." Bickerstaff interprets that difference in terms of its moral value and not simply its remunerativeness, basing his evaluation less upon each man's specific business practices than upon his general manner of living.

Paolo offers the best of both worlds, for his "Habitation . . . has at once the Air of a Nobleman and a Merchant." Paolo's domestic setting manifests his qualities of "Benevolence and Integrity" as reflected in his servants, who display "Affection to their Master, and Satisfaction in themselves,"[12] as well as in his table, which "is the Image of Plenty and Generosity, supported by Justice and Frugality." While Paolo combines the bountiful display of the lord with the careful economy of the businessman, the narrative carefully distinguishes his brand of generosity from aristocratic excess, because it is founded upon prudence. Avaro, as his name implies, illustrates only the most negative aspects of the merchant stereotype. He has only one servant, whose "careful Countenance" complements the spacious but barren "great House" and the "suspicious Aspect" of its Master.

Although the boy's father is "ravish'd" by the parsimonious habits of Avaro, Bickerstaff soon sets him straight: "This *Paolo* (said I) grows wealthy by being a common Good; *Avaro*, by being a general Evil: *Paolo* has the Art, *Avaro* the Craft of Trade." Steele's language highlights the way in which Paolo transforms craft—associated with the "mechanic" or laboring classes—into the genteel discipline of art. Paolo's possession of the art of trade, his generosity and *noblesse oblige*, enable him to mingle private success with public benefit: "When *Paolo* gains, all Men he deals with are the better." In the *Tatler*'s sketch of Paolo we find foreshadowed the commercial munificence that becomes central to the *Spectator*'s representations of tradesmen. In this third stage, instantiated in the Spectator Club's wealthy overseas merchant, Sir Andrew Freeport, the trader supersedes the gentleman in terms of his value to the nation at large.

Not only do the *Spectator*'s narratives distinguish between tradesmen and gentry, but they also single out trade from among other occupations. In No. 21, Mr. Spectator laments the fact that "the three great Professions of Divinity, Law and Physick" are "over-burdened with Practitioners, and filled with Multitudes of Ingenious Gentlemen that starve one another." In contrast, a "well-regulated Commerce . . . flourishes by Multitudes, and gives Employment to all its Professors." The possibilities of a "trading Nation" are so great that "there are very few in it so dull and heavy" that they cannot prosper. Unsuccessful children, then, reflect not upon the deficits of trade, but upon the shortsightedness of those parents who choose their sons' occupations with regard to "their own Inclinations" instead of "the Genius and

Abilities of their Children." As a moving instance of this deplorable situation, Addison deploys the story of Will Wimble, a character Mr. Spectator meets during his prolonged visit to Sir Roger's country home (No. 108). The "younger Brother to a Baronet," the middle-aged Will has been "bred to no Business and born to no Estate." He spends his time supervising his brother's game and endearing himself to the neighboring gentry through small offices and smaller gifts. Will's extreme good nature and obvious care for others prompts the Spectator's compassionate concern that "so good an Heart and such busy Hands were wholly employed in Trifles; that so much Humanity should be so little beneficial to others, and so much Industry so little advantageous to himself." He wonders what good Will's "useful tho' ordinary Qualifications" might have done "to his Country or himself" if otherwise employed, and blames the situation, once again, upon those "great Famil[ies]" who would rather see their younger sons "starve like Gentlemen, than thrive in a Trade or Profession that is beneath their Quality."

Will Wimble seems in no danger of physical diminishment, at least while he enjoys such proficiency at fishing and trapping. Rather, his lack of a productive occupation attenuates his ability to enact the role of virtuous citizen. Mr. Spectator clearly singles out trade as the most likely route to success: "It is the Happiness of a trading Nation, like ours, that the younger Sons, tho' uncapable of any liberal Art or Profession, may be placed in such a Way of Life, as may perhaps enable them to vie with the best of their Family."[13] He goes on to speculate that "It is not improbable but *Will.* was formerly tried at Divinity, Law, or Physick; and that finding his Genius did not lie that Way, his Parents gave him up at length to his own Inventions: But certainly, however improper he might have been for Studies of a higher Nature, he was perfectly well turned for the Occupations of Trade and Commerce." Thus in an essay devoted to "The Art of Growing Rich" (No. 283), Mr. Spectator writes, "I regard Trade not only as highly advantageous to the Commonwealth in general; but as the most natural and likely Method of making a Man's Fortune; having observed, since my being a Spectator in the World, greater Estates got about *Change*, than at *Whitehall* or *St. James*'s." Wealth is available to "every Man of good Common Sense" if he practices "Thrift," "Diligence," and "Method in Business," all of which are "attainable by Persons of the meanest Capacities." These essays figure commercial largesse by its accessibility to anyone, regardless of status, education, or even intelligence; all it takes is the proper application of "method" and one can "most certainly be Rich."[14]

Spectator No. 346 uses a quotation from Cicero to contrast aristocratic display with the "constant Benignity in Commerce" available to the trader.

For unlike other men, the mercantile man can arrive at *"that highest Fruit of Wealth, to be liberal without the least Expence of a Man's own Fortune."* This point recalls Defoe's famous metaphor: *"an estate's a pond, but a trade's a spring, . . . an inexhausted current, which not only fills the pond, and keeps it full, but is continually running over, and fills all the lower ponds and places about it."*[15] The *Spectator*'s portrait of Sir Andrew Freeport personifies the belief that mercantile endeavor benefits not only the members of the British nation, but also the world at large.[16] When Mr. Spectator initially introduces the Spectator Club to his readers, he places the city merchant third in "Consideration" behind the country squire Sir Roger de Coverly and the unnamed Templar (No. 2). Yet by No. 549, six issues from the first series' end, Sir Andrew and Mr. Spectator are the club's "sole remaining Members." The merchant's longevity testifies to his eminence; although in that number Mr. Spectator prints a letter from Sir Andrew describing the merchant's proposed retirement, it is, I think, no accident that Sir Andrew is the last to go. Throughout the *Spectator*'s many numbers, it becomes increasingly clear that the values espoused and enacted by Sir Andrew are precisely those virtues that will enable the middle classes to prosper: industry, method, and the judicious application of capital. It hardly surprises us, therefore, that Sir Andrew's favorite "frugal Maxim" is "A Penny saved is a Penny got" or that he argues that "Diligence makes more lasting Acquisitions than Valour, and . . . Sloth has ruin'd more Nations than the Sword" (No. 2). As the quintessential self-made man, Sir Andrew symbolizes England's own imperialist potential: "He has made his Fortunes himself; and says that *England* may be richer than other Kingdoms, by as plain Methods as he himself is richer than other Men."

The periodical persistently establishes Sir Andrew as a mercantile Everyman, whose "plain Methods," as well as commercial successes, are available to all careful men of business. Yet the merchant's rise into the ranks of the elite—embodied in his designation as "Sir"—has been consistently taken for granted, whether in the text of the *Spectator* itself or in critics' readings of that text. Whereas Tom Trueman must give up his position as trader in order to be styled a gentleman, Sir Andrew achieves his gentlemanly status through his mercantile efforts: we assume that he, like the trader knighted for his "good Services" in *Spectator* No. 299, has earned rather than inherited his title. Before the reader even meets Sir Andrew, he has obtained the very status that the text goes on to prove he deserves. As is the case with gender difference, the periodical assumes that which it is in the process of affirming. Sir Andrew's title blurs precisely those distinctions—between nobleman and citizen, land and trade—that the portrayal itself, in its attempt to demonstrate the merchant's superiority, must necessarily uphold.

Sir Andrew's final correspondence with Mr. Spectator, in which he describes his "considerable Purchase" of "Substantial Acres and Tenements" (No. 549), ostensibly emphasizes the difference between the traditional or aspiring gentleman who would view such an acquisition as an opportunity for leisure, and the merchant, who proposes to run his estate along the same principles he had formerly applied to his business. In the administration of his country estate, Sir Andrew puts into practice the Whig economic view he had earlier theorized in No. 232. Instead of the handouts which, spent on food and drink, serve only to promote "the Trade of the Victualler, and the Excises of the Government," he argues there that providing the poor with the opportunity to work "would be equally beneficial both to the landed and trading Interests," for the "Goods which we export are indeed the Product of the Lands, but much the greatest Part of their Value is the Labour of the People." In contrast to his more traditional predecessors, including the Spectator himself,[17] Sir Andrew transforms land into the same labor-intensive system commonly lauded as one of trade's greatest assets. He tells Mr. Spectator that "My Gardens, my Fishponds, my Arable and Pasture Grounds shall be my several Hospitals, or rather Work-houses, in which I propose to maintain a great many indigent Persons, who are now starving in my Neighbourhood" (No. 549).

Yet we do well to remember that Sir Andrew enacts his difference within the context of the most powerful and persistent of aristocratic prerogatives—the large country estate.[18] Having earlier colonized the globe in his role as overseas merchant—for, according to Mr. Spectator, "there is not a Point in the Compass but blows home a Ship in which he is an Owner" (No. 2)—Sir Andrew subsequently manipulates his estate from his privileged position as landowner. In both situations, he takes over in order to reform, justifying usurpation through his claim of aiding others. As a merchant, he expressed the "constant Benignity in Commerce" not available to other men (No. 346); as a landowner, he will be equally charitable by "setting my poor Neighbours to Work, and giving them a comfortable Subsistence out of their own Industry" (No. 549). Sir Andrew redefines charity to mean not the sporadic though well-meaning hospitality of the country squire, but the ability to make men self-sufficient. In this way, he transforms the trader's stereotyped parsimony into a superior generosity: "Sir ROGER gives to his Men, but I place mine above the Necessity or Obligation of my Bounty" (No. 174).

For Sir Andrew, landed property simply provides an opportunity for industry: "I have got a fine Spread of improveable Lands, and in my own Thoughts am already plowing up some of them, fencing others; planting Woods, and draining Marshes." Although he writes that "as I have my Share in the Surface of this Island, I am resolved to make it as beautiful a Spot as any in Her Majesty's Dominions," it soon becomes clear that for Sir Andrew beauty equals utility: "at least there is not an Inch of it which shall not be cultivated to the best Advantage, and do its utmost for its Owner." Under Sir Andrew's mercantile thumb, land has become a form of "mobile property," available for the same kinds of manipulation and calculation previously applied to his "floating Capital"—"tost upon Seas or fluctuating in Funds" (No. 549)—methods whose success has enabled Sir Andrew's purchase of this estate in the first place.[19] Sir Andrew makes the association himself: "As in my Mercantile Employment, I so disposed of my Affairs, that from whatever Corner of the Compass the Wind blew, it was bringing home one or other of my Ships; I hope, as a Husband-man, to contrive it so, that not a Shower of Rain, or a Glimpse of Sunshine, shall fall upon my Estate without bettering some part of it, and contributing to the Products of the Season." Sir Andrew triumphs not by denying the agrarian concerns of his noble opponents, in particular Sir Roger, but by addressing and even improving those concerns through a felicitous application of mercantile principles. Eliding the natural and the cultivated, the squire and the merchant, the material and the moral, Sir Andrew epitomizes the new model of economic man who easily unites private interest and public benefit under the silken flag of Industry.

Wants Made Pleasures

> Nature has implanted in us Two very strong Desires, Hunger for the Preservation of the Individual, and Lust for the Support of the Species; . . . But reasonable Creatures correct these Incentives, and improve them into elegant Motives of Friendship and Society. . . . By this Cultivation of Art and Reason, our Wants are made Pleasures, and the Gratification of our Desires, under proper Restrictions, a Work no Way below our noblest Faculties.
> —*Tatler* No. 205

The success of the *Tatler*'s and *Spectator*'s representations of the trader as gentleman depended upon an acknowledged correlation between individual prosperity and benefit to society at large. We have seen the embodiment of this achievement in the city merchant turned country squire, Sir Andrew Freeport. Yet it is noteworthy that in the numerous discussions of and by Sir Andrew, we find only one mention of his family. In No. 232, Mr. Spectator describes how the merchant divides his time between town and country, business and pleasure: "His Time in Town is given up to the Publick, and the Management of his private Fortune; and after every three or four Days spent in this Manner, he retires for as many to his Seat within a few Miles of the Town, to the enjoyment of himself, his Family, and his Friend [i.e., Mr. Spectator]." The virtual exclusion of Sir Andrew's family from the pages of the *Spectator* marks the more general status of the family as both necessary to, and repressed within, economic discourse.

Classical models defined male virtue in terms of the disinterested activity of the citizen within the city-state. In the emerging eighteenth-century model, however, the locus of virtue shifts, as does the importance of economic disinterest, as the family competes with the *polis* as the arena in which men might demonstrate their merit. In this context, a man becomes a good and worthy member of society by performing successfully the duties of husband and father. In Chapter 4 I claimed that mercantilist theory posited the trader as more of a gentleman than the landed squire or aristocrat by virtue of his superior ability to benefit others while also improving himself. Family plays a key role in that discussion, for in its status as both self and other, the intimate family reconciles the seemingly conflictual demands of self-interest and community. The bourgeois view refigures economic interest as an asset instead of a liability: as interests pursued in the name of the family, relations of production and exchange become benevolent rather than selfish, nurturing rather than ruthless; in other words, such interests become family values *avant la lettre*.

As a way to explicate this intersection of the familial and the economic, I want to modify the position taken by Albert O. Hirschman in *The Passions and the Interests: Political Arguments for Capitalism Before Its Triumph*.[20] Hirschman argues for a shift from the Augustinian perception of three comparable passions—the desire for money and possessions, the desire for power, and sexual desire—to a belief in the late seventeenth century that economic activity could emerge as a benign form of interest rather than a destructive passion, and could serve to counteract the tyrannical abuse of power. Although Hirschman's analysis is particularly helpful in understanding the early eighteenth-century view of economic activity as personally benevolent and socially useful—a *"doux commerce"*—his emphasis on the relation between economics and politics ignores the third passion of sexual lust. I believe that the ideology of a domestic, benevolent, companionate masculinity becomes a way not of sublimating passions to interests, but rather of integrating the two, within the context of the sentimental nuclear family. Just as the softening and sweetening aspects of commerce ostensibly act to attenuate the harsher and more dangerous qualities of ambition,[21] so too does the construction of what I term a *douce famille* serve similarly to civilize men's more intemperate and immoderate appetites on economic, sociopolitical, and sexual levels. Economic interest thereby forms the basis for a family setting in which both ambition and sexual desires can be met, albeit in new ways. The family setting transforms sexual lust into the pure love that will produce healthy and delightful offspring;[22] educating and providing for these children satisfies the desire for fame. The family is an attractive entity precisely in that it allows men a place where the desires for material goods, for glory, and for sexual gratification could all be integrated in a form that ostensibly benefited others as well as themselves.

The *Tatler* and *Spectator* attempted to neutralize lust by changing it from an undifferentiated appetite, the product of an instinct for survival possessed by all creatures, to rational desire for a select person. In numerous narratives, the family purifies desire through its economic function: not only does the mutual comfort of sexual pleasure smooth out the choppy seas of life, but the demands of life itself, in particular the need to provide for and educate a family, also convert unrestrained passion into "a perpetual Spirit of Benevolence, Complacency, and Satisfaction" (*Spectator* No. 128). In *Tatler* No. 49, Steele describes love as desire that can be met; ostensibly, this fulfillment will lead to the stability represented by the balanced frigate of *Spectator* No. 128, where "Care and Chearfulness go Hand in Hand," or the anchored ship depicted by Daniel Defoe in his marital conduct book, *Conjugal Lewdness*: "the Pleasure of a married State consists wholly in the Beauty of the Union, the sharing Comforts, the doubling all Enjoyments; 'tis the Settlement of Life; the Ship is always in a Storm till it finds this safe Road, and here it comes to an Anchor."[23]

Yet as we have seen in the previous chapter, such ideals of connubial bliss could be all too easily forestalled by the unruly desires of women, whose material lusts often rivaled their sexual appetites in their ability to disrupt the safe harbor of familial existence. Two contemporary works expose, in different ways, the worm within the matrimonial rose. By arguing that nuptial desire must itself be carefully regulated, Defoe challenges Steele's notion that marriage is the state that chastens lust by transforming it into love. The very title of his book, *Conjugal Lewdness; or, Matrimonial Whoredom: A Treatise concerning the Use and Abuse of the Marriage Bed,* affirms marital sexuality as a source of anxiety rather than respite, a blessed state that can, at any turn, become a hell. Defoe counsels the use of reason to attain "matrimonial chastity" first through the judicious choice of a marriage partner, and then through constant vigilance in the marriage bed. In *The Fable of the Bees*, by contrast, Bernard Mandeville concerns himself less with sexual behavior per se than with polite society's hypocritical attitudes toward desire itself—a criticism developed partly in response to the writings of Richard Steele.[24]

Whereas Steele decries the fact that "a brutal Desire call'd Lust is frequently concealed and admitted" under the "rever'd Name" of Love (No. 49), Mandeville deconstructs the very distinction between love and lust by arguing that love is simply the name we give to those who conceal their lust well. He writes that "a Man need not conquer his Passions, it is sufficient that he conceals them. Virtue bids us subdue, but good Breeding only requires we should hide our Appetites." If society defines virtue as the ability to conquer those appetites that define the human condition, yet must at the same time depend for its continuance upon behavior defined as vice—namely, the pursuit of those very appetites—then it must invent the means to reconfigure them. As a result, even the word for sexual desire becomes taboo: "the very Name of the Appetite, tho' the most necessary for the Continuance of Mankind, is become odious, and the proper Epithets commonly join'd to Lust are *Filthy* and *Abominable*."[25]

Mandeville endeavors to lionize lust as a fundamental element in human existence; for Steele, however, lust serves the necessary function of distinguishing passion domesticated by the familial setting from desire forever displaced, unsatisfied, and incomplete: "they who are instigated by the Satyr [of Lust], are ever tortur'd by Jealousies of the Object of their Wishes; often desire what they scorn, and as often consciously and knowingly embrace where they are mutually indifferent" (*Tatler* No. 49). The number's principal illustration compares "*Florio*, the generous Husband" with "*Limberham*, the kind Keeper" in order to analyze "the different Effects" that love and lust "produce in the Mind."[26] In the exemplary marriage, Florio and his wife Amanda enjoy the "Goods of Life," both material and emotional, in the context of benevolent and confident friendship. Amanda provides the justification for Florio's worldly endeavors, for he "sees it the End of all his Ambition to make her Life one Series of Pleasure and Satisfaction"; moreover, his ability to fulfill her desires comprises his own gratification: "*Amanda*'s Relish of the Goods of Life is all that makes 'em pleasing to *Florio*." In short, the couple use the fruits of ambition to enhance their relationship.

In contrast to the contentment experienced by Amanda, Limberham's mistress, Corinna, "lives in constant Torment." Although her plentiful and luxurious possessions, the dividends of her liaison, "make her the Envy of all the strolling Ladies in Town," Corinna nevertheless understands that "she her self is but Part of *Limberham*'s Household-stuff, and is as capable of being dispos'd of elsewhere, as any other Moveable." While Amanda enjoys objects, Corinna knows herself to be one. Like the fairy-tale sister who produces pearls and rubies with each word, Corinna's staged demonstrations of affection translate into material goods: "A kind Look or falling Tear is worth a Piece of Brockade, a Sigh is a Jewel, and a Smile a Cupboard of Plate." Indeed the statement that Limberham can be even more "magnificently bountiful" than a "*Persian* Prince" when he is assured that Corinna has been faithful to him calls to mind another work by Defoe, *Roxana, or the Fortunate Mistress* (1724), in which the unscrupulous heroine amasses her considerable fortune in part through the generosity of princes and kings. Although Corinna is particularly adroit in obtaining tokens of Limberham's devotion, the goods she receives are ultimately dispensable, because she feels no affection for him. Limberham, in turn, typifies the man activated by lust: he purchases, spends, and expends, but all for nought. Rather than ameliorating his own position, Corinna's improvement serves literally to deplete him. The passage's economic terminology underlines the *Tatler*'s critique of domestic situations determined by lust rather than by love: "With this great *Oeconomy* and *Industry* does the unhappy *Limberham purchase* the constant Tortures of Jealousy, the Favour of *spending* his Estate, and the Opportunity of *enriching* one by whom he knows he is hated and despis'd" (my emphasis).

Although at first blush it might seem possible to blame Corinna's abuse of Limberham upon the fact that they are unmarried, the *Spectator* provides numerous portraits of even married women who demand material goods and fail to respond with emotional ones. Such examples from the previous chapter as the wife who used the "Rhetorick" of tears to requisition luxury items from her overly benevolent spouse (No. 252), and the modern wives of Hensberg, who carry not husbands but lace and lapdogs from the besieged city (No. 499), reveal the viper lurking within the earthly Eden that the authors of the *Tatler* and *Spectator* claim is marriage. That is, the very family setting which, by sanctioning men's labor and refining their desires, should act to civilize men's appetites could also, and ironically, provide men an opportunity to indulge those very appetites within the structures of marriage itself. I end this section with a reading of two letters to the *Spectator* that, while seeming to decry the intemperate behaviors of women, also censure the excesses of men.

In No. 295, Mr. Spectator responds to a letter from "Josiah Fribble, *Esq.*" bemoaning his wife's inflexible demand for her four hundred pounds of "*Pin-money*" in spite of the fact that *he* wants to apply that money toward a "Provision" for their many children. Mr. Spectator proceeds to show the absurdity of the concept of pin money by taking it literally:

> Should a Man unacquainted with our Customs be told the Sums which are allowed in *Great Britain*, under the Title of *Pin-money*, what a prodigious Consumption of *Pins* would he

> think there was in this Island? *A Pin a Day*, says our frugal
> Proverb, *is a Groat a Year*, so that according to this Calcula-
> tion, my Friend *Fribble*'s Wife must every Year make use of
> Eight Millions six hundred and forty thousand *new Pins*.

Although he subsequently concedes that "our *British* Ladies alledge they
comprehend under this general Term several other Conveniences of Life,"
Mr. Spectator cannot pass up the opportunity to castigate women's notorious love of "Dress and Trifles," thereby providing in himself an example
of the very "malicious World" he appears to reprove: "I cou'd therefore
wish, for the Honour of my Country-women, that they had rather call'd it
Needle-money, which might have implied something of Good-housewifry,
and not have given the malicious World occasion to think, that Dress and
Trifles have always the upper-most Place in a Woman's Thoughts." Such
rhetoric, while providing the rationale for depriving women of the money
they might legally have contracted for, cannot ultimately obscure the more
weighty aspects of the subject.[27] Pin money, by providing women with independence, might buy the potential for sexual license: Josiah Fribble notes
that if he should "credit" his "Malicious Neighbors," his wife's pin money
"has not a little contributed" to the "several Children" for whom he is
struggling to provide, ironically through a reappropriation of that very
money. Mr. Spectator confirms such a possibility: "Mr. *Fribble* may not,
perhaps, be much mistaken, where he intimates, that the supplying a Man's
Wife with *Pin-money*, is furnishing her with Arms against himself, and in a
manner becoming accessary to his own Dishonour." He supports this claim
by adding "that in proportion as a Woman is more or less beautiful, and
her Husband advanced in Years, she stands in need of a greater or less number of *Pins*, and upon a Treaty of Marriage, rises or falls in her Demands
accordingly."

Pin money provides a further threat to marital stability in the form of financial independence. Mr. Spectator cites "several of my fair Reasoners"
who defend the practice by arguing for it as a kind of advance alimony, "in
case their Husband proves a Churl or a Miser." Mustering themselves such
an "Allowance" functions, according to Mr. Spectator, not unlike the practice of those "over-cautious Generals" who "never engage in a Battel without securing a Retreat, in case the Event should not answer their Expectations." Rather, he implies, women should follow the model of "your greatest
Conquerors," who "have burnt their Ships, or broke down the Bridges behind them, as being determined either to succeed or die in the Engagement." He soon makes the comparison explicit: "I should very much suspect
a Woman who takes such Precautions for her Retreat, and contrives Meth-

ods how she may live happily, without the Affection of one to whom she joins herself for Life." Women's financial dependence underpins the complaisance so necessary to a successful marriage; as Mr. Spectator bluntly puts it, "Separate Purses, between Man and Wife, are, in my Opinion, as unnatural as separate Beds." Accordingly, men find such dependence emotionally and erotically stimulating: "There is no greater Incitement to Love in the Mind of Man, than the Sense of a Person's depending upon him for her Ease and Happiness." For women, the subordination inherent in such dependence reinforces their cultivation of the traits that will make them desirable, and thereby protected: "a Woman uses all her Endeavours to please the Person whom she looks upon as her Honour, her Comfort, and her Support." Samuel Richardson was to echo this sentiment four decades later, when in a letter to the *Rambler* disparaging the mercenary marital customs of his age he contends that "settlements are expected, that often, to a mercantile man especially, sink a fortune into uselessness: and pin-money is stipulated for, which makes a wife independent, and destroys love, by putting it out of a man's power to lay any obligation upon her, that might engage gratitude, and kindle affection."[28]

Ironically, the belief that men's love stems from responsibility and women's from indebtedness actually promotes the very attitudes that the essays by Addison and Richardson are intended to reform. That is, husbands must toil and wives demand in order to provide and receive the very "obligations" that determine their relationship to each other. The commodification that results from this process of defining gender roles in economic terms finds clever expression at the end of the *Spectator* paper. Mr. Spectator first retells a story from Plato's *Alcibiades*, in which Socrates, traveling through Persia, comes across large portions of land earmarked for the different parts of the Queen's dress, lands the Spectator drolly claims "might not be improperly called the Queen of *Persia's Pin-Money*." He follows with a contemporary example concerning the "Perverse Widow" who had many years before refused Sir Roger de Coverly's generous offer of marriage:

> he had disposed of an hundred Acres in a Diamond-Ring, which he would have presented her with, had she thought fit to accept it; and [said] that upon her Wedding-Day she should have carried on her Head fifty of the tallest Oaks upon his Estate. He further informed me, that he would have given a Colepit to keep her in clean Linnen, that he would have allowed her the Profits of a Windmill for her Fans, and have presented her, once in three Years, with the Sheering of his Sheep for her Under-Petticoats.

In this passage, the delightful turn of Addison's wit can soften or at least delay the satirical blow: like Limberham's mistress Corinna, such a woman depletes rather than enhances her husband's resources. Yet while women's material desires are here the subject of clever male critique, those desires also disclose an arena of male anxiety. Sir Roger concludes his narrative by telling Mr. Spectator that "though he did not care for fine Cloaths himself, there should not have been a Woman in the Country better dressed than my Lady *Coverly*." Pin money could operate as a kind of bribe, a way to purchase a more desirable woman: as Mr. Spectator himself noted, the older the man, and the younger, prettier, or more well-bred the woman, the more "pins" he must give her. Furthermore, while the wife of Josiah Fribble might use hers to discharge gambling debts, pin money was usually designed as "an annual sum allotted to a woman for personal expenses in dress, etc." (*OED*); thus pin money was proportional to status in part because of the greater sums needed to outfit genteel women properly. As a wife's private expenditure, pin money was under her control;[29] it revealed her position, but also flaunted her husband's success in obtaining and providing for her. By ascribing to women a natural love of ornament, trifles, and luxury, men could place themselves in the morally superior role of their monitors or censors, even as they simultaneously benefited from such feminine display.

As I have shown in the previous chapter, women's bodies played a crucial role in the discursive war distinguishing the middle classes from their aristocratic and genteel counterparts. In this context, discussions of interclass marriages provided a means of criticizing the prideful display associated with the upper classes by commending the middle-class qualities of domestic regulation. Defoe, in fact, devotes an entire chapter of *Conjugal Lewdness* to the dangers "Of marrying with Inequality of Blood." His first example describes a woman "scandalously . . . treated" by an impoverished noble family simply for being "beneath them in Degree," despite the fact that she is well-behaved, well-educated, and indeed that "her Fortune has been the very raising, or at least, restoring the Circumstances of the Person who has taken her."[30] His second and more extensive illustration concerns a man with "vast Fortune" but of "no Family," who marries a poorer but noble-blooded woman. The woman, forced by a covetous mother to marry below her station, disdains her husband, turning his own children against him. Her haughtiness makes his life miserable, although he married her not for her status or money (he could have had a much wealthier woman) but rather for qualities he mistakenly thought she possessed: "good Temper, Sense and Sincerity." The most interesting part of the chapter concerns a dialogue between this lady and a well-meaning "noble Lord of an antient Family," who attempts to reform her arrogance by describing historical changes in the relations between the "Nobility" and the "Commons" in England. Sounding more like Defoe with each sentence, the nobleman proceeds to explain that "great Numbers of [Commoners] are of noble Families," since the Gentry frequently bring "their Sons up to Industry and Trade," successfully raising "innumerable Families out of nothing"; furthermore, he adds, the nobility "often go into the City to get Fortunes for our Sons; and many noble Families, sunk by the Folly and Luxury of their Predecessors, are restored, by marrying into the Families of those that you call Mechanicks." Our ladyship, unfortunately for her husband, remains unconvinced.[31]

Spectator No. 299 presents a more humorous version of this situation, in which the story of the "plain Jack Anvil" who becomes "Sir John Enville" offers an exemplary tale for men. After a brief preface, Mr. Spectator uncharacteristically lets his writer's letter speak for itself, as "a Representation of those Calamities and Misfortunes which a weak Man suffers from wrong Measures, and ill-concerted Schemes of Life." The letter begins by claiming to have been inspired by the recently published narrative of Josiah Fribble (No. 295), for the writer believes his own "Case . . . no less deplorable than that of Squire *Fribble*." Jack/John is a poor working man made good. A successful ironmonger who used his considerable savings as capital, at twenty-five he "became a bold Trader both by Sea and Land, which in a few Years raised me a very great Fortune." Knighted for his "good Services" at thirty-five, he lived happily in the city as Sir John Anvil. Noting that he was "in . . . Temper very Ambitious, I was now bent upon making a Family, and accordingly resolved that my Descendants should have a Dash of good Blood in their Veins." This sentence is a crucial one, for the ambition Sir John describes is that of pride rather than wealth; his desire for noble heirs portends his downfall. Once he has begun wooing "the Lady *Mary Oddly*, an indigent young Woman of Quality," his story becomes increasingly facetious, as it satirizes the excessive requirements of his fiancée. To expedite the betrothal process, he gives her "*Charte Blanche*"; he found she "was very concise in her Demands, insisting only that the Disposal of my Fortune, and the Regulation of my Family, should be entirely in her Hands." Moreover, Sir John tells us that her impoverished "Father and Brothers," who at first "appear'd exceedingly averse to this Match" are "at present . . . so well reconciled, that they Dine with me almost every Day, and have borrowed considerable Sums of me; which my Lady *Mary* very often twits me with, when she would shew me how kind her Relations are to me."

Lady Mary makes up in "Spirit" for what she lacked in portion, an energy exhibited primarily through aristocratic display. She changes her husband's name from Anvil to Envil to Enville; dismisses his "careful Servants," instituting in their place "a couple of Black-a-moors, and three or four very genteel Fellows in Laced Liveries" in addition to a noisy "*French*-woman"; "reform[s]" his house, filling it with so much glass and china that he is afraid to move about; and holds weekly receptions from which he is pointedly excluded. In addition to making him a stranger in his own home, Lady Mary also finds methods of estranging him from his children. She even usurps his prerogative with regard to the public realm, for he states that "she thinks her self my superior in Sense, as much as she is in Quality, and therefore treats me like a plain well-meaning Man, who does not know the World."

Lady Mary illustrates a different form of wifely dishonor from the aristocratic "Fulvia" (*Spectator* No. 15), who treats her husband as steward rather than friend and support. While the latter eschews the patient domestic virtues for the glitter of public life, so that a missed first night at the opera becomes for her an event as catastrophic as the death of a child, Lady Mary sins by bringing those aristocratic values into her home. Exhibiting many of the characteristics associated stereotypically with the decadent aristocrat (although, in contrast to the wife of Josiah Fribble, she is not accused of sexual infidelity), Lady Mary consumes what is modish rather than lasting. A woman who uses objects—and objectifies people, including her own children—in order to reinforce her misguided sense of self-importance, she believes that superior blood entitles her to conjugal dominance. An economic rather than political virago, she does not treat her husband as her steward but becomes one herself.

Lady Mary's ancestry, and the lack of deference it permits, serve as a warning to all men in their choice of a marriage partner as well as in their making of a marriage contract. More generally, the letter educates its male readers into the right—and wrong—ways of becoming a gentleman. Sir John errs by confusing birth with value. As a merchant already honored for his national service, he has no need to marry "up" in order to claim gentility; his marriage subverts rather than solidifies his gentlemanly position. Sir John's pitiable narrative demonstrates that it is unnecessary, even detrimental, for the merchant, who has recently been elevated in his own right, to valorize outmoded aristocratic values. The following section provides evidence for a different mode of gentility, by exploring the periodicals' representations of a relationship in which aspiration can be a benevolent virtue rather than a vain and destructive vice.

The Father-Son Partnership

> It is the most beautiful Object the Eyes of Man can behold,
> to see a Man of Worth and his Son live in an entire unre-
> served Correspondence. The mutual Kindness and Affection
> between them give an inexpressible Satisfaction to all who
> know them. It is a sublime Pleasure which encreases by the
> Participation. It is as sacred as Friendship, as pleasurable as
> Love, and as joyful as Religion.
> —*Spectator* No. 192

Just as Keith Wrightson has responded to the work of Lawrence Stone by arguing that it is unwise to make too sharp a distinction between "patriarchal" and "companionate" marriages,[32] so too do I believe that the new configuration of fatherhood that emerges in the pages of the *Tatler* and *Spectator* partakes of related and competing ideological positions with regard to men's perceived paternal role. In this period, the role of the "sentimental father" arises among the middle ranks both as a product of changing economic relations—landed property into commerce—and as a way to distinguish middle-class or business virtue from the honorable characteristics associated with the aristocracy and landed gentry. The paternal characteristics that I am terming sentimental are not, of course, exclusive to the middle classes. Yet the *Tatler* and *Spectator* represent such attributes in a manner that marks them as a form of partnership impossible within families in which inheritance was determined by "the need to keep together the estate upon which the standing of gentry families depended."[33] In contrast, partible inheritance, as well as the opportunity for sons to join their father in the family business,[34] permitted a form of economic affiliation that could also carry moral and emotional weight. We find the most extreme form of this father-son partnership manifested in the type I call the "fraternal father." He, like the father in the Cornelii family described in *Spectator* No. 192, "lives with his Sons like their eldest Brother." It is clearly no accident that the Cornelii are a family of "eminent Traders": their benevolent familial relations, because publicly inscribed, earn "Returns" that are societal as well as pecuniary: "their Friendship, Good-will, and kind Offices, are disposed of joyntly as well as their Fortune; so that no one ever obliged one of them, who had not the Obligation multiplied in Returns from them all."

Changes in economic structures underlie all of the moral characteristics associated with the sentimental father. A father's lack of filial partiality (*Tatler* No. 235)—emulating Noah rather than Jacob—manifests itself materially in partible inheritance or business partnership rather than primogeniture; financial liberality (*Tatler* No. 60) can result from the fact that the son's learning to manage the family fortune is also in his father's interest; sympathy, empathy, and understanding (*Spectator* No. 263) are possible in part because father and son function together within the same or a similar system. The "transplanted Self-love" described in *Spectator* No. 192, whereby "All the Enjoyments and Sufferings which a Man meets with, are regarded only as they concern him in the Relation he has to another," is in part transplanted self-interest. The idealized image of the sentimental father, who protects, supports, advises, and understands his son or sons is thus a composite portrait. Formed, on the one hand, in light of the middle-class fraternal ideal, he also develops in contrast to the traditionally authoritative patriarchal father: the king who decrees rather than discusses, has complete control over familial resources, and competes for those resources with his heir or heirs. As we shall see, these texts associate this type of father primarily with the aristocracy and gentry. In *Tatler* No. 189, for example, Bickerstaff contrasts desirably empathetic parent-child relations, in which parents "repeat their Lives in their Offspring; and their Concern for them is so near, that they feel all their Sufferings and Enjoyments as much as if they regarded their own proper Persons," with the brutishly competitive situation of "the common Race of 'Squires in this Kingdom [who] use their Sons as Persons that are waiting only for their Funerals, and Spies upon their Health and Happiness, as indeed they are by their own making them such."

The patriarchal father personifies the negative aspects of aristocratic paternity: selfishness, profligacy, competitiveness, and insensitivity. Taking its motto from Terence—"My son should enjoy these things equally with me, or even more, because youth is more appropriate for these things"—*Spectator* No. 496 denigrates those fathers who unbecomingly pursue their own pleasures at the expense of their sons. Not only do these men provide a negative role model by failing to teach their sons "to resist the Impetuosity of growing Desires," but they also deplete the stock that should allow their offspring to live honorable lives: "Narrowness in their Circumstances has made many Youths to supply themselves as Debauchees, commence Cheats and Rascals." *Tatler* No. 189 offers a very near example of such parental misrule in a branch of Bickerstaff's own family, in which children's desires are sacrificed to those of their father rather than being compatible with them. Unlike good fathers, who favorably "repeat their Lives in their Offspring," bad ones keep perpetuating the same sins:

> When one of the Family has, in the Pursuit of Foxes, and in
> the Entertainment of Clowns, ran out the Third Part of the
> Value of his Estate, such a Spendthrift has dressed up his el-
> dest Son, and married what they call a Good Fortune, who has

supported the Father as a Tyrant over them, during his Life, in
the same House or Neighbourhood: The Son in Succession
has just taken the same Method to keep up his Dignity, till the
Mortgages he has eat and drank himself into, have reduced
him to the Necessity of sacrificing his Son also, in Imitation of
his Progenitor.[35]

Portraits of such men are complemented, and conquered, by the presence
of their opposite, the fraternal father. In addition to promoting a critique of
patriarchal attitudes, the fraternal ideal acts to buttress a belief in liberal individualism. In *The Sexual Contract*, Carole Pateman contends that by obscuring that part of the social contract that depends upon men's subordination of women, contract theory, far from being opposed to patriarchal right,
reinscribes that right in a new configuration: "Modern patriarchy is fraternal
in form and the original contract is a fraternal pact."[36] Thus while the concept of a cooperative fraternal fatherhood might seem seductive in its
promise of male relations apparently stripped of hierarchy and dominance,
Pateman's analysis reminds us of such a concept's dark underside. In spite of
Defoe's analogy between a trading partnership and a marriage, since both
are "engaged in for better or for worse, till the years expire,"[37] in this period
the only true contract, and therefore partnership, can exist between men.[38]
And what makes that partnership and its underlying model of egalitarianism
possible is the subordination of women. These new, increasingly middle-
class representations of masculine virtue, modeled upon the relations between the sentimental father and his "towardly" son (*Spectator* No. 263),
reinscribe oppressive relations, albeit in new forms. Such fraternal patriarchy serves as both a basis for the capitalist endeavor and as a means of perpetuating women's subordination and exploitation.

The *Spectator* presents the sentimental father as exemplary in large part
because he combines patriarchal and fraternal roles. Such mentoring can
cross both party lines and class positions. No. 346 tells the story of "Tom the
Bounteous" who, although "so known a Tory," supports others on a collegial
rather than a paternal level by "lend[ing] at the ordinary Interest, to give
Men of less Fortune Opportunities of making greater Advantages," while
No. 330 includes a letter from the eighteen-year-old "Son of a Merchant of
the City of *London*" who is rescued from both aristocratic profligacy and professional oblivion after his own father's death by a country "Gentleman."
The son, whose mother has also died, inherits a modest estate, but "without
Friend or Guardian to instruct me in the management or Enjoyment of it"
soon encounters bad company and worse debt. Later, in an attempt at self-
reformation, he begins to "study the Law," but, again bereft of advice, fails

to progress: "I trifled away a whole year in looking over a thousand intricacies without Friend to apply to in case of doubt." Good-hearted but ill-guided, our correspondent is eventually delivered by a "relation" who, observing in him "a good inclination," carries him to his country seat. Under the "Favour and Patronage" of this virtuous man, the youth blossoms: his mentor provides him with books, horses, and good conversation; inspires him with confidence; and, most important, inclines him toward virtue. The youth writes that his patron has achieved such influence by blending superior knowledge, experience, and position with sympathetic understanding: "he has an Authority of a Father over me, founded upon the Love of a Brother." The young man formulates his letter to the *Spectator* as both a tribute to his mentor and an exhortation to other men in similar positions to follow such a beneficent example.[39] Such commendable behavior, he writes, is desirable for all men who have achieved some kind of success, because it costs nothing and returns much: "others may gain Preferments and Fortunes from their Patrons, but I have, I hope, received from mine good Habits and Virtues."

While these representations of idealized paternal benevolence emphasize the father's or guardian's concern for "the Virtue and Disposition of his Children, [rather] than their Advancement or Wealth" (*Spectator* No. 192), the commercial man is a better father precisely because of his superior ability to be "liberal without the least Expense of [his] own Fortune" (*Spectator* No. 346), to share his mobile resources with his sons rather than compete with them for limited ones. Similar to the process through which potentially dangerous masculine sexual desire is purified when directed toward a chaste spouse, so too is wealth rendered honest only when attached to virtuous behavior, thus serving to moralize worldly success: "Good Habits are what will certainly improve a Man's Fortune and Reputation; but on the other Side, Affluence of Fortune will not as probably produce good Affections of the Mind" (*Spectator* No. 192).

Spectator No. 240 illustrates the benevolent qualities of these relations through a letter that tells the story of a trader saved from "criminal Pleasures, some Excesses, and a general loose Conduct" by "the handsome Behaviour of a learned, generous, and wealthy Man," of no relation, who takes the correspondent under his wing. Described, indeed, as a "good Angel," this man puts his "Friendship," "Advice," and money at the youth's disposal, giving him "the Use of any Part of his Fortune, to apply the Measures he should propose to me, for the Improvement of my own." A veritable sentimental son, the narrator reflects, "I assure you I cannot recollect the Goodness and Confusion of the good Man when he spoke to this Purpose to me without melting into Tears." He is able to put his gratitude into practice not through direct returns to his mentor, who is far from needing them, but "by being ready to serve others to my utmost Ability, as far as is consistent with the Prudence" his protector prescribes. Perhaps the correspondent's greatest gift from his mentor is not the "Ease and Plenty" made possible by the use of his assets, but his having learned from him "the Government of my Passions, and Regulation of my Desires."

The idea that men must learn from other men the virtues of self-control recalls the discussion of the rake in *Tatler* No. 27: represented as "the most agreeable of all bad Characters," a rake's "Faults proceed not from Choice or Inclination, but from strong Passions and Appetites, which are in Youth too violent for the Curb of Reason, good Sense, good Manners and good Nature. . . . His Desires run away with him through the Strength and Force of a lively Imagination, which hurries him on to unlawful Pleasures, before Reason has Power to come to his Rescue." One could argue that in this depiction, "Reason" personifies the benevolent older guardian figure, whose timely intervention turns a bad young man good, or keeps a good one that way. In this sense, the rake is in many ways a fatherless son.

Spectator No. 248 extends the attributes of benevolent paternity to encompass possibilities for all men by comparing the worthy and public actions performed by those in "conspicuous Stations of Life" with the good works of the more common folk. Mr. Spectator points out that the former are in fact obliged by their "great Talents and high Birth . . . to exert some noble Inclinations for the Service of the World" as part of their inheritance, for, if ignored, "such Advantages become Misfortunes, and Shade and Privacy are a more eligible Portion." Romanticizing noble behavior can, however, obscure the "heroick" possibilities available to men "in lower Scenes of Life": "It is in every Man's Power in the World who is above meer Poverty, not only to do things worthy but heroick."[40] By practicing the "Self-Denial" that is the "great Foundation of civil Virtue," all men can be in a position to help others. The essay juxtaposes actions by those who "in the domestick Way of Life deny themselves many Advantages, to satisfy a generous Benevolence which they bear to their Friends oppressed with Distresses and Calamities" with those "great and exalted Spirits [who] undertake the Pursuit of hazardous Actions for the Good of others, at the same Time gratifying their Passion for Glory." It is not that the gentleman has less interest in helping other men, but that the commercial man has more resources with which to do so.

Two letters epitomize the number's most sentimental moments. The first concerns a pair of brothers: Lapirus, a younger son, has inherited from his father a "great Estate . . . by reason of the dissolute Behaviour of the First-born." "Shame and Contrition," however, have reformed the profligate brother, who has become, according to Mr. Spectator, "as remarkable for his good Qualities as formerly for his Errors." Lapirus, now in the role of father, reinstates the traditional succession in the following letter:

> *Honoured Brother,*
>
> I enclose to you the Deeds whereby my Father gave me this House and Land: Had he lived till now he would not have bestowed it in that Manner; he took it from the Man you were, and I restore it to the Man you are.

Lapirus's mixture of fraternal and paternal generosity obscures the fact that his own position is diminished, if not outright destroyed, by his good deed. While he might sign himself "Your affectionate Brother," his action reinscribes patriarchal succession, thereby turning him into a dispossessed son. The second letter, in contrast, presents an example of fraternal affection which may very well surpass any other portrait in the *Tatler* or *Spectator* series. Explicitly categorized as a love letter by Mr. Spectator's comment—"I think there is more Spirit and true Gallantry in it than in any Letter I have ever read from *Strephon* to *Phillis*"—this missive describes an encounter between two tradesmen, which Mr. Spectator inserts "even in the mercantile honest Stile in which it was sent":

> *Sir,*
>
> I have heard of the Casualties which have involved you in extreme Distress at this Time; and knowing you to be a Man of great Good-nature, Industry, and Probity, have resolved to stand by you. Be of good Chear, the Bearer brings with him five thousand Pounds, and has my Order to answer your drawing as much more on my Account. I did this in Haste, for Fear I should come too late for your Relief; but you may value your self with me to the Sum of fifty thousand Pounds; for I can very chearfully run the Hazard of being so much less rich than I am now, to save an honest Man whom I love.

Described by Mr. Spectator as a "City Romance," this narrative rewrites the *Tatler*'s earlier example of "Heroick Love in the City" in which the trader "Tom Trueman" wins his bride by saving her father from economic ruin at the hands of a corrupt factor (No. 213). Paradoxically, Trueman is exemplary both because he rescues the father and because he forgoes the economic benefits incurred by such deliverance. In the *Spectator* story, however, no woman is necessary to inspire male bonding. The increasing consignment of women to an allegedly isolated domestic sphere positions them as the necessary centerpiece of the nuclear family in their roles of wife and mother and, ironically, as the least important members of that intimate unit. In this period, women's protective, nurturing, and even moral qualities are shadowed by the greater possession of those same characteristics by men.

The *Spectator*'s most damning portrait of paternal relations gone awry configures illegitimacy as paternal betrayal.[41] No. 203 relegates women who give birth to illegitimate children solely to their childbearing role, for the essay never mentions their sexual behavior; removed from judgment, they are neither condemned nor pitied. It is as if they exist only as repositories for the seed of those "young Patriarchs," who, "like heedless Spendthrifts that squander away their Estates before they are Masters of them, have raised up their whole stock of Children before Marriage." Not only do the men in this "Generation of Vermin" dissipate their assets, but they also misuse their time and energies. The consummate bad businessmen, these youths apply themselves with "indefatigable Diligence" to the wrong things. Extraordinarily inventive in pursuing their "vicious Amour[s]," they misapply their resources by channeling them improperly. As Mr. Spectator notes, they "might conquer their corrupt Inclinations with half the Pains they are at in gratifying them." The potent libertine, as he is represented in this text, betrays not his mistress but his legal wife, should he have one, and, most important, his progeny. Society itself, according to Mr. Spectator, colludes in such licentious behavior by using terminology that condemns victims rather than perpetrators: "And here I cannot but take notice of those depraved Notions which prevail among us, and which must have taken Rise from our natural Inclination to favour a Vice to which we are so very prone, namely, that *Bastardy* and *Cuckoldom* should be looked upon as Reproaches, and that the Ignominy which is only due to Lewdness and Falsehood, should fall in so unreasonable a manner upon the Persons who are Innocent."

In the same number, Addison uses the voice of a wronged son to make his powerful argument against the fathering of illegitimate children. In this most pathetic of epistles, we find represented all that the sentimental father shuns. Plagued by "continual Uneasiness" and "continual Anxiety," this far from prodigal son is both infantilized and feminized. Deprived of paternal "Tenderness . . . Love and Conversation," kept at "so vast a Distance" and treated so haughtily that he cannot express his feelings or communicate his situation to his father, he is also unable to "render him the Duties of a Son." Uneducated for any occupation or profession but that of "Gentleman" while wholly dependent upon his father's doubtful "Assistance," the writer feels himself "a Monster strangely sprung up in Nature, which every one is ashamed to own."

This representation focuses its reforming attention not upon the wife or mother, who must be virginal before and chaste within marriage to insure the legitimacy of her husband's heirs, but upon the chastity of the man himself, who must restrict the fulfillment of his appetites to the sphere of lawful marriage; status as father should follow, not precede, position as husband. The letter ends with the correspondent's request for Mr. Spectator's advice about his unhappy situation, with particular regard to the "part, I being unlawfully born, may claim of the Man's Affection who begot me, and how far in your Opinion I am to be thought his Son, or he acknowledged as my Father." Although Mr. Spectator does not here respond directly, his sympathy regarding the letter implies that even if legal ties are absent, emotional, moral, and material obligations are very much extant. By distinguishing the products of custom from supposedly natural "Affections," this text can criticize cultural norms at the same time as it reaffirms them. Just as Mr. Spectator's desire "to make the word *Wife* the most agreeable and delightful Name in Nature" (No. 490) elides nature and culture, instinct and law, so too does the construction of the sentimental father represent as intrinsic to all virtuous men attributes specific to a distinctive group at a particular historical moment.

I have argued that in the eighteenth century, the shift from the *polis* to the family as the sphere of masculine virtue configures the intimate family as justification for men's pursuit of both passions and interests. The movement into a fraternal representation of familial relations via a father and son partnership—an association seemingly cooperative, benevolent, and without hierarchies of power and dominance—erases the oppressive implications, for both men and women, of that new masculine role. As the sentimental father develops into the sentimental man, men (as sons) are being socialized to assume the role of the active producer as if their life depended on it, for indeed it does; and these sons are taught to sustain their position through the subordination and objectification of desirably dependent women. Despite the formulation of a *doux commerce*, mercantile relations are neither benevolent nor cooperative. Thus while the emerging ideology of a moral fatherhood made possible by commercial relations seems to be about good connections among certain men, this investment in sentimental masculinity can also express both the guilt and the human cost of these relations.

9 A Women's Magazine? Masculine Subjectivity in Periodicals for and by Women

Throughout this study I have argued that in the earliest periodical literature written by men, the need to monitor and reform women functioned as a crucial component of a developing class-based archetype of masculinity, a masculinity that transformed the autocratic patriarchal father into the sentimental husband whose supposedly tender rule over wife and children revealed a new form of gender dominance. These representations of a masculinity presented as available to all men necessitated a concomitant categorization of all women by the ostensibly universal quality of sex, a process that placed them into a group perceived as both separate from men and subordinate to them. While eighteenth-century periodical literature frequently distinguished among women in different stages of life or from divergent class positions, these virgins and widows, servant maids and their mistresses all participated in the same range of emotional, intellectual, and bodily attributes that supposedly differentiated them from men. Although the bulk of those qualities, as I have shown, related to women's increasingly circumscribed place within both the physical domain of the home and the psychological realm of their relations to husband and children, it is important to remember that such placement was not exclusive to women. The first chapter of this book emphasized the way in which an ideology of companionate masculinity constructed men's domestic roles as provider for and protector of their families as justification for their prosperity in the public arena, while subsequent readings of periodical literature demonstrated how early examples of the genre constituted editorial authority by appropriating the paternal role of advisor and reformer. In these texts, men's supervision of women's domestic responsibilities—both practical and emotional—served also to delineate men's own gendered identity. Thus the ability to view women as Women—beings determined by sex rather than birth, title, or wealth and therefore defined by attributes linked to that sex (attributes we class for convenience under the heading of "femininity")—depended upon and worked in tandem with men's textual organization of women and of themselves.

To target women in their dual roles of subject and audience as an indispensable component of the periodical enterprise, even to promulgate an explicit connection between women's position as a "definable 'special interest' group" and the emergence of the genre itself,[1] seems basic to any reading of early periodical literature. In addition, women's increased literacy and desire for education, especially among the middling classes, and their correspondent turn to periodicals as a source of entertainment and instruction, allowed women to play a part that was integral both economically and ideologically to the periodical venture.[2] I contend, however, that there exists a fundamental difference between the important work of analyzing women's place in the emergence of periodical literature and postulating—as do virtually all the scholars who have examined these texts—that such attention was equivalent to the production of a "women's periodical" or a "women's magazine."[3]

The notion of gender difference that solidified in later periods has permeated our collective vision so thoroughly that these critics' otherwise perceptive readings of early eighteenth-century periodicals seem, for the most part, blinded to men's inscription in the text. While scholars have unproblematically employed the terms "women's periodical" or "women's magazine" to describe publications supposedly focusing on women from Dunton forward, I maintain that these formulations, particularly when applied to texts written before 1770, unthinkingly erase men's consequential and even predominant place in the domestic realm.[4] Thus for critical minds that have been steeped in precisely the reified distinctions between the sexes that eighteenth-century periodicals were instrumental in creating, such terms as "women's periodical" or "women's magazine" automatically and necessarily mean the exclusion of men. To take one of many possible examples of this practice, the authors of *Women's Worlds: Ideology, Femininity and the Women's Magazine* clearly acknowledge the difference between the eighteenth century and the centuries that followed: "In the eighteenth century writers and readers appear to have been actively engaged in a *process*, or *struggle*, to establish gender difference as both unambiguous and oppositional, providing 'masculinity' and 'femininity' with different and special social and textual content. Through the nineteenth and twentieth centuries we see this difference *institutionalised* and *entrenched textually in the women's magazine.*"[5] Yet their readings of eighteenth-century periodicals assume that very institutionalization and textual entrenchment of gender difference by positing the genre of the women's magazine as one in which men are at best peripheral, if not altogether absent.

It should be evident that expressions like "women's magazine" or "women's periodicals" are anachronistic. Dunton might have dedicated certain issues of his *Athenian Mercury* to the nominal use of "the Ladies," but as earlier readings of that publication revealed, the term referred to a particular realm of experience—love and marriage—rather than to a specific audience: Dunton published questions on these topics from both sexes, and from the testimony of further queries, it is apparent that both men and women read the answers. To demonstrate just how convoluted the situation was, we do well to remember that Peter Motteux called the October 1693 number of his *Gentleman's Journal* the *Lady's Journal* since it contained an extraordinary amount of contributions by women; from the outset he designed his journal to appeal to women as well as to men. The interpenetration of public and private effected by men's authoritative familial role functioned, paradoxically, to obviate any exclusive alignment of the domestic with the feminine, even if such authority persisted in associating women primarily with their wife-and-mother roles.

To read the body of critical literature devoted to the so-called women's magazine with a perspective trained upon dialectical gender construction becomes, then, a vexed as well as vexing process. My first reaction to the critical literature was to wonder if I had read the same primary texts; thereafter I remained openmouthed at the results of this assumption of an ideology of separate spheres. While solecisms abound, perhaps the most striking is the blatant effacement of men. Thus in an otherwise insightful essay, Helene Koon compares Eliza Haywood's *Female Spectator* with the periodical written by Addison and Steele as follows: "The *Female Spectator* portrays a world as different as if it had been created on another planet; attention is strictly devoted to women's affairs, and men are only peripheral."[6] Although I shall be devoting the bulk of this chapter to an explication of the precise ways in which men are not peripheral but pivotal to Haywood's publication, I want here to address the issue more generally. As I have argued throughout, under the ideology of gender that operated for most of the eighteenth century, there could be no such condition as "separate spheres"; as a group defined by sex, women comprised an important subset of the ostensibly universal realm of experience and existence constituted as male. Thus the idea of a "women's magazine" as a publication written exclusively for women is not only anachronistic but also oxymoronic. That is, there could be nothing "for women" that was not necessarily defined, monitored, or in some way circumscribed by men.

I will begin with a brief examination of the *Visiter* (1724), a weekly periodical ostensibly addressed specifically to women (although, tellingly, it is narrated by a male), in order to show that the text's stance of acute deference to "the Ladies" served to do little more than promote a process of gender construction already at work in earlier publications. While the anonymously authored *Visiter* appears to be only old wine in old bottles, Eliza Haywood's *Female Spectator* (1744–46), commonly referred to as "the first periodical for women written by a woman,"[7] would seem to testify to a drastic change in periodical methodology. I contend, however, that the authority Haywood vests in her female narrators does not transform its genre but operates within a sex-gender system in which men precede as well as predominate.[8] In addition to their implicit, ubiquitous part in shaping women's identity, men play a clear-cut role in Haywood's periodical as examples and correspondents, reformers and targets of reform. If, as I will show, differences among women are increasingly elided under the prototype of female domesticity, so that femininity is presented, for the most part, as a seamless and unified position, attention to the disparate and contradictory portrayals of men, and thus to emergent notions of contradictory masculinities within these texts, reveals the dark underside of the roles both men and women were being socialized to play.[9]

Designing Men: The 'Visiter'

In its introductory issue, offered free to the public on June 18, 1723, the *Visiter*'s editor asserts that he will avoid the "Absurdities" necessarily associated with politics by resolving never to "touch upon any thing which in the least relates to Publick Affairs." Instead, he will confine himself "to those Subjects, that tend to the Improvement of the Mind and Manners, as they are relative to a Domestick Life." He also declares that in his explications of virtues as well as vices, "The Ladies I design as my most peculiar Care." Throughout the periodical's fifty-one numbers, the Visiter reinforces his initial claims of a distinct agenda for women readers by an attitude of intense sympathy for their romantic plight (expressed in the first number as the desire to show "tenderness and humanity toward those who suffer from passion") as well as by the continual assertion of men's necessary role in championing women's cause: "To consult the Honour and promote the Happiness of the Fair Sex, is the distinguishing Character of every Gentleman" (No. 37).

While the *Visiter*'s exemplary position as the protector and defender of its women readers, which included in part a plea for the expansion of their limited educational opportunities, might seem to situate the periodical as an important precursor in the development of the women's magazine,[10] all of the above characteristics were, as I have shown in earlier chapters, fundamental to the genre of the social periodical from the outset. Although such miscellany publications as Motteux's *Gentleman's Journal* and Steele's *Tatler* contained an assortment of foreign and domestic news, these sections were part of an endeavor designed to amuse and instruct, one that clearly distinguished itself from the partisan nature of newspapers. Attending to women might function as a lucrative marketing strategy in the highly volatile world of early publishing, but this practice did not a women's magazine make. Moreover, periodical editors and eidolons consistently employed the roles of lover, knight, teacher, father-confessor, and guardian as a means of relating to and configuring their male—as well as female—audience. Although Shevelow might claim that the *Visiter* "replaces the morally superior stance of the earlier periodicals with a sentimental paternalism tempered further by a declared attitude of empathy,"[11] readings of those antecedent texts have revealed the myriad ways in which precisely such "sentimental paternalism" contributed to the shaping of new forms of masculine identity. I find nothing in the *Visiter*'s pages that differs in any substantial way from what has preceded it; the periodical's essays and letters consistently confirm as well as refine an oppositional model of gender relations in which men, enacting the contradictory roles of rake and knight, provide women with both a source of danger and a means of succor.

The editor of the *Visiter* evidently recognizes the imbrication of women's interests with those of men when he writes that since women's "Happiness, or Misery, must chiefly depend upon the good or ill Behaviour of the other Sex towards them, I shall think myself obliged to observe their Actions; and do assure them, that no one publick or private Mark of Vice or Villainy, that extends toward the Prejudice of the Fair Sex, shall escape my Notice" (No. 1). Women's perceived vulnerability to men's opinions as well as their appetites sets up a dynamic in which men become the overt and implicit focus of reforming attention. The editor's habitual acceptance of a libidinal economy that constructs male sexuality as both voracious and insatiable, as well as of a sexual double standard that blames women for men's actions,[12] sets up the periodical's need to educate men in self-control. If the *Visiter* is truly to help women, it must target men as the sex to be scrutinized and regulated. The sensitive man—that is to say, the Visiter himself—can neither question nor alter the "General Custom" that punishes the female victims of male "Villainy," for such privilege justifies his own position as knight errant. Thus what Shevelow terms the publication's "gallantly paternalistic" relation to its women readers depended in large part upon a correspondingly paternalistic attention to other men.[13]

A closer look at two numbers from the middle of the periodical's run reveals the ways in which the text's stance as condescending purveyor to women permeates its editorial posture and thus unavoidably hampers its repeated claim that women had equal status in the eyes of the paper. At the end of *Visiter* No. 25, the eidolon seems to attribute sexual difference to social rather than natural causes when he states that he "cou'd never find that there was any Difference made between the Male and Female of any Species, except the Humane." Yet the essay itself, by offering an origin narrative in which the sexes fall from a literally Edenic state of perfect equality into relations of dominance and submission, neatly combines biology and custom in its explanation of male supremacy. The Visiter presents himself as biblical exegete, returning to the Garden of Eden to find the source of men's tyranny over women. In contrast with those traditional interpretations that comprehend male dominance as inherent within the creation story itself, the Visiter's account of prelapsarian gender relations surprisingly posits woman's place as one of intellectual and emotional parity with men: "Man was designed for a sociable Animal; the great Creator at first pronounced it not good for him to be alone, and therefore in his infinite Mercy created a Partner for him of equal Abilities in Mind, that she might be a Companion and Counsellor in his Solitude." While the woman possesses "superior Beauty in Person" for the man's "Solace and Delight," the man is not adjured in turn to support or even protect her. Rather, the account presents the "happy Pair" as "mutually to enjoy the Benefits and Comforts of Life." Indeed, as the editor goes on to state, "It is not reasonable to believe that there was any Superiority intended; where perfect Happiness was designed, that cou'd have no Place: Their joyous Hours were to pass in the reciprocal Offices of tender Love and mutual Friendship; and I very much question, whether the Words *Obedience* and *Command* had any Explanation in their Language."

It is only after the fall, when the couple has no means to satisfy their resultant "Thirst of Power" except upon each other, that disaster strikes: "as Man was endow'd with the greatest Share of Strength, he perverted that Qualification, which was certainly meant to preserve his more helpless Partner from the Insults of any other Creature, to a Right ruling over her. Custom (that Rooter of Absurdities) has ever since given a Sanction to it; and we now have the Folly and Arrogance, to imagine it grounded upon the Decrees of the Almighty." Thus the masculine strength, a biological characteristic, that should serve to protect women becomes instead the trait that allows men to dominate them; and biology is subsequently sustained by social practice. Although the essay goes on to argue that men's tyranny over women ultimately comes back to haunt them, for while "it is absolutely necessary for one Side to submit" to the other, "there can be no such thing as Happiness, where either does it in any great degree," the narrator never truly questions men's supposedly unfounded power over women. In other words, the essay accepts as given the very difference it had earlier exposed as a social construction. Men, the male editor dictates, should refrain from dictating to women not out of respect for women's inherent equality, but because such behavior will lead to the destruction of home, family, and often of men themselves: "A Woman that is not capable of governing her self, will make a very ill Figure under Government; or if she does in Appearance submit to it, will very likely have some private Pleasures, some hoarded Satisfactions, that she can enjoy uncontroul'd." As the fictional examples in Eliza Haywood's *Female Spectator* will later demonstrate, wives who are treated too harshly by their husbands often seek out "Pleasures" and "Satisfactions" elsewhere. The story of Manilius and his young bride Sabina, which the periodical offers as "Warning" to husbands "not to urge or exasperate a Wife too much" (Book 10), furnishes a blatant illustration.

Thus the *Visiter*'s seemingly egalitarian critique of "Custom" founders upon the rocks of a gender difference that demands men's role as powerful protectors of the women endangered by men's own licentious desires. *Visiter* No. 37, which takes its motto from Dryden—"Unhappy Sex! Whose Beauty is your Snare, / Exposed to Tryals, made too frail to bear"—uses a letter from a presumed male correspondent to condemn libertines and, in the process, to define masculinity. This missive, which corroborates earlier and subsequent sentiments of the Visiter himself,[14] explicates the ways in which the rake and protector function as two sides of the same base coin. In this dynamic, chivalry provides the form of control that keeps "Custom," which is to say male dominance, in place by positing men's guardianship of women as a natural relationship fundamental to masculinity itself:

> To consult the Honour and promote the Happiness of the Fair
> Sex, is the distinguishing Character of every Gentleman. We
> need not have recourse to the laudable Maxims of Knight-
> Errantry, for confirming this Truth. The establish'd Rules of

> Politeness and Good Manners oblige us to it. To take Advantage
> of the Weakness, and impose on the Credulity of any Persons,
> is base and ungenerous: but how much more so, to betray the
> Innocence, and expose the Reputation of those, who naturally
> depend on us for Protection and Support? There is something
> so shocking in such a Conduct, that the Man who attempts it,
> must needs be divested of the common Principles of Humanity.

Most women are vulnerable because they lack the requisite experience to distinguish true love from false, the sincere lover from the "Cameleon" who will employ even religion as a "Mask to cover the baseness of [his] Designs." However, while the letter here defines the Real Man by a compassionate concern for defenseless femininity, the partial nature of a world that categorically censures any unlicensed sexual behavior by women compromises his knightly position: "General Custom has given it for the Men, and has cast the Whole of the Infamy on that Sex which can least bear it, as upon the whole it least deserves it." Consequently, if society, delineating men as inherently rapacious, sets up a structure that blames women for their own seduction, then women's recourse can only be modesty: "So that all the Women can do, is, to prevent the Occasion of their Misfortunes; to be strictly on their Guard at all Times, and in all Places and Companies; so as never by their Looks, Words or Gestures, to encourage any Freedoms which are not perfectly consistent with Civility and Good Manners." The correspondent also counsels an expansion of women's instruction as a guard against defilement, for those "who are most expos'd to the Artifices, and in most Danger from the Attempts of designing Men, are Women of a narrow and confin'd Education; such as have not been acquainted with the Manners of the Age they live in, nor with the Treatment they must expect when they come into the World."[15]

But even modesty cannot fully protect women from men, for as the writer himself has earlier noted, the "Civility and Good Manners" that would seemingly attest to male sincerity could themselves be feigned. Women must therefore defer to men's superior experience and thus become once again their wards, just as they must depend upon men to educate them into the knowledge that will supposedly safeguard them. Whereas Shevelow maintains, "Although the *Visiter* commented that to address the interests of women meant to address men as well, its perspective demonstrates that women were its principal intended readers,"[16] I contend that the periodical's own ideology of gender effectively negated such a possibility. Through his sympathetic correspondent, the Visiter accepts "Custom" with its blame-the-victim stance in part because such a belief underpins the image of masculinity that justifies both his role and his publication. By contrast, most eighteenth-century women possessed neither the experience nor the authority to play such a benevolent part. What happens to the periodical's defining role as women's champion when the editor is a woman writing to those of her own sex? The following reading of Eliza Haywood's popularly and critically acclaimed production, the *Female Spectator*, will expose men's significant place in an endeavor purportedly for and by women.

The 'Female Spectator' and the Male Gaze

Only recently has Eliza Haywood emerged from relative obscurity to assume her standing as one of the early eighteenth century's most important literary figures. Although many of the facts surrounding her life remain distressingly vague,[17] the diligent efforts of a number of recent scholars have illuminated more clearly than ever before the range and complexity of Haywood's oeuvre.[18] As "the author of more than seventy pieces in six genres over four decades, one who played a key role in the novel's evolution and defined central issues in the portrayal of eighteenth-century female subjectivity,"[19] Haywood deserves a place beside that other prolific and resourceful practitioner of the literary trade, Daniel Defoe.

By the time Haywood launched her most successful and enduring periodical publication, the *Female Spectator*, in 1744, she was, as Robert Mayo notes, "an old hand at the wheel of public taste—as dramatist, journalist, translator, and popular author of romances and secret histories."[20] A failed career on the stage forced Haywood to turn in 1719 to the writing of fiction; her first production, *Love in Excess*, was a tremendous popular success (although not necessarily a critical one), vying with "*Gulliver's Travels* (1726) and *Strange Surprising Adventures of Robinson Crusoe* (1719), [as] one of the three most popular works of fiction before *Pamela* (1740)."[21] In the late 1720s, Pope's representation of Haywood in the second book of his *Dunciad* and *Dunciad Variorum* as "yon Juno of majestic size," who is the reward in the bookseller's pissing contest, had, as Blouch observes, "a complicated effect on Haywood's later reputation," whereby her "appearance among the dunce authors whom Pope satirizes, and more specifically the kind of appearance she makes, has affected critical scholarship regarding her ever since."[22] Yet Haywood did not, as most critics have alleged, disappear from view during the 1730s. Instead she "maintained a literary career during the decade, producing, in fact, her most ambitious experiments in genre to date."[23] She returned to the theater as both actor and writer, and continued to "trade on her reputation as a novelist," producing in 1732 a third edition of her fictional works. As she would later do with respect to the *Female Spectator*, Haywood marshaled popular sentiment in the name of literary production: "Both of Haywood's reputations, personal and literary, had become economic commodities that served as currency in the London literary community."[24]

Although Haywood's turn in the 1740s to what her first biographer, George Whicher, described as a second career as a moral novelist might seem to underlie the production of her overtly didactic *Female Spectator*,[25] Haywood had earlier made a number of forays into the periodical genre. Both the 1724 *Tea-Table* and the first rendition of *The Parrot*, authored by a "Mrs. Penelope Prattle" in 1728, have been variously attributed to Haywood;[26] moreover, Blouch notes the possibility of an early version of the *Female Spectator* advertised in the *Whitehall Evening Post* for December 9, 1731.[27] Yet neither of the extant publications makes any kind of concerted effort to address a female audience, either through subject matter or the composition of their collective authors; that honor was reserved for Haywood's enormously successful periodical venture, the twenty-four monthly "Books" of the *Female Spectator*.[28]

Haywood fluidly incorporated her prodigious expertise into the decidedly new character of the Female Spectator, replete with a club comprised of three female acquaintants: a "Wife," a "Widow of Quality," and a "Young Lady." Although explicitly modeled after the highly successful *Spectator*, the publication seemed designed in part to address its predecessor's glaring omission of women from the masculine domain of the Spectator Club. Indeed the *Female Spectator* effected a seeming revolution in periodical form through its deliberate construction of women as both scrutinizers and objects of scrutiny, as editors and audience alike. The periodical's introductory number presents its three club members as paragons of ideal femininity: Mira, valued both for her own wit and education and for her harmonious marriage to "a Gentleman every way worthy of so excellent a Wife," epitomizes the conjugal state;[29] the "Widow of Quality" manages to participate in the all the "modish Diversions of the Times" while still retaining her "Innocence and Honour"; Euphrosine, the accomplished daughter of a wealthy merchant, illustrates filial obedience. In contrast to the Spectator Club, whose members retained—almost to a fault—their individual voices and points of view,[30] the Female Spectator presents her association as "one Body, of which I am the Mouth," a family of women whose distinct experiences are gathered in the name of Femininity itself.

I contend, however, that beneath this mask of female unity and feminine self-sufficiency lies the text's deference to a literary authority delineated as particularly masculine and embodied in the persona of Mr. Spectator.[31] In other words, the *Female Spectator* hinged on the relationship between, on the one hand, an increasing awareness of certain subjects as belonging to a "feminine" realm in which women might reign supreme and, on the other hand, a masculine approbation that, as I will show, also included extensive male participation. We find these dual forces identified in a panegyric printed in the *Gentleman's Magazine* for December 8, 1744, acknowledging the receipt of the eighth book of the *Female Spectator*:

> Yet fair philosophers in virtue's cause,
> Conspicuous merit claims a just applause!
> Thrice worthy league! your gen'rous plan pursue,
> And take this tribute to your labours due:
> Were your great predecessor yet on earth,
> He'd be the first to speak your page's worth:
> There all the foibles of the fair you trace;
> There do you shew your sex's truest grace;
> There are the various wiles of man display'd,
> In gentle warnings to the credulous maid;
> Politely pictur'd, wrote with strength and ease,
> And while the wand'rer you reclaim, you please:
> Whether the fair, yet glows the blooming maid,
> Or a gay bride to hymen's porch is led
> Or a matron busy'd with domestick cares,
> Or as a widow for her loss despairs,
> Learn'd in the weaker sex in every state,
> *You* shew a *judgment* more than *man's* complete.
> Women, the heart of women best can reach;
> While men from maxims—you from practice teach.[32]

Sanctioning these possibly suspect feminine "labours" by draping them in the fabric of a literary authority implicitly defined as male, this "tribute" combines the endorsement of the poet, the male editors of the successful *Gentleman's Magazine*, and, most important, the absent Spectator himself in detailing the publication's numerous virtues. In this eulogy, the enthusiastic support of the great Spectator—"the first to speak your page's worth"—positions him as a veritable guardian angel, watching over the work of the women who are then constituted as his wards and pupils. The seemingly novel idea of female authority deriving from female experience—experience from which men would be naturally excluded—rests upon a foundation of domesticity that ironically posits men as the center of women's existence. This ideology follows a logical progression: if marriage is presented as women's *raison d'être*,

and if both custom and law give men ultimate control in the conjugal relationship, then women's happiness depends first upon their choice of a partner, and then upon their ability to coexist harmoniously with him. Not surprisingly, these two themes—how to choose the right man and how to get
along if one has chosen the wrong one—dominate the first two volumes of
the *Female Spectator*.

While the periodical seems to inch toward an ideology of separate spheres
in which women function as the repository of moral value, the Female Spectator's own didactic voice is authorized by her esteemed male predecessor.
Ironically, Haywood's reconsideration of the all-male Spectator Club depends upon her association's circumscription within the very limitations espoused by that august body. As my reading of the *Female Spectator*'s narratives will reveal, women's education and reformation occur most often at the
hands of men or in relation to them. Women's fundamental submission to
male authority within the domestic sphere means that women can provide
warning before the fact, or sympathy after it, but are virtually powerless in
terms of effecting any kind of decisive change.

By way of example, the lamentable tale of the hapless Monyma, oppressed
by a parsimonious father (Book 20), is a familiar type in the annals of periodical literature. After thwarting her marriage to the man she loves,
Monyma's father barters her to a physically repulsive older man whose only
charms are financial: "The grand Motive," Monyma tells the Female Spectator, "is, that the Person to whom my ill Stars have rendered me amiable,
desires no Money with me, and has it besides greatly in his Power to be serviceable to my Father in his way of Business." Monyma recounts her story
not in expectation of any direct relief to herself but rather with the desire
that the narrator's rhetoric might affect others: "The only Ease under this
heavy Affliction I can enjoy is, in the Hope my Story will influence you to
say something in your perswasive Manner that may have its due Weight with
other Parents, (for I despair of mine being moved, even with an Angel's Eloquence): Unhappy as I am, I wish not to have any Sharer in the same Fate,
though I am afraid too many have and will: That the Number may decrease,
however, is the sincere Prayer of . . . MONYMA."

After an initial expatiation on the sins of avarice, the narrator responds to
her correspondent's sad situation in language that could have come directly
from the *Athenian Mercury*. Regretting that Monyma had not written
sooner, she offers belated support for filial resistance, stating that "there is
no one Member of our Club, not even *Euphrosine* herself, who is the most
perfect Pattern of an implicit Obedience I ever knew, but is of Opinion, that
Monyma, circumstanced as she was, and under a former Engagement, might

have refused entering into a second without incurring any just Censure from the World." However, she acknowledges that she would not have counseled Monyma to have gone as far as a secret marriage with her young lover, for that would have been a "Breach of Duty." Yet her instructions regarding Monyma's comportment when married to the man she detests go far beyond the advice of any predecessor when she states that "We therefore hope *Monyma's* good Sense will enable her to endeavour a Forgetfulness of every thing that may occasion a Melancholly in herself, or a Dissatisfaction to her Husband:—Virtue, Religion, Reputation, Reason, and Interest all concur to exact it from her; and, in fulfilling their Dictates, she can only expect to find any true Ease or Consolation."

The Female Spectator's inability to ameliorate her correspondent's miserable situation reminds us that the "Dictates" she counsels Monyma to obey were of course all male dictates—instigated and implemented by men. In this period, the reforming gaze of men necessarily colors women's attention to other women. The *Female Spectator* typifies this situation by incorporating into the clearly female persona of its primary eidolon characteristics generally associated with men, including a broad range of worldly experience and a capacity for sophisticated analytical thought. Most interesting is the way in which the narrator facilely marshals a questionable past in the name of societal reform. While previous critics have glossed over the morally dubious content of the Female Spectator's introductory remarks as representing nothing more than a mirror of Haywood's own supposedly dissolute life,[33] I maintain that Haywood purposely bestows upon her narrator a discursive license conventionally given only to men. Unlike the women whose stories she will relate, the Female Spectator can walk through fire without being burned; moreover, her textual authority results from the burnishing of experience with the cloth of "Reflection." In contrast to her associates in the periodical endeavor, the Female Spectator remains unmarked by domestic affiliation, her account devoid of any mention of husband or even parents. Unhampered by familial ties, this forebear to herself resides outside the very domestic situation she uses to characterize and evaluate other women. Lacking a feminine gendered identity as defined through traditional affiliations to men, the narrator, whose relation to men is uniquely discursive, can function as the absent male in the *Female Spectator* family. Her narrative position combines Isaac Bickerstaff's extensive worldly experience with Mr. Spectator's more detached observations of human behavior:

> I have run through as many Scenes of Vanity and Folly as the
> greatest Coquet of them all.—Dress, Equipage, and Flattery,
> were the Idols of my Heart.—I should have thought that Day

lost which did not present me with some new Opportunity of shewing myself.—My Life, for some Years, was a continued Round of what I then called Pleasure, and my whole Time engrossed by a Hurry of promiscuous Diversions.—But whatever Inconveniences such a manner of Conduct has brought upon myself, I have this Consolation, to think that the Public may reap some Benefit from it:—The Company I kept was not, indeed, always so well chosen as it ought to have been, for the sake of my own Interest or Reputation; but then it was general, and by Consequence furnished me, not only with the Knowledge of many Occurrences, which otherwise I had been ignorant of, but also enabled me, when the too great Vivacity of my Nature became tempered with Reflection, to see into the secret Springs which gave rise to the Actions I had either heard, or been Witness of,—to judge of the various Passions of the human Mind, and distinguish those imperceptible Degrees by which they become Masters of the Heart, and attain the Dominion over Reason.—A thousand odd Adventures, which at the Time they happened made slight impression on me, and seemed to dwell no longer on my Mind than the Wonder they occasioned, now rise fresh to my Remembrance, with this Advantage, that the Mystery I then, for want of Attention, imagined they contained, is entirely vanished, and I find it easy to account for the Cause by the Consequence. (Book 1)

As opposed to the strict and limited background of most young women, the Female Spectator's own "Experience, Genius, and Education more liberal than is ordinarily allowed to Persons of [her] Sex" qualify her as a philosopher of the human psyche. Her ability to "judge" and "distinguish," her concern for the "secret Springs" of human behavior, her observations and analyses, all function, I maintain, to associate her with a discursive mode conventionally designated an exclusively masculine prerogative. In addition, the narrator's self-conscious use of the exemplum as her primary instructional mode further identifies her with a predominantly masculine moral and philosophical tradition. Theorizing from her "Observations of human Nature" that "Curiosity had . . . a Share in ev'ry Breast," she develops a narrative technique that will enable her to employ that inquisitiveness in the name of improvement: "my Business, therefore, was to hit this reigning Humour in such a Manner, as that the Gratification it should receive from being made acquainted with other People's Affairs, should at the same time teach every one to regulate their own" (Book I). *Pace* Shevelow, whose reading of the *Fe-*

male Spectator contends that the power of Haywood's fictional anecdotes overshadows the authority of the editor herself,[34] I contend that the Female Spectator demonstrates complete mastery over the narrative technique that she describes in the final book as one in which "Edification and delightful Entertainment would be so blended, as to render it an Impossibility to divide them, and every Reader be compelled to grow wiser and better without intending or seeking to be so."

The Female Spectator's analytical command positions her as distinct from the members of her club, whose influence derives solely from their idealized performance of domestic roles. There is nothing particularly new in the periodical's postulation of these characters as exemplifying the three stages of a woman's life; such prototypes, as we have seen, filled the pages of earlier periodical literature. What is different, however, is the way the women's shared possession of a goodness delineated in specifically female terms levels the social distinctions that, as I have shown, played such an important part in the Spectator Club. As all three typify different aspects of the same pattern, the daughter of a merchant meshes seamlessly with an upper-class widow. The text's erasure of differences among women depends, however, upon a corresponding amplification of the opposition between women and men. Just as in the *Spectator* men from diverse economic and political positions could unite in relation to a common Other comprised of women, so too does the *Female Spectator* construct a comparable narrative situation in which all women become sisters in their struggle against the voracious appetites of men. Haywood employs the familiar figure of the usually aristocratic rake as a means through which to alert her female readers to the ubiquitous hazards of uncontrolled male sexuality. Yet at the same time as she upholds the traditional view of masculinity as inherently dangerous, she fills her publication with more recently available images of a manly benevolence embodied in particularly middle-class terms. Men in their roles as husbands and fathers dominate the exemplary tales that pervade the first volume, while the contributions of supposed male correspondents, whose offerings of treatises, advice, and tutelage expand the periodical's domestic focus into the realms of politics, ethics, and natural philosophy, shape in turn the essays of later volumes. By examining men's dual roles as heads of household and liaisons to the public arena, this reading demonstrates men's pivotal position in both the text of the *Female Spectator* and the domain of experience and behavior designated feminine.

•

Although rife with stories of familial relations gone awry, the *Female Spectator* nevertheless treats the family in its ideal form as an intrinsically benevolent structure, devoid of generational conflict or sibling rivalry. Like the *Tatler* before it, the text employs instances of both virtuous and vicious parental behavior as example as well as warning to its readers of both sexes. While women as mothers are certainly present in the text, their position as wives generally eclipses their maternal role. Notably, the publication's first correspondent, a disconsolate mother, provides an instance of maternal failure;[35] the memorable story of the exemplary Alithea, which will be discussed more fully below, uses motherhood as a way to win back an unfaithful husband. Numerous tales, in combination with the Female Spectator's appended editorial comments, attest to an unquestioned acceptance of fathers as dominant figures within the family. Almost without exception, paternal behavior functions to determine familial bliss or domestic misery, thereby confirming the sentiment earlier expressed by Mr. Spectator himself: "I have hardly ever observed the married Condition unhappy, but for want of Judgment or Temper in the Man" (No. 479).

An essay from the middle of the third volume on the subject of second marriages discloses a parental double standard that in turn uncovers the publication's theory of male-female relations. While on the one hand the narrator finds nothing troubling in the remarriage of a widowed father, and in fact counsels second wives to extend the love they feel for their new husbands to those children whose "being *his* will endear them to her, the same as if she had an equal Part in them herself," she notes that widowed mothers, on the other hand, should refrain from the execrable act of "giving up the dear Pledges of a former Tenderness as a kind of Sacrifice to a second Passion." The reason, she soon explains, has to do with the "Power of a Step-Father" over those children:

> Every one knows a Wife is but the second Person in the Family:—A Husband is the absolute Head of it;—can act in every thing as he pleases, and though it is a great Misfortune to lose either of our Parents while young, and unable to take Care of ourselves, yet is the Danger much greater when the Place of a Father is fill'd up by a Stranger, than it can be under a Mother in-law.—The Reason is obvious;—the one can do of himself, what the other can only accomplish by the Influence she has over her Husband. (Book 16)

Such blatant admission of men's unequivocal power in the household informs all of the *Female Spectator*'s domestic chronicles. Although at first blush the story of Panthea, debauched by an evil father (Book 2) and that of Euphrosine, protected by a compassionate one (Book 3), would seem to have little in common, both narratives exemplify the text's acceptance of an ideology in which fathers, whether good or bad, retain complete power over, as well as primary responsibility for, the lives of their vulnerable offspring. The Female Spectator acknowledges such accountability by beginning her history of the unhappy Panthea with the claim that in order fully to understand her situation, one must "trace her Misfortunes to their Fountain Head, which, indeed, was from the first Moment of her Being." While Panthea's illegitimate birth (her father, the "subtle and opulent *Lacroon*," was married, but not to Miletta, her mother) implicates both parents,[36] her mother's sudden death in Panthea's adolescence tellingly leaves Lacroon the sole arbiter of his daughter's fate. In contrast to what one would expect from such a demonstrated profligate, he brings Panthea to his home, informs her of her birth, and owns her publicly, thereby treating her "with all the Marks of a paternal Care and Affection." Her life seemingly normalized, she falls in love with the aptly named Fidelio, whom her father approves because of his high birth.

Lacroon's corrupt actions, however, soon interrupt the loving courtship of Panthea and Fidelio. To save his own neck, Lacroon arranges to pander his lovely daughter to the powerful and "amorous" Imperio, for he was "resolv'd to make no Scruple to offer her up a Sacrifice to Shame, if by her Prostitution he could be preserved from the just Prosecution of his Enemies." When the virtuous Panthea responds that she would rather die than become Imperio's mistress, her artful father extorts compliance by appealing to her filial "tenderness," thus forestalling his own ruin through hers. Although noting that the bulk of society, following the "Custom" excoriated in the earlier *Visiter*, has since blamed Panthea for her loss of honor, the Female Spectator reproves this severity by arguing that "her Youth, and the Authority of a Father, than whom she had no other Friend, may plead some Excuse for her Want of that Fortitude and Resolution, which alone could have preserved her Virtue." She declares instead that "'Tis on *Lacroon* alone that the just Censures of her Fall should light:—*Lacroon*, guilty of Crimes unnumber'd, yet of none more unnatural, more detestable than this of separating two Hearts, which seem'd by Heaven united, and seducing and betraying his own Child to Infamy and Perdition." While Haywood's use of "betray" appears highly justified, "seduce" seems an interesting—and loaded—term for discussing father-daughter relations. Yet the word's multiple meanings—to mislead as well as to violate—serve to highlight Panthea's no-win situation: while her chastity depends upon mustering the "Fortitude" and "Resolution" to defy her father's brutal request, as a dutiful daughter she can possess neither attribute, for her will must reflect her father's. Led astray by a belief in her father's decency, Panthea, like Iphigenia before her, is destroyed by her father's sacrifice as well as by the society that invests him with the power to perform it. Using the tender bond of filial love as a means to manipulate rather than protect his daughter, Lacroon epitomizes the malevolent paternity made possible by an ideology of patriarchal control.

One would expect that the extended narrative from the next book of the *Female Spectator* would stand in every way opposite to the story of the execrable Lacroon, for Euphrosine's merchant father provides "an Example for many others to imitate" in his "amiable" treatment of her. He is a father who not only consults but also solicits his daughter's desire with regard to a prospective suitor and, in the process, cements family harmony. Yet I submit that even this "worthy Family," whose relations Haywood paints in the most glowing colors, necessarily partakes in a gender dynamic in which paternal authority eradicates female desire. In a striking irony, Euphrosine's father declares that she has earned her will by forfeiting it: "you well deserve to be left to the Freedom of your Choice," he tells her, "by your Readiness to resign it." Indeed the story's formal structure further muffles the young woman's voice—as well as her sexual subjectivity—by having the Female Spectator relay the events, rather than Euphrosine, herself a member of the club.

Serving as an example of the proper attitude toward wealth as well as toward children, the narrative, whose eulogistic tone recalls the *Spectator*'s essay on the Cornelii family (No. 192), divulges relations of class in addition to those of gender by reiterating the connection between mercantile benevolence and sentimental family relations.[37] The story goes as follows: Euphrosine was courted by a very rich and significantly older gentleman. While her father has willingly deferred to his "Daughter's Inclinations," the belief that her father approves of the match shapes Euphrosine's own proclivity. However, a sickly physical appearance and the lack of her customary "Chearfulness and Vivacity" betray her true unhappiness to her family. When pressed eventually by the impatient suitor, the father confers with his daughter, explaining that although her five siblings will benefit from this match (each will receive a "considerable Addition" to his or her own fortune from a share of the portion Euphrosine's wealthy suitor has agreed to forfeit), she should nevertheless consult her own desire, for he believes "that true Felicity does not consist in Wealth alone"; moreover, he "think[s] it both unjust and cruel to make those wretched to whom I have given Being." He then asks whether she can love this man "as it will be your Duty to do if you become his Wife?" When Euphrosine docilely replies that she would always "fulfil her Duty," her father subsequently informs her that "there were two ways of fulfilling a

Duty;—the one merely because it was so, and the other, because it afforded *a Pleasure to oneself.*" Noting that her recent "Melancholly" would seem to imply that the match was "far from being agreeable" to her, he cautions his daughter not to sacrifice her own peace of mind to the former kind of duty. "Emboldened by so much Goodness," Euphrosine acknowledges that disinclination for her suitor had been overruled by "implicit Obedience" to her father, and is lavishly praised in the manner described above.[38]

In each account, it is not the daughter's behavior—both Panthea and Euphrosine are uniformly chaste and obedient—but that of the father which determines each young woman's state of suffering or tranquillity. The stories of the "penetrating" father of Beliza, who discerns that her suitor Cleophil is more interested in his daughter's portion than her love (Book 3), and that of the understanding father to the heiress Celemena, who supports her infatuation for a music master out of concern for her health and happiness (Book 7), provide further testimony to the significance of fatherly love. Although the text's numerous examples of relations between fathers and daughters do not all succeed in attaining this benevolent standard, the *Female Spectator* consistently presents paternal authority as preferable to its absence. Those young women who eschew familial guidance inevitably find themselves wedded to abusive charlatans. As an attempt to warn her correspondent Sarah Oldfashion of the danger of treating her pleasure-loving daughter too harshly, the Female Spectator tells the story of a certain Christabella, who, while cleverly devising a stratagem to escape imprisonment by an overcautious father, climbs literally into the hands of an impostor who then forces her to beg for her own money (Book 5). The narrator presents her tale not as vindication of Christabella's actions but instead as a warning to other parents to use psychology rather than severity with their children: "It is certain that the Fate of so disobedient a Daughter, cannot excite much Commiseration in the World; but it ought to be a Warning to all Parents who wish to see their Children happy, to study carefully their Dispositions before they go about to treat them with ungentle Means, and rather condescend to *sooth* an obstinate Temper than *Compel* it to a Change." The strategy for maintaining parental (read paternal) control may change, but that control remains in force.

Implicitly confirming the text's fantasy of a best of all possible worlds in which fathers act as they should, the passage also speaks to children's utter dependence upon such fathers for their own happiness. As will be the case in marriage, men determine women's lives; a woman's only hope is in being born to—or in choosing—the right man. The Female Spectator's tales of marital relations reflect her conviction that "it is not by Force our Sex can hope to maintain their Influence over the Men"; her "infallible Maxim" for her women readers is "that whenever we would truly conquer we must seem to yield" (Book 10). Thus while an early number openly criticizes the foolish husband of the intelligent Altizeera, who "thinks he must have a Judgment superior to his Wife, because he is a *Man*, and that it becomes him to contradict every thing she says and does, because he is a *Husband*" (Book 2), the text nevertheless uniformly counsels passivity as women's sole means of combating male abuse.

Although the periodical contains numerous examples of such exemplary complaisance,[39] most interesting for our purposes is the story of the beleaguered Alithea (possibly a reference to the virtuous and in many ways passive maiden in Wycherley's *The Country Wife*), who responds to her husband Dorimon's infidelity and escalating hostility with only an increase in devotion. The essay's narrative structure constitutes Alithea's exceptional behavior as a feminine norm by positioning it as the centerpiece of Book 6, a treatise on the particularly feminine quality of "Good-Nature": "as all other Vices, so a Sourness of Humour is also more unbecoming in Women than in Men." Consequently, those women who fail to imitate what is often inimitable behavior become somehow less than women: "deservedly shunn'd and hated by the more gentle of [their] own Sex, and ridicul'd and laugh'd at by all in general of the other."

Alithea's tale offers a poignant variation on the theme of the ideal second wife, whom the Female Spectator counsels to treat her husband's children as if they were her own, by adding a maternal element to wifely amiability. Upon discovering that her unfaithful husband, Dorimon, has fathered a child by his mistress, who has subsequently deposited the boy with a nurse, Alithea adopts the boy as her own—visiting him weekly with food and clothing more fitting his station, even bringing him to her own house when she knows Dorimon will be absent. Returning home one day earlier than expected, he discovers his wife playing with an unknown child; when Alithea, after great pains—she does not want to discomfit him in any way—finally informs him that the boy is his illegitimate son, Dorimon at last recognizes his wife's merit and dismisses his mistress: "Good God! cried he, am I awake!—Can it be possible there is such a Woman in the World!"

Dorimon's understandable amazement at such a paragon of wifehood is not shared by the Female Spectator, whose closing comments reveal the contradiction within her exemplum. While on the one hand she states that "there is no Particular in the Conduct of the amiable *Alithea* that ought to be omitted, or may not serve to shew how much a perfect Good-Nature may enable us to sustain, and to forgive," on the other hand she warns that she "would have no Husband . . . depend on this Example, and become a *Dorimon* in expectation of finding an *Alithea* in his Wife." Thus while women must "seem to yield" in order "truly [to] conquer" (Book 10), these examples demonstrate that semblance becomes too easily elided with reality. That is, women's prosperity rests upon their ability to internalize so completely an ideology of domesticity in which men reign supreme that their own passions become not just stifled but nonexistent.[40]

The rhetoric of passivity that counsels women's necessary deference to their fathers' or husbands' desires does not, however, mean that women must absent themselves entirely from realms of experience and authority designated male. While highly critical of those pleasure-loving women who live in their families "like a Stranger," the Female Spectator simultaneously censures "Those Men . . . who think, that all the Learning becoming in a Woman is confined to the Management of her Family" (Book 10). The periodical attempts to lessen the potential dangers of instruction in such subjects as philosophy, geography, and history by employing the time-honored convention that this education will make women only "more obedient Daughters, more faithful Wives, more tender Mothers, more sincere Friends, and more valuable in every other Station of Life."[41] In addition, and perhaps even more powerfully, the text blunts the potential danger of this instruction by swathing it in the words of numerous, and most probably fictional, male correspondents.[42] Men serve as the intellectual ambassadors who will escort women through dialogues on government (Book 9) or diatribes on tea-drinking (Book 8), on nature walks through the English countryside (Books 15 and 19) or to a shipwreck off the coast of Sumatra (Book 18). Under male guidance, women might even make repeated trips to the mythical "Topsy-Turvy Island" that serves as an allegory for English corruption (Books 16 and 18).[43] For a publication supposedly advocating a separate agenda for its women readers or functioning as a conduct book for domestic femininity,[44] the *Female Spectator* is surprisingly occupied with problems that would seem to fall outside the sphere of domestic relations.

In this text, men's central place within the family functions as both microcosm of and supplement to their work within the public sphere. In addition to the numerous articles concerned with men's relation to children and wives, the periodical includes pieces on such issues as familial, economic, and emotional relations among men; men in the military; men's escalating abuse of gaming, speculation, and luxury; and men's role in politics. Haywood employs numerous strategies for interposing men into her text. We have already seen how she uses examples, both positive and negative, of fathers and husbands as a means of authorizing particular forms of gendered relations. In the following pages I wish to expand upon those representations by analyzing men's crucial role as the subjects and correspondents who develop the text's construction of both male and female gender and class identities.

•

Like most would-be reformers, the Female Spectator proves her own importance by pointing out to supposedly oblivious readers how drastically their own times have degenerated. Since she holds the male sex ultimately responsible for the fate of women as well as for their own well-being, her corrective gaze falls with particular severity upon men: "Vanity, Affectation, and all Errors of that Nature are infinitely less excuseable in the Men than in the Women, as they have so much greater Opportunities than we have of knowing better" (Book 15). The early and seemingly unrelated discussions of "Effeminacy" in the military (Book 2) and the destruction wrought upon all levels of society by the contagious "Itch of Gaming" (Book 3) confirm a belief in masculinity as necessarily invested in an ethos of self-sacrifice. The narrator reproaches the indolent soldier for the same reason that she condemns the man of business who neglects his shop in the hope of "getting more by *Play*": each ignores, rather than sacrifices himself to, societal needs—be they those of the nation at large or of individual families. In contrast to those reforming predecessors who consistently identified the dangerous pursuit of luxury and pleasure with women, the *Female Spectator* singles out men's deviation from the manly ideal as the severest threat to English society.

The essay in the second book wittily ridicules those men who put physical indulgence above the requirements of their country. Like Addison and Steele censuring the women who wore French brocades during the War of the Spanish Succession, or who valued goods above their own husbands, Haywood attacks those men who lament not the deleterious situation of their nation at war but "the Want of any of those Commodities, the Interruption of our Commerce prevents from being imported." She finds such masculine "Over-Delicacy" particularly calamitous when enacted by men in the military. As "Diversion" to her readers, as well as an implied rebuke to the soldier himself, she publishes a copy of a bill owing to a friend from a "Gentleman now in the Army." Such crucial items as almond paste, gloves, and orange water were "the Ammunition this doughty Hero, it seems, took with him; the Loss of which, had it happen'd to have fallen into the Enemy's Hands, would probably have given him more Concern than the routing of the whole Army, provided his own dear Person had escaped without a Scar." She hopes that this ruinous "Effeminacy" will be worn off by experience, as such men learn "that if they would soar to Glory, they must entirely throw aside all of the *softening Luxuries of their Silken Youth*" (my italics). In contrast to numerous essays in the earlier *Spectator*, which represented the fop as more attractive to women than the man of sense, Haywood's euphonious formulation sensualizes these men while at the same time emasculating them. She contends that women's rightful predilection for "military Gentlemen" derives not from the fact that they wear a "red Coat," for "*that* many others do, who sometimes sit behind a Counter, and what is worse, have not the Heart to draw a Sword, or fire a Pistol," but rather from their assumed role as women's defenders: "a Soldier is supposed, at least, to have Courage to defend, in any Exigence, all who are under his Protection." Interestingly, the essay expands the traditionally aristocratic attribute of physical courage to fit all men: "the Character of a brave Man is, of all other, most esteem'd in the World, as that of a Coward is most contemn'd." The Female Spectator ridicules the "fine Gentleman" who takes perfume to the trenches because he pays too much attention to his own body and not enough to those bodies he is supposedly there to safeguard.

While luxurious desires pose a threat to national security by softening the soldier, the Female Spectator notes that a fervor for affluence without the requisite toil has similarly endangered England's economic condition by destroying its middle class. She dates the germ of this "extravagant Itch of Gaming, which, like the Plague, has spread its Contagion through all Degrees of People" to "the fatal Year 1720," when the "alluring Prospect of making a great Fortune at once, and without any Labour or Trouble, so infatuated the Minds of all the Ambitious, the Avaricious, and the Indolent, that for a Time there seemed an entire Stagnation of all Business but what was transacted by the *Brokers* in *Change-Alley*." The subsequent decades have transformed cards from a source of "Amusement" on a winter's night to the "Employment of the Year"; the Female Spectator blames this private gambling, as well as the more public form of speculation on stocks precipitated by the South Sea Bubble, for the undoing of "three Parts in four of the middling Class": "To this unhappy Propensity is greatly owing that so many Shops lately well stock'd and flourishing, are now shut up even in the Heart of the City, and their Owners either Bankrupts or miserable Refugees in foreign Parts." While numerous texts, including the *Spectator* itself, demonstrated the ruinous effects of gaming upon both women and men of the upper classes, the *Female Spectator* confines its attack to those whose welfare depends upon "honest" work—namely, men of the middle ranks. Thus while offhandedly remarking that women are "known to be so fond of appearing fine and gay, that it is no wonder the Tradesmen's Wives should even exceed their Husbands in the Article of Dress," the narrator does not represent such lavish feminine display as in any way responsible for the decimation of bourgeois enterprise. Her narrative, reminiscent of that told in George Lillo's play *The London Merchant* (1731), locates *men's* sartorial splendor as the cause of financial ills:

> No Difference [is] made between the young Nobleman and the City-Prentice, except that the latter is sometimes the greater Beau:—Gold-headed Canes, Watches, Rings, Snuff-Boxes, and lac'd Wastcoats, run away with the Fortune that should set him up in Business, and frequently tempt him to defraud his Master, who perhaps also, taken up with his own private Pleasures, examines too little into his Shop-Affairs, and when the Till is drained, borrows a while to support his darling Pride, then sinks at once to Ruin and Contempt. (Book 3)[45]

As in the earlier *Night-Walker*, the narrator's description of the ruin incurred when the "City-Prentice" emulates his superiors reinforces a belief in behaviors appropriate to each class as well as each sex. The periodical further delineates the "innumerable Inconveniences" that occur whenever people "behave in a Fashion unbecoming of their Rank" by describing in the sixteenth book a voyage to "a little Republic in the Atlantic Ocean, called the Topsy-Turvy Island." Haywood chooses as the supposed source of this tale the correspondent Eumenes, who presents himself as an unabashed apologist for both the middling class and the status quo: "But as I am more particularly concerned for the Reputation, Interest, and Happiness of the Citizens of *London*, than for any other Division or Degree of People in his Majesty's Dominions, my Family, for a long Generation, having had the Honour to be of the Number, and I myself now am, I would fain engage the *Female Spectator* to make it her Endeavour to convince them, that there is nothing on the other Side of *Temple-Bar* which it will be for their Advantage to imitate." Eumenes's pride in his socioeconomic position combines with his authority as narrator to establish a supposedly natural and beneficent order of both gender and class relations. By presenting the inhabitants of Topsy-Turvy Island as "Lunatics," Eumenes's history solidifies an ideology of intrinsic difference between men and women as well as between "Nobility" and "Mechanics":

> Their very Habits and Recreations seem to denote them Enemies, not only to common Sense, but also to Nature:—The Men affecting to wear soft *effeminate* Garb, and the Women one altogether *masculine*:—Their Heroes sit for three Hours together, sipping warm Water and Sugar, and their Virgins breakfast upon Brandy:—The Nobility take a Pride in driving Coaches, or running like Lackeys by the Side of them; and the

> Mechanics forsake their Shops, to ride about the Town in
> State like so many Magnifico's.

Such reversals lead, of course, only to destruction. Eumenes trots out a fa-
vored comparison as warning to the periodical's readers: "*London* has been
called a second *Rome*, and we have flattered ourselves that the Comparison
was just; but pray Heaven we may never be too like it in its Decline; let us
remember from what an envy'd Height that famous City fell, when Luxury
and Pride debased the Minds of its Inhabitants."[46]

Eumenes's attack reaffirms the *Female Spectator*'s earlier statement of its
reforming principles: "To check the enormous Growth of Luxury, to reform
the Morals, and improve the Manners of an Age, by all confess'd degenerate
and sunk" (Book 8). In a second installment of his saga, further detailing the
island's decline (Book 19), Eumenes recapitulates the terms of the Female
Spectator's own attack on gaming in Book 3: "Certain it is, notwithstanding,
that they were once a wise and gallant People; but Avarice on the one Hand,
and Luxury on the other, have poisoned and enervated all their nobler Passions, and rendered them, both in public and private Life, no less deserving
of Contempt than formerly they were of Veneration and Esteem." As in
Haywood's England, gaming has become the "chief Business, as well as
Amusement" of the inhabitants who worship only the "goddess Fortune."
The Female Spectator's response to Eumenes's contribution accurately summarizes a view of "Virtue" that applies particularly to men: "When a Nation
devotes itself to such Studies and Amusements as can no way contribute to
the Glory or Interest of their Country, or to their own particular Reputation, they will infallibly become by degrees divested of all Sense of Virtue,
and, like the *Topsy-Turvyans*, grow the Slaves of Vice and Folly."

Like Eumenes, "John Careful" demonstrates a particular concern for the
trading classes. Writing in Book 8 to warn other husbands about the dangers
of women's immoderate use of tea, he appeals to an ethos that explicitly links
time with money. In distinction to those middle-class husbands who support
their wives' imitation of the unemployed aristocracy, John Careful bemoans
the way in which the endless ritual of the tea-table occasions "the Loss of
Time both as to the Mistress and Servants"; moreover, he wittily notes that
"the Regularity of the Tea-Table occasions a Want of Regularity in every
Thing beside."[47] As Mr. Careful's narrative demonstrates, a man's domestic
and economic "Interest and Happiness" depend upon his ability to regulate
his wife's behavior. The Female Spectator's initial response to this epistle assumes an expectation of female solidarity on the part of her women readers:
"I dare say one Half of my Readers will expect me to be very angry at this
Declamation against an Amusement my Sex are generally so fond of."

Tellingly, she also assumes that half her readers are male! However, resorting to Bickerstaff's very diction, she maintains instead that "it is the firm Resolution of our Club to maintain strict Impartiality in these Lucubrations; and were any of us ever so deeply affected by the Satire, (which thank Heaven we are not) we should, notwithstanding, allow it to be just."

The periodical's claim to an impartial moral authority that is universal (and hence male) rather than partial to the female sex informs what is arguably the Female Spectator's most interesting and perplexing interchange: that with the correspondent who identifies himself as "Curioso Politico" (Book 8). His vituperative letter takes the Female Spectator to task for having pretended to things above her reach. Yet he seems more irate that she has failed to deliver on her earlier pledge to provide information that extends far beyond women's ken than at the fact that she has promised such information in the first place: "did you never reflect that People would grow uneasy at the Disappointment, when, instead of that full and perfect Account of the most momentous Actions you made them hope, they find themselves for several Months together entertained only with Home-Amours, Reflections on Human Nature, the Passions, Morals, Inferences, and Warnings to your own Sex;—the most proper Province for you, I must own, but widely inconsistent with the Proposals of your first setting out." Curioso Politico implies that the periodical's failure to address issues of war and politics preempts its narrator's earlier claims of literary authority: "Are you not under most terrible Apprehensions that, instead of the Woman of Experience, Observation, fine Understanding, and extensive Genius you would pass for, you should be taken for an idle, prating, gossiping old Woman, fit only to tell long Stories by the Fire-side for the Entertainment of little Children or Matrons, more antiquated than yourself?" By associating what is for the most part an accurate description of the publication's content—"Home-Amours, Reflections on Human Nature, the Passions, Morals, Inferences, and Warnings to your own Sex"—with the idle gossip of superannuated women, Curioso Politico's attack operates not only to denigrate the specific methodology of the *Female Spectator* but also to dismiss the entire periodical enterprise as "in no way fit for the polite Coffee-Houses, or to satisfy Persons of an inquisitive Taste."

In her spirited defense, the narrator shifts the terms of the controversy from issues of gender to those of genre. That is, she does not distinguish between realms of experience and literary authority appropriate to each sex, but instead contrasts the reportorial concerns of newspapers with the more expository design of the periodical undertaking.[48] Claiming that many of the topics with which Curioso Politico seems concerned "come not within the

Province of a *Female Spectator*;—such as Armies marching,—Battles fought,—Towns destroyed,—Rivers cross'd, and the like," she notes the redundancy of attending to such issues: "I should think it ill became me to take up my own, or Reader's Time, with such Accounts as are every Day to be found in the public Papers." Her movement outside the dichotomy imposed by gender also enables her to break down any rigid demarcation of public and private as she exonerates her periodical by emphasizing the public benefit that results from the reform of private vice: "the better we regulate our Actions in *private Life*, the more we may hope of *public Blessings*, and the more we shall be enabled to sustain *public Calamities*."

Following the reforming tradition of her august predecessor Mr. Spectator, the narrator further diminishes the separation between public and private, male and female, by extolling the universal benefits of her periodical enterprise: "To check the enormous Growth of Luxury, to reform the Morals, and improve the Manners of an Age, by all confess'd degenerate and sunk, are the great Ends for which these Essays were chiefly intended; and the Authors flatter themselves that nothing has been advanced, but may contribute in a more or less Degree to the accomplishing so glorious a Point." The description of her corrective strategy makes no distinction between men and women; vice, virtue, the passions—all are construed as human attributes rather than those apportioned by sex.

And yet, as the attack, whether spurious or authentic, of Curioso Politico has demonstrated, women in this period have not been authorized a universal voice. The Female Spectator herself acknowledges such a lack of editorial authority in her response to a letter from "Leucothea" in Book 15 asking why she has not paid more attention to the foibles of men. She writes that "I had not a sufficient Idea of my own Capacity, to imagine, that any Thing offered by a *Female Censor* would have so much Weight with the Men as is requisite to make that Change in their Conduct and Oeconomy, which, I cannot help acknowledging, a great many of them stand in very great need of." While the statement is somewhat disingenuous, its sincerity belied by the presence of numerous earlier attacks on male behavior as well as by the fact that the essay continues with a potent assault upon those civilian men who boyishly sport military costume, the assertion nevertheless betrays an anxiety with regard to women's place vis-à-vis men. No male eidolon, by comparison, ever questions the appropriateness of his advice to a female audience; his masculinity not only ensures but even enhances his right to scrutinize, as well as necessarily to correct, women's behavior.

Paradoxically, however, the very periodical tradition that enables the Female Spectator to assert a supposedly universal reforming voice simultaneously undermines that voice, for those earlier texts were instrumental in the process of establishing a gender difference that defined moral authority as the primary province of men. On the one hand, the presence of its female eidolon and her club of women enables the *Female Spectator* to articulate a rhetoric of particular concern for its women readers as justified by the bonds of a supposed sympathy; the narrator tells a female correspondent that "As I am a Woman, I am more interested in their [women's] Happiness" (Book 15). On the other hand, this affiliation is circumscribed by the text's need for men's approval and participation. While Haywood's publication might therefore push at the boundaries of that sphere established within periodical literature as the particular domain of women, it in no way reconfigures the broader design. Throughout the *Female Spectator*, women, whether editors, correspondents, or readers, remain confined to a subset of the universal sphere designated male. Putting the men back into our reading of the *Female Spectator* not only enables us to analyze with greater acumen the dialectically constituted relations between women and men, but also forces us to rethink the terms of a literary history of the eighteenth century that accepts far too comfortably the notion of an unbridgeable chasm between public and private, male and female.

Afterword

Both the public and the private labors involved in producing this book—reading, writing, presenting, discussing, rereading and rewriting—have provided invaluable opportunities to reflect upon my understanding of gender ideologies, as conceived in the eighteenth century and espoused today. From my earliest undergraduate immersion in feminist theory to more recent considerations of the relationship between gender studies and eighteenth-century studies,[1] I have questioned an account of gender that, whether deliberately or unwittingly, claims to analyze the female sex as detached from the male half of the species except in the latter's exclusive role as women's oppressors. The dialectical approach to gender formation that I have advocated throughout this book does not attempt to remove women from discussion; nor does it try to deny or to minimize in any way men's responsibility for the subordination of women. Rather, my goal has been to create a way of talking about gender that simultaneously challenges the conventions of western European, male-dominated thought and the revisions of modern feminism by exposing both sexes to a concurrent critical gaze. In this way, I hope to offer a theoretical framework that will help men and women to support each other in the practical struggle to undermine and eradicate existing structures of oppression.

Beyond the specific historical scope of this study, I believe that one of the key issues this book raises is whether it is productive to view feminism as a liberating discourse if it cuts itself off from a dialectical understanding of gender formation. As the last chapter demonstrated, we find the problematics of separatism clearly exemplified in the combined eighteenth-century presentation and twentieth-century interpretation of Eliza Haywood's *Female Spectator*. Written at a historical moment in which women were increasingly granted a literary presence and tendered as a publication specifically addressed to women by women, the *Female Spectator* has been commonly read as the articulation of a distinct, and at times even subversive, woman's voice, a voice audibly different from any attributed to men. But the discourse that both eighteenth-century rhetoric and modern critical practice have represented as separate and discrete turns out to be as much about men as it is about women. Moreover, since male authority invariably circumscribed and perhaps still circumscribes women's entrance into print, the changing structures of that authority must be carefully and constantly scrutinized if we are ever to break free of a conception of gender that seamlessly elides the masculine and the universal.

For me, one of the most fascinating and, I believe, important results of writing this book has been the discovery of the ways in which eighteenth-century ideology provides a nascent form of, and thus a unique access to, our own current relationship to gender. The earlier era's creation of a beneficial, inevitable, and supposedly natural separation between the sexes has given rise to a discourse of gender that investigates the construction of femininity as somehow distinct from the equally fabricated set of norms and behaviors constitutive, in any given culture and period, of masculine gender identity. Just as separatist thinking failed to offer any real liberation from male domination by necessarily binding women to men as exemplifying that from which women must separate, so too does the strand of feminism that examines femininity without a comparable attention to its counterpart in masculinity keep women confined within the universalist assumption that, by problematizing women, correspondingly exempts men from critical view. Unraveling the tapestry that manifests the cumulative work of many centuries demands, then, feminism's assiduous and often uneasy consideration of the masculine half of the gender equation. Whether or not I have managed to meet this challenge, I hope that by proposing men, I have succeeded in offering my readers an alternative theory of, as well as methodology for, examining the construction of gender in the eighteenth century as well as in our own.

Reference Matter

Notes

All citations from Addison and Steele's *Tatler, Spectator*, and *Guardian* refer to the editions below; they will be included in the text by issue number.

The Tatler, ed. Donald F. Bond, 3 vols.
(Oxford: Clarendon Press, 1987).

The Spectator, ed. Donald F. Bond, 5 vols.
(Oxford: Clarendon Press, 1965).

The Guardian, ed. John Calhoun Stephens
(Lexington: University Press of Kentucky, 1982).

Introduction

1. Whereas the study of women's oppression has, by now, an impressive critical tradition and a developed body of scholarship, only recently have critics paid similar attention to masculinity as an equally historical, and comparably pernicious, social construction. Yet while practitioners of the discipline of men's studies have challenged productively the biases of feminist thinking, their work, like that of their feminist counterparts, often fails to recognize the relational quality of gendered identity. Some important exceptions may be found in the work of Michael Kimmel, particularly his article entitled "The Contemporary 'Crisis' of Masculinity in Historical Perspective," *The Making of Masculinities: The New Men's Studies*, ed. Harry Brod (London: Allen and Unwin, 1987), 121–53, and in Michael Roper and John Tosh's introduction to their volume *Manful Assertions: Masculinities in Britain since 1800* (London: Routledge, 1991), 1–24. Moreover, an increasing number of eighteenth-century scholars have begun to constitute a new

field—that of eighteenth-century gender studies—by endeavoring to theorize gender both historically and dialectically. See, for example, G. J. Barker-Benfield, *The Culture of Sensibility: Sex and Society in Eighteenth-Century Britain* (Chicago: University of Chicago Press, 1992); Kristina Straub, *Sexual Suspects: Eighteenth-Century Players and Sexual Ideology* (Princeton, N.J.: Princeton University Press, 1992); Jill Campbell, *Natural Masques: Gender and Identity in Fielding's Plays and Novels* (Stanford, Calif.: Stanford University Press, 1995); Anthony Fletcher, *Gender, Sex and Subordination in England 1500–1800* (New Haven: Yale University Press, 1995); and Michael McKeon, "Historicizing Patriarchy: The Emergence of Gender Difference in England, 1660–1760," *Eighteenth-Century Studies* 28, no. 3 (1995): 295–322.

2. *Illuminations*, ed. Hannah Arendt (New York: Schocken Books, 1969), 263.

3. Kathryn Shevelow, *Women and Print Culture: The Construction of Femininity in the Early Periodical* (London: Routledge, 1989).

Chapter One

1. *Life and Errors of John Dunton, Late Citizen of London, Written by Himself in Solitude* [1705] (New York: Burt Franklin, 1969), vol. 1, 249.

2. According to John G. Ames, "Public journals before 1690 were, almost entirely, restricted to temporary news and politics; to the heated discussion of controverted subjects of an ecclesiastical character; and to mere catalogues of books lately published; to papers written for the improvement of trade; and to sheets of nonsense" (*The English Literary Periodical of Morals and Manners* [Mt. Vernon, Ohio: Republican Publishing Co., 1904], 7).

3. Kathryn Shevelow, *Women and Print Culture: The Construction of Femininity in the Early Periodical* (London: Routledge, 1989) and Terry Eagleton, *The Function of Criticism: From "The Spectator" to Post-Structuralism* (London: Verso, 1984).

4. I employ the term "social periodical" in order to emphasize both the periodical's self-defined role as an arbiter of social norms and the imbrication of those social norms with literary and aesthetic ones.

5. Ian Watt, *The Rise of the Novel* (Berkeley: University of California Press, 1957). For other studies of the novel also explicitly concerned with relations of class and genre, see Lennard Davis, *Factual Fictions: The Origins of the English Novel* (New York: Columbia University Press, 1983); Nancy Armstrong, *Desire and Domestic Fiction: A Political History of the Novel* (New York: Oxford University Press, 1987); Terry Lovell, *Consuming Fiction* (London: Verso, 1987); Michael McKeon, *The Origins of the English Novel, 1600–1740* (Baltimore: Johns Hopkins University Press, 1987); J. Paul Hunter, *Before Novels: The Cultural Contexts of Eighteenth-Century English Fiction* (New York: Norton, 1990); and Catherine Gallagher, *Nobody's Story: The Vanishing Acts of Women Writers in the Marketplace, 1670–1820* (Berkeley: University of California Press, 1994).

6. Anthony Fletcher, *Gender, Sex and Subordination in England 1500–1800* (New Haven: Yale University Press, 1995), 383.

7. I am thinking in particular of the pioneering essay by Laura Mulvey entitled "Visual Pleasure and Narrative Cinema," *Screen* 16, no. 3 (Autumn 1975).

8. *The History of Sexuality, Vol. 2: The Use of Pleasure* (New York: Vintage, 1986), 213.

9. Ibid., 253.

10. Ibid.

11. See in particular Davis, *Factual Fictions*, and Hunter, *Before Novels*.

12. *Athenian Mercury*, No. 3 (Mar. 31, 1691).

13. F. W. Bateson, "Addison, Steele and the Periodical Essay," *The New History of Literature: Dryden to Johnson*, ed. Roger Lonsdale (New York: Peter Bedrick Books, 1987), 132. J. H. Plumb notes the pervasive authority of these texts even into the twentieth century: "The collected *Spectator* . . . was reprinted over and over again, and Addison was the model essayist in thought as well as in style when I was a boy at school" ("The Commercialization of Leisure in Eighteenth-Century England," *The Birth of a Consumer Society*, ed. Neil McKendrick, John Brewer, and J. H. Plumb [Bloomington: Indiana University Press, 1982], 284).

14. On this process, see Linda Nicholson, *Gender and History: The Limits of Social Theory in the Age of the Family* (New York: Columbia University Press, 1986). Nicholson's analysis of the simultaneous historical emergence of the categories of "family" and the "state" out of those "kinship systems, which at one time had been the major mechanisms for regulating food production and distribution, sexuality, crime and punishment, etc." (2) allows us to conceptualize both the patriarchal elements that underpin the modern family and the "progressive domination of the state and later the market over kinship" (196–97).

15. Hunter, *Before Novels*, 86.

16. Jeremy Black, *The English Press in the Eighteenth Century* (London: Croom Helm, 1987), xiv–xv. Moreover, Black notes that "journals that are widely accepted as newspapers did and do not devote themselves to current affairs only. Items characteristic of eighteenth-century magazines can be found in abundance in the newspapers of the period. The distinction between the two is more one of size and frequency than of content" (ibid.). In this light, it is important to recall that many early publications maintained a fluidity between different forms of discourse: although considered periodicals, Motteux's *Gentleman's Journal*, Defoe's *Review*, and Steele's *Tatler* all included lengthy sections of current news.

17. "Of Either Sex" was later added to the title when the editors agreed in its thirteenth number, comprised of questions sent in by a "Gentleman" and "relating to *Love* and *Marriage*," that women might also contribute queries.

18. A number of other periodicals also used the question-and-answer blueprint, but Dunton felt that having originated the idea he owned title to it and resented those who infringed upon his "territory": "Commonplace as it is today, in Dunton's time it was an innovation to be guarded jealously . . . Dunton scolded Tom Brown [editor of the *London Mercury*] and Daniel Defoe for their exploitation of the idea" (Gilbert McEwen, *The Oracle of the Coffeehouse: John Dunton's "Athenian Mercury"* [San Marino, Calif.: The Huntington Library, 1972], 28). The other important periodical to use questions and answers in this period was the *British Apollo* (1708–11).

19. David Cressy, "Literacy in Seventeenth-Century England: More Evidence," *Journal of Interdisciplinary History* 8, no. 1 (Summer 1977): 150.

20. See in particular Altick's discussion of aristocratic controls on working-class education in this period, in *The English Common Reader: A Social History of the Mass Reading Public, 1800–1900* (Chicago: University of Chicago Press, 1957), 30–31.

21. Cressy, "Literacy," 147.

22. Altick, *English Common Reader*, 45–46.

23. Hunter, *Before Novels*, 75–81.

24. See Bertha Monica Stearns, "The First English Periodical for Women," *Modern Philology* 28 (1930): 45–59 and "Early English Periodicals for Ladies," *PMLA* 48 (1933): 38–60; Alison Adburgham, *Women in Print: Writing Women and Women's Magazines from the Restoration to the Accession of Victoria* (London: Allen and Unwin, 1972); Cynthia White, *Women's Magazines 1693–1968* (London: Michael Joseph, 1970); and Kathryn Shevelow, *Women and Print Culture*.

25. "I will not meddle with the *Spectator*—let him [i.e., Richard Steele] fair-sex it to the world's end" (*Journal to Stella*, Feb. 8, 1712; cited in Shevelow, 98).

26. Hunter, *Before Novels*, 246. In his influential series of essays on the "Pleasures of the Imagination" (*Spectator* Nos. 411–421), Addison classes the new with the great (or sublime) and the beautiful as particular sources of delight: "Every thing that is *new* or *uncommon* raises a Pleasure in the Imagination, because it fills the Soul with an agreeable Surprise, gratifies its Curiosity, and gives it an Idea of which it was not before possest" (No. 412).

27. Hunter, *Before Novels*, 14. Although my book, especially Chap. 2, concerns itself primarily with the *Athenian Mercury*, Dunton also produced a range of other "Athenian" publications, including *Athenae Redivivae: or The New Athenian Oracle* (1704), *The Athenian Catechism* (1704), *The Athenian Spy* (1704, 1709, and 1720), *Athenian Sport* (1707), *Athenianism* (1710), and *Athenian News: or, Dunton's Oracle* (1710). For an analysis of these texts' importance to the novel, see chap. 1 of Hunter's *Before Novels*.

28. Charles Knight, "Bibliography and the Shape of the Literary Periodical in the Early Eighteenth Century," *The Library* 8, no. 3 (1986): 244. The term "middle style" derives from Samuel Johnson, who ends his life of Addison with the following advice: "Whoever wishes to attain an English style, familiar but not coarse, and elegant but not ostentatious, must give his days and nights to the volumes of Addison" (*Lives of the English Poets* [London: J. M. Dent and Sons, 1954], vol. 1, 368). See as well the analysis by Bateson, who maintains that "Addison's prose style is probably the best, considered simply as style, in the whole range of English literature" (119).

29. Ames, *English Literary Periodical*, 151.

30. See Stephen Botein, Jack R. Censer, and Harriet Ritvo, "The Periodical Press in Eighteenth-Century English and French Society: A Cross-Cultural Approach," *Comparative Studies in Society and History* 23, no. 3 (July 1981): 474–75.

31. Altick, *English Common Reader*, 46.

32. See the useful discussion in Louis T. Milic, "Tone in Steele's *Tatler*," *Newsletters to Newspapers: Eighteenth-Century Journalism*, ed. Donovan Bond and W. Reynolds McLeod (Morgantown: West Virginia University Press, 1977), 33–45.

33. Richmond Bond has aptly delineated the chicken-and-egg problem involved in assessing the relationship of readers to texts: "With more readers at hand more journals were published to satisfy their desire, and more papers prompted more readers as well as more reading by the established readers" (*Growth and Change in the Early English Press* [Lawrence: University of Kansas Libraries, 1969], 9).

34. Although it did not signal the end of government intervention, of which the Stamp Tax is probably the most notorious example.

35. Describing the various changes that turned England into a "well-developed print society" by the end of the eighteenth century, Terry Belanger states that "until the Licensing Act expired in 1695, printing was rigorously restricted to London, the two university towns, and York"; after 1695, "the number of printers and presses both in London and the provinces expanded rapidly" ("Publishers and Writers in Eighteenth-Century England," *Books and Their Readers in Eighteenth-Century England*, ed. Isabel Rivers [New York: St. Martin's, 1982], 6, 8).

36. Richmond Bond catalogues the exponential leap in serial publications across the eighteenth century: "In 1711, the year the *Spectator* commenced its immortal life, there were sixty-six journals in the British Isles, in 1750 ninety, in 1775 one hundred forty, and in 1800 two hundred sixty-five. . . . In all there were approximately twenty-five hundred journals, one kind and another, by the end of the eighteenth century" (*Growth and Change*, 4).

37. Watt, *Rise*, 43. Watt notes that while the cost of books in the eighteenth century is roughly comparable to those today, incomes themselves averaged only a tenth of our own, which meant that novels, even in their least expensive form, were affordable only for the highest reaches of the middle ranks (40).

38. Peter Stallybrass and Allon White, *The Politics and Poetics of Transgression* (Ithaca: Cornell University Press, 1986), 95.

39. Ames writes that "the practice of publishing periodical papers afforded a more certain and rapid remuneration than the printing of books, and induced many men to attempt to gain a livelihood from this form of publication" (152).

40. Botein et al., "Periodical Press," 474–75.

41. Ames, *English Literary Periodical*, 151.

42. John E. Willis, Jr., "European Consumption and Asian Production in the Seventeenth and Eighteenth Centuries," *Consumption and the World of Goods*, ed. John Brewer and Roy Porter (London: Routledge, 1993), 141. Describing the popularity as well as ubiquity of London's coffee-houses, Willis notes that "many prosperous middle-class Londoners spent part of every day in a particular coffeehouse" (ibid.).

43. James R. Sutherland, "The Circulation of Newspapers and Literary Periodicals, 1700–30," *The Library*, 4th ser., 15, 1 (June 1934): 124.

44. *The Structural Transformation of the Public Sphere* was published in German in 1962. Although a small section was translated into English and published in *New German Critique* 1, 3 in 1974, the full text was not translated until 1989 by Thomas Burger (Cambridge, Mass.: MIT Press).

45. Stallybrass and White, *Politics and Poetics*, 96. See also G. J. Barker-Benfield's analysis of the shift from the alehouse to the coffee-house as a site for "the elaboration of public male culture" in *The Culture of Sensibility: Sex and Society in Eighteenth-Century Britain* (Chicago: University of Chicago Press, 1992), 89–90.

46. J. H. Plumb, "The Commercialization of Leisure," 269.

47. Mr. Spectator is citing Gratian in an analysis of the term "taste" and its proper use in literary criticism that *Spectator* editor Donald Bond contends would "lay the foundations for most eighteenth-century speculation on the subject in England" (Vol. 3: 527).

48. Lovell, "Subjective Powers? Consumption, the Reading Public, and Domestic Woman in Eighteenth-Century England," *The Consumption of Culture 1600–1800*, ed. Ann Bermingham and John Brewer (London: Routledge, 1995), 25.

49. Thus G. J. Barker-Benfield writes that *"The Spectator* attempted to associate its standards of taste with classical authority, symbolically heading its papers with Greek or Latin mottoes; this attempt, however, coexisted with *The Spectator*'s association of itself with the popularized consumerism symbolized by tea and china, and it addressed a readership drawn from both sexes" (169).

50. John Locke, *Two Treatises of Government*, ed. Peter Laslett (Cambridge: Cambridge University Press, 1988), II: §27.

51. See Barker-Benfield, *Culture of Sensibility*; and John Brewer, "'The Most Polite Age and the Most Vicious': Attitudes Towards Culture as a Commodity, 1660–1800," *The Consumption of Culture 1600–1800*, ed. Ann Bermingham and John Brewer (London: Routledge, 1995), 341–61.

52. Campbell, *The Romantic Ethic and the Spirit of Modern Consumerism* (Oxford: Basil Blackwell, 1987), 157.

53. Ibid., 35.

54. Cf. Michael McKeon: "Class criteria gradually 'replace' status criteria: which is to say not that the regard for status is obliterated but that it is subsumed under and accommodated to the more dominant and insistent regard for financial income and occupational identity" (*The Origins of the English Novel, 1600–1740* [Baltimore: Johns Hopkins University Press, 1987], 163).

55. Campbell, *Romantic Ethic*, 153.

56. Ibid.

57. Armstrong, *Desire and Domestic Fiction*.

58. Moreover, Eagleton and Shevelow are representative of a widespread phenomenon in eighteenth-century studies. In *Married Women's Separate Property in England, 1660–1833* (Cambridge, Mass.: Harvard University Press, 1990), Susan Staves notes a similar tendency in the work of Lawrence Stone and Randolph Trumbach. She writes that "both historians have succumbed to a bourgeois illusion that there can be a clear separation between, on the one hand, a public and economic sphere, and, on the other, a private domestic sphere of true feeling and personal authenticity. In this aspect of their work, they have accepted the very ideological formulation created by eighteenth-century advocates of domesticity" (223). While I do not in any way contend that either Shevelow or Eagleton has "accepted" bourgeois ideology, I do believe that their important studies might be further enriched by greater attention to the relation between public and private, male and female.

59. Lawrence Klein's essay, "Gender and the Public/Private Distinction in the Eighteenth Century: Some Questions about Evidence and Analytical Procedure" (*Eighteenth-Century Studies* 29, no. 1 [1995]: 97–109), is salutary in reminding us of the complex and often overlapping usages of these terms. Moreover, his statement that "The gender of these eighteenth-century 'publics' cannot be determined by an a priori commitment to the publicity of men and the privacy of women" (105) clearly confirms my own arguments with regard to the ideological division of public and private spheres.

60. As expressed, for example, in Steele's motto for the early *Tatler*, taken from Juvenal: "Quicquid agunt Homines nostri Farrago Libelli [Whate'er men do, or say, or think, or dream, / Our motley paper seizes for its theme]."

61. This formulation alludes to the subtitle—"Private Vices, Publick Benefits"—of Bernard Mandeville's controversial *Fable of the Bees*.

62. Numerous studies have criticized liberal discourses for excluding women and perpetuating gendered relations of domination and subordination, a position anticipated in the seventeenth century by Mary Astell. (See Ruth Perry, "Mary Astell and the Feminist Critique of Possessive Individualism," *Eighteenth-Century Studies* 23, no. 4 [Summer 1990]: 444–57.) Particularly valuable critiques include Susan Moller Okin, "Women and the Making of the Sentimental Family," *Philosophy and Public Affairs* 11, no. 1 (1981): 65–88; Linda Nicholson, *Gender and History: The Limits of Social Theory in the Age of the Family* (New York: Columbia University Press, 1986); Joan Landes, *Women and the Public Sphere in the Age of the French Revolution* (Ithaca: Cornell University Press, 1988); Carole Pateman, *The Sexual Contract* (Stanford, Calif.: Stanford University Press, 1988); and Nancy Fraser, "What's Critical about Critical Theory? The Case of Habermas and Gender," in *Unruly Practices: Power, Discourse, and Gender in Contemporary Social Theory* (Minneapolis: University of Minnesota Press, 1989), 113–43.

63. While contemporary thinking resolutely places economic relations into the sphere marked public, Habermas reminds us that until the seventeenth century, when economics took on its modern meaning, the term was "limited to the sphere of tasks proper to the *oikodespotes*, the *pater familias*, the head of the household" (*Structural Transformation*, 20).

64. Indeed, he even goes so far as to use the term "restricted patriarchal nuclear family." Stone's description of this family type comprises part three of the abridged edition of *The Family, Sex and Marriage in England, 1500–1800* (Harmondsworth: Penguin, 1977).

65. In revising both her earlier argument with Teresa Brennan ("'Mere Auxiliaries to the Commonwealth': Women and the Origins of Liberalism," *Political Studies* 27, no. 2 [June 1979]: 183–200) and prior, "patriarchal" ways of reading contract theory as an escape from the tyranny of the father, Pateman contends in *The Sexual Contract* that it is not fathers but brothers who make the original contract that defines civil society, and that such a contract is sexual as well as social: "The sons overturn paternal rule not merely to gain their liberty but to secure women for themselves." Accordingly, contract is not opposed to patriarchy, but is instead "the means through which modern patriarchy is constituted" (2), albeit in the new form of fraternal relations: "Political right originates in sex-right or conjugal right. Paternal right is only one, and not the original, dimension of patriarchal power. A man's power as a father comes after he has exercised the patriarchal right of a man (a husband) over a woman (wife)" (3).

66. For a compelling study of the implications of economically based power relations for the twentieth-century family, see Susan Moller Okin's *Justice, Gender and the Family* (New York: Basic Books, 1989), in particular chap. 7, "Vulnerability within Marriage."

67. According to Arendt, "The distinctive trait of the household sphere was that in it men lived together because they were driven by their wants and needs. . . . The realm of the *polis*, on the contrary, was the sphere of freedom, and if there was a relationship between these two spheres, it was a matter of course that the mastering of the necessities of life in the household was the condition for freedom of the *polis*" (*The Human Condition* [Chicago: University of Chicago Press, 1958], 30–31).

68. Ibid., 46.

69. Ibid., 28.

70. Thus Arendt notes that "the rise of the social coincided historically with the transformation of the private care for private property into a public concern. Society, when it first entered the public realm, assumed the disguise of an organization of property-owners who, instead of claiming access to the public realm because of their wealth, demanded protection from it for the accumulation of more wealth" (68).

71. "Women and slaves belonged to the same category [of necessity] and were hidden away not only because they were somebody else's property but because their life was 'laborious,' devoted to bodily functions" (Arendt, 72).

72. For a provocative article that questions the validity of a notion of separate spheres even for the nineteenth century, see Amanda Vickery, "Golden Age to Separate Spheres? A Review of the Categories and Chronology of English Women's History," *Historical Journal* 36, no. 2 (1993): 383–414. I am grateful to Lawrence Klein for this reference.

73. Michael Kimmel, "The Contemporary 'Crisis' of Masculinity in Historical Perspective," *The Making of Masculinities: The New Men's Studies*, ed. Harry Brod (London: Allen and Unwin, 1987), 123.

74. In *Making Sex: Body and Gender from the Greeks to Freud* (Cambridge, Mass.: Harvard University Press, 1990), Thomas Laqueur argues that in the eighteenth century, a shift occurred from a "one-sex model," which formulated women's reproductive organs as a lesser version of men's, to a "two-sex model" that reconceived female reproductive physiology as intrinsically different from that of men. Such a representation of biological difference was, and continues to be, used to justify gender difference, female inferiority, and thus women's exclusion from a myriad of male-designated realms.

75. Bermingham, "Elegant Females and Gentlemen Connoisseurs: The Commerce in Culture and Self-Image in Eighteenth-Century England," *The Consumption of Culture 1600–1800*, 492.

76. Fletcher, *Gender, Sex and Subordination*, 411, 407.

77. Michael McKeon, "Historicizing Patriarchy: The Emergence of Gender Difference in England, 1660–1760," *Eighteenth-Century Studies* 28, no. 3 (1995): 300.

78. My thinking on this subject has been particularly influenced by the teaching of Elizabeth Spelman and the late Ricky Sherover-Marcuse. First, I believe that as with the category of "oppressed," "oppressor" is a role rather than an inherent identity—a role that can be unlearned. Second, and this is a concept essential to the premise of this book, I maintain that the act of oppressing or subordinating an individual or group works simultaneously to construct an identity for the person or people in the role of oppressor. While men's oppression might be more difficult to identify because it is perpetrated by society at large rather than by a particular group, men's role in oppressing women also contributes significantly to their devaluation. For valuable insight into processes whereby men themselves become dehumanized, see Albert Memmi's analysis of the colonizer in *The Colonizer and the Colonized* (Boston: Beacon Press, 1965) and the chapter on "Domination-Subordination" in Jean Baker Miller, *Toward a New Psychology of Women* (Boston: Beacon Press, 1976).

79. The historians Leonore Davidoff and Catherine Hall note that possibly "the

single greatest distinction between the aristocracy and the middle class was the imperative for members of the latter to actively seek an income rather than expect to live from rents and the emoluments of office while spending their time in honour-enhancing activities such as politics, hunting or social appearances" (*Family Fortunes: Men and Women of the English Middle Class, 1780–1850* [Chicago: University of Chicago Press, 1987], 20).

80. Roberta Hamilton, *The Liberation of Women: A Study of Patriarchy and Capitalism* (London: Allen and Unwin, 1978), 23–28, 37–50; Sheila Rowbotham, *Women, Resistance and Revolution* (New York: Vintage, 1972), 19–30. Cf. as well Alice Clark's statement that in "the seventeenth century the idea is seldom encountered that a man supports his wife; husband and wife were mutually dependent and together supported their children" (*The Working Life of Women in the Seventeenth Century* [New York: A. M. Kelley, 1978], 12).

81. This is Richard Sennett's view in *The Fall of Public Man*; it is, of course, also the viewpoint proposed by the "sentimental" family historians such as Stone and Trumbach, and assimilated by the many others who build upon their work.

82. See, for example, Alan Macfarlane's critical review of Stone (*History and Theory* 18, no. 1 [1979]), in which he argues that Stone's "description of life in the Early Modern Period bears little resemblance to the society which is revealed to a number of us who have studied the period" (106). He rejects in particular Stone's "central psychological assumption" of affective changes. In addition, historians have challenged the demographic basis of the claims made by members of the Cambridge Group, particularly Peter Laslett, that for the majority of people household size changed very little from the sixteenth to the nineteenth centuries. See also the discussion in Nicholson, *Gender and History*, 109–11.

83. See Hamilton, *Liberation of Women*, 39–40.

84. Kimmel, "The Contemporary 'Crisis' of Masculinity," 125.

85. See the discussion of debt in Chap. 4, note 19.

86. Victor J. Seidler, *Rediscovering Masculinity: Reason, Language and Sexuality* (London: Routledge, 1989), 161.

87. See Laqueur's *Making Sex*, especially chap. 5, "Discovery of the Sexes," and Keith Thomas, "The Double Standard," *Journal of the History of Ideas* 20 (1959): 195–216.

88. Seidler, *Rediscovering Masculinity*, 22.

89. My formulation alludes to Patricia Meyer Spacks's ground-breaking study of eighteenth-century female sexuality, "Ev'ry Woman is at Heart a Rake" (*Eighteenth-Century Studies* 8 [1974–75]: 27–46); her title derives, of course, from Pope's second "Moral Essay: Of the Characters of Women" (1735).

90. The most famous example of the rake-sodomite is John Wilmot, Earl of Rochester. See the readings of his poems in Alan Bray, *Homosexuality in Renaissance England* (New York: Columbia University Press, 1982/1995), 49–50, and in Randolph Trumbach, "The Birth of the Queen: Sodomy and the Emergence of Gender Equality in Modern Culture, 1660–1750," *Hidden from History: Reclaiming the Gay and Lesbian Past*, ed. Martin Duberman, Martha Vicinus, and George Chauncey, Jr. (New York: Meridian, 1989), 130–33.

91. Bray, *Homosexuality*, 104. See also Trumbach, "Sodomitical Subcultures,

Sodomitical Roles, and the Gender Revolution of the Eighteenth Century: The Recent Historiography," *'Tis Nature's Fault: Unauthorized Sexuality During the Enlightenment*, ed. Robert P. Maccubin (Cambridge: Cambridge University Press, 1987), 109–21.

92. Bray, chap. 4, "Molly"; and Trumbach, "London's Sodomites: Homosexual Behavior and Western Culture in the Eighteenth Century," *Journal of Social History* 11 (1977): 1–33.

93. Cf. McKeon: "The early modern shift from a sexual system of hierarchy to one of difference may be seen as a shift to the system of heterosexuality, reciprocally inseparable from its dialectical antithesis, homosexuality—which is therefore also a crucial part of the system" ("Historicizing Patriarchy," 308).

94. Barker-Benfield writes, "By mid-century, businessmen had long recognized the value to them of cultivating refinement; it enhanced their reputation and their status. Their clubs and societies were established to encourage 'mutual consideration,' 'mutual benevolence,' and 'friendly feeling' between men, generating what one club called 'principles of Benevolence, Charity, and Humanity'" (91). See also Brewer, "Commercialization and Politics," in *The Birth of a Consumer Society*.

95. Trumbach, "Birth of the Queen," 133–35. Here I disagree slightly with Trumbach, who contends that this meaning of effeminate had "disappeared" by the early eighteenth century, so that "an adult effeminate male was likely to be taken for an exclusive sodomite." See also the chapters on effeminacy in the studies by Barker-Benfield and Fletcher.

Chapter Two

1. Jürgen Habermas's representation of the bourgeois public sphere as developing out of the *Intimsphäre* of the family reminds us of the inextricable relation between family structures and literary forms. See *The Structural Transformation of the Public Sphere*, trans. Thomas Burger (Cambridge, Mass.: MIT Press, 1989).

2. Armstrong and Tennenhouse, "The Literature of Conduct, the Conduct of Literature: An Introduction," *The Ideology of Conduct: Essays on Literature and the History of Sexuality* (London: Methuen, 1987), 12.

3. Published by John Dunton, the *Ladies Dictionary* claimed in its preface to be a "Dictionary for the Use of the Fair-Sex, (which may serve as a Secret Oracle, to Consult in all difficult Cases) being the First Attempt of this kind that has appeared in English." The quoted passage is found under the heading "Reason considered in humane affairs" (441). In addition to reprinting numerous responses from Dunton's periodical, the *Athenian Mercury*, the dictionary also plagiarized material from many of the seventeenth-century authorities on "feminine" issues, from Thomas Heywood's tales of famous women to the Marquis of Halifax's *Advice to a Daughter*. For a painstaking analysis of the publication's expropriations, see the study by Gertrude Noyes, "John Dunton's *Ladies Dictionary*, 1694," *Philological Quarterly* 21, no. 2 (1942): 129–45.

4. In "Literature and Social Mobility," David Daiches comments that "English culture is full of examples of *nouveaux riches* seeking instruction in the graces of life. That instruction was provided for them in all kinds of ways, and from a much earlier

period than is generally supposed" (159). Thus while the simultaneous "education and entertainment of the middle classes," as a process that played such an important role in Dunton's *Athenian Mercury* (as well as in the success of the *Tatler* and *Spectator* two decades later) was not a new phenomenon, Daiches nevertheless distinguishes the periodicals' approach from that of earlier conduct manuals: "The sixteenth- and seventeenth-century manuals . . . give evidence of social mobility, but the social situation that underlies them is much less determinate than in the early eighteenth century, when we see large numbers of prosperous citizens, with their wives and daughters, grooming themselves for genteel life. Of course, prosperous Elizabethan citizens did the same, but as individuals rather than as a class" (161). (*Aspects of History and Class Consciousness*, ed. István Mészáros [London: Routledge and Kegan Paul, 1971], 152–72.)

5. For a perceptive analysis of the editor role, and particularly of the relation of the journal editor to the editor of epistolary fiction, see Robert Iliffe, "Author-Mongering: The 'Editor' between Producer and Consumer," *The Consumption of Culture 1600–1800*, ed. Ann Bermingham and John Brewer (London: Routledge, 1995), 167–92.

6. For a discussion of this process with particular regard to feminine gender construction, see Kathryn Shevelow's discussion of "The Reformist Agenda and the Woman Reader," *Women and Print Culture: The Construction of Femininity in the Early Periodical* (London: Routledge, 1989), 32–37.

7. Stephen Parks, *John Dunton and the English Book Trade* (New York: Garland, 1976), 77.

8. Gilbert McEwen, *The Oracle of the Coffee House: John Dunton's "Athenian Mercury"* (San Marino, Calif.: The Huntington Library, 1972), 18.

9. Parks, *John Dunton*, 74.

10. Ibid., 75–76. Connection to the "Universities" was also an important part of the term "Athenianism": "For Dunton, Oxford was the Athens of England" (McEwen, *The Oracle*, 27). In her reading of "Athenian Iconography," Kathryn Shevelow describes an emblem for the *Young Students' Library* representing the Athenian Society as "a quasi-judiciary panel of experts": "The Society, much inflated in numbers, sits at a long table (presumably in the 'courtroom' of the coffee house), veiled to signify their anonymity, surrounded by illustrations of the four seats of learning, Athens, Rome, Oxford and Cambridge" (82).

11. Victor Seidler, *Rediscovering Masculinity: Reason, Language and Sexuality* (London: Routledge, 1989), 3.

12. Originally designated for "the first Tuesday of every month," these numbers became fortnightly in Vol. 8, No. 10 (Oct. 1, 1692) and weekly early in 1693, with Vol. 9, No. 22 (Feb. 25, 1693).

13. The use of the term "magazine" to describe a storehouse for literary articles only entered contemporary usage in 1731 with Edward Cave's extremely successful *Gentleman's Magazine*.

14. For a comprehensive analysis of the miscellaneous qualities of Motteux's publication, see Dorothy Foster, "The Earliest Precursor of Our Present-Day Monthly Miscellanies," *PMLA* 32 (1917): 22–58.

15. Robert Cunningham, *Peter Anthony Motteux 1663–1718: A Biographical and Critical Study* (Oxford: Basil Blackwell, 1933), 50.

16. Margaret J. M. Ezell maintains that in addition to its "tiny but secure niche in literary history," Motteux's journal provides an important case study of the diverse textual practices that functioned to incorporate coterie modes of literary production into an overtly commercial enterprise. In particular, her article focuses on the periodical's dependence upon "a thriving community of women readers and writers, previously invisible to our eyes because of their adherence to coterie literary practices but, in the pages of the *Gentleman's Journal*, entering the commercial arena through Motteux's new literary form" ("The *Gentleman's Journal* and the Commercialization of Restoration Coterie Literary Practices," *Modern Philology* 89, no. 3 [Feb. 1992]: 323, 338).

17. Motteux, like many Huguenots, had fled France in 1685 upon the revocation of the Edict of Nantes. See Cunningham, *Peter Anthony Motteux*, for an assessment of Motteux's early years in Normandy (1–8).

18. Ibid., 14–15; Foster, "Earliest Precursor," 23.

19. Jan. 1692, 1.

20. He is described in the "Epistle Dedicatory" as "Lord Steward of Their Majesties Household, Lord-Lieutenant of the City of *Derby*, Knight of the Noble Order of the Garter, and One of Their Majesties Most Honourable Privy Council."

21. Jan. 1692, "Epistle Dedicatory," A_2.

22. Ibid.

23. Jan. 1692, 1.

24. Ezell, "The *Gentleman's Journal*," 327.

25. Foster notes that Motteux had other models in addition to *Le Mercure Galant* for his epistolary mode: "In spite of the numbers and popularity of the newspapers, news-letters, both printed and in manuscript, were still for sale in London for country correspondence, with space left at the beginning and end for the personal address and private items of news, and with a vacant fourth page destined to serve as the envelope" (24–25). (For a further history of these news-letters, see James Sutherland's *The Restoration Newspaper and its Development* [Cambridge: Cambridge University Press, 1986], 6–8.) While it seems reasonable to assume that the entrepreneurial Motteux incorporated some of the personal quality of the news-letter into his own journal-letter, Ezell argues that the letter form served another function as well, by assisting "in the creation of a friendly community of readers and more broadly invit[ing] their participation in the process of writing the journal." Thus she speculates that Motteux's choice of letter format had "another possible source than the commercial news-letter, namely, the mode of circulation in manuscript coterie circles" (328).

26. Oct. 1693, 324–25.

27. See Dryden's earlier development of this trope in the fifth stanza of his Killigrew Ode (my thanks to James Winn for calling my attention to this passage):

> Art she had none, yet wanted none;
> For Nature did that want supply:
> So rich in treasures of her own,
> She might our boasted stores defy:
> Such noble vigour did her Verse adorn,
> That it seemed borrowed where 'twas only born.
>
> (lines 71–76).

28. May 1692, 9–11.

29. In an essay entitled an "Account of the charms and miseries of love for young beauties" (July 1693), Motteux again demonstrates his characteristic combination of sensitivity and conventionalism in his attempt to exonerate women's oft-censured misuse of their attractions: "The ways that lead Men to Command and Glory are not open to the fair Sex, and they have nothing to advance themselves besides the Endowments of Beauty. Is it not just then that they preserve and raise its Lustre with Care and Industry? because some Men are too much sway'd by their Passions, must not women be allowed to display their Charms? It may as justly be requir'd that the Planets and Stars may cease to shine, because some Nations admiring their Brightness have worshipped them. Beauty makes the Glory of Women, as Valour that of Men" (223).

30. Motteux also uses a physiognomic explanation to argue for women's learning: see the essay contained in the *Lady's Journal* entitled "That Women may apply themselves to Liberal Arts and Sciences" (Oct. 1693, 335–39).

31. In *The Culture of Sensibility*, G. J. Barker-Benfield shows how the belief that women possessed a greater delicacy of nerves and fibers than men meant that women had more sensibility but less capacity for learning. See chap. 1, "Sensibility and the Nervous System" (Chicago: University of Chicago Press, 1992).

32. Entry under the heading "Young men, Admonitions to them in sundry matters highly concerning them," 523. In an earlier entry entitled "Husband," he had been informed of the character of a good husband, as well as of such a husband's duty toward his wife.

33. Vol. 2, No. 15 (July 14, 1691); the following number gives the men a similar prayer for a good wife.

34. Interestingly, however, both Motteux's *Gentleman's Journal* and Steele's *Tatler* attempted in more general ways to ameliorate the unhappy situation of single women: Motteux proposed a "Lottery" through which indigent "Maids" and "Batchelors" might win enough money to set up housekeeping together (Apr. 1694) while Steele's eidolon Bickerstaff refers to a "Scheme" to "take off the dead Stock of Women in City, Town, and Country," thereby relieving "all *British* Females, who at present seem to be devoted to involuntary Virginity" (No. 195). Although Bickerstaff later mentions "the numberless Crowd of Damsels I have proposed to take Care of" (No. 205), perhaps he found the task too daunting, for there is no further discussion of his "Scheme."

35. The *Ladies Dictionary* reprints a number of these responses: "Friendship between Persons of a different Sex"; "Friendship . . . may it continue if either Marry?"; "Love, what is it?"; "Husband, whether lawful for a Young Lady to pray for one"; "Wife, advice about choosing a good one" (cited in Noyes, 142). The *Ladies Dictionary* also includes entries about husbands' and wives' "Characters," "Marriage State Instructions," and "Duty" toward each other.

36. McEwen, *The Oracle*, 154.

37. *Ladies Dictionary*, "Books, Directions to Ladies about Reading Them," 69.

38. It seems possible that the plagiarizing Dunton took this response from Hannah Woolley's reflection in *The Gentlewoman's Companion* (1675) that "Most in this

depraved later age think a woman learned and wise enough if she can distinguish her husband's bed from another's" (288; cited in David Roberts, *The Ladies: Female Patronage of Restoration Drama 1660–1700* [Oxford: Clarendon Press, 1989], 17).

39. *Ladies Dictionary*, "Behaviour, in conversation," 70.

40. Ibid.

41. In contrast to both the *Athenian Mercury* and the *Night-Walker*, two narratives from later periodicals give the responsibility for redemption solely to the female. A short story titled "The Prudent Wife: Or, the Lewd Husband Reclaim'd," in which a woman does not accuse her husband when she finds him with her maid, but rather wins him with love and patience (John Tipper's *Delights for the Ingenious* [Mar. 1711]) reproduces almost exactly the situation in Colly Cibber's popular play, *The Careless Husband* (1704). In "The Fair Counselor: Or, the Young Lady's Conduct after Marriage, A Dialogue between Charlotte and Olivia," Charlotte uses her own experience and that of other women to instruct Olivia in the proper methods by which to reclaim her "indifferent" husband (*The Young Ladies Miscellany* [1723]). See as well the analysis of Eliza Haywood's continuation and crystallization of these attitudes in Chap. 9.

42. In "The First English Periodical for Women," Bertha Monica Stearns argues that Dunton's steadily growing dependence "upon feminine favor" for the popularity of the *Athenian Mercury* caused him to venture "in 1693, a short-lived periodical called the *Ladies Mercury*" (*Modern Philology* 28 [1930]: 45). Although both McEwen (103) and Parks (104) seem to take for granted Dunton's publication of the *Ladies Mercury*, Shevelow's assessment is more cautious. She writes that Dunton "for a short time may have generated the companion publication, the *Ladies Mercury* (1693), entirely devoted to 'feminine' concerns" (64).

43. Feb. 27, 1693.

44. This number included answers to all of the questions posed in the first number of the *Ladies Mercury*.

45. Theodore Hatfield, for example, calls it "a dreary collection of grave-faced pornography" ("John Dunton's Periodicals," *Journalism Quarterly* 10, no. 3 [1933]: 215).

Chapter Three

1. The same narrative appears three years later in Dunton's *Ladies Dictionary* under the heading "Six Nights Rambles of a Young Gentleman through the City." Surprisingly, Stephen Parks, Dunton's most comprehensive bibliographer, misses the *Athenian Mercury* reference and cites only the *Dictionary* article as the precedent for Dunton's periodical entitled the *Night-Walker*. (Stephen Parks, *John Dunton and the English Book Trade* [New York: Garland, 1976].)

2. "In 1691 the officers and more prosperous inhabitants of Tower Hamlets, London, formed an association to suppress immorality which led to the founding of a London Society for the Reformation of Manners" (John Addy, *Sin and Society in the Seventeenth Century* [London: Routledge, 1989], 213).

3. The *Night-Walker* was produced monthly from Sept. 1696 to Apr. 1697. The last number announced that "Some particular reasons have occasioned the change of

the Person concerned in this Undertaking, but 'tis hoped without any disadvantage to it or to the publick, tho we must own that Gentlemans Accomplishments to be very great and not easily matched." Dunton's first wife, Elizabeth Annesley, who had been of great assistance to him in his business, was at that time very ill; she died in May of 1697.

4. A recent exception to this trend, Elizabeth Bennett Kubek uses the *Night-Walker* as one of her primary examples of "texts by male writers that represent urban women and their 'histories' as objects to be sexually, visually, or verbally consumed." Placing Dunton's publication into a broader sociocultural context, Kubek's article examines the ways in which such narratives, by "representing all urban women as prostitutes, and thus always already commodities," attempt to mediate the threat posed by women's uncontained sexual behavior. However, her emphasis upon men's textual control of women fails to notice the repercussions of such control upon men, who, as I will argue, must simultaneously reimagine and reform themselves ("Women's Participation in the Urban Culture of Early Modern London: Images from Fiction" in *The Consumption of Culture 1500–1800*, ed. Ann Bermingham and John Brewer [London: Routledge, 1995], 441, 443).

5. Graham, *The Beginnings of English Literary Periodicals: A Study of Periodical Literature 1665–1715* (New York: Oxford University Press, 1926), 55–56.

6. Ibid., 56.

7. Dunton himself claimed to have published more than six hundred works during his lifetime (Parks, *John Dunton*, 43); Parks's own checklist cites 185 publications launched by Dunton. Swift lampooned Dunton's Athenianism in *A Tale of A Tub* and Pope placed him among his crew of dunces. See J. Paul Hunter's useful reinterpretation of Dunton's part in the ancients-moderns debate in *Before Novels: The Cultural Contexts of Eighteenth-Century English Fiction* (New York: W. W. Norton, 1990).

8. In addition to the full-length studies of Dunton by Gilbert McEwen and Stephen Parks, J. Paul Hunter's *Before Novels* provides a conspicuous exception to this trend. Larding his extensive work with references to Dunton's life as well as with readings of Dunton's various literary productions, Hunter emphasizes the *Athenian Mercury*'s contribution to the beginnings of the English novel; moreover, he singles out Dunton as a "representative type of the new man who, despite an ingrained respect for authority and a conservative religious temperament, championed modernism and worshiped the dawn of every day as a pointer to an improved future" (99).

9. In Chap. 7 I examine the ways in which Addison and Steele mitigated the tensions between the moral and the commercial. For a useful analysis of twentieth-century readers' aversion to the didactic see chap. 9 in Hunter's *Before Novels*, in which Hunter contends that the description "Religious in subject matter, didactic in intent . . . fits most published writings and an astounding amount of private discourse in the late seventeenth and early eighteenth centuries in England—so fully so as almost to constitute a definition of taste, desire, and habit. The difficulty this focus has caused for modern readers is hard to calculate and almost impossible to exaggerate" (225).

10. Defoe's *Review*, Apr. 7, 1709, quoted in Richmond Bond, *"The Tatler": The Making of a Literary Journal* (Cambridge, Mass.: Harvard University Press, 1971),

72–73. See as well the discussion in Vern Bullough's study "Prostitution and Reform in the Eighteenth Century," in *'Tis Nature's Fault: Unauthorized Sexuality during the Enlightenment*, ed. Robert P. Maccubin (Cambridge: Cambridge University Press, 1987): 61–74.

11. Mandeville, *A Modest Defense of the Public Stews* (London, 1724), 54.

12. Addy, *Sin and Society*, viii.

13. Ibid., 128.

14. Ibid.

15. Ibid., 211–13.

16. Bond, *"The Tatler,"* 72.

17. Addy, *Sin and Society*, 213.

18. "Inspirational tracts offering *Advices, Cautions, Disswasives, Monitors*, and *Rebukes* were printed by the Society for violators of the Sabbath, profane swearers, drunkards, gamesters, unclean persons, soldiers, and seamen, and appropriate sermons were preached at meetings of the reformers" (Bond, *"The Tatler,"* 72).

19. Dunton, *Life and Errors*, vol. 1, 28.

20. Ibid., 29.

21. Ibid., 38.

22. Parks, *John Dunton*, 20, 45.

23. *The Lord's Last Sufferings*, Stephen Jay's *Daniel in the Den*, John Shower's *Sermon Preacht upon the Death of Mrs. Anne Barnardiston*, and *The House of Weeping*, touted as "the most proper book yet extant to be given on funeral occasions" (Parks, *John Dunton*, 16).

24. Ibid.

25. Hunter, *Before Novels*, 101.

26. In his "Account of the Societies for Reformation of Manners," Josiah Woodward notes that the founding members "prosecuted their Business, increasing their Number by the Addition of Persons of considerable Note, and of the best Character; some of whom, tho' they were of different Opinions from those of the *Establish'd Church*, as to some points concerning Religion, were willing to unite their Strength in the common cause of Christianity, and engage in so Noble a Design, that had done so much Good" (7).

27. The "Instrument" begins as follows: "We who are Inhabitants of the Cities of *London* and *Westminster*, and Parishes adjacent, both in the Counties of *Middlesex* and *Surry*, having an Eye to the Honour of God and the King, and the publick Benefit of the Nation: And being encouraged by the late happy Success that hath attended the industrious Endeavours of the *Tower-Hamlets*; whereby (according to a Method mentioned in their printed Paper, or Instrument, *That declaring honest and joynt design for the general suppressing of* Bawdy-houses, *&c.*) they have with more than ordinary Diligence, and great expence of their Time and Money, in the space of two or three Years, (as lately Affidavit hath been made before the Bench of Justices at *Hick's Hall*,) not only brought to due Punishment, according to Law, seven or eight hundred Criminals; but also generally routed those naughty Houses, which formerly abounded amongst them. And being influenced by that good old Principle or Axiom, *Bonum quo communius, eo melius*, resolve to use our hearty Endeavours, that so good a Work may no longer be confined within such narrow Limits, but be farther promoted for more general Advantage. WHERE-FORE we agree, upon our own Costs and Charges to imploy and maintain a competent Number of such fitting Persons, as we shall choose, to assist the several Constable and other Officers, in the Wards of the

said City of *London*, and in other of the said adjacent Parishes, in putting into Execution those good Laws aforesaid; *viz.* by observing and taking notice of all those, that for the time to come, shall impudently dare, in Rebellion against the Laws of God and Man, to Swear and Curse, to profane the Lord's day, or be guilty of the loathsome Sin of Drunkenness; also, by searching out the lurking Holes of Bawds, Whores, and other filthy Miscreants, in order to their Conviction and Punishment according to Law" (24–25 [mismarked "29" in text]).

28. In his study of the *Tatler*, Richmond Bond remarks that the Society's first twelve lists, published in 1707, contained more than ten thousand names (72); the anonymous author of "The Thirtieth Account of the Progress Made in the Cities of *London* and *Westminster*, And Places adjacent, By the *Societies* for Promoting a *Reformation* of *Manners*," ironically appended to the 1725 edition of Bernard Mandeville's *A Modest Defense of the Public Stews*, makes the seemingly outrageous claim that "The Total Number of Persons prosecuted by the Societies, in and near *London* only, for Debauchery and Prophaneness, for 33 Years last past, are calculated at Eighty Nine Thousand Three Hundred Ninety Three" (60).

29. Vol. 1, No. 1 (Sept. 1696), sig. B₁v. All further references to the *Night-Walker* will be included in the text.

30. Woodward, "Account of the Societies," 8.

31. Ibid., 8–13.

32. Here I concur with Kubek: "These narratives reassured men of their power over women in an urban society where social 'place' seemed unstable, and provided female readers with an image of their own sexuality that, while ostensibly erotic, reinforced conventional standards of virtue and domesticity" (445). Again, my explicit concern is the ways in which the *Night-Walker* influenced male readers in controlling both their own sexuality and that of women.

33. Other issues regarding the origins and authenticity of Dunton's periodical include not only the authorship of the outside narratives, but also the probability of the Night-Walker's actual encounters in the London streets. Although it is of course impossible to authenticate the narrator's claims, I would stress the importance of the way in which these situations are represented as having actually happened. In particular, the idea of the women's life stories originating from the women themselves rather than from Dunton lends sympathy as well as authority to both the women and their stories.

34. Cf. Parks, *John Dunton*: "Although ostensibly highly moral, the content of the periodical was in fact mildly salacious" (72); and Gilbert McEwen: the periodical's subjects "were almost entirely 'exposures' of sexual adventures, in spite of the writer's insistence that his aim was to reform" (*The Oracle of the Coffee House: John Dunton's "Athenian Mercury"* [San Marino, Calif.: The Huntington Library, 1972], 215).

35. For an example of the Night-Walker's interesting technique—as well as of Dunton's moralizing style—here is the account of the narrator's initial encounter: "The *First Night* I travers'd the *Pall-Mall*, and read the Face of every unmask'd Lady I met; and if mask'd, I started some Question that still gave me an indication of their Temper, endeavouring to light upon as *refin'd* yet *modest piece of Wickedness* as I could: At last having made (as I thought) the *best of the Market*, away we walk'd to drink upon the Bargain: So, after several Glasses, and some little insignificant Prittle-prat-

tle, I fix'd my Eyes upon her, and said, *Madam, methinks I read some Lines and Characters of Goodness in your Face, which are not yet absolutely defac'd: Your Education, I am confident, has not been unhappy: Pray be free, and tell me, Are you yet Proof against the Lashes of your Conscience?* Sir (said she) your Design I know not, but I dare not believe it to be ill, you having made such an inquisitive Prologue. No indeed (reply'd I) my Request proceeds purely from a generous Pity at your Misfortunes, which are sufficiently slavish. Alas Sir! (said she, and sigh'd) 'tis a slavish Riddle *to chuse what I hate;* I have repeated these Actions, but never without regret and self-abhorrency for such a Folly:——This I had peculiar to myself, that I never was Mercenary, thinking it a greater baseness to *sell* my Heaven, than *give* it; I was first betray'd by keeping company with a Lady that was not *over-modest,* but not thinking to engage my self, till one of her Gallants weaken'd my Resolves, and at last——I know not what; but I was ruin'd, for all my Resolves are now too weak to resist, never being able to hold out a quarter of a year together; but *secure my Honour for this once by Secrecy,* and not watching me to my Lodgings: And I hope the Novelty of this Enterprize may have new Effects upon me, and keep me from doing such Actions as must be repented of, or I am undone" (Vol. 1, No. 1, p. 2; the narrative is reprinted verbatim from the "Account of Six Nights Rambles" recorded in the *Athenian Mercury,* Vol. 3, No. 3 [1691]).

36. My reading here clearly diverges with that of Kubek, cited above.

37. Cf. the *Ladies Dictionary* entry under "Jealousie": "If I, for one, am guilty of this Tickling Sin, my Bastards Heir my Estate, I can put them off with little, but if my Wife be faulty, I must be a drudge for other men's Children, which is insufferable" (240–41).

38. *Tatler* No. 162.

39. After discussing the part that pleasure plays in conception, Mandeville goes on to remark that "it is hard to imagine, that so many alert Members, which can exert themselves in such a lively Manner on this Occasion [i.e., conception], should be at all other Times in a state of perfect Tranquillity; for, besides that Experience teaches us the contrary, this handsome Disposition would be entirely useless, if Nature had not provided a prior Titillation, to provoke Women at first to enter upon Action; and all our late Discoveries in Anatomy, can find out no other Use for the *Clitoris,* but to whet the Female Desire by its frequent Erections; which are, doubtless as provoking as those of the *Penis,* of which it is a perfect Copy, tho' in miniature" (30).

40. Ibid., 36–38.

41. For a useful analysis of the relevance of Juvenal's satire for the misogynistic tradition of the Restoration and eighteenth century, see chap. 5 of Felicity Nussbaum's *The Brink of All We Hate: English Satires on Women 1660–1750* (Lexington: University Press of Kentucky, 1984).

42. Bullough, "Prostitution and Reform," 61. In contrast, however, to the eighteenth-century reformers Bullough considers, Dunton's periodical viewed prostitution as a problem for all classes and both sexes.

43. Roy Porter and Lesley Hall, *The Facts of Life: The Creation of Sexual Knowledge in Britain, 1650–1950* (New Haven: Yale University Press, 1995), 27; the quotation derives from Henry Fielding's *An Enquiry into the Causes of the Late Increase in Robbers* (London: A. Millar, 1751), 47.

44. There is, however, one place in which the narrator comments on the larger socioeconomic context, advocating legal reform as opposed to solely individual change. In his response to the story of a Long Acre prostitute who leaves an abusive husband and can find no other way to maintain herself, the Night-Walker comments: "This instance doth naturally afford matter for the following Reflections, *viz.* That it is highly necessary there should be care taken for imploying the Poor, and Constraining such as are able to work. If effectual Methods were faln upon to provide for those two Cases, the Reformation of this horrid abuse by strowling Women, would become very easie, much sin and miserie would be prevented, and the Nation in a great measure cleansed from that horrid Uncleanness, with which it is at present defil'd; but of this we see little hopes till Magistrates and Ministers do Universally and Cheerfully concur in the work according as their respective Stations oblige them" (Vol. 2, No. 1 [Jan. 1697], 30). See Bullough, "Prostitution and Reform," for an analysis of the failure of most economic solutions for prostitution during the eighteenth century.

45. *Gender, Sex and Subordination in England, 1500–1800* (New Haven: Yale University Press, 1995), 219.

46. It is illuminating to compare the Night-Walker's narrative with the position of Jonas Hanway later in the eighteenth century. According to Bullough, "Hanway believed that one of the major causes of prostitution was the obligation of girls to furnish a dowry when they married. Since many girls in the lower classes could not afford dowries, they turned to prostitution as an alternative to marriage. As a partial solution, he urged that the English royal family give a number of poor girls dowries on occasions such as the birth of an heir to the crown" (Letter 5 to Robert Dingley, Esq.: Being a Proposal for the Relief and Employment of Friendless Girls and Repenting Prostitutes [London, 1758]; cited in Bullough, "Prostitution and Reform," 71).

47. Indeed a similar situation occurs in the second number (Oct. 1696, 13–15), in which the Night-Walker is reminded of the story of a man, who, although impotent, wanted an heir to his estate. He sends his wife—much against her will—to town, where she then concocts an elaborate scheme, ending in her impregnation by a ship's captain. Although the initial liaison is successfully accomplished, the woman, having "once broken the bounds of Modesty," can no longer restrain herself from further encounters, and brings disgrace and ruin upon herself and her husband. Yet the blame is placed less upon the woman herself than upon her husband's "foolish pride" in wanting an heir.

Chapter Four

1. Richard Steele, *The Englishman*, 1st ser., No. 4 (1713).

2. "The Code of Honour and Its Critics: The Opposition to Duelling in England 1700–1850," *Social History* 5, 3 (Oct. 1980): 409–34.

3. Moreover, John Loftis notes that whereas the similarities between the play and Steele's essays have always been common knowledge, less recognized is the fact that *The Conscious Lovers* was planned and perhaps in part composed while Steele was writing the essays that appear in his major periodicals. (*Steele at Drury Lane* [Berkeley: University of California Press, 1952], 184.)

4. Charles Wilson, *England's Apprenticeship 1603–1763*, 2nd ed. (New York: Longman, 1984), x. For other useful discussions of the increasingly powerful interdependence of land and trade, see Keith Wrightson, *English Society 1580–1680* (London: Hutchinson, 1982); Lawrence Stone and Jeanne C. Fawtier Stone, *An Open Elite? England 1540–1880* (Oxford: Oxford University Press, 1986); Leonore Davidoff and Catherine Hall, *Family Fortunes: Men and Women of the English Middle Class, 1780–1850* (Chicago: University of Chicago Press, 1987); and Peter Earle, *The Making of the English Middle Class: Business, Society and Family Life in London, 1660–1730* (Berkeley: University of California Press, 1989).

5. In *An Open Elite?*, Stone and Stone contest the existence of an "open elite" by demonstrating that in the 340-year period of their study, only 157 men of business—7 per cent of all owners—purchased major estates in the three counties they examined (283). As a possible cause for the perpetuation of the myth, they cite "a confusion between the undoubted purchase of land by merchants as a secure form of investment, with a desire by them to establish an elite county family by purchasing a seat and adopting the way of life of a country squire" (289).

6. See, for example, the story of Sir John Enville in *Spectator* No. 299, discussed in part two of Chap. 8. The odious Brangton family in Frances Burney's *Evelina* (1778) is possibly one of the more virulent later examples.

7. Stone and Stone maintain that the sense of gentility shared by the elite and those of the middle station meant that instead of resenting their superiors, the aspiring middle classes "eagerly sought to imitate them, aspiring to gentility by copying the education, manners, and behaviour of the gentry. They sent their children to boarding-schools to learn social graces, they withdrew their wives from work to put them in the parlour to drink tea, they patronized the theatres, the music-rooms, the print-shops, and the circulating libraries, and they read the newspapers, the magazines, and the novels. Their attitude thus provided the glue which bound together the top half or more of the nation by means of an homogenized culture of gentility that left elite hegemony unaffected" (*Open Elite*, 291). See also Neil McKendrick's "The Consumer Revolution of Eighteenth-Century England" in *The Birth of a Consumer Society* (Bloomington: University of Indiana Press, 1982), for the ways in which consumption both allowed for and problematized mobility between classes.

8. *The Plays of Richard Steele*, ed. Shirley Strum Kenny (Oxford: Clarendon Press, 1971), IV.ii.50–53.

9. The play itself provides one example: the plot hinges on Bevil junior's fear of his father's disapproval of the woman he loves, who has neither connections nor money. The problem is resolved when Indiana, a supposed orphan, turns out to be Sealand's long-lost daughter; Sealand gives her, of course, half of the extensive dowry promised to Lucinda and Bevil junior is able to unite sexual desire with filial piety.

10. This publication was in part calculated to reinstate Steele in his place as Governor of the Royal Company of Comedians. See John Loftis's introduction to Richard Steele, *The Theatre 1720*, ed. Loftis (Oxford: Clarendon Press, 1962), ix.

11. *The Theatre*, No. 3.

12. For a reading of this number, see the first section of Chap. 8.

13. I.ii.164–70.

14. Cf. Edward and Lillian Bloom: "In the early eighteenth century, it was ax-

iomatic that England's power depended on her wealth and her wealth on her trade" (*Joseph Addison's Sociable Animal* [Providence: Brown University Press, 1971], 59); and Lee Andrew Elioseff's "Review Essay": "Mercantilist theory in early eighteenth-century England argued, in effect, that the glory and security of the nation are safer in the hands of men of business virtue than they are in the hands of the more aristocratic military" (*Eighteenth-Century Studies* 6 [1973]: 377). See as well the discussion in chap. 4 of Michael McKeon's *The Origins of the English Novel*, where he details the process of what he calls "supersession—the replacement of all the outworn fictions of status orientation by the emergent criteria of class" ([Baltimore: Johns Hopkins University Press, 1987], 223).

15. *Spectator* No. 2.

16. Defoe, *The Complete English Tradesman* [1726] (Gloucester: Alan Sutton, 1987), chap. 22, "Of the Dignity of Trade in England," 219. Compare Addison's somewhat balder statement of the same sentiment in *Freeholder* No. 42 (May 14, 1716): "as an Island, it has not been thought agreeable to the true *British* Policy to make Acquisitions upon the Continent. In lieu, therefore, of such an Increase of Dominion, it is our Business to extend to the utmost our Trade and Navigation. By this Means we reap the Advantages of Conquest, without Violence or Injustice; we not only strengthen ourselves, but gain the Wealth of our Neighbours in an honest Way; and, without any Act of Hostility, lay the several Nations, of the World under a kind of Contribution" (ed. James Leheny [Oxford: Clarendon Press, 1979]).

17. In "Women and the Making of the Sentimental Family" (*Philosophy and Public Affairs* 11, no. 1 [1981]), Susan Moller Okin writes: "The legitimation of male rule both within and outside the family is reinforced—despite challenges to it inherent in individualism—on the grounds that the interests of the family are totally united, that family relations, unlike those outside, are based only on love, and that therefore husbands and fathers can be safely entrusted with power within the household and with the right of representing their families' interests in the political realm" (74).

18. See also the merchant-turned-gentleman Mr. Charwell, of *Guardian* No. 9 (1713), who replaces the traditional aristocratic family—centerpiece of a system derived from feudalism and based on rigid economic hierarchies—with a new, ostensibly egalitarian order in the form of a town comprised of 1,000 individual families.

19. B. L. Anderson, "Money and the structure of credit," *Business History* (1970), 98; qtd. in John Brewer, "Commercialization and Politics," *The Birth of a Consumer Society*, 213. While the topic of debt and credit is an enormous one, I have found most useful Brewer's analysis cited above, which focuses upon the importance of private (as opposed to public) indebtedness (205–6), the "almost universal" quality of such debt (207), and the often devastating effects of this precarious credit system upon traders. For a more general discussion, see "The Pyramid of Debt and Credit" in Charles Wilson's *England's Apprenticeship 1603–1763*, 206–25; a helpful account of the effects of credit on the middle classes in particular can be found in Peter Earle's discussion of "trusting" in *The Making of the English Middle Class*. Earle reminds us that although the extent of credit liability "may not seem all that much by the standards of today's mortgage-ridden citizens, . . . it was a worrying problem in a world of personal credit where the whole edifice was built on confidence in the ability of the debtor to pay and very few debts were supported by collateral. A casual remark in a

coffee-house or tavern might lead creditors to suspect that their debtor had no 'bottom' and to close in quickly for repayment" (120).

20. John Barrell writes that as a result of the "awareness that more and more landed estates were kept whole only by infusions of money from the City," as well as recognition that "the ownership of land was . . . also an *interest*: a political interest, of course, and an economic one," owning land "was no longer a convincing guarantee that one's interests were identical with the permanent interests of the state." As ties between land and trade increased, "ownership of land was inevitably and increasingly involved in an economy of credit, where values and virtues were unstable, and where a man was estimated not by an 'objective' standard, but in terms of an opinion of his credit worthiness which was liable to fluctuate whatever the source of his income" (*An Equal, Wide Survey: English Literature in History 1730–80* [London: Hutchinson, 1983], 39–40).

21. See J. G. A. Pocock, *Virtue, Commerce and History* (Cambridge: Cambridge University Press, 1985), 110.

22. Ibid., 111–12.

23. Ibid., 114. For eighteenth-century views on "Credit," see the discussion in Pocock, *The Machiavellian Moment* (Princeton, N.J.: Princeton University Press, 1975), 452–58; see as well Edward and Lillian Blooms, *Joseph Addison's Sociable Animal*, 56–57, for their reading of "Public Credit" in *Spectator* No. 3.

24. Yet despite acknowledging that the merchant's profession renders him more vulnerable than other men, Mr. Spectator nonetheless concludes the essay by emphasizing his greater importance to society at large: "the Merit of the Merchant is above that of all other Subjects; for while he is untouched in his Credit, his Handwriting is a more portable Coin for the Service of his Fellow-Citizens, and his Word the Gold of *Ophir* in the Country wherein he resides."

25. Defoe, *Complete English Tradesman*, chap. 15, 132.

26. Ibid.

27. Ibid. Defoe's description of the tradesman's devastation, like that of Steele before him, employs the violent imagery of victimization: "like an arrow that flies in the dark, [malicious rumor] wounds unseen. . . . [T]he poor tradesman feels the wound, receives the deadly blow, and is perhaps mortally stabbed in the vitals of his trade, I mean his trading credit, and never knows who hurt him" (136). Indeed Defoe names such slander "committing a trading murder" (137).

28. Ibid., 133.

29. Ibid., 135. Cf. *The Ladies Dictionary* (1694) under the heading "Behaviour, in conversation": "Virginity is an inclosed Garden, it should not admit of any Violation, the very report can cast a Blemish on it" (73).

30. Vol. 1, No. 16 [1704], 78. (*Defoe's "Review,"* 1704–1711, Reproduced from the Original Editions, with Introduction and Notes by Arthur Wellesley Secord [Published for Facsimile Text Society by Columbia University Press, 1938].)

31. *Tatler* No. 29. Steele had himself fought a duel while serving in the army; *The Christian Hero* was designed in part as an expiation of such youthful escapades. (Ed. Rae Blanchard [Oxford: Oxford University Press, 1932].)

32. *The Conscious Lovers*, Preface.

33. See, for example, *Spectator* No. 82: "Our Gentry are, generally speaking, in

debt; and many Families have put it into a kind of Method of being so from Generation to Generation." Compare Brewer's stress upon the ways in which the gentry took advantage of the system: "The patricians simply passed on their own indebtedness to the trader by taking credit and failing to pay their bills promptly, or, sometimes, not at all. No grievance was felt more strongly than this hidden subsidy to aristocratic wealth" (198). For a later novelistic example, see Frances Burney's *Cecilia* (1782), in which the overextended Mr. Harrel must ultimately resort to suicide.

34. He interestingly adds that if allowed to choose for themselves, men would probably value wisdom or virtue, women wit or good-nature.

35. In his comprehensive study, *The Duel in European History* (Oxford: Oxford University Press, 1989), Victor Kiernan maintains that the duel was a mode of self-display that, like hunting, demonstrated courage and thus created fear in the ruled (15). And yet, while "A duel proved courage, and courage proved power," Kiernan cites Thomas Hobbes as a means of exposing "the paradox always inherent in it, that it was forced on most men by 'the fear of dishonour, in one, or both the combatants: who engaged by rashness, are driven into the lists to avoid disgrace' [*Leviathan*, chap. 10]" (95).

36. In *The Idea of Honour in the English Drama, 1591–1700* (Gothenburg Studies in English, vol. 6, 1957), C. L. Barber postulates that the rise of the concept of honor reflected a need on the part of some gentry for an ethos different from that of the rest of society, and especially from that of the Puritans. Citing Ruth Kelso's study of "The Doctrine of the English Gentleman in the Sixteenth Century," he suggests that as the middle classes began to increase in wealth and importance, thus lessening distinctions between the classes in terms of dress, way of living, wealth, armorial bearings, even occupation, the gentry felt the need for a distinguishing code of their own. Barber writes that they "obviously needed a word to denote their ideal of character and their code of conduct; traditional ones like *virtue* were repugnant to them as they refer to bourgeois qualities, so it is very natural for *honour*, with its specifically upper-class associations, to be used more and more, and especially to be used in the sense of 'honourable,' when it can replace the middle-class *virtue*. The heroes of Restoration comedy exalt honour, and claim to be men of honour, but often refer to virtue with contempt" (99–100).

37. Note also Samuel Richardson's character Sir Charles Grandison, who repeatedly exhibits the superior courage of refusing to duel. (*The History of Sir Charles Grandison* [1753–54], [Oxford: Oxford University Press, 1986].)

38. Steele gives an explicit instance of this process in *Tatler* No. 207, when Bickerstaff uses his three nephews, who are to be raised as a scholar, a courtier, and a trader, to exemplify "the Denomination of a Gentleman"; he writes that the "Tradesman who deals with me in a Commodity which I do not understand with Uprightness, has much more Right to that Character, than the Courtier who gives me false Hopes, or the Scholar who laughs at my Ignorance."

39. Moreover, "honesty," when applied to women, also connoted sexual rather than moral integrity.

40. I am grateful for Wendy Jones's useful elaboration of this issue with regard to Richardson's hero in her talk entitled "'A saint in his heart and a rake in his address': *Sir Charles Grandison* and the Dilemma of Virtuous Libertinism" (Paper delivered at

the 1991 conference of the American Society for Eighteenth-Century Studies, Pittsburgh, Pa.).

41. Steele, *The Theatre*, No. 16. See also Richardson who, like Addison and Steele before him, carefully distinguishes true honor from false. In contrast to those who find their value in the eyes of others, Sir Charles Grandison "is not so much a coward, as to be afraid of being branded for one"; his code of honor is both Christian, and internal: "I live not to the world: I live to myself, to the monitor within me" (Vol. 1, 206).

42. Victor Kiernan notes that "'Honour' has always a twofold nature, external as well as internal. The word has sometimes stood for the tangible rewards bestowed by society on those who obey its rules: the *cursus honorom*, or sequence of offices to which a public man in Rome was elected, or the 'honour,' or fief, bestowed by the crown on a high feudal vassal in England" (*Duel*, 17).

43. *Theatre* Nos. 19 and 26; *Tatler* Nos. 25, 26, 28, 29, 31, 38, and 39. In *Tatler* No. 93, Bickerstaff describes his own ludicrous attempts to prepare himself for the challenge presented by those "Enemies" to his writings who "design to demand the fashionable Way of Satisfaction for the Disturbance my Lucubrations have given them."

44. As Kiernan points out, the "two gravest transgressions were a blow, and an accusation of lying. Either implied treatment as an inferior: a nobleman is above any need to tell falsehoods" (*Duel*, 48). Donna Andrew states, "Since a gentleman's word was his honour, calling him a liar questioned both his courage and his status as a gentleman" ("Code," 411).

45. Vol. 1, No. 18 [1704], 86–87.

46. Vol. 1, No. 16 [1704], 79. The second instance occurs in Vol. 7, No. 113 [1710], where Defoe uses the duel and the anecdote to explain his own nonconfrontational response to the slanderous attacks of other journals: "The Case, I confess, seems intollerably hard, that when a Man's Wife proves a Whore, and he has the most unsufferable Affront in Nature, that then he must stake his Life upon even Terms with the Adulterer" (451).

47. Steele, *The Conscious Lovers*, IV.i.210–11. Further references to the play will be cited in the text.

48. Loftis, *Steele at Drury Lane*, 199.

49. Cf. Rose Zimbardo, who contends that "in the last two decades of the seventeenth century and the first decade of the eighteenth there is to be found in the most widely heard molders of popular opinion, Anglican divines, a new *feeling* about *feeling*," with significant impact on the drama: "Drama no longer teaches by demonstrating to the understanding, but by evoking in audiences *feeling* for characters (personages, imitations of 'particular men') whose *feelings* the audience is drawn to share and to emulate" ("Imitation to Emulation: 'Imitation of Nature' from the Restoration to the Eighteenth Century," *Restoration* 2, 2 [Fall 1978]: 6–7).

50. Laura Brown, *English Dramatic Form, 1660–1750* (New Haven: Yale University Press, 1981), 147. See her useful exposition of "Dramatic Moral Action," 145–48.

51. Isabella's distrust is portrayed as directly related to her own bad experience of having been jilted by a man who "left to marry an Estate" (II.ii.118–19). The conflation of woman and property here suggests the brutalities of the marriage market, a constant motif in the play: the heiress Lucinda Sealand describes her situation as that

of an animal, "barter'd for, like the Beasts of the Fields" (III.i.182–3). Yet I contend that Steele's considered attention to women's plight, both in this play and throughout his oeuvre, is nonetheless mitigated by the gendered roles he also consistently advocates; women's delineation as "property" is a necessary concomitant of a notion of gender difference defined in economic terms.

52. In *Phormio and Other Plays*, trans. Betty Radice (Harmondsworth: Penguin, 1975).

53. Barber notes the irony of this situation: "the ridiculous thing is that the outraged gallant challenging the seducer of his sister is often busily engaged in the seduction of the other man's sister" (*Idea of Honor*, 276).

54. James Thompson, *Models of Value: Eighteenth-Century Political Economy and the Novel* (Durham: Duke University Press, 1996), 20. Yet as Thompson also notes, Steele resolves the possible conflict between individual worth and class status through the use of "romance conventions": "The incognita is eventually recognized as having the requisite genealogical credentials to marry into the male protagonist's class, and so the question of whether individual qualities are determined by class and breeding is, as usual, begged" (ibid.).

Chapter Five

1. *Gender, Sex and Subordination in England 1500–1800* (New Haven: Yale University Press, 1995), 19. In contrast to most historians of gender, who focus almost exclusively on women, Fletcher clearly recognizes the crucial entwinement of masculinity and femininity in the construction of gendered identity: "We need to investigate fully and deeply the ways in which authority over women sustained men's sense of themselves as men. Civility and politeness on the one hand, and sexual prowess on the other, begin to look like two sides of the same coin" (346).

2. Kathryn Shevelow, *Women and Print Culture: The Construction of Femininity in the Early Periodical* (London: Routledge, 1989), 94–95.

3. See Ruth H. Bloch, "Untangling the Roots of Modern Sex Roles: A Survey of Four Centuries of Change," *Signs* 4, 2 (1978): 237–52, for a useful discussion of the predominant shift in defining the social relation of the sexes from one of similarity, in the sixteenth and seventeenth centuries, to a view in the eighteenth and nineteenth centuries that stressed distinctness. Bloch states that although each view predominated at times in the past, neither eclipsed the other; similarly, I would argue for the coexistence of contradictory views of masculinity. See also Thomas Laqueur's analysis of a comparable transformation in the perception of women's reproductive difference from men in *Making Sex: Body and Gender from the Greeks to Freud* (Cambridge, Mass.: Harvard University Press, 1990), especially chap. 5.

4. Cott, "Passionlessness: An Interpretation of Victorian Sexual Ideology 1790–1850," *Signs* 4, 2 (1978): 223.

5. Shevelow writes that Steele's "ideal masculine figures . . . articulated in the *Tatler* the point he would dramatize in *The Conscious Lovers*: that the realization of an ideal family necessitated a new standard of behavior—and structure of feeling—for men constructed in relationship with their daughters and wives" (117).

6. "The Contemporary 'Crisis' of Masculinity in Historical Perspective," *The*

Making of Masculinities: The New Men's Studies, ed. Harry Brod (London: Allen and Unwin, 1987), 122–23.

7. The notion of complementarity necessarily depends upon a belief in a fundamental incommensurability between the sexes. This doctrine, as I noted in Chap. 1, takes its justification from the fact that each sex is fulfilling its supposedly natural function.

8. See the discussion in Chap. 3 of the first number of the *Night-Walker* (Sept. 1696), dedicated to the "Whoremasters of London and Westminster," in which Dunton directs his reforming address toward men because only they held women as property to be defiled.

9. See Fletcher, chap. 1, "Men's Dilemmas," and Randolph Trumbach: "In that older [pre-eighteenth-century] pattern, the debauchee or libertine who denied the relegation of sexuality to marriage had been able to find, especially in cities, women and boys with whom he might indifferently, if sometimes dangerously, enact his desires. In the modern pattern, most men conceived first of all that they were male, because they felt attraction to women, and to women alone" ("Sodomitical Subcultures, Sodomitical Roles, and the Gender Revolution of the Eighteenth Century: The Recent Historiography," *'Tis Nature's Fault: Unauthorized Sexuality during the Enlightenment*, ed. Robert P. Maccubin [Cambridge: Cambridge University Press, 1987], 118).

10. Spacks, "Ev'ry Woman is at Heart a Rake," *Eighteenth-Century Studies* 8 (1974–75): 27. The plot of Samuel Richardson's third epistolary novel, *Sir Charles Grandison* (1753–54), hinges, at least in part, upon this delicate situation. Although it becomes increasingly clear that the beautiful and virtuous Harriet Byron is the fit mate for the exemplary hero, Grandison's previous—as well as concealed—commitment to an Italian noblewoman precludes his making any kind of amatory advances toward the woman he so greatly admires. Harriet's struggle, like Grandison's own, entails negotiating the conflicting claims of duty and desire.

11. Marquis of Halifax, "The Lady's New-Year's Gift: or, Advice to a Daughter," *The Works of George Savile, Marquis of Halifax*, ed. Mark N. Brown (Oxford: Clarendon Press, 1989), 369–70.

12. See John Berger, *Ways of Seeing* (Harmondsworth: Penguin, 1972), chap. 3.

13. Richard Dammers, *Richard Steele* (Boston: Twayne, 1982), 61; Richmond Bond, *"The Tatler": The Making of a Literary Journal* (Cambridge, Mass.: Harvard University Press, 1971), 167.

14. See Nos. 13, 15, 22, and 48.

15. One of the best examples of the difference between being only beautiful, and thus proud and arrogant, and less comely, but thereby pleasing, occurs in *Spectator* No. 33, the story of the sisters Laetitia and Daphne. The fair Laetitia hears nothing but praise all her life; Daphne, who is plain, must cultivate other charms. Of course in the end it is Daphne who gets the man: a young gentleman, first smitten by the beautiful sister, soon tires of her "haughty Impertinence" and is able to appreciate the "good Humour" and "agreeable Conversation" of Daphne, to the point of deciding to marry her.

16. The point is made again in No. 67 in a somewhat different form: Bickerstaff talks of establishing a "Charitable Society" to send circulars through the penny post "tell[ing] People of their Faults in a friendly and private Manner, whereby you may know what the World thinks of 'em, before it is declared to the World that they are

thus faulty." But those who "will not be reform'd by it, must be contented to see the several Letters printed, which were not regarded by 'em, that when they will not take private Reprehension, they may be try'd further by a publick one."

17. Berger, *Ways of Seeing*, 46.

18. However, while Bickerstaff might be vicious with regard to female gossips, his own talent for tattle, borne out by the periodical's contemporary popularity as well as by numerous editions in volume form, gives unambiguous testimony of the successful incorporation of feminine verbal modes into the masculine realm of cultural authority. On this point see also Shevelow, *Women and Print Culture*, 97–98.

19. For attention to coquettes (and their reformation), see also Nos. 9, 107, 109, 120, and 126.

20. See No. 22, where Pacolet brings Bickerstaff a letter from "Amanda" in which she revels in her powers to make men unhappy.

21. In the *Iliad*, they are named as "loveliness and desirability" (*The Iliad of Homer*, trans. Richmond Lattimore [Chicago: University of Chicago Press, 1961]).

22. Addison's rendition of this setting—"the Earth beneath them sprung up in Lotuses, Saffrons, Hyacinths, and a Bed of the softest Flowers for their Repose"— clearly recalls the love scene in the ninth book of *Paradise Lost*, itself derived directly from Homer:

> "For never did thy beauty since the day
> I saw thee first and wedded thee, adorned
> With all perfections, so inflame my sense
> With ardor to enjoy thee, fairer now
> Than ever, bounty of this virtuous tree."
>   So said he, and forbore not glance or toy
> Of amorous intent, well understood
> Of Eve, whose eye darted contagious fire.
> Her hand he seized, and to a shady bank,
> Thick overhead with verdant roof enbow'red
> He led her, nothing loath, flow'rs were the couch,
> Pansies, and violets, and asphodel,
> And hyacinth, earth's freshest softest lap.
>   (lines 1029–41)

23. The fact that this "Discretion" is actually deception is duly noted by the *Female Tatler*, No. 108 (Mar. 22, 1710). Upon witnessing a young woman "amuze the Company for some time, with that Art which is vulgarly called *Lying*," the narrator learns that she has been given "*Authority for this Latitude of Discourse*" by a recent *Tatler*, in which "'Squire Bickerstaff joynes with Old *Homer*, not only to excuse but to recommend a Lye; a Lye twice told: I could scarcely believe my Eyes," the narrator continues, "to see a Crime paum'd upon us for a Moral . . . " (cited in Donald Bond, *Tatler* Vol. 2: 333).

24. Here the classic text would be not the *Iliad*, but Virgil's *Aeneid*.

25. Shevelow, *Women and Print Culture*, 102.

26. See Kathryn Shevelow, "Fathers and Daughters: Women as Readers of the *Tatler*" in *Gender and Reading*, ed. Elizabeth A. Flynn and Patrocino P. Schweickart (Baltimore: Johns Hopkins University Press, 1986), 107–23.

27. Bickerstaff shies away from the husband role: No. 117 tells the story of the accidental death of his first, and only, love. See also Marmaduke Myrtle, the eidolon of Steele's periodical *The Lover* (1714), who is characterized most fully by his unrequited love for "Mrs. Ann Page."

28. Ironically, this is the very way Jenny will come to feel about her husband, Tranquillus.

29. "The Father's House and the Daughter in It," *Daughters and Fathers*, ed. Lynda Boose and Betty Flowers (Baltimore: Johns Hopkins University Press, 1988), 31–32.

30. This number was written by Thomas Tickell (cited in Donald Bond, *Tatler* Vol. 2, 137).

31. See the useful discussion of this topic in Fletcher, particularly chap. 6, "Prologue: Prescription and Honour Codes."

32. The fact that the woman covets china is telling: throughout these texts, china, like luxury apparel, symbolizes women's desires run rampant, often at the expense of husbands.

33. Fletcher writes that "Honour consisted in part of displaying the reason and strength of character attributed to men as the source of discipline for the weaker sex" (105). Indeed he speculates that the community ritual of charivari or "rough music" functioned to chasten ineffectual husbands as much, if not more than, their overly strident wives: "There is good reason to think that charivari was always directed primarily, if only implicitly in some cases, against the husband and that its message was directed at other husbands. The crucial issue was his personal and sexual control over his wife" (271–72).

34. Bond, *"The Tatler": The Making of a Literary Journal* (Cambridge, Mass.: Harvard University Press, 1971), 172.

35. We find an extended illustration of this reforming process in Steele's third play, *The Tender Husband* (1705). Here the main male character, Clerimont Senior, encourages his mistress Fainlove to dress as a "pretty Gentleman" in order to conduct an amour with his wife. Interestingly, what Clerimont wishes to expose is not his wife's sexual infidelity but a licentiousness learned from traveling abroad. Manifested most dangerously in card playing, this vice is less pernicious in and of itself than in what it leads to—the disruption of domestic order: "all Household Care, regard to Posterity, and fear of Poverty, must be Sacrific'd to a Game at Cards—" (*The Plays of Richard Steele*, ed. Shirley Strum Kenny [Oxford: Clarendon Press, 1971], I. i).

36. For another example of a fatherless young woman gone astray, see *Tatler* No. 198 for the story of the unhappy "Caelia," who enters unknowingly into a bigamous marriage.

37. In *Spectator* No. 449, the story of the exemplary daughter Fidelia, Mr. Spectator writes that in "love to our Wives there is Desire, to our Sons there is Ambition; but in that to our Daughters, there is something which there are no Words to express. Her life is designed wholly domestick, and she is so ready a Friend and Companion, that every thing that passes about a Man, is accompanied with the Idea of her Presence. Her Sex is naturally so much exposed to Hazard, both as to Fortune and Innocence, that there is, perhaps, a new Cause of Fondness arising from that Consideration also."

Chapter Six

1. Thus while in the *Tatler's* last number (271) Steele credits Addison with "the finest Strokes of Wit and Humour in all Mr. *Bickerstaff*'s Lucubrations" as well as help with specific "noble Discourses," Addison's actual share amounted to one-fifth. Robert Otten maintains that Steele "wrote 49 issues completely by himself and contributed a share in 22 other numbers," while Richmond Bond claims 47 complete papers for Addison. (Otten, *Joseph Addison* [Boston: Twayne, 1982], 69; Richmond Bond, *"The Tatler": The Making of a Literary Journal* [Cambridge, Mass.: Harvard University Press, 1971], 20.) By comparison, Donald F. Bond assesses Addison's share in the *Spectator* as follows: of the original 555 numbers, Addison wrote 202 of the "independent essays" that contained no contributed letters, while Steele wrote 89; of papers made up wholly or in part of letters or contributed matter Addison wrote 49 and Steele 162 (Vol. 1, lix).

2. Useful readings of this ostensible neutrality may be found in Terry Eagleton, *The Function of Criticism from "The Spectator" to Post-Structuralism* (London: Verso, 1984); Edward and Lillian Bloom, *Joseph Addison's Sociable Animal: In the Market Place, On the Hustings, In the Pulpit* (Providence: Brown University Press, 1971); and Lee Andrew Elioseff's "Review Essay: Joseph Addison's Political Animal: Middle-Class Idealism in Crisis," *Eighteenth-Century Studies* 6 (1973): 372–81.

3. Eagleton, *Function of Criticism*, 22.

4. In "The Legal Status of the English Woman in Early Eighteenth-Century Common Law and Equity" (*Studies in Eighteenth-Century Culture* 4 [Madison: University of Wisconsin Press, 1975]), Janelle Greenberg writes that although "women were accorded more legal rights than is generally acknowledged" (172), nevertheless under common law, a woman's ability to own property and chattel, to bequeath by will, and to make contracts was extant only so long as she was a single woman, or a *feme sole*. When a woman married, she became a *feme covert*: "she surrendered those rights and fell prey to a whole series of disabilities which placed her in the same legal category as wards, lunatics, idiots, and outlaws" (ibid.). For our purposes, Greenberg's most important point is that "it was not women *per se* who were subject to disabilities at common law but rather married women, *feme coverts*, who were disabled because of their association with people presumed to be more capable than they, namely, their husbands" (175). See also Susan Staves's valuable and extensive examination of this topic in *Married Women's Separate Property in England, 1660–1833* (Cambridge, Mass.: Harvard University Press, 1990).

5. Donald Bond notes that "Although the Preliminaries of Peace were not made known until the following autumn . . . , the Tory ministers were already conducting secret negotiations with the enemy, and rumours of peace were now circulating, particularly after the death of the young Emperor Joseph I on 17 Apr, N.S. (reported in the *Post Boy* of 19 Apr. [1711], two days before the publication of this number)" (*Spectator* Vol. 1, 192–93).

6. Since most readers had long been aware of Steele's authorship, Richmond Bond suspects that there may have been additional motivations behind Steele's resolve to end the *Tatler*. Although political compromise with the powerful Tory leader Sir Robert Harley, who had been a subject of Steele's satire some months earlier,

"cannot now be demonstrated to the point of full acceptance, . . . it seems plausible as a major factor in Steele's decision and perhaps as the strongest" (*"The Tatler,"* 186). See also pp. 59–69 for Bond's discussion of overt political issues within the *Tatler*.

7. My reading here clearly takes issue with that of Ros Ballester, who, by viewing spectating as a "traditionally feminine pastime," argues that in the *Spectator*, "the figure of the early eighteenth-century lady . . . comes to represent the boundary or margin of that sensitive and disinterested critical awareness that they [i.e., Addison and Steele] sought to encourage in their (male) readers" (*Seductive Forms: Women's Amatory Fiction* [Oxford: Clarendon Press, 1992], 39–40).

8. *The Narrative Act: Point of View in Prose Fiction* (Princeton, N.J.: Princeton University Press, 1981), 138.

9. Ibid., 137, note 35.

10. Eagleton, *Function of Criticism*, 18.

11. "Bibliography and the Shape of the Literary Periodical in the Early Eighteenth Century," *The Library* 8, no. 3 (Sept. 1986): 241.

12. "Commercialization and Politics," *The Birth of a Consumer Society*, ed. Neil McKendrick, John Brewer, and J. H. Plumb (Bloomington: Indiana University Press, 1982), 216–17.

13. Ibid., 222.

14. Sennett, *The Fall of Public Man* (New York: Random House, 1977), 81.

15. Ibid., 84.

16. Ibid.

17. Women, of course, were largely excluded from coffee-houses; they had, however, other means of access to the *Spectator*, such as privately purchased copies.

18. Bloom and Bloom, *Joseph Addison's Sociable Animal*, 13.

19. John Locke, *Two Treatises of Government*, ed. Peter Laslett (Cambridge: Cambridge University Press, 1988), II: §82.

20. See, for example, the "Cott-Quean" of No. 482, whose wife, in a letter to Mr. Spectator, bemoans her lot, claiming that she would rather he were "a Man of a rough Temper, that would treat me harshly sometimes, than of such an effeminate busie Nature in a Province that does not belong to him."

21. See G. J. Barker-Benfield, *The Culture of Sensibility: Sex and Society in Eighteenth-Century Britain* (Chicago: University of Chicago Press, 1992), chap. 1.

22. In "Foucault, Femininity, and the Modernization of Patriarchal Power" (*Feminism and Foucault*, ed. Irene Diamond and Lee Quinby [Boston: Northeastern University Press, 1988]), Sandra Lee Bartky criticizes Foucault's *Discipline and Punish* for its treatment of all bodies as if they were one, thus failing to analyze the specific ways in which the "feminine body" is gendered and made "docile" by disciplinary practices. She cites three categories through which to examine the disciplinary practices that "produce a body in which gesture and appearance is recognizably feminine": "those that aim to produce a body of a certain size and general configuration; those that bring forth from this body a specific repertoire of gestures, postures, and movements; and those that are directed toward the display of the body as an ornamental surface" (64). Although Bartky goes on to talk about how women have come to internalize "patriarchal standards of bodily acceptability," I am interested in her

categories for the way they provide a framework for thinking about the shaping of the female body within a political context that is at the same time defined as overtly antipolitical.

23. The *OED* defines *virago* as "A man-like, vigorous, and heroic woman; a female warrior; an amazon."

24. *The Freeholder*, No. 4 (Jan. 2, 1716), ed. James Leheny (Oxford: Clarendon Press, 1979).

25. Or a man picks up a mirror: see the discussion of the Fop in the next chapter.

26. For the latter, see Diane Dugaw, *Warrior Women and Popular Balladry 1650–1850* (Cambridge: Cambridge University Press, 1989).

27. See Anthony Fletcher, *Sex, Gender and Subordination in England 1500–1800* (New Haven: Yale University Press, 1995).

28. The previous number explained that these neighboring republics used to come together upon their borders for a week out of every year, at which time those who had not already made a choice of mate would do so. These choices lasted through all further meetings; any boys that resulted from the couplings would be sent to live with the men, while girls remained with the women.

29. Fletcher recounts a similarly outraged male response to a "transvestite fashion, a new kind of female modishness, which had caused a spate of male comment since the 1570s" (23). The imprecations of these earlier writers, who denounced such women as hermaphrodites, Amazons, even monsters, show that, in the sixteenth century as in the eighteenth, clothing played a fundamental role in both establishing and maintaining gender norms.

30. *Between Men: English Literature and Male Homosocial Desire* (New York: Columbia University Press, 1985), 50.

Chapter Seven

1. In *Luxury: The Concept from Eden to Smollett* (Baltimore: Johns Hopkins University Press, 1977), John Sekora asserts that by the eighteenth century, "luxury had become a fluid and complex concept in which moral, religious, economic and political attitudes were mixed into a vague and contradictory amalgam" (48). Yet he maintains that despite significant variations in authors' usage of the term, "luxury probably *was* the greatest single social issue and the greatest single commonplace" in the eighteenth century (75). In this chapter, I am concerned less with explicating the general expression of attitudes towards luxury in Addison and Steele's periodicals than I am with examining the ways in which their journals employed a millennia-old debate in the service of contemporary class and gender ideologies. See Sekora's important study for a comprehensive historical analysis of luxury, as well as a specific treatment of eighteenth-century views about it.

2. "More or less narrowly, social rank is linked to the possession of a fortune, but only on the condition that the fortune be partially sacrificed in unproductive social expenditures such as festivals, spectacles, and games. . . . In so-called civilized societies, the fundamental *obligation* of wealth disappeared only in a fairly recent period" (Georges Bataille, "The Notion of Expenditure," *Visions of Excess: Selected Writings, 1927–1939* [Minneapolis: University of Minnesota Press, 1985], 123).

3. See Lorna Weatherill, *Consumer Behaviour and Material Culture in Britain 1660–1760* (London: Routledge, 1988), 14.

4. The pioneering work on this subject is to be found in *The Birth of a Consumer Society: The Commercialization of Eighteenth-Century England*, ed. Neil McKendrick, John Brewer, and J. H. Plumb (Bloomington: Indiana University Press, 1982). See in particular the first two chapters, written by McKendrick: "The Consumer Revolution of Eighteenth-Century England" and "The Commercialization of Fashion." While McKendrick regards the blurring of class boundaries as primarily a later eighteenth-century phenomenon, I believe that anxiety about such an occurrence was also present in the earlier part of the century. For a plethora of recent essays continuing the debates about eighteenth-century consumption, see the first and third volumes in the "Consumption and Culture" series: *Consumption and the World of Goods*, ed. John Brewer and Roy Porter (London: Routledge, 1993) and *The Consumption of Culture 1600–1800*, ed. Ann Bermingham and John Brewer (London: Routledge, 1995).

5. Maxine Berg, *The Age of Manufactures 1700–1820* (New York: Oxford University Press, 1986), 172.

6. Kaja Silverman, "Fragments of a Fashionable Discourse," *Studies in Entertainment: Critical Approaches to Mass Culture*, ed. Tania Modleski (Bloomington: Indiana University Press, 1986), 147. While I clearly agree with Silverman's assessment that "class distinctions have 'softened' and gender distinctions have 'hardened' since the end of the eighteenth century," I believe that readings of periodicals from the early eighteenth century establish that such a process was taking place in that period as well.

7. J. H. Plumb places these publications at the crux of the intersection of profit, leisure, and the emerging middle classes. See "The Commercialization of Leisure in Eighteenth-Century England" in *The Birth of a Consumer Society*.

8. Mandeville, *The Fable of the Bees*, ed. F. B. Kaye (Oxford: Clarendon Press, 1929), I: 115.

9. Such thinking is epitomized in Eliza Haywood's attack on the luxurious male soldier in her *Female Spectator*.

10. *Spectator* Nos. 281 and 275, respectively.

11. *Warrior Women and Popular Balladry 1650–1850* (Cambridge: Cambridge University Press, 1989), 139, 144.

12. See Louis Landa, "Pope's Belinda, The General Emporie of the World, and the Wondrous Worm" and "Of Silkworms and Farthingales and the Will of God," both reprinted in *Essays in Eighteenth-Century English Literature* (Princeton, N.J.: Princeton University Press, 1980) and Laura Brown, *Ends of Empire: Women and Ideology in Early Eighteenth-Century England* (Ithaca: Cornell University Press, 1993). The quotation comes from Pope's *The Rape of the Lock* (Canto V, line 11), a poem discussed by both critics.

13. Brown, *Ends of Empire*, 16.

14. In *On Human Finery* (London: Hogarth, 1976), Quentin Bell argues that prior to the eighteenth century, "The nobleman, like the lady, was a creature incapable of useful work; war and sport were the only outlets for his energy, and a high degree of conspicuous leisure was expected of him. Equally, it was important that he should in his own person be a consumer" (141; qtd. in Silverman, 140).

15. As Silverman has noted, prior to the eighteenth century, "the elegance and richness of male dress equalled and often surpassed that of female dress . . . , so that in so far as clothing was marked by gender, it defined visibility as a male rather than a female attribute" ("Fragments," 139).

16. See Jill Campbell's article entitled "Lady Mary Wortley Montagu and the Historical Machinery of Female Identity," in *Women, Gender and Eighteenth-Century Literature*, ed. Beth Fowkes Tobin (Athens: University of Georgia Press, 1994), 64–85.

17. Landa, "Belinda," 180.

18. Ibid., 189. For a helpful summary of eighteenth-century mercantilist views with specific regard to luxury, see Sekora, *Luxury*, 310, note 10. In addition, Beverly Lemire's study *Fashion's Favourite: The Cotton Trade and the Consumer Revolution in Britain 1660–1800* (Oxford: Oxford University Press, 1991), offers a historically detailed and theoretically grounded analysis of the effects of the cotton industry, both imported and domestic, upon Britain's material and social economy.

19. McKendrick, "The Consumer Revolution of Eighteenth-Century England," in *Birth of a Consumer Society*, 16. See also Joyce Appleby, "Ideology and Theory: The Tension between Political and Economic Liberalism in Seventeenth-Century England," *American Historical Review* 81 (1976): 499–515.

20. See, for example, chap. 5, "Mandeville and His Critics," in Thomas Horne's *The Social Thought of Bernard Mandeville: Virtue and Commerce in Eighteenth-Century England* (London: Macmillan, 1978); Sekora, *Luxury*, 114–15; and McKendrick, "Consumer Revolution," 16–19. McKendrick notes the ironic fact that by the end of the eighteenth century a "Doctrine of Beneficial Luxury," as exemplified in Adam Smith's *Wealth of Nations*, had become acceptable rather than scandalous: "The pursuit of luxury could now be seen as socially desirable, for as the growth of new wants stimulated increased effort and output, improved consumption by all ranks of society would further stimulate economic progress" (19).

21. Landa, "Pope's Belinda," 180.

22. *The Spinster* is presented as the first number of a journal "To be continued Occasionally"; no other issues, if they existed, have survived. (*Tracts and Pamphlets by Richard Steele*, ed. Rae Blanchard [Baltimore: Johns Hopkins University Press, 1944], 549–56.)

23. Steele, *Spinster*, 551.

24. Ibid.

25. See, for example, Laura Brown: "Spinning was originally a household industry, dominated by women who produced yarn for their families and for personal sale. With the growth of wage labor, the spinster, previously an essential participant in domestic manufacture, was progressively excluded from productive work, except as a wage-earner in a pauper trade. The currency of 'spinster' as a derogatory term for a useless female dependent dates from this period of transformation (1719) and records the extent and effect of the changes in the attitudes toward women" (*Ends of Empire*, 93–94).

26. Steele, *Spinster*, 552.

27. Ibid., 555.

28. Ibid., 554.

29. Richard Steele, *The Theatre 1720*, ed. John Loftis (Oxford: Clarendon Press, 1962).

30. All quotations are taken from this number of the periodical.

31. *The Freeholder* ran from December 23, 1715, to June 29, 1716 (ed. James Leheny [Oxford: Clarendon Press, 1979]).

32. Note again the elision of the fashionable with the martial in the letter that comprises *Spectator* No. 102. Proposing to set up an "Academy for the training up of young Women in the *Exercise of the Fan*, according to the most fashionable Airs and Motions that are now practised at Court," the letter begins: "Women are armed with Fans as Men with Swords, and sometimes do more Execution with them."

33. According to the *OED*, a contemptuous term for "A man that acts the housewife, that busies himself unduly or meddles with matters belonging to the housewife's province." The dictionary cites the *Freeholder* quotation as one of its examples. See also *Spectator* No. 482.

34. Joan Thirsk, "Fantastical Folly," qtd. in Lemire, *Fashion's Favourite*, 8. Lemire's own study details the results of the damage to British woolen manufactures inflicted by the cotton industry.

35. See Peter Stallybrass and Allon White's discussion of the relation of coffee-houses to the public sphere in *The Politics and Poetics of Transgression* (Ithaca: Cornell University Press, 1986), 94–100.

36. Bickerstaff notes that "These in Truth have not been inconsiderable; for, besides those weekly Contributions which I receive from *John Morphew* [Steele's distributor], and those annual Subscriptions which I propose to my self from the most elegant Part of this great Island, I daily live in a very comfortable Affluence of Wine, Stale Beer, *Hungary* Water, Beef, Books, and Marrow-Bones, which I receive from many well-disposed Citizens; not to mention the Forfeitures which accrue to me from the several Offenders that appear before me on Court-Days" (No. 162). Bickerstaff's "Courts of Justice" will be discussed below.

37. Bickerstaff's use of the term here conjoins a number of different meanings: luxury in the sense of excess, as in "luxuriance"—"superabundant growth or development, exuberance"; luxury in the sense of costliness, as in "the habitual use, or indulgence in what is choice or costly, whether food, dress, furniture, or appliances of any kind"; and luxury as distinguished from necessity: "Something which conduces to enjoyment or comfort in addition to what are accounted the necessaries of life. Hence, in recent use, something which is desirable but not indispensable" (all definitions taken from the *OED*). For a discussion of the changing nature of luxury, see Sekora, *Luxury*.

38. Indeed "dead" might mean not only lifeless, but also useless or unproductive: "Not fulfilling the normal and ostensible purpose" (*OED*, definition 15).

39. See Kristina Straub's analysis of the ways in which the male actor functions as spectacle in the first chapter of *Sexual Suspects: Eighteenth-Century Players and Sexual Ideology* (Princeton, N.J.: Princeton University Press, 1992).

40. See No. 113, in which Bickerstaff describes the effects, offered at auction, of the young man who was "carried off dead upon the taking away of his Snuff-Box." Listed, for example, are: "A large Glass-Case, containing the Linnen and Clothes of the Deceased; among which are, Two embroidered Suits, a Pocket Perspective, a

Dozen Pair of Red-heeled Shoes, Three Pair of Red Silk Stockings, and an Amber-headed Cane."

41. For a valuable analysis of the history of and attitudes toward this controversial item of female dress, see Kimberly Chrisman's article "Unhoop the Fair Sex: The Campaign Against the Hoop Petticoat in Eighteenth-Century England," *Eighteenth-Century Studies* 30, no. 1 (Fall 1996): 5–23. Chrisman contends that "the origins, innovations, fluctuations, and failings of the hoop demonstrate the tenacity of eighteenth-century Englishwomen in their struggle for sexual autonomy" (7); the hoop's history also elucidates the tenacious attempts of eighteenth-century English*men* to extirpate the formidable carapace.

42. Ibid., 16.

43. Yet as "a highly-charged sexual symbol," which excited men by the possibility of what might be revealed by an accidental—or sometimes even calculated—fall, the hoop petticoat "seemed to attract as many men as it repulsed" (ibid., 18–19).

44. Brown, *Empire*, 116. Louis Landa's essay "Of Silkworms and Farthingales" asserts that the passage, in which Bickerstaff "maintains that the animal and physical worlds are properly exploited for the embellishment of women" (208), operates within a larger trend in which the lady of fashion "will be seen to play a vital part in a universe rationally designed and providentially ordered to accommodate her" (199). We find here the same passive construction as in Addison's own essay: by whom will she be seen? Landa's grammar thus elides the supposed "Will of God" with the will of men: "Because the eighteenth century held firmly to the Aristotelian conviction that nature does nothing in vain, it found a rationale for the lady of fashion in the cosmic scheme of things. And perhaps it is not untenable to maintain that the lady of fashion, like the seas, the mountains, and other artifacts of nature, was herself part of that design and harmony in the universe which truly demonstrated the existence of a deity."

45. Brown, *Empire*, 118.

46. Ibid.

47. Landa, "Of Silkworms and Farthingales," 208.

48. Cf. Sekora, *Luxury*: "In that conviction originates the practice of defining putative instances of luxury with juridical precision, a process greatly accelerated by the Romans" (30).

49. "A moral component is sutured into and inseparable from the concept of culture or cultivation in this eighteenth-century usage from the start" ("Subjective Powers? Consumption, the Reading Public, and Domestic Woman in Early Eighteenth-Century England," *The Consumption of Culture*, 24).

50. Cf. also No. 98, in which Mr. Spectator had satirized women's extravagant headgear: "There is not so variable a thing in Nature as a Lady's Head-dress: Within my own Memory I have known it rise and fall above thirty Degrees. About ten Years ago it shot up to a very great Height, insomuch that the Female Part of our Species were much taller than the Men. The Women were of such an enormous Stature, that *we appeared as Grass-hoppers before them*: At present the whole Sex is in a Manner dwarfed and shrunk into a Race of Beauties that seems almost another Species. . . . [Women] are at present like Trees new lopped and pruned, that will certainly sprout up and flourish with greater Heads than before."

51. See Carole Fabricant's discussion of the relationship between landscape gardening and domestic tourism, "The Literature of Domestic Tourism and the Public Consumption of Private Property," *The New Eighteenth Century*, ed. Felicity Nussbaum and Laura Brown (New York: Methuen, 1987), 254–75.

52. For a useful examination of this belief in early modern England, see chap. 4, "The Weaker Vessel," in Anthony Fletcher's *Gender, Sex and Subordination in England 1500–1800* (New Haven: Yale University Press, 1995).

53. The quoted words constitute the epigraph to *Spectator* No. 15, taken from Ovid's *Ars Amatoria*.

54. *The Rape of the Lock*, Canto I, line 100.

55. Conversely, women turn people—namely, men—into objects. See the discussion of No. 499, below.

56. See No. 66, written by Steele, in which Mr. Spectator admonishes those parents who educate daughters by focusing on their bodies at the expense of their minds.

57. Addison further satirizes this aspect of female behavior in No. 281, a dream-vision in which Mr. Spectator witnesses "the Dissection of a *Coquet's Heart.*" In the essay, the operator demonstrates a "Weather-glass" he had fashioned from the "thin reddish Liquor" extracted from a coquette's pericardium. Instead of acquainting its maker "with the Variations of the Atmosphere," this barometer "showed him the Qualities of those Persons who entered the Room where it stood. He affirmed also, that it rose at the Approach of a Plume of Feathers, an embroidered Coat, or a Pair of fringed Gloves; and that it fell as soon as an ill-shaped Perriwig, a clumsy pair of Shoes, or an unfashionable Coat came into his House: Nay, he proceeded so far as to assure us, that upon his Laughing aloud when he stood by it, the Liquor mounted very sensibly, and immediately sunk again upon his looking serious. In short, he told us, that he knew very well by this Invention whenever he had a Man of Sense or a Coxcomb in his Room."

58. An unsettling contemporary echo of this sentiment in *Esquire* magazine (May 1994) reveals that men's anxiety about accommodating women's desire did not end with the eighteenth century. Placed under the heading "How to Be a Man, 1994," the article by Harry Stein entitled "The Post-Sensitive Man Is Coming! The Post-Sensitive Man Is Coming! (And Boy Is He Pissed)" denounces the feminist male as a modern version of the Ladies Man, a "faux man" created only because "It's what we thought women wanted. After all, this new, improved man—communicative and noncompetitive, secure enough both to support women as they assumed their place in the world and to happily compensate for their absence at home, *basically a woman with a penis*—definitely wasn't any guy's invention" (59, my italics). Tellingly, the author must revert to another socially constructed stereotype—that of the Rake—to elucidate what "contradictory creatures" real men really are: "At once sensitive and capable of terrific insensitivity. Thoughtful and crude. Supportive and self-absorbed. And, in almost every circumstance, able somehow to think hard about two things at once. Like, say, a domestic-policy briefing and what's under the tight, pinstripe business suit of the woman delivering it. What we're at last willing to say aloud is, Sorry, this is the way it is; it can't be socialized away. Nor would we want it to be" (63).

59. No. 156 notes that "the pleasantest of all the Women's Equipage are your regular Visitants; these are Volunteers in their Service without Hopes of Pay or Prefer-

ment: It is enough that they can lead out from a publick Place, that they are admitted on a publick Day, and can be allowed to pass away Part of that heavy Load, their Time, in the Company of the Fair."

60. *SEL* 22 [1982], 415, 414.

61. This letter, which Donald Bond contends is "very likely genuine," was substituted in the octavo and duodecimo editions for the number printed in the folio.

62. "Wherever Nature designs a Production, she always disposes Seeds proper for it, which are as absolutely necessary to the Formation of any moral or intellectual Excellence, as they are to the Being and Growth of Plants; and I know not by what Fate and Folly it is, that Men are not taught to reckon him equally absurd that will write Verses in Spite of Nature, with that Gardiner that should undertake to raise a Junquil or Tulip without the Help of their respective Seeds" (No. 404).

63. We find a classical precedent for Will Honeycomb's version of this story in a passage from Juvenal's sixth satire, which compares the dissolute behavior of contemporary Roman wives to the virtuous example of Alcestis:

> They see upon the stage a Grecian wife
> Redeeming with her own her husband's life;
> Yet in her place would willingly deprive
> Their lords of breath to keep their dogs alive.

(*Juvenal's Satires with the Satires of Persius*, trans. William Gifford [1802], [London: Everyman, 1992], lines 657–60.)

64. Cf. Fletcher, in *Gender, Sex and Subordination*: "Patriarchy has always carried the whiff of marital violence because it is a scheme of gender relations based upon dominance and submission" (202).

65. Ironside has a noteworthy literary ancestor as well—Homer's wise Nestor.

66. Barker-Benfield, *Culture of Sensibility*, 159.

67. See Ann Bermingham, who in "Elegant Females and Gentleman Connoisseurs: The Commerce in Culture and Self-Image in Eighteenth-Century England" (*The Consumption of Culture*, 489–513) contends that "as an exercise of taste and judgment," connoisseurship "was a demonstration of sexual difference" (502). Paying particular attention to men, her essay offers important insight into the processes through which the acts of looking and judging served to establish masculine subjectivity.

Through the mechanisms of connoisseurship, Ironside clearly distinguishes himself from such ladies' men as the Oxford student "Simon Sleek," a self-described "Academical Beau." Sleek's letter to the *Guardian* reveals, moreover, a correlation between tea-tables and other parts of female equipage: "As it is necessary to have the Head clear, as well as the Complexion, to be perfect in this part of Learning, I rarely mingle with the Men, (for I abhor Wine) but frequent the Tea Tables of the Ladies. I know every part of their Dress, and can name all their Things by their Names" (No. 10).

68. Cf. No. 114, in which "Tom Plain" protests that "Your Predecessor, the *Spectator*, endeavour'd, but in vain, to improve the Charms of the fair Sex, by exposing their Dress whenever it launched into Extremities. Among the rest the great Petticoat came under his Consideration, but in Contradiction to whatever he has said they still resolutely persist in the Fashion. . . . Many are the Inconveniences that accrue to Her Majesty's loving Subjects from the said Petticoats, as hurting Mens Shins,

sweeping down the Ware of industrious Females in the Street, &c. I saw a young Lady fall down, the other Day, and, believe me Sir, she very much resembled an over-turned Bell without a Clapper."

69. Other essays in this series are contained in Nos. 109, 116, 118, 132, and 134.

70. See Fletcher, in *Gender, Sex and Subordination*: "Manhood consisted in ex-hibiting the sexual and physical strength which was necessary to keep a wife out of circulation" (18–19).

71. John Calhoun Stephens, note 2 to *Guardian* No. 109, 700–701. The motto can still be found on the edge of British pound coins.

72. Recollect Carole Pateman's contention in *The Sexual Contract* that access to women's bodies provides an essential component of both the marriage contract and contract theory in general.

73. Although it appears relatively late in the *Guardian* series (slightly less than two-thirds of the way through the 175 numbers), Ironside's lion nevertheless makes its appearance in the same number in which the Guardian has described his literal and figurative kinship with "*Isaac Bickerstaff* of famous Memory" (No. 98). Ironside notes that the head he shall erect "is to open a most wide and voracious Mouth, which shall take in such Letters and Papers as are conveyed to me by my Correspon-dents, it being my Resolution to have a particular Regard to all such Matters as come into my Hands though the Mouth of the Lion." In No. 114, where he announces that "the Lion's Head . . . is now erected," he proudly notes that the Lion "is indeed a proper Emblem of *Knowledge* and *Action*, being all Head and Paws."

74. Stephens, note 5 to *Guardian* No. 134, 721.

Chapter Eight

1. Rae Blanchard, "Richard Steele and the Status of Women" *Studies in Philology* 26 (1929): 325–55; Kathryn Shevelow, *Women and Print Culture: The Construction of Femininity in the Early Periodical* (London: Routledge, 1989).

2. Shevelow, *Women and Print Culture*, 140–41.

3. *Family Fortunes: Men and Women of the English Middle Class, 1780–1850* (Chi-cago: University of Chicago Press, 1986), 13.

4. See Neil McKendrick, John Brewer, and J. H. Plumb, *The Birth of a Consumer Society: The Commercialization of Eighteenth-Century England* (Bloomington: Indiana University Press, 1982).

5. Expounded in chap. 22, "Of the Dignity of Trade in England More than in Other Countries," of Daniel Defoe's *The Complete English Tradesman* [1726] (Glouces-ter: Alan Sutton, 1987), this belief is also espoused in *Spectator* No. 108: "It is the Happiness of a trading Nation, like ours, that the younger Sons, tho' uncapable of any liberal Art or Profession, may be placed in such a Way of Life, as may perhaps enable them to vie with the best of their Family: Accordingly we find several Citizens that were launched into the World with narrow Fortunes, rising by an honest Indus-try to greater Estates than those of their elder Brothers." See also the discussion in Keith Wrightson, *English Society 1580–1680* (London: Hutchinson, 1982), 28–30.

6. John Barrell, *An Equal, Wide Survey: English Literature in History 1730–80* (London: Hutchinson, 1983), 22.

7. Pateman, *The Sexual Contract* (Stanford, Calif.: Stanford University Press, 1988), 84. Although Locke's *Second Treatise* explicitly states that parental control extends only as far as children are unable to care for themselves, his constant and seemingly unconscious shift from "Parents" to "Fathers" and from "Children" to "Sons" patently belies his attempt to include women in his theory. Thus whereas at the age of discretion, "The *Father's Empire* then ceases, and he can from thence forwards no more dispose of the liberty of his Son, than that of any other Man" (II: §65), daughters, by their very omission, are aligned with the ranks of "Lunaticks," "Ideots," and "Madmen"—those creatures who, because they "come not to such a degree of Reason, wherein [they] might be supposed capable of knowing the Law, and so living within the Rules of it" (II: §60), are therefore deemed incapable of freedom because devoid of rationality (II: §63). (John Locke, *Two Treatises of Government*, ed. Peter Laslett [Cambridge: Cambridge University Press, 1988].)

8. Pateman, *The Sexual Contract*, 84; Locke, *Two Treatises*, II: §61.

9. First expounded by Freud in *Totem and Taboo* (written 1912–13; published 1918), this theory returns in *Moses and Monotheism* (1939). See Pateman's reading in *The Sexual Contract*, especially 108–10.

10. In the Greek *polis*, writes J. G. A. Pocock, property "was both an extension and a prerequisite of personality"; property endowed its owner with the autonomy and the leisure necessary to be a virtuous citizen. Furthermore, the possession of property was fundamentally at odds with the "partial" demands of business: activities of "trade, exchange or profit . . . were hardly compatible with the activity of citizenship." The economic disinterest provided by property made possible political interest: "In the form of *oikos* within *polis*, property appears as an item within the scheme of relationships which are essentially political and obtain between citizens set free by their property to engage in them" (*Virtue, Commerce, and History* [Cambridge: Cambridge University Press, 1985], 103, 104).

11. In *Married Women's Separate Property in England, 1660–1833*, Susan Staves writes, "Part of the schizophrenia of bourgeois culture was to repress the importance of the very market achievements that gave the bourgeoisie its wealth and power, to insist on nonmonetary motives for action and nonmonetary sources of value, and to cry up the worth of psychic achievements. . . . In the realm of the family, especially, bourgeois ideology insisted that the right basis was not economic but affective" ([Cambridge, Mass.: Harvard University Press, 1990], 223).

12. See the comparable description in *Spectator* No. 2 of Sir Roger de Coverly's sympathetic relation to his servants.

13. Compare a similar passage in Defoe: "As so many of our noble and wealthy families are raised by, and derive from trade, so it is true, and, indeed, it cannot well be otherwise, that many of the younger branches of our gentry, and even of the nobility itself, have descended again into the spring from whence they flowed, and have become tradesmen; and thence it is, that, as I said above, our tradesmen in England are not, as it generally is in other countries, always of the meanest of our people. . . . Trade itself in England is not, as it generally is in other countries, the meanest thing the men can turn their hand to; but, on the contrary, trade is the readiest way for men to raise their fortunes and families; and therefore it is a field for men of figure and of good families to enter upon" (*Complete English Tradesman*, chap. 22, 213).

14. This number was penned by Eustace Budgell, who contributed 29 papers to the first series of the *Spectator*; along with Thomas Tickell, he also aided Addison in the periodical's continuation in 1714.

15. Defoe, *Complete English Tradesman*, chap. 22, 215. Defoe had earlier placed this formulation into the mouth of the wealthy merchant Sir Robert Clayton, who appears as a character in his novel *Roxana* (1724).

16. This view also informs the representations of trade in George Lillo's *The London Merchant* (1733). See in particular the impassioned speeches by the merchant Thorowgood and his apprentice Trueman that open the play's third act.

17. Mr. Spectator, we should remember, lives off of the earnings of "a small Hereditary Estate . . . [that] has been delivered down from Father to Son whole and entire, without the Loss or Acquisition of a single Field or Meadow, during the Space of six hundred Years" (No. 1). At the same time, however, Mr. Spectator is also, as I argued in Chap. 7, a "trader in virtue," enjoying the profits of his periodical enterprise.

18. See the discussion in Lawrence Stone and Jeanne C. Fawtier Stone, *An Open Elite? England 1540–1880* (Oxford: Oxford University Press, 1986), especially 283–89.

19. Sir Andrew's retirement demonstrates his ability to mix material wealth with spiritual riches. He is thus an exemplary portrait of virtue both because he cares for his own salvation and because his retirement benefits others.

20. See in particular Part One: "How the Interests were Called upon to Counteract the Passions," in Hirschman, *The Passions and the Interests* (Princeton, N.J.: Princeton University Press, 1977).

21. Ibid., 56–66.

22. Cf. the motto for *Tatler* No. 95, from Virgil's *Georgics*, 2.523–4, in the English translation by Dryden:

> His little Children climbing for a Kiss,
> Welcome their Father's late return at Night;
> His faithful Bed is crown'd with chast delight.

23. Daniel Defoe, *Conjugal Lewdness; or, Matrimonial Whoredom: A Treatise concerning the Use and Abuse of the Marriage Bed* [1727], ed. Maximillian E. Novak (Gainesville, Fla.: Scholars' Facsimile and Reprints, 1967), 97.

24. *The Fable of the Bees* (1714), 52–53.

25. Ibid., 72, 143.

26. Steele clearly appropriated his negative exemplar from the title character of Dryden's comedy *The Kind Keeper; or, Mr. Limberham* (performed 1678, published 1680); Dryden's Limberham, however, agrees to marriage at the play's end.

27. For an analysis of the complex legal circumstances surrounding pin money, see Susan Staves's essay in *Studies in Eighteenth-Century Culture* 14 (1985): 47–77, as well as the more extended examination in her *Married Women's Separate Property in England, 1660–1833*.

28. *The Rambler* No. 97 [Feb. 19, 1751] (*The Yale Edition of the Works of Samuel Johnson*, vol. 3, ed. W. J. Bate and Albrecht B. Strauss [New Haven: Yale University Press, 1969]).

29. Women's independence with regard to pin money is noted in the *OED* example that follows the quotation from *Spectator* No. 295; it is taken from Blackstone's *Commentaries* (1766): "If she has any pinmoney or separate maintenance, it is said she may dispose of her savings thereout by testament, without the control of her husband." See Staves for the complications surrounding women's actual possession of their pin money.

30. Defoe, *Conjugal Lewdness*, 252.

31. Ibid., 252–58.

32. Wrightson, *English Society*, 104. My agreement with this point is based, however, less on the evidence Wrightson supplies than the belief that all marriages were, and continue to be, inherently patriarchal by virtue of the "sexual contract." See the discussion of Carole Pateman's *Sexual Contract* in Chap. 1.

33. Wrightson, *English Society*, 112.

34. Davidoff and Hall, *Family Fortunes*, 205–6.

35. Not only do sons suffer the faults of unprincipled fathers; the exigencies of landed inheritance can also serve to harness admirable father to reprobate sons. See, for example, the story of "Ruricola" in *Spectator* No. 192.

36. Pateman, *The Sexual Contract*, 77.

37. Defoe, *The Complete English Tradesman*, chap. 16, 153.

38. Chap. 21 of Defoe's *Complete English Tradesman* deals in great detail with the proper relation of wives to their husbands' businesses. While highly critical of "gentlewomen" who marry traders but shun their occupation, Defoe commends those women who become knowledgeable about their husbands' commercial affairs. Yet we should note that Defoe approves such expertise not for its own sake, but for the sake of women's ability to maintain the enterprise for their children in the event of a husband's death. Women's place in business becomes natural—in contrast to the "unnatural" widow who might "think herself above having children by a tradesman"—only when it maintains the line between men: "I have known many a widow that would have thought it otherwise below her, has engaged herself in her husbands's business, and carried it on, purely to bring her eldest son up to it, and has preserved it for him, and which has been an estate to him, whereas otherwise it must have been lost, and he would have had the world to seek for a new business" (204).

39. Compare the dialogue between Sir Roger de Coverly and Sir Andrew Freeport in *Spectator* No. 174: in No. 330, however, wealth is to be found in guidance rather than in labor.

40. Cf. also *Tatler* No. 202: "I would have every Thing to be esteemed as Heroick which is great and uncommon in the Circumstances in the Man who performs it. Thus there would be no virtue in human Life which every one of the Species would not have a Pretence to arrive at, and an Ardency to exert."

41. Steele had himself fathered an illegitimate child, but unlike the examples cited in this text, he did not disown her. Richard Dammers writes, "During his time in the Footguards [1694] Steele engaged in amorous adventures and received for his trouble a baby girl, born to Elizabeth Tonson, sister of Steele's future publisher. To his credit, he acknowledged the child and later brought her into his home" (*Richard Steele* [Boston: Twayne, 1982], 3).

Chapter Nine

1. See the authors of *Women's Worlds*, who contend that "the emergence of the early modern 'magazine' as a form went hand-in-hand with the development of a specific address to female readers as a definable 'special interest' group. From its first inception, in its earliest form as the single-essay periodical, the magazine's publishers and authors felt obliged to attract the attention of female readers by invoking their interests as discrete and important." This statement ignores, however, the actual "earliest form" of the question-and-answer periodical. (Ros Ballester, Margaret Beetham, Elizabeth Fraser and Sandra Hebron, *Women's Worlds: Ideology, Femininity and the Women's Magazine* [London: Macmillan, 1991], 48.)

2. Indeed, catering to women, with their perceived leisure time, could ensure both moral and financial success. For a particularly useful examination of the relation between middle-class female education and women's consumption of periodical literature see Peter John Miller, "Eighteenth-Century Periodicals for Women" (*History of Education Quarterly* 11 [Fall 1971]: 279–86); for an analysis of female readership in this period, see Jan Fergus, "Women, Class, and the Growth of Magazine Readership in the Provinces, 1746–1780," *Studies in Eighteenth-Century Culture* 15 (Madison: University of Wisconsin Press, 1986): 41–56; and Kathryn Shevelow, *Women and Print Culture: The Construction of Femininity in the Early Periodical* (London: Routledge, 1989). Moreover, as Fergus notes, magazines were a "bargain compared to book-length works of fiction, offering for sixpence a variety of short and long tales, essays, and so on" (44).

3. The use of the term ranges from book title to defining rubric. The former describes Cynthia White's *Women's Magazines 1693–1968* (London: Michael Joseph, 1970); Alison Adburgham's *Women in Print: Writing Women and Women's Magazines from the Restoration to the Accession of Victoria* (London: George Allen and Unwin, 1972); and *Women's Worlds*, cited above. Although Bertha Monica Stearns, in "Early English Periodicals for Ladies" (*PMLA* 48 [1933]: 38–60), uses the more demure term "ladies' magazines," her perspective is similar. Examples of the latter include Miller's article cited above and chap. 5, "Gender Specialization and the Feminine Curriculum: The Periodical for Women," in Shevelow's *Women and Print Culture*. Such thinking has become, clearly, an eighteenth-century truism: in his otherwise discerning essay on the commodification of culture, John Brewer mistakenly calls the *Athenian Mercury* "a periodical that catered predominantly for women"; moreover, he goes on to write that "there were women's periodicals like the *Athenian Mercury*, the *Ladies Mercury*, *The Visiter*, and the *Town and Country Magazine*" ("'The Most Polite Age and the Most Vicious': Attitudes towards Culture as a Commodity, 1660–1800," *The Consumption of Culture 1600–1800*, ed. Ann Bermingham and John Brewer [London: Routledge, 1995], 356).

4. I do not, however, mean to claim that there is no such thing as a "woman's magazine," either in the eighteenth century or today. The contents of the *Lady's Magazine, or Entertaining Companion for The Fair Sex*, first published in 1770 and highly successful for the sixty years that followed, included material significantly different from that of earlier publications and heralded the shift to a format that continues to define women's magazines to the present day. Although an analysis of this magazine

falls beyond the range of this study, for a useful examination see the article by Jean E. Hunter, "The Lady's Magazine and the Study of Englishwomen in the Eighteenth Century," *Newsletters to Newspapers: Eighteenth-Century Journalism*, ed. Donovan Bond and W. R. McLeod (Morgantown: West Virginia University Press, 1977), 103–17. My concern, then, is not for the use of the term itself but for its anachronistic application to periodicals published in the first two-thirds of the eighteenth century.

5. Ballester et al., *Women's Worlds*, 5; emphasis added.

6. Helene Koon, "Eliza Haywood and the *Female Spectator*," *Huntington Library Quarterly* 42 (1978): 45.

7. Shevelow, *Women and Print Culture*, 167.

8. In her "Afterword" to *Women and Print Culture*, Kathryn Shevelow notes this inescapable limitation when she compares her own more chastened history of women's emergence into print with Virginia Woolf's celebratory portrait of writing women in *A Room of One's Own*: "My history, on the other hand, begins with men writing—writing by, for, and as women. Their writing was complemented by women represented as writing within the structures dominated (textually and extra-textually) by men. My history chronicles women taking on those structures and in some ways reformulating them, but remaining situated firmly within the dominant patriarchal ideology" (198). And yet, while Shevelow clearly acknowledges male influence, her passing reference to "dominant patriarchal ideology" testifies to another kind of critical oversight. As this book has argued throughout, periodical literature played a vital role in constructing, rather than simply espousing, ideologies of masculinity. My problem is not with Shevelow's interpretation of such ideology but with her understanding of how it works: men dominate women not through separation but through circumscription and control.

9. My emphasis here and throughout this study upon men's own circumscription within bourgeois ideology necessarily distinguishes my approach from that of Deborah J. Nestor, who in "Representing Domestic Difficulties: Eliza Haywood and the Critique of Bourgeois Ideology" (*Prose Studies* 16, no. 2 [Aug. 1993]: 1–26) views Haywood's periodical as in many ways subversive of the ideal of femininity promulgated, in large part, by Addison and Steele. Although I find Nestor's readings of specific narratives and narrative structures within the *Female Spectator* uniformly convincing, I disagree strongly with the fundamental premise of domestic ideology that underpins her argument—that the "virtuous woman" occupies "a privileged position within the now exalted domestic realm" (1).

10. Shevelow titles her section on the *Visiter* "Defining the Territory of the Women's Periodical" (*Women and Print Culture*, 159–67).

11. Ibid., 161.

12. A letter in *Visiter* No. 37 asserts that "General Custom has given it for the Men, and has cast the Whole of the Infamy on that Sex which can least bear it, as upon the whole it least deserves it."

13. Shevelow, *Women and Print Culture*, 161.

14. See in particular Nos. 8, 29, and 42.

15. Here the Visiter concurs with the editors of the *Athenian Mercury*; see in particular the reading of Vol. 12, No. 4 (Chap. 2), which advocates education as the best guard against loss of chastity.

16. Shevelow, *Women and Print Culture*, 150–51. The parenthetical sentence that follows—"(All early women's periodicals clearly included men in their audience, but as a sub-audience secondary to women.)"—demands our attention. First and foremost, it patently refutes the concept, accepted by Shevelow herself as well as by the other critics mentioned above, of a periodical designed expressly, indeed exclusively, for women. Moreover, Shevelow's ability to present men as a "sub-audience secondary to women" problematically ignores a domestic ideology in which men were always the primary forces. Thus the parenthesis marginalizes what I believe to be a central focus in these early texts.

17. For a detailed explication of both erroneous facts and current information, see Christine Blouch, "Eliza Haywood: Questions in the Life and Works," Ph.D. dissertation (University of Michigan, 1991). Many of Blouch's findings have also been published in an article titled "Eliza Haywood and the Romance of Obscurity," *SEL* 31, no. 3 (Summer 1991): 535–51.

18. Book chapters or full-length studies of Haywood include works by Katherine Sobba Green, Mary Anne Schofield, Jane Spencer, Dale Spender, Janet Todd, and Marilyn Williamson—all cited in Blouch, chap. 6, "Eliza Haywood: An Annotated Critical Bibliography." This chapter also contains a useful bibliography of Haywood's own works. For major studies published subsequent to Blouch's bibliography, see chapters on Haywood in Ros Ballester, *Seductive Forms: Women's Amatory Fiction from 1684–1740* (Oxford: Clarendon, 1992) and Catherine Craft-Fairchild, *Masquerade and Gender: Disguise and Female Identity in Eighteenth-Century Fictions by Women* (University Park: Pennsylvania State University Press, 1993), as well as the two articles by Deborah J. Nestor: "Representing Domestic Difficulties," cited above, and "Virtue Rarely Rewarded: Ideological Subversion and Narrative Form in Haywood's Later Fiction," *SEL* 34 (1994): 579–97.

19. Blouch, "Eliza Haywood: Questions," 4. All further citations from this source.

20. *The English Novel in the Magazines 1740–1815* (Evanston: Northwestern University Press; London: Oxford University Press, 1962), 85.

21. John Richetti, *Popular Fiction Before Richardson: Narrative Patterns 1700–1739* (Oxford: Clarendon Press, 1969), 179.

22. Blouch, 111.

23. Ibid., 149.

24. Ibid., 154.

25. *The Life and Romances of Mrs. Eliza Haywood* (New York: Columbia University Press, 1915), 23; qtd. in Blouch, 185.

26. In addition to Blouch's attributions, see Stearns, "Early English Periodicals," 51; Walter Graham, *English Literary Periodicals* (New York: Thomas Nelson and Sons, 1930), 103, 105; and Adburgham, *Women in Print*, 78. The second version of the *Parrot*, written in the persona of an actual bird, appeared in nine weekly issues in 1746, within months of the close of the *Female Spectator*. For readings of these rare texts, see Kathryn M. Burton, "An Addison in Petticoats: Eliza Haywood and the Periodical Essay" (Ph.D. dissertation, 1993).

27. The advertisement stated that the first number was to be "continued weekly by a *Club* of Gentlemen. In which, Essays on Moral Subjects, Pieces of Poetry, and

Polite Criticism, Wit, Humour, Fable and Satyr (without any Mixture of Party or Politicks) will be inserted, after the Manner of the *Tatlers, Spectators,* &c." (qtd. in Blouch, 155). Blouch speculates that this early *Female Spectator* "fits well into Haywood's patterns of using the genre—repeating titles, experimenting with collective authorship, and adapting Addison's and Steele's titles—and is consistent with both her early and late-career persistence in pseudonymous periodical publication" (156). Although the periodical has unfortunately remained obscure, I am interested in the way a "Club of Gentlemen" could construe themselves as spectators of women.

28. The periodical's printing history testifies to its popularity: Blouch claims that there were "at least eight English editions in the next ten years," in addition to its publication as *La Nouvelle Spectatrice* in France in 1751 and a last English issue in 1771 (211), while Mayo notes seven English editions (93), still a significant output in this period. (Compare, for example, the seven editions each of the *Tatler* and *Guardian* published between 1740 and 1800.) Because of the confusion in pagination among different editions, I will follow Ann Messenger in citing the text by book number only. ("Educational *Spectators*: Richard Steele, Joseph Addison, and Eliza Haywood," *His and Hers: Essays in Restoration and Eighteenth-Century Literature* [Lexington: University Press of Kentucky, 1986].)

29. Cf. Haywood's dedication of Vol. 1 to "Her Grace the Dutchess of *Leeds*," in which the author praises this "shining Pattern" not for her heritage, rank, or beauty, but rather for "those innate Graces which no Ancestry can give, no Titles can embellish, nor no Beauty atone for the Want of." The Duchess's domestic virtues are both proven and enhanced by her choice of a partner: "You singled out Him who alone was worthy of You." Thus the Duchess's primary virtue is conjugal virtue; and her most important characteristic her ability, in league with her husband, to restore the "Fame" of the now debased institution of marriage.

Haywood also utilized the characters of Mira and her husband as the respective authors of two late conduct books, *The Wife* and *The Husband. In Answer to the Wife,* both published in 1756. For readings of these texts, see Nestor, "Representing Domestic Difficulties," 16–21.

30. See in particular *Spectator* No. 34.

31. Robert Mayo reminds us that Haywood was not alone in cashing in on the respectability conferred by titular association with the esteemed *Spectator*: "There were only a few years between 1740 and 1815 when some latter-day *Spectator* or *Guardian* was not politely bowing its way onto the stage in London, Dublin, or Edinburgh . . . [Addison and Steele's] writings were everywhere regarded as models of elegance among those classes increasingly preoccupied with manners and self-realization" (72).

32. The poem is cited in Messenger, *His and Hers,* 260, note 8, as well as in the introduction to Gabriel Firmager's recent edition of *The Female Spectator: Being Selections from Mrs. Eliza Haywood's Periodical, First Published in Monthly Parts (1744–6)* (Bristol Classics Press, 1993), 8.

33. See, for example, Ballester et al., *Women's Worlds,* 57. By arguing that the contradictions within the Female Spectator's autobiographical narrative—"She exemplifies folly but she pronounces wisdom; her morality derives from her immortality"—reflect the conflicts within sentimental ideology itself, Barbara Benedict's reading of-

fers a notable exception. (*Framing Feeling: Sentiment and Style in English Prose Fiction 1745–1800* [New York: AMS Press, 1994], 28.)

34. See Shevelow, *Women and Print Culture*, 171–74, as well as the more detailed explication of this process in her article "Rewriting the Moral Essay: Eliza Haywood's *Female Spectator*," *Reader* 18 (1985): 19–31.

35. "Sarah Oldfashion," who writes in Book 5 seeking help in governing her gadabout daughter, fails to heed the advice she has been given; she subsequently writes to blame the Female Spectator for the fact that Biddy, whom she has sent to a kind of solitary confinement in Cornwall, has absconded with a neighbor's groom (Book 15).

36. Indeed the narrator particularly chastises Miletta for her refusal to recognize her daughter, even after she has wed Panthea's father: "A strange Caprice in some Women! they are asham'd of the Fruits of their Sin, tho' not of the Sin itself."

37. See the epigraph to the third part of Chap. 8. Listen in turn to the Female Spectator's exclamation: "Oh! what could the greatest Acquisition of Fortune bestow, in any degree of Competition with those pure and unmixed Raptures, which arise from the disinterested Love and Friendship between Persons of the same Blood!—It is sure a Pleasure which no Words can paint;—no Heart unfeeling it conceive!—A Pleasure inspired by Nature, confirmed by Reason, heavenly in itself, and laudable before God and Man."

38. Euphrosine's siblings have observed her aversion; when they interrupt the conference to beg their father "not to suffer any Considerations of Interest to them to prevail on him to render a Sister, so justly dear to them, unhappy, by a Match which they were well convinced, tho' never from herself, could not be agreeable to her," he jubilantly informs them that their "Suit is granted before you thought of asking it:—Neither Euphrosine, nor any one of you, shall ever be compelled by my Authority, as a Father, to give your Hands where your Hearts do not first lead the way."

39. See in particular the Female Spectator's account in Book 12 of "Eudosia" and "Constantia," described as "two of my particular Acquaintance, who have reclaim'd their Husbands, and recovered the Love they once thought wholly lost, with Interest."

40. My reading clearly differs from that of Nestor, who maintains that Dorimon's disbelief with regard to Alithea's virtue "makes the overall effect of the narrative subversive to the very patriarchal ideology it appears to uphold," a process Nestor sees as seconded by the Female Spectator herself. ("Representing Domestic Difficulties," 15.)

41. For an influential later example of this argument, see Mary Wollstonecraft's *A Vindication of the Rights of Woman* (1792).

42. Mayo shares my sense that Haywood's numerous correspondents "sound suspiciously like the Author herself" (85). Yet Haywood's decision to impersonate male voices has gone curiously unremarked by those critics who consistently read the *Female Spectator* as a periodical addressed by women to women.

43. We should here recall Haywood's earlier career as an allegorical and political writer; see in particular *Memoirs of a Certain Island Adjacent to the Kingdom of Utopia* (1725), which chronicles the aftermath of the South Sea Bubble, and *The Adventures of Eovaai, Princess of Ijaveo* (1736), a thinly disguised attack on Walpole.

44. Two articles in particular exemplify these respective positions: Helene Koon's "Eliza Haywood and the *Female Spectator*," cited above, and James Hodges's "The *Fe-*

male Spectator, a Courtesy Periodical," *Studies in the Early English Periodical*, ed. Richmond P. Bond (Chapel Hill: University of North Carolina Press, 1957), 153–82.

45. A letter from the irate Leucothea in Book 15 reprimands the Female Spectator, albeit somewhat erroneously, for "confin[ing] all your Satire to our Sex, without giving One Fling at the Men, who, I am sure, deserve it as much to the full, if not more, than we do." Her tirade is particularly interesting in the way it argues for a parity between the excesses of the fop and the coquette: "I defy the most strict Examiner to find any one Folly in us, that they do not abound with in an equal Degree:—If we have our Milliners, Mantuamakers, and Tire-women to take up our Time, have they not their Taylors, Barbers; aye, and their Face-menders too, to engross as much of theirs?—Are there not as many Implements on the Toylet of a Beau, as there can be on one of the greatest Coquet among us?—Does he not take the same Pains to attract, and is as much fond and proud of Admirations?—Are not the Men in general affected with every new Mode, and do they not pursue it with equal Eagerness?—Are there any of the fashionable Diversions (call them as absurd as you will) that they do not lead into by their Example?"

46. For an analysis of Rome's downfall, see John Sekora, *Luxury: The Concept from Eden to Smollett* (Baltimore: John Hopkins University Press, 1977).

47. See Beth Kowaleski-Wallace's analysis of this letter as well as of the broader economic and ideological circumstances surrounding tea drinking in "Tea, Gender, and Domesticity in Eighteenth-Century England," *Studies in Eighteenth-Century Culture* 23, ed. Carla H. Hay and Sydney M. Conger (E. Lansing, Mich.: Colleagues Press, 1994), 131–45.

48. My reading of this passage clearly takes issue with the perspective offered by the authors of *Women's Worlds*, who contend that "With Haywood's *Female Spectator* we see the articulation of a separation between the public and private spheres on the basis of gender distinction through the association of specific forms with specific genders—the newspaper as masculine and public, the magazine as private and feminine" (61).

Afterword

1. This was the subject of a roundtable discussion that I organized and chaired at the 1994 Northeast American Eighteenth-Century Studies conference, held in New York City. The participants were Jill Campbell, George Haggerty, Lawrence Klein, and Kristina Straub.

Bibliography

Abelove, Henry. "Some Speculations on the History of Sexual Intercourse during the Long Eighteenth Century in England." *Genders* 6 (Fall 1989): 125–30.

Adburgham, Alison. *Women in Print: Writing Women and Women's Magazines from the Restoration to the Accession of Victoria*. London: Allen and Unwin, 1972.

Addison, Joseph. *The Freeholder*. Ed. James Leheny. Oxford: Clarendon Press, 1979.

Addy, John. *Sin and Society in the Seventeenth Century*. London: Routledge, 1989.

Altick, Richard. *The English Common Reader: A Social History of the Mass Reading Public 1800–1900*. Chicago: University of Chicago Press, 1957.

Ames, John Griffith, Jr. *The English Literary Periodical of Morals and Manners*. Mt. Vernon, Ohio: Republican Publishing, 1904.

Amussen, Susan. *An Ordered Society: Gender and Class in Early Modern England*. New York: Blackwell, 1988.

Andrew, Donna. "The Code of Honour and Its Critics: The Opposition to Duelling in England 1700–1850." *Social History* 5, no. 3 (Oct. 1980): 409–34.

Appleby, Joyce. "Ideology and Theory: The Tension between Political and Economic Liberalism in Seventeenth-Century England." *American Historical Review* 81 (1976): 499–515.

Arendt, Hannah. *The Human Condition*. Chicago: University of Chicago Press, 1958.

Armstrong, Nancy. *Desire and Domestic Fiction: A Political History of the Novel*. New York: Oxford University Press, 1987.

Armstrong, Nancy, and Leonard Tennenhouse. "The

Literature of Conduct, the Conduct of Literature: An Introduction." *The Ideology of Conduct: Essays on Literature and the History of Sexuality.* Ed. Armstrong and Tennenhouse. London: Methuen, 1987. 1–24.

The Athenian Gazette: or Casuistical Mercury, Resolving all the most Nice and Curious Questions proposed by the Ingenious. [After the first number titled *The Athenian Mercury.*] London, Printed for John Dunton, 1691–97.

The Athenian Spy: Discovering the Secret Letters which were sent from the Athenian Society By the Most Ingenious Ladies of Three Kingdoms. Relating to the Management of their Affections. London, 1704.

Ballester, Ros. *Seductive Forms: Women's Amatory Fiction.* Oxford: Clarendon Press, 1992.

Ballester, Ros, Margaret Beetham, Elizabeth Fraser, and Sandra Hebron. *Women's Worlds: Ideology, Femininity and the Woman's Magazine.* London: Macmillan, 1991.

Barber, C. L. *The Idea of Honour in the English Drama 1591–1700.* (Gothenburg Studies in English Vol. 6, 1957.) Folcroft Library Editions, 1972.

Barker-Benfield, G. J. *The Culture of Sensibility: Sex and Society in Eighteenth-Century Britain.* Chicago: University of Chicago Press, 1992.

Barker, Gerard. *Grandison's Heirs: The Paragon's Progress in the Late Eighteenth-Century Novel.* Newark: University of Delaware Press, 1985.

Barrell, John. *An Equal, Wide Survey: English Literature in History, 1730–80.* London: Hutchinson, 1983.

Barrett, Michèle. *Women's Oppression Today: Problems in Marxist-Feminist Analysis.* New York: Schocken Books, 1980.

Bataille, Georges. "The Notion of Expenditure." *Visions of Excess: Selected Writings, 1927–1939.* Minneapolis: University of Minnesota Press, 1985.

Bateson, F. W. "Addison, Steele and the Periodical Essay." *The New History of Literature: Dryden to Johnson.* Ed. Roger Lonsdale. New York: Peter Bedrick Books, 1987. 117–35.

Belanger, Terry. "Publishers and Writers in Eighteenth-Century England." *Books and Their Readers in Eighteenth-Century England.* Ed. Isabel Rivers. New York: St. Martin's, 1982. 5–25.

Beljame, Alexander. *Men of Letters and the English Public in the Eighteenth Century.* Ed. Bonomy Dobrée. London: Kegan Paul, Trench, Trubner and Co., 1948.

Benedict, Barbara M. *Framing Feeling: Sentiment and Style in English Prose Fiction 1745–1800.* New York: AMS Press, 1994.

Benjamin, Walter. "Theses on the Philosophy of History." *Illuminations.* Ed. Hannah Arendt. New York: Schocken Books, 1969.

Berg, Maxine. *The Age of Manufactures 1700–1820.* New York: Oxford University Press, 1986.

Berger, John. *Ways of Seeing.* Harmondsworth: Penguin, 1972.

Bermingham, Ann. "Elegant Females and Gentlemen Connoisseurs: The Commerce in Culture and Self-Image in Eighteenth-Century England." *The Consumption of Culture 1600–1800.* Ed. Ann Bermingham and John Brewer. London: Routledge, 1995. 489–513.

———, and John Brewer, eds. *The Consumption of Culture 1600–1800.* London: Routledge, 1995.

Black, Jeremy. *The English Press in the Eighteenth Century*. London: Croom Helm, 1987.

Blanchard, Rae. "Richard Steele and the Status of Women." *Studies in Philology* 26 (1929): 325–55.

Bloch, Ruth. "Untangling the Roots of Modern Sex Roles: A Survey of Four Centuries of Change." *Signs* 4, no. 2 (1978): 237–52.

Bloom, Edward A., and Lillian D. Bloom. "Addison on 'Moral Habits of the Mind.'" *Journal of the History of Ideas* 21 (1960): 409–27.

———. *Joseph Addison's Sociable Animal: In the Market Place, On the Hustings, In the Pulpit*. Providence: Brown University Press, 1971.

Blouch, Christine. "Eliza Haywood: Questions in the Life and Works." Ph.D. Dissertation: University of Michigan, 1991.

———. "Eliza Haywood and the Romance of Obscurity." *SEL* 31, no. 3 (Summer 1991): 535–51.

Bond, Richmond P. "Growth and Change in the Early English Press." Lawrence: University of Kansas Libraries, 1969.

———. Introduction. *Studies in the Early English Periodical*. Ed. Bond. Chapel Hill: University of North Carolina Press, 1957. 3–43.

———. *"The Tatler": The Making of a Literary Journal*. Cambridge, Mass.: Harvard University Press, 1971.

Boose, Lynda E. "The Father's House and the Daughter in It: The Structures of Western Culture's Daughter-Father Relationship." *Daughters and Fathers*. Ed. Lynda E. Boose and Betty S. Flowers. Baltimore: Johns Hopkins University Press, 1988. 19–74.

Botein, Stephen, Jack Censer, and Harriet Ritvo. "The Periodical Press in Eighteenth-Century English and French Society: A Cross-Cultural Approach." *Comparative Studies in Society and History* 23, no. 3 (July 1981): 464–90.

Boursay, Peter. *The English Urban Renaissance: Culture and Society in the Provincial Town 1660–1770*. Oxford: Clarendon Press, 1989.

Bray, Alan. *Homosexuality in Renaissance England*. New York: Columbia University Press, 1982/1995.

Brennan, Teresa, and Carole Pateman. "'Mere Auxiliaries to the Commonwealth': Women and the Origins of Liberalism." *Political Studies* 27, no. 2 (June 1979): 183–200.

Brewer, John. "Commercialization and Politics." *The Birth of a Consumer Society: The Commercialization of Eighteenth-Century England*. Ed. Neil McKendrick, John Brewer, and J. H. Plumb. Bloomington: Indiana University Press, 1982. 197–262.

———. "'The Most Polite Age and The Most Vicious': Attitudes Towards Culture as a Commodity, 1660–1800." *The Consumption of Culture 1600–1800*. Ed. Ann Bermingham and John Brewer. London: Routledge, 1995. 341–61.

———, and Roy Porter, eds. *Consumption and the World of Goods*. London: Routledge, 1993.

Brown, Laura. *Alexander Pope*. Oxford: Basil Blackwell, 1985.

———. *Ends of Empire: Women and Ideology in Early Eighteenth-Century English Literature*. Ithaca: Cornell University Press, 1993.

————. *English Dramatic Form, 1660–1750*. New Haven: Yale University Press, 1981.

Bullough, Vern L. "Prostitution and Reform in Eighteenth-Century England." *'Tis Nature's Fault: Unauthorized Sexuality during the Enlightenment*. Ed. Robert P. Maccubin. Cambridge: Cambridge University Press, 1987. 61–74.

Burton, Kathryn M. "An Addison in Petticoats: Eliza Haywood and the Periodical Essay." Ph.D. Dissertation: Florida State University, 1993.

Campbell, Colin. *The Romantic Ethic and the Spirit of Modern Consumerism*. Oxford: Basil Blackwell, 1987.

Campbell, Jill. "Lady Mary Wortley Montagu and the Historical Machinery of Female Identity." *Women, Gender and Eighteenth-Century Literature*. Ed. Beth Fowkes Tobin. Athens: University of Georgia Press, 1994. 64–85.

————. *Natural Masques: Gender and Identity in Fielding's Plays and Novels*. Stanford, Calif.: Stanford University Press, 1995.

Castronovo, David. *The English Gentleman: Images and Ideals in Literature and Society*. New York: Ungar, 1987.

The Challenge, Sent by a Young Lady to Sir Thomas——. Or, the Female War &c. London, 1697.

Chrisman, Kimberly. "Unhoop the Fair Sex: The Campaign Against the Hoop Petticoat in Eighteenth-Century England." *Eighteenth Century Studies* 30, no. 1 (Fall 1996): 5–23.

Clark, Alice. *The Working Life of Women in the Seventeenth Century*. 1919. New York: A. M. Kelley, 1968.

Clark, Lorenne M. G. "Women and Locke: Who owns the apples in the Garden of Eden?" *The Sexism of Social and Political Theory*. Ed. Clark and Lange. Toronto: University of Toronto Press, 1979. 16–40.

Clark, Lorenne M. G., and Lynda Lange. Introduction. *The Sexism of Social and Political Theory: Women and Reproduction from Plato to Nietzsche*. Ed. Clark and Lange. Toronto: University of Toronto Press, 1979.

Clarke, Samuel. "A Discourse of Natural Religion." 1706. *British Moralists, 1650–1800*. Ed. D. D. Raphael. Oxford: Clarendon Press, 1969. Vol. 1: 191–225.

Cott, Nancy. "Passionlessness: An Interpretation of Victorian Sexual Ideology 1790–1850." *Signs* 4, no. 2 (1978): 219–36.

Cressy, David. *Literacy and the Social Order: Reading and Writing in Tudor and Stuart England*. Cambridge: Cambridge University Press, 1980.

————. "Literacy in Seventeenth-Century England: More Evidence." *Journal of Interdisciplinary History* 8, no. 1 (Summer 1977): 141–50.

Cunningham, Robert Newton. *Peter Anthony Motteux 1663–1718: A Biographical and Critical Study*. Oxford: Basil Blackwell, 1933.

Daiches, David. "Literature and Social Mobility." *Aspects of History and Class Consciousness*. Ed. István Mészáros. London: Routledge and Kegan Paul, 1971. 152–72.

Dammers, Richard H. *Richard Steele*. Boston: Twayne, 1982.

————. "Richard Steele and *The Ladies Library*." *Philological Quarterly* 62, no. 4 (Fall 1983): 530–36.

Davidoff, Leonore, and Catherine Hall. *Family Fortunes: Men and Women of the English Middle Class, 1780–1850*. Chicago: University of Chicago Press, 1987.

Davies, Kathleen M. "Continuity and Change in Literary Advice on Marriage." *Marriage and Society: Studies in the Social History of Marriage*. Ed. R. B. Outhwaite. London: Europa Publications, 1981. 58–80.

Defoe, Daniel. *The Complete English Tradesman*. 1726. Gloucester: Alan Sutton Publishing, 1987.

———. *Conjugal Lewdness; or, Matrimonial Whoredom. A Treatise concerning the Use and Abuse of the Marriage Bed*. 1727. Ed. Maximillian E. Novak. Gainesville, Fla.: Scholars' Facsimile and Reprints, 1967.

———. *Defoe's "Review."* 1704–1711. Reproduced from the original editions, with introduction and notes by Arthur Wellesley Secord. Published for Facsimile Text Society for Columbia University Press, 1938.

———. *Roxana, or, The Fortunate Mistress*. 1724. Harmondsworth: Penguin, 1982.

Delights for the Ingenious: Or, a Monthly Entertainment For the Curious of Both Sexes. By John Tipper. London, 1711.

The Diarian Miscellany: Consisting of All the Useful and Entertaining Parts, both Mathematical and Poetical, extracted from the Ladies' Diary, From the beginning of that work in the year 1704, down to the end of the year 1733. [Early numbers by John Tipper.] London, 1733.

Dugaw, Diane. *Warrior Women and Popular Balladry 1650–1850*. Cambridge: Cambridge University Press, 1989.

Dunton, John. *The Life and Errors of John Dunton, Late Citizen of London, Written by Himself in Solitude*. 2 vols. 1705. New York: Burt Franklin, 1969.

Eagleton, Terry. *The Function of Criticism: From "The Spectator" to Post-Structuralism*. London: Verso, 1984.

Earle, Peter. *The Making of the English Middle Class: Business, Society and Family Life in London, 1660–1730*. Berkeley: University of California Press, 1989.

Ellis, Aytoun. *The Penny Universities: A History of the Coffee-House*. London: Secker and Warburg, 1956.

Elioseff, Lee Andrew. *The Cultural Milieu of Addison's Literary Criticism*. Austin: University of Texas Press, 1963.

———. "A Review Essay: Joseph Addison's Political Animal: Middle-Class Idealism in Crisis." *Eighteenth-Century Studies* 6 (1973): 372–81.

Elshtain, Jean Bethke. *Public Man, Private Woman: Women in Social and Political Thought*. Princeton, N.J.: Princeton University Press, 1981.

Ezell, Margaret J. M. "The *Gentleman's Journal* and the Commercialization of Restoration Coterie Literary Practices." *Modern Philology* 89, no. 3 (Feb. 1992): 323–40.

———. *The Patriarch's Wife: Literary Evidence and the History of the Family*. Chapel Hill: University of North Carolina Press, 1987.

Fabricant, Carole. "The Literature of Domestic Tourism and the Public Consumption of Private Property." *The New Eighteenth Century*. Ed. Felicity Nussbaum and Laura Brown. New York: Methuen, 1987. 254–75.

Fergus, Jan. "Women, Class, and the Growth of Magazine Readership in the

Provinces, 1746–1780." *Studies in Eighteenth-Century Culture* 16. Ed.
O. M. Brack. Madison: University of Wisconsin Press, 1986. 41–56.

Firmager, Gabriel, intro. and ed. *The Female Spectator: Being Selections from Mrs. Haywood's Periodical, First Published in Monthly Parts (1744–46)*. Bristol: Bristol Classics Press, 1993.

Flax, Jane. *Disputed Subjects: Essays on Psychoanalysis, Politics and Philosophy*. New York and London: Routledge, 1993.

———. "Postmodernism and Gender Relations in Feminist Theory." *Signs* 12, no. 4 (Summer 1987): 621–43.

Fletcher, Anthony. *Gender, Sex and Subordination in England 1500–1800*. New Haven: Yale University Press, 1995.

Flynn, Carol Houlihan. "Defoe's Idea of Conduct: Ideological Fictions and Fictional Reality." *The Ideology of Conduct*. Ed. Armstrong and Tennenhouse. London: Methuen, 1987. 73–95.

Foster, Dorothy. "The Earliest Precursor of Our Present-Day Monthly Miscellanies." *PMLA* 32 (1917): 22–58.

Foucault, Michel. *The History of Sexuality, Volume I: An Introduction*. Trans. Robert Hurley. New York: Vintage, 1980.

———. *The History of Sexuality, Volume II: The Use of Pleasure*. Trans. Robert Hurley. New York: Vintage, 1986.

———. *The History of Sexuality, Volume III: The Care of the Self*. Trans. Robert Hurley. New York: Vintage, 1988.

Fraser, Nancy. "What's Critical about Critical Theory? The Case of Habermas and Gender." *Unruly Practices: Power, Discourse, and Gender in Contemporary Social Theory*. Minneapolis: University of Minnesota Press, 1989. 113–43.

Furtwangler, Albert. "The Making of Mr. Spectator." *Modern Language Quarterly* 38 (1977): 21–39.

Gay, John. "The Present State of Wit, in a Letter to a Friend in the Country." 1711. Augustan Reprint Series 1, no. 3, 1947.

The Gentleman's Journal: or the Monthly Miscellany. By Way of Letter to a Gentleman in the Country. Consisting of News, History, Philosophy, Poetry, Musick, Translations, &c. [By Peter Anthony Motteux.] London, 1692–94.

Gerzon, Mark. *A Choice of Heroes: The Changing Faces of American Manhood*. Boston: Houghton Mifflin, 1982.

Graham, Walter. *The Beginnings of English Literary Periodicals: A Study of Periodical Literature 1665–1715*. New York: Oxford University Press, 1926.

———. *English Literary Periodicals*. New York: Thomas Nelson and Sons, 1930.

Greenberg, Janelle. "The Legal Status of the English Woman in Early Eighteenth-Century Common Law and Equity." *Studies in Eighteenth-Century Culture* 4. Ed. Harold Pagliaro. Madison: University of Wisconsin Press, 1975. 171–85.

The Guardian. Ed. John Calhoun Stephens. University Press of Kentucky, 1982.

Habermas, Jürgen. "The Public Sphere: An Encyclopedia Article (1964)." *New German Critique* 1, no. 3 (1974): 49–55.

———. *The Structural Transformation of the Public Sphere*. 1962. Trans. Thomas Burger. Cambridge, Mass.: MIT Press, 1989.

Halifax, George Savile, Marquis of. "The Lady's New-Year's Gift: or, Advice to a Daughter." 1688. *The Works of George Savile, Marquis of Halifax*. Ed. Mark N. Brown. Oxford: Clarendon Press, 1989. 363–406.

Hamilton, Roberta. *The Liberation of Women: A Study of Patriarchy and Capitalism.* London: George Allen and Unwin, 1978.

Hartsock, Nancy. *Money, Sex, and Power: Toward a Feminist Historical Materialism.* Boston: Northeastern University Press, 1983.

Hatfield, Theodore M. "John Dunton's Periodicals." *Journalism Quarterly* 10, no. 3 (1933): 209–25.

Haywood, Eliza. *The Female Spectator*. London, 1744–46.

———. *The Parrot. By Mrs. Penelope Prattle*. London, 1724.

———. *The Parrot*. London, 1746.

———. *The Tea-Table*. London, 1724.

Hill, Christopher. *Reformation to Industrial Revolution*. Harmondsworth: Penguin, 1967.

Hill, Peter Murray. "Two Augustan Booksellers: John Dunton and Edmund Curll." Lawrence, Kansas: University of Kansas Libraries, 1958.

Hirschman, Albert O. *The Passions and the Interests: Arguments for Capitalism Before Its Triumph*. Princeton, N.J.: Princeton University Press, 1977.

Hodges, James. "The *Female Spectator*, a Courtesy Periodical." *Studies in the Early English Periodical*. Ed. Richmond P. Bond. Chapel Hill: University of North Carolina Press, 1957. 153–82.

Hohendahl, Peter Uwe. *The Institution of Criticism*. Ithaca: Cornell University Press, 1982.

———. "Jürgen Habermas: 'The Public Sphere' (1964)." *New German Critique* 1, no. 3 (1974): 45–48.

Horkheimer, Max, and Theodor W. Adorno. *Dialectic of Enlightenment*. 1944. New York: Continuum, 1972.

Horne, Thomas A. *The Social Thought of Bernard Mandeville: Virtue and Commerce in Early Eighteenth-Century England*. London: Macmillan, 1978.

Hunter, Jean E. "The Lady's Magazine and the Study of Englishwomen in the Eighteenth Century." *Newsletters to Newspapers: Eighteenth-Century Journalism*. Ed. Donovan Bond and W. R. McLeod. Morgantown: West Virginia University Press, 1977. 103–17.

Hunter, J. Paul. *Before Novels: The Cultural Contexts of Eighteenth-Century English Fiction*. New York: W. W. Norton, 1990.

The Iliad of Homer. Trans. Richmond Lattimore. Chicago: University of Chicago Press, 1961.

Iliffe, Robert. "Author-Mongering: The 'Editor' between Producer and Consumer." *The Consumption of Culture 1600–1800*. Ed. Ann Bermingham and John Brewer. London: Routledge, 1995. 167–92.

Juvenal. "The Sixth Satire." *Juvenal's Satires with the Satires of Persius*. Trans. William Gifford. 1802. London: Everyman, 1992.

Kahn, Coppelia. *Man's Estate: Masculine Identity in Shakespeare*. Berkeley: University of California Press, 1981.

Kaplan, Cora. "Pandora's Box: Subjectivity, Class and Sexuality in Socialist

Feminist Criticism." *Sea Changes: Culture and Feminism*. London: Verso, 1986. 147–76.

Kaplan, E. Ann. "Is the Gaze Male?" *Powers of Desire: The Politics of Sexuality*. Ed. Ann Snitow, Christine Stansell, and Sharon Thompson. New York: Monthly Review Press, 1983. 309–27.

Kaufman, Michael, ed. *Beyond Patriarchy: Essays by Men on Pleasure, Power, and Change*. New York: Oxford University Press, 1987.

Kay, Donald. *Short Fiction in the "Spectator."* University of Alabama Press, 1975.

Kelly, Joan. "Family Life: A Historical Perspective." *Household and Kin: Families in Flux*. Ed. Amy Swerdlow, Renate Bridenthal, Joan Kelly, and Phyllis Vine. New York: Feminist Press, 1981. 1–39.

Kelso, Ruth. *The Doctrine of the English Gentleman in the Sixteenth Century*. (University of Illinois Press, 1929.) Gloucester: Peter Lang, 1964.

Ketcham, Michael G. *Transparent Designs: Reading, Performance and Form in the "Spectator" Papers*. Athens: University of Georgia Press, 1985.

Kiernan, Victor. *The Duel in European History*. Oxford: Oxford University Press, 1989.

Kimmel, Michael, ed. *Changing Men: New Directions in Research on Men and Masculinity*. California: Sage Publications, 1987.

———. "The Contemporary 'Crisis' of Masculinity in Historical Perspective." *The Making of Masculinities: The New Men's Studies*. Ed. Harry Brod. London: Allen and Unwin, 1987. 121–53.

———. "From Lord and Master to Cuckold and Fop: Masculinity in Seventeenth-Century England." *University of Dayton Review* 18, no. 2 (Winter-Spring 1986–87): 93–109.

———. Introduction. *"Mundus Foppensis" and "The Levellers."* No. 248: Augustan Reprint Society. Los Angeles: UCLA, William Andrews Clark Memorial Library, 1988.

Kinsley, William. "Meaning and Format: Mr. Spectator and His Folio Half-Sheets." *ELH* 34 (1967): 482–94.

Klein, Lawrence E. "Gender and the Public/Private Distinction in the Eighteenth Century: Some Questions about Evidence and Analytical Procedure." *Eighteenth-Century Studies* 29, no. 1 (1995): 97–109.

———. "Gender, Conversation and the Public Sphere in Early Eighteenth-Century England." *Textuality and Sexuality: Reading Theories and Practices*. Ed. Judith Still and Michael Worton. Manchester: Manchester University Press, 1993. 100–15.

Kleinberg, Seymour. "The New Masculinity of Gay Men, and Beyond." *Beyond Patriarchy*. Ed. Michael Kaufman. New York: Oxford University Press, 1987. 121–38.

Knight, Charles A. "Bibliography and the Shape of the Literary Periodical in the Early Eighteenth Century." *The Library* 8, no. 3 (Sept. 1986): 232–48.

Koon, Helene. "Eliza Haywood and the *Female Spectator*." *Huntington Library Quarterly* 42 (1978): 43–55.

Kowaleski-Wallace, Beth. "Tea, Gender, and Domesticity in Eighteenth-Century

England." *Studies in Eighteenth-Century Culture* 23. Ed. Carla H. Hay and Sydney M. Conger. E. Lansing, Mich.: Colleagues Press, 1994. 131–45.

Kubek, Elizabeth Bennett. "Women's Participation in the Urban Culture of Early Modern London: Images from Fiction." *The Consumption of Culture 1600–1800*. Ed. Ann Bermingham and John Brewer. London: Routledge, 1995. 440–54.

The Ladies Dictionary, Being a General Entertainment For the Fair Sex: A Work Never attempted before in English. London: Printed for John Dunton, 1694.

The Ladies Mercury. London, 1694.

Landa, Louis. "Of Silkworms and Farthingales and the Will of God." *Essays in Eighteenth-Century English Literature*. Princeton, N.J.: Princeton University Press, 1980. 199–217.

———. "Pope's Belinda, The General Emporie of the World, and the Wondrous Worm." *Essays in Eighteenth-Century English Literature*. Princeton, N.J.: Princeton University Press, 1980. 178–98.

Landes, Joan. *Women and the Public Sphere in the Age of the French Revolution*. Ithaca: Cornell University Press, 1988.

Langford, Paul. *A Polite and Commercial People: England 1727–1783*. New York: Oxford University Press, 1989.

Lanser, Susan. *The Narrative Act: Point of View in Prose Fiction*. Princeton, N.J.: Princeton University Press, 1981.

Laqueur, Thomas. *Making Sex: Body and Gender from the Greeks to Freud*. Cambridge, Mass.: Harvard University Press, 1990.

Laslett, Peter. *The World We Have Lost*. New York: Charles Scribner's Sons, 1965.

Leites, Edmund. *The Puritan Conscience and Modern Sexuality*. New Haven: Yale University Press, 1986.

Lemire, Beverly. *Fashion's Favourite: The Cotton Trade and the Consumer Revolution in Britain 1660–1800*. Oxford: Oxford University Press, 1991.

Lillo, George. *The London Merchant*. 1731. Ed. William H. McBurney. Lincoln: University of Nebraska Press, 1965.

Locke, John. *Two Treatises of Government*. Ed. Peter Laslett. Cambridge: Cambridge University Press, 1988.

Loftis, John. *Comedy and Society from Congreve to Fielding*. Stanford, Calif.: Stanford University Press, 1959.

———. *Steele at Drury Lane*. Berkeley: University of California Press, 1952.

Lovell, Terry. *Consuming Fiction*. London: Verso, 1987.

———. "Subjective Powers? Consumption, the Reading Public, and Domestic Woman in Eighteenth-Century England." *The Consumption of Culture 1600–1800*. Ed. Ann Bermingham and John Brewer. London: Routledge, 1995. 23–41.

Macfarlane, Alan. *The Culture of Capitalism*. Oxford: Basil Blackwell, 1987.

———. "Review of Lawrence Stone, *The Family, Sex and Marriage in England, 1500–1800*." *History and Theory* 18, no. 1 (1979): 103–26.

MacKinnon, Catharine A. "Feminism, Marxism, Method and the State: An Agenda for Theory." *Signs* 7, no. 3 (1982): 515–44.

Mandeville, Bernard. *An Enquiry into the Origin of Honour and the Usefulness of Christianity in War*. London, 1732.

————. *The Fable of the Bees.* 1714. Ed. F. B. Kaye. 2 vols. Oxford: Clarendon Press, 1954.

————. *A Modest Defense of the Public Stews: or, an Essay upon Whoring.* London, 1724.

Marshall, David. *The Figure of Theater: Shaftesbury, Defoe, Adam Smith and George Eliot.* New York: Columbia University Press, 1986.

Mason, John. *Gentlefolk in the Making: Studies in the History of English Courtesy Literature and Related Topics from 1531 to 1774.* Philadelphia: University of Pennsylvania Press, 1935.

Mason, Philip. *The English Gentleman: The Rise and Fall of an Ideal.* London: André Deutsch, 1982.

Mayo, Robert D. *The English Novel in the Magazine 1740–1815.* Evanston: Northwestern University Press; London: Oxford University Press, 1962.

McEwen, Gilbert D. *The Oracle of the Coffee House: John Dunton's "Athenian Mercury."* San Marino, Calif.: The Huntington Library, 1972.

McKendrick, Neil, John Brewer, and J. H. Plumb. *The Birth of a Consumer Society: The Commercialization of Eighteenth-Century England.* Bloomington: University of Indiana Press, 1982.

McKenzie, Alan T. *Certain, Lively Episodes: The Articulation of Passion in Eighteenth-Century Prose.* Athens: University of Georgia Press, 1990.

McKeon, Michael. "Historicizing Patriarchy: The Emergence of Gender Difference in England, 1660–1760." *Eighteenth-Century Studies* 28, no. 3 (1995): 295–322.

————. *The Origins of the English Novel, 1600–1740.* Baltimore: Johns Hopkins University Press, 1987.

McVeagh, John. *Tradefull Merchants: The Portrayal of the Capitalist in Literature.* Boston: Routledge and Kegan Paul, 1981.

Messenger, Ann. "Educational *Spectators*: Richard Steele, Joseph Addison, and Eliza Haywood." *His and Hers: Essays in Restoration and Eighteenth-Century Literature.* Lexington: University Press of Kentucky, 1986. 108–47.

Milic, Louis T. "Tone in Steele's *Tatler.*" *Newsletters to Newspapers: Eighteenth-Century Journalism.* Ed. Donovan H. Bond and W. Reynolds McLeod. Morgantown: West Virginia University Press, 1977. 33–48.

Miller, Peter John. "Eighteenth-Century Periodicals for Women." *History of Education Quarterly* 11 (Fall 1971): 279–86.

Milton, John. *Paradise Lost.* 1674. New York: Norton, 1975.

Mulvey, Laura. "Visual Pleasure and Narrative Cinema." *Screen* 16, no. 3 (Autumn 1975).

Nestor, Deborah J. "Representing Domestic Difficulties: Eliza Haywood and the Critique of Bourgeois Ideology." *Prose Studies* 16, no. 2 (Aug. 1993): 1–26.

————. "Virtue Rarely Rewarded: Ideological Subversion and Narrative Form in Haywood's Later Fiction." *SEL* 34 (1994): 579–97.

Nicholson, Linda. *Gender and History: The Limits of Social Theory in the Age of the Family.* New York: Columbia University Press, 1986.

The Night-Walker: or Evening Rambles in search after Lewd Women, with the Conferences Held with Them, &c. [By John Dunton.] London, 1696–97.

Noyes, Gertrude. "John Dunton's *Ladies Dictionary*, 1694." *Philological Quarterly* 21, no. 2 (1942): 129–45.

Nussbaum, Felicity. *The Brink of All We Hate: English Satires on Women, 1660–1750.* Lexington: University Press of Kentucky, 1984.

Okin, Susan Moller. *Justice, Gender, and the Family.* New York: Basic Books, 1989.

———. "Women and the Making of the Sentimental Family." *Philosophy and Public Affairs* 11, no. 1 (1981): 65–88.

Otten, Robert M. *Joseph Addison.* Boston: Twayne, 1982.

Parks, Stephen. *John Dunton and the English Book Trade.* New York: Garland, 1976.

Pateman, Carole. *The Sexual Contract.* Stanford, Calif.: Stanford University Press, 1988.

Perry, Ruth. *The Celebrated Mary Astell: An Early English Feminist.* Chicago: University of Chicago Press, 1986.

———. "Mary Astell and the Critique of Possessive Individualism." *Eighteenth-Century Studies* 23, no. 4 (Summer 1990): 444–57.

———. *Women, Letters and the Novel.* New York: AMS Press, 1980.

Pleck, Joseph. "American Fatherhood in Historical Perspective." *Changing Men.* Ed. Michael Kimmel. Beverly Hills, Calif.: Sage Publications, 1987. 83–97.

———. *The Myth of Masculinity.* Cambridge, Mass.: MIT Press, 1981.

Plumb, J. H. "The Commercialization of Leisure in Eighteenth-Century England." *The Birth of a Consumer Society.* Ed. Neil McKendrick, John Brewer, and J. H. Plumb. Bloomington: Indiana University Press, 1982. 265–85.

Pocock, J. G. A. *The Machiavellian Moment: Florentine Political Thought and the Atlantic Republican Tradition.* Princeton, N.J.: Princeton University Press, 1975.

———. *Virtue, Commerce and History.* Cambridge: Cambridge University Press, 1985.

Poovey, Mary. "Fathers and Daughters: The Trauma of Growing up Female." *Men by Women.* Ed. Janet Todd. New York: Holmes and Meier, 1981. 39–58.

———. *The Proper Lady and the Woman Writer: Ideology as Style in the Works of Mary Wollstonecraft, Mary Shelley, and Jane Austen.* Chicago: University of Chicago Press, 1984.

Porter, Roy, and Lesley Hall. *The Facts of Life: The Creation of Sexual Knowledge in Britain 1650–1950.* New Haven: Yale University Press, 1995.

"Proposals for a National Reformation of Manners, Humbly Offered to the Consideration of our Magistrates and Clergy." London, 1694.

Richardson, Samuel. *The History of Sir Charles Grandison.* 1753–54. Oxford: Oxford University Press, 1986.

Richetti, John. *Popular Fiction Before Richardson: Narrative Patterns 1700–1739.* Oxford: Clarendon, 1969.

Rogers, Katharine. "Dreams and Nightmares: Male Characters in the Feminine Novel of the Eighteenth Century." *Men by Women.* Ed. Janet Todd. New York: Holmes and Meier, 1981. 9–24.

Roper, Michael, and John Tosh. "Introduction: Historians and the Politics of Masculinity." *Manful Assertions: Masculinities in Britain since 1800.* London: Routledge, 1991. 1–24.

Rotundo, E. Anthony. "Patriarchs and Participants: A Historical Perspective on

Bibliography

Fatherhood." *Beyond Patriarchy*. Ed. Michael Kaufman. New York: Oxford University Press, 1987. 64–80.

Rowbotham, Sheila. *Women, Resistance and Revolution*. New York: Vintage, 1972.

Sedgwick, Eve Kosofsky. *Between Men: English Literature and Male Homosocial Desire*. New York: Columbia University Press, 1985.

Segal, Lynne. *Slow Motion: Changing Masculinities, Changing Men*. New Brunswick: Rutgers University Press, 1990.

Seidler, Victor J. *Rediscovering Masculinity: Reason, Language and Sexuality*. London: Routledge, 1989.

Sekora, John. *Luxury: The Concept from Eden to Smollett*. Baltimore: Johns Hopkins University Press, 1977.

Sennett, Richard. *The Fall of Public Man: On the Social Psychology of Capitalism*. New York: Random House, 1977.

Shevelow, Kathryn. "Fathers and Daughters: Women as Readers of the *Tatler*." *Gender and Reading*. Ed. Elizabeth A. Flynn and Patrocino P. Schweikart. Baltimore: Johns Hopkins University Press, 1986. 107–23.

———. "Rewriting the Moral Essay: Eliza Haywood's *Female Spectator*." *Reader* 18 (1985): 19–31.

———. *Women and Print Culture: The Construction of Femininity in the Early Periodical*. London: Routledge, 1989.

Silverman, Kaja. "Fragments of a Fashionable Discourse." *Studies in Entertainment: Approaches to Mass Culture*. Ed. Tania Modleski. Bloomington: Indiana University Press, 1986.

Spacks, Patricia Meyer. *Desire and Truth: Functions of Plot in Eighteenth-Century English Novels*. Chicago: University of Chicago Press, 1990.

———. "Ev'ry Woman is at Heart a Rake." *Eighteenth-Century Studies* 8 (1974–75): 27–46.

———. *Gossip*. New York: Knopf, 1985.

The Spectator. 5 vols. Ed. and intro. Donald F. Bond. Oxford: Clarendon Press, 1965.

Spencer, Jane. *The Rise of the Woman Novelist: From Aphra Behn to Jane Austen*. Oxford: Basil Blackwell, 1986.

Spring, Eileen. "Law and the Theory of the Affective Family." *Albion* 16 (Spring 1984): 1–20.

———. *Law, Land, and Family: Aristocratic Inheritance in England, 1300–1800*. Chapel Hill: University of North Carolina Press, 1993.

Stallybrass, Peter, and Allon White. *The Politics and Poetics of Transgression*. Ithaca: Cornell University Press, 1986.

Staves, Susan. "A Few Kind Words for the Fop." *SEL* 22 (1982): 413–28.

———. *Married Women's Separate Property in England, 1660–1833*. Cambridge, Mass.: Harvard University Press, 1990.

———. "Pin Money." *Studies in Eighteenth-Century Culture* 14. Ed. O. M. Brack. Madison: University of Wisconsin Press, 1985. 47–77.

Stearns, Bertha Monica. "Early English Periodicals for Ladies (1700–1760)." *PMLA* 48 (1933): 38–60.

———. "The First English Periodical for Women." *Modern Philology* 28 (1930): 45–59.

Steele, Richard. *The Christian Hero*. 1701. Ed. Rae Blanchard. Oxford: Oxford University Press, 1932.

———. *The Plays of Richard Steele*. Ed. Shirley Strum Kenny. Oxford: Clarendon Press, 1971.

———. *The Englishman: A Political Journal*. Ed. Rae Blanchard. Oxford: Oxford University Press, 1955.

———. *Richard Steele's Periodical Journalism*. Ed. Rae Blanchard. Oxford: Clarendon Press, 1959.

———. *The Theatre 1720*. Ed. John Loftis. Oxford: Clarendon Press 1962.

———. *Tracts and Pamphlets of Richard Steele*. Ed. Rae Blanchard. Baltimore: Johns Hopkins University Press, 1944.

Stone, Lawrence. *The Crisis of the Aristocracy 1558–1641*. Oxford: Oxford University Press, 1967.

———. *The Family, Sex and Marriage in England 1500–1800*. Harmondsworth: Penguin, 1977.

———. "Literacy and Education in England 1640–1900." *Past and Present* 42 (1969): 69–139.

———, and Jeanne C. Fawtier Stone. *An Open Elite? England 1540–1880*. Oxford: Oxford University Press, 1986.

Straub, Kristina. *Sexual Suspects: Eighteenth-Century Players and Sexual Ideology*. Princeton, N.J.: Princeton University Press, 1992.

Sutherland, James R. "The Circulation of Newspapers and Literary Periodicals, 1700–30." *The Library*, 4th ser., 15, no. 1 (June 1934): 110–24.

———. *The Restoration Newspaper and its Development*. Cambridge: Cambridge University Press, 1986.

The Tatler. 3 vols. Ed. and intro. Donald F. Bond. Oxford: Clarendon Press, 1987.

Terence. *The Andrian Woman. Phormio and Other Plays*. Trans. Betty Radice. Harmondsworth: Penguin, 1975.

Thirsk, Joan. "Younger Brothers in the Seventeenth Century." *The Rural Economy of England*. London: Hambledon Press, 1984. 335–57.

Thomas, Keith. "The Double Standard." *Journal of the History of Ideas* 20 (1959): 195–216.

Thompson, E. P. *Customs in Common*. New York: Norton, 1991.

Thompson, James. *Models of Value: Eighteenth-Century Political Economy and the Novel*. Durham: Duke University Press, 1996.

Todd, Janet. *Sensibility: An Introduction*. London: Methuen, 1986.

———. *The Sign of Angellica: Women, Writing and Fiction, 1660–1800*. London: Virago, 1989.

Tompkins, Jane P. "The Reader in History: The Changing Shape of Literary Response." *Reader-Response Criticism: From Formalism to Post-Structuralism*. Ed. Jane P. Tompkins. Baltimore: Johns Hopkins University Press, 1980. 201–32.

Trumbach, Randolph. "The Birth of the Queen: Sodomy and the Emergence of Gender Equality in Modern Culture, 1660–1750." *Hidden from History:*

Reclaiming the Gay and Lesbian Past. Ed. Martin Duberman, Martha Vicinus, and George Chauncey, Jr. New York: Meridian, 1989. 129–40.

———. "London's Sodomites: Homosexual Behavior and Western Culture in the Eighteenth Century," *Journal of Social History* 11 (1977): 1–33.

———. *The Rise of the Egalitarian Family: Aristocratic Kinship and Domestic Relations in Eighteenth-Century England.* New York: Academic Press, 1978.

———. "Sodomitical Subcultures, Sodomitical Roles, and the Gender Revolution of the Eighteenth Century: The Recent Historiography." *'Tis Nature's Fault: Unauthorized Sexuality during the Enlightenment.* Ed. Robert P. Maccubin. Cambridge: Cambridge University Press, 1987. 109–21.

Turner, James G. "Pope's Libertine Self-Fashioning." *The Eighteenth Century* 29, no. 2 (1988): 123–44.

———. "Properties of Libertinism." *'Tis Nature's Fault: Unauthorized Sexuality during the Enlightenment.* Ed. Robert P. Maccubin. Cambridge: Cambridge University Press, 1987. 75–87.

Vickery, Amanda. "Golden Age to Separate Spheres? A Review of the Categories and Chronology of English Women's History." *The Historical Journal* 36, no. 2 (1993): 383–414.

The Visiter. London, 1723.

Watt, Ian. *The Rise of the Novel.* Berkeley: University of California Press, 1957.

Weatherill, Lorna. *Consumer Behaviour and Material Culture in Britain 1660–1760.* London: Routledge, 1988.

Weber, Harold. *The Restoration Rake-Hero: Transformations in Sexual Understanding in Seventeenth-Century England.* Madison: University of Wisconsin Press, 1986.

Weber, Max. *The Protestant Ethic and the Spirit of Capitalism.* 1930. London: Allen and Unwin, 1990.

White, Cynthia. *Women's Magazines 1693–1968.* London: Michael Joseph, 1970.

Willis, John E. Jr. "European Consumption and Asian Production in the Seventeenth and Eighteenth Centuries." *Consumption and the World of Goods.* Ed. John Brewer and Ray Porter. London: Routledge, 1993. 133–47.

Wilson, Charles. *England's Apprenticeship 1603–1763.* 2nd ed. New York: Longman, 1984.

Woodward, Josiah. "An Account of the Societies for Reformation of Manners, in England and Ireland." London, 1699.

Wright, Louis B. *Middle-Class Culture in Elizabethan England.* Chapel Hill: University of North Carolina Press, 1935.

Wrightson, Keith. *English Society, 1580–1680.* London: Hutchinson, 1982.

Wycherley, William. *The Country Wife.* 1675. New York: W. W. Norton, 1991.

The Young Ladies Miscellany: or, Youth's Innocent and Rational Amusement . . . Written for the Particular Diversion and Improvement of the Young Ladies of Mrs. Bellamy's School. [By Daniel Bellamy the Elder.] London, 1723.

Zimbardo, Rose. "Imitation to Emulation: 'Imitation of Nature' from the Restoration to the Eighteenth Century." *Restoration* 2, no. 2 (Fall 1978): 2–9.

Zwinger, Lydia. *Daughters, Fathers, and the Novel: The Sentimental Romance of Heterosexuality.* Madison: University of Wisconsin Press, 1991.

Index

In this index an "f" after a number indicates a separate reference on the next page, and an "ff" indicates separate references on the next two pages. A continuous discussion over two or more pages is indicated by a span of page numbers. *Passim* is used for a cluster of references in close but not consecutive sequence.

Kiernan, Victor, 259n35, 260nn42,44
Kimmel, Michael, 27, 98
Klein, Lawrence, 242n59
Knight, Charles, 123
Koon, Helene, 206
Kubek, Elizabeth Bennett, 251n4,
    253n32, 254n36

The Ladies Dictionary, 34f, 47, 49, 58,
    246n3, 249n35, 250n1, 254n37,
    258n29
Ladies' man, 33, 102, 120, 137f,
    160–61, 272nn58–59
The Ladies Mercury, 3, 54–58, 250n42
Landa, Louis, 137–40 *passim*, 153,
    271n44
Landes, Joan, 18
Lanser, Susan, 121
Laqueur, Thomas, 244n74
Leisure, 9, 22, 134–38 *passim*, 148,
    150, 161, 268n14
Lemire, Beverly, 269n18
Libertinism, 31–32, 44, 65, 84–87
    passim, 97, 99, 110, 116, 202,
    259n40, 262n9. *See also* Rake
Lillo, George, 227, 276n16
Locke, John, 17, 23f, 126, 178–79,
    275n7
Loftis, John, 255n3
Lovell, Terry, 16, 155, 271n49
Luxury, 5, 17–18, 101, 134–40 *passim*,
    147–50 *passim*, 155, 228, 230,
    264n32, 267n1, 269n18, 270n37

McEwen, Gilbert, 50, 239n18, 253n34
Macfarlane, Alan, 245n82
McKendrick, Neil, 256n7, 268n4,
    269n20
McKeon, Michael, 28, 242n54,
    246n93, 256n14
Male gaze, 8, 97–108 *passim*, 119–20,
    127, 132, 171–74 *passim*, 216
Male sexuality, 8–9, 31–33, 52–54
    passim, 65, 86, 95, 97, 171–75,
    208–9, 218, 251n4. *See also* Chaste
    heterosexuality; Libertinism

Mandeville, Bernard, 46, 61, 69, 75,
    242n61, 254n39
Masculinity, 1–5, 204–5, 232–33,
    244n78; bourgeois family man, 3,
    5, 18–31 *passim*, 161–62, 169–70,
    180; chivalric, 36–38 *passim*, 42–47,
    94, 208–11 *passim*; exemplary, 7,
    24–25, 58, 75–78, 92–93, 105–6,
    116f, 178, 200, 261n5; paternal
    role, 47–51, 100, 120, 200, 208–9;
    productive role, 7, 145–58 *passim*,
    162–66; sentimental, 7, 9, 23f, 28,
    97–98, 196–203 *passim*. *See also*
    Fathers; Gender; Husband; Male
    sexuality; Patriarchy
Mayo, Robert, 212, 281nn28,31,
    282n42
Men's studies, 27, 237n1
Mercantilism, 82, 137–42 *passim*, 153,
    177, 187, 256n14, 269n18
Merchant, overseas, 80–82 *passim*,
    173–75, 182, 258n24; as gentleman,
    4, 78–81 *passim*, 95, 257n18. *See
    also* Freeport, Sir Andrew;
    Sealand, Mr.; Trader
Mercure Galant, 40
Middle ranks, 7, 69–71 *passim*, 124,
    135–40 *passim*, 226–27. *See also*
    Class identity
Mirror, 103–8 *passim*, 124, 160,
    267n25
A Modest Defense of the Public Stews
    (Mandeville), 61, 69, 254n39
Motteux, Peter Anthony, 3f, 39–47,
    52, 206, 248n17, 249n29
Myrtle, Charles (in *Conscious Lovers*),
    93–95

Nestor, Deborah, 279n9, 282n40
Nicholson, Linda, 239n14
The Night-Walker, 3, 36, 52, 58–75
    passim, 102, 109, 227, 250nn1,3,
    251n4, 253nn32–35, 254n42,
    255nn44,46, 262n8
Nonpartisan spirit, 119, 122–25 *passim*,
    178

Library of Congress Cataloging-in-Publication Data

Maurer, Shawn L.
    Proposing men : dialectics of gender and class in the eighteenth-century English periodical / Shawn Lisa Maurer.
        p.   cm.
    Includes bibliographical references and index.
    ISBN 0-8047-3353-8
        1. English essays—18th century—History and criticism.
2. English prose literature—18th century—History and criticism.
3. English prose literature—Men authors—History and criticism.
4. Literature and society—Great Britain—History—18th century.
5. English periodicals—History—18th century.   6. Gender
identity in literature.   7. Social classes in literature.   8. Masculinity
in literature.   9. Sex role in literature.   10. Men in literature
I. Title
PR925.M32   1998
052'.09'034—dc21   98-16809
                                                                      CIP
                                                                      Rev.

∞   This book is printed on acid-free, recycled paper.

Original printing 1998

Last figure below indicates year of this printing:
07   06   05   04   03   02   01   00   99   98

Designed by James P. Brommer
Typeset in 10/12.7 Janson and Shelley Allegro